LORD CHATHAM

Pitt and the Seven Years' War

O. A. SHERRARD

Lord Chatham

PITT AND THE SEVEN YEARS' WAR

THE BODLEY HEAD

First published in 1955

Printed in Great Britain by
THE GARDEN CITY PRESS LIMITED, LETCHWORTH, HERTS
for JOHN LANE THE BODLEY HEAD LIMITED
28 Little Russell St., London, W.C.1

Preface

This book, though an entity in itself, is also the second volume of my Life of Lord Chatham. It deals with the period from November 1755, when he was dismissed from his post as Paymaster, to October 1761, when he resigned the Seals as Secretary of State. Historically, the facts of the period are well known. I hope I have described them in sufficient detail for the ordinary reader and at not too wearisome length for the expert. As the main event was the conquest of Canada, I have thought it as well to begin with a résumé of American-Canadian affairs, so that Pitt's place in the broad sweep of history may be the better appreciated. In this portion—the first six chapters—there has inevitably been a measure of overlapping from the moment when Pitt appears upon the scene. I have tried to keep it to a minimum and to use it for emphasising some feature of Pitt's thought or policy which was perhaps too lightly passed over before. I have omitted detailed reference to Indian affairs, which will, I think, come in more conveniently and no less appropriately at a later stage. So much for the mechanics of the book. Now for a word on Pitt.

Biographically, the bare facts are not so interesting as Pitt's relations to them and to his contemporaries. His achievements were so tremendous that they tend to overlay his relations with his colleagues, and it has too easily been assumed that his famous Ministry was an efficient machine, each part doing its proper work and all combining to produce the perfect result. Perhaps in consequence it has been customary to pass over Pitt's first Ministry and the succeeding 'interministerium' exceedingly briefly. It would not, I think, be much exaggeration to say that historians generally regard the first Ministry as a false dawn which not only did not lead on to the perfect day but could never have done so; and the 'interministerium' as a manifestation of Pitt's awkwardness and inexperience. It seems to be suggested that Pitt should have realised from the first that he needed Newcastle as much as Newcastle needed him; that the two formed the perfect coalition and that without their mutual aid neither was capable of solving England's problems. I have not found it so. I have read and re-read and read again the correspondence of the times, and the more I read the more clear it seems to me that Newcastle needed Pitt but the less clear that Pitt needed Newcastle. Equally. the 'interministerium,' so far from being an exhibition of intransigence on Pitt's part, seems a desperate rearguard action which Pitt lost, to his own and his country's lasting misfortune. And finally, entering the coalition stands out as Pitt's one great mistake. It gave him nothing worth while, and took from him everything that mattered. Like Achilles' wrath it was the spring of woes unnumbered, extending its baleful influence over the rest of Pitt's life, and so over England's destiny. It stole from him that serenity of mind which characterised him during his first Ministry; it destroyed his power to pursue his own policies unhampered and unopposed, and it deprived him of the right and opportunity, though not the regretful wish, to create and build up his own party in the House. I fancy, though admittedly without proof, that its effect on his health was incalculably bad. The outstanding features of the coalition were the increasing loneliness of Pitt, the increasing weight on his shoulders, the increasing opposition which he had to face from his so-called colleagues. Not one of them shared his views, not one of them saw his vision, not one of them contributed one iota to his genius, his dynamism, his inspiration. Newcastle's main function was not, as usually suggested, to peddle in patronage, nor yet to manage finance. His real contribution to the coalition, given reluctantly enough, was occasionally to persuade the King to accept Pitt's proposals—a useful function, so far as it went, but one which should not have been necessary, if Newcastle had not himself so often and so deliberately decried Pitt in the royal presence. For the rest, he was a hindrance and a trouble. Pitt was great in spite of the coalition, not because of it. By entering it, he made the one fatal mistake which led slowly but inexorably to the tragic end. The might-have-beens of history are generally as doubtful as they are useless; but if there is one more certain than another, it is, surely, that the coalition would never have come into being if the 'interministerium' had lasted a few weeks longer, perhaps no more than another fortnight. Neither King nor Newcastle could have resisted the threefold impact of Kolin, Hastenbeck and Closterseven. Pitt would have come back on his own terms and master of his own house. What he might then have done scarcely bears thinking of. No man carried history more evidently on his back, but he brought to it not only his genius and ability, not only his hopes and fears, not only his errors and happy chances, but also his ignorance of the future. Had he but known! A short fortnight, but how long in the retrospect!

This book has been written from the angle I have tried to describe. I recognise that it is not the ordinary view, and I can hardly hope that historians will accept it either generally, or gladly, or immediately. I can only say that it is based on the evidence as I have seen it, and is supported by quotations from the original sources which could have been many times multiplied, had I not already quoted more freely than I altogether like.

As in my first volume, the bibliography is limited to works from which I have quoted directly or indirectly. Those who are interested will find more complete bibliographies in Basil Williams' *Life of William Pitt, Earl of Chatham,* or Brian Tunstall's *William Pitt, Earl of Chatham.*

LAKE SUPERIOR
Mon
LAKE MICHIGAN
LAKE HURON
Frontenac
Toronto
LAKE ONTARIO
Niagara
Presque
LAKE ERIE
Le Boeuf
PENNSY
Venango
Pittsburg
Fort Duquesne
MARY
R. POTOMA
R. MONONGAHELA
VIRGI
R. OHIO
CAROLI
R. MISSISSIPPI
GEORGIA
LOUISIANA
Mobile
New Orleans
FLORIDA
GULF OF MEXICO
CUBA

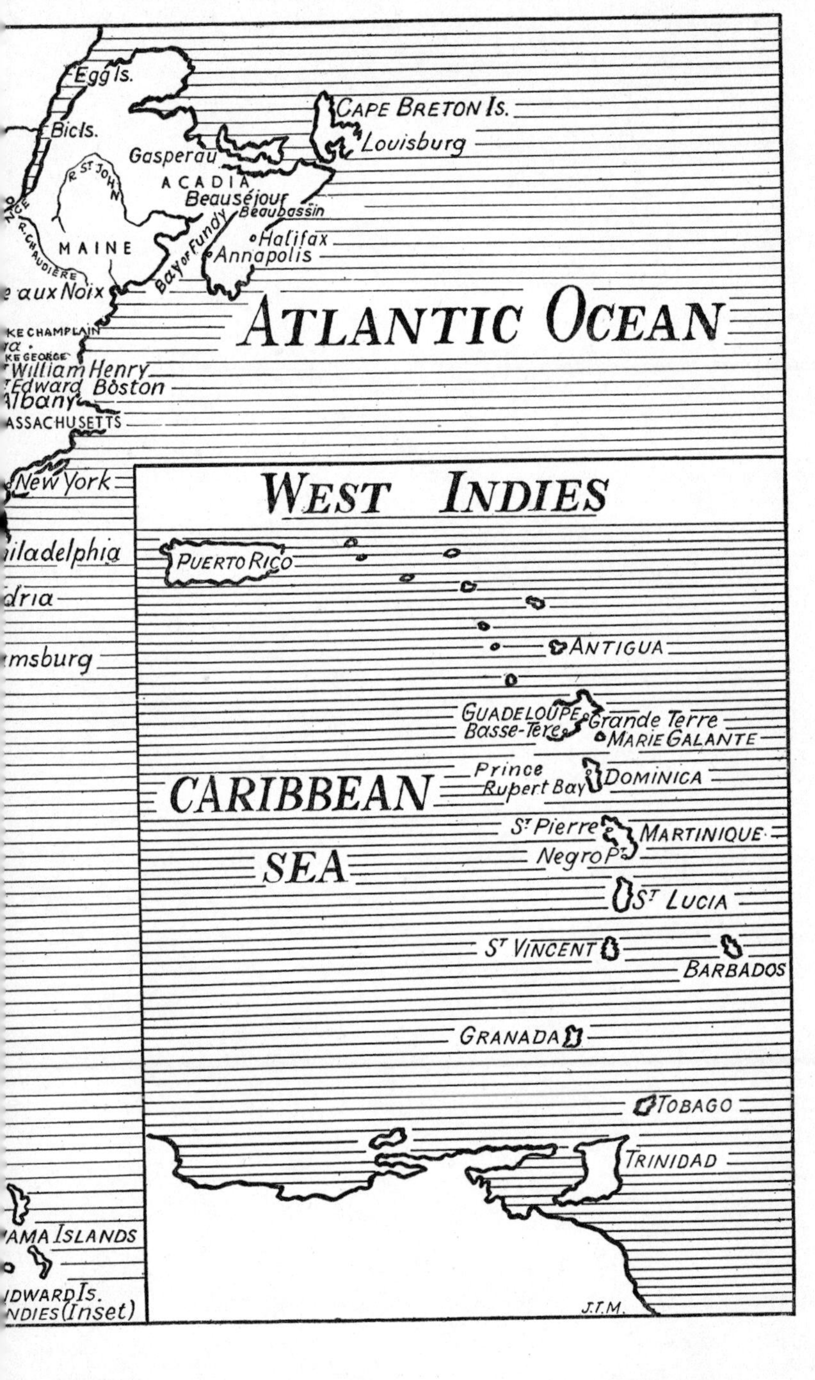
Egg Is.
Bic Is.
CAPE BRETON Is.
Louisburg
Gasperau
ACADIA
R. ST JOHN
Beauséjour
Beaubassin
Halifax
Annapolis
Bay of Fundy
MAINE
R. CHAUDIÈRE
e aux Noix
ATLANTIC OCEAN
William Henry
Edward
Boston
lbany
ASSACHUSETTS
New York
WEST INDIES
iladelphia
PUERTO RICO
dria
msburg
ANTIGUA
GUADELOUPE
Basse-Terre
Grande Terre
MARIE GALANTE
Prince Rupert Bay
DOMINICA
CARIBBEAN SEA
ST Pierre
MARTINIQUE
Negro Pt
ST LUCIA
ST VINCENT
BARBADOS
GRANADA
TOBAGO
TRINIDAD
AMA ISLANDS
DWARD Is.
NDIES (Inset)
J.T.M.

Contents

PREFACE 5

1 THE COLONIES IN AMERICA 13

2 GUSTS AND FLURRIES 32

3 THE EUROPEAN OUTLOOK 43

4 SLITHERING INTO WAR 56

5 DISMISSAL 70

6 'THE MISCARRIAGE UPON THE OHIO' 80

7 INTERLUDE 92

8 EAST AND WEST 112

9 NEWCASTLE FALLS 124

10 PITT ARRIVES 145

11 BYNG 163

12 FOREIGN AFFAIRS 170

13 A COURT INTRIGUE 184

14 THE INTERMINISTERIUM 195

15 THE ROCHEFORT EXPEDITION 214

16 NADIR 228

17 DISJUNCTIVE COALESCENCE 245

18 TROUBLES AT HOME 258

19 MINOR OPERATIONS 267

20 NEWS FROM AMERICA 280

21 ENTER BUTE 297

22 THE ROOT OF ALL EVIL 309

23 MINDEN 318

24 AMERICA AGAIN 330

25 'DAPPLINGS FOR PEACE' 340

26 PROBLEMS OF PEACE 351

27 THE NEW KING 368

28 THE SEARCH FOR PEACE 374

29 THE WILES OF BUTE 386

30 IS IT PEACE? 396

BIBLIOGRAPHY 423

INDEX 427

I

THE COLONIES IN AMERICA

(i)

During its course, the Seven Years' War was sometimes called Pitt's War. The title was well conceived, for, though it began before he had attained power and ended after he had lost office, his was the outstanding figure, and his the will to victory. At all points, he looms up vast and solitary amidst a crowd of lesser men, carrying the war on his shoulders and giving it a meaning that few grasped at the time and not all the world has yet fully understood.

It was a complicated and unusual war, raging fiercely in America and on the high seas for well over a year before it was officially declared, and having two halves that were wholly distinct yet vitally interconnected. One half, the American, was rooted in the past and evolved slowly out of local rivalries; the other, the continental, sprang suddenly out of a realignment of European powers, designed for purposes which had nothing to do with America and not much with England. The immediate upshot was the conquest of Canada and the foundation of the Indian Empire. The more remote results are still working themselves out.

It is now generally known as the Seven Years' War, but that is merely the latest of its titles and, except chronologically, the least enlightening. For the contemporary Englishman it began as the usual nondescript war with France. All he knew was that there was some trouble in America, some squabbling over boundaries, a tiresome state of things resulting in a tiresome war. Before long the struggle would, of course, degenerate into the usual fighting in Flanders and become complicated by an invasion of Hanover. There seemed to be no answer to that very ungentlemanly, but one was bound to admit highly effective, trick of the French, which put a stranglehold on England through her King and his

European entanglements, compelling her to give up her conquests in the West Indies in order to ransom Hanover.[1] It was exasperating, but facts had to be faced. The average Englishman had no doubt that the war would result in a peace restoring the *status quo ante,* for as Hervey had said, 'England is always a great loser by a war while it lasts, and can never be a great gainer when it concludes.'[2] Even the Prime Minister, the Duke of Newcastle, felt that the only hope of reaching any other conclusion lay in a system of wholesale bribery to keep the peace in Europe, which might leave England free to make some impression in America, securing perhaps an adjustment of the ragged boundaries of Acadia (Nova Scotia). It was worth trying, though in his view the only thing that mattered was the preservation of the 'old system' and the balance of power on the Continent, let events fall out in America as they would.

The war began with a series of disasters which confirmed the contemporary Englishman in his worst fears. It continued, unexpectedly, in a blaze of glory which filled him with intoxication too delirious to last, so that before long he suffered the normal reaction, and in a fit of victorious indigestion gave the war its first actual title. It became known as the German war and fell into disrepute. English historians, such as Mahon, who wrote not long after the event, found it little more than a series of episodes, glorious but untitled; and for the older American historians, such as Bancroft, it was merely the preliminary to the sterner business of the struggle for independence. Later in the nineteenth century, Seeley linked it with the War of the Austrian Succession, which had preceded it, and the War of American Independence, which followed after, and declared that the three together formed 'the great decisive duel between England and France for the possession of the New World'[3]—a view which, in spite of the nature of the decision, became generally accepted, even by American historians. From such a standpoint it was a short and easy step to regard the war as a vast imperial conception. 'One of the main objects of the war,' Lecky declared, 'was the creation of a great colonial empire.'[4] But Lecky and those who

[1] 'Every petty Prince who is a match for Hanover is too powerful for England; nor is it a question any longer what nations can cope with Great Britain, but what little Landgrave is too formidable to the Electorate.' Walpole. *George II*, I 297.

[2] Ilchester. *Lord Hervey and His Friends,* p. 236.

[3] *Expansion of England,* p. 33.

[4] *History of England in the Eighteenth Century,* II, p. 511.

thought with him were foreshortening facts. Originally the war had no particular object; like Topsy, it just growed. Neither the English nor the French Ministers, neither Louis XV nor George II, who slithered down into the cauldron together, set out with any intention of creating a great colonial empire. Even in America, where the ambition was rather more in evidence, it had lurked mostly in the imagination of one man—La Galissonière, who was once Governor of Canada but had left some seven years before the trouble began. Pitt and Pitt alone gave cohesion and meaning to a war which when he took it over was a sorry mess of largely unrelated defeats.

It is not therefore surprising that recently there has been a subtle change of outlook, not wholly denying but rather modifying the claims previously made. Pitt's relations with the Empire are altered; he is no longer the creator but the saviour. This is the view expressed by Sir Charles Grant Robertson, who says 'William Pitt was not, as he has often erroneously been called, the Founder of the First British Empire; but unquestionably he saved it in the great Ministry (1757-1761).'[1] Not that Sir Charles was being entirely original. When, on the 31st of October 1761, Sir Thomas Chitty, the Lord Mayor of London, laid the first stone of Blackfriars Bridge in honour of William Pitt, he laid with it an inscription hoping the bridge would remain a monument 'to the man who, by the strength of his genius, the steadiness of his mind, and a certain kind of happy contagion of his probity and spirit . . . recovered, augmented, and secured the British Empire, in Asia, Africa and America, and restored the ancient reputation and influence of his country amongst the nations of Europe.'[2]

Amidst these variations of interpretation, perhaps room may be found for one more, a further development bringing the circle full round; for there is a sense in which Pitt can be called the founder not only of the first but of all British empires because of the new meaning which he gave both to the word and to the conception.

(ii)

The British Empire, as a title, is of comparatively modern growth. It seldom appears in eighteenth-century writings.[3] I

[1] Grant Robertson. *Chatham and the British Empire,* p. xi. [2] Almon III. 382.

[3] One of the few occasions is to be found in an anonymous pamphlet of 1749, '*An Examination of the Principles and an Enquiry into the Conduct of the Two Brothers*' —i.e. Pelham and Newcastle—where it is used (p. 37) to emphasise the folly of restoring Cape Breton to the French by the Treaty of Aix.

think it is to be found in only three of Pitt's reported speeches (1st May 1771, 1st February 1775, and 30th May 1777), though there are perhaps half a dozen other occasions, all in the latter part of his life, on which he referred to 'empire' without an epithet. Empire was, on the whole, an alien conception, liable to be confused with the Holy Roman variety, which loomed much larger in the eighteenth-century eyes than its British counterpart. What came most easily to the lips of Pitt and his contemporaries were titles such as the Colonies, the Plantations, or the Dominions of the King.

This trick of speech emphasises a point which tends to be overlooked—that colonies are not necessarily the same as empire. There are historically two different forms of colonisation reaching back to the classical world—the Greek and the Roman—and the difference between the two is very marked. The Greek Colonies had their origin, sometimes in civil discord, sometimes in the need to reduce surplus population, but generally in a desire to establish trade relations with foreign countries. The settlers took with them the Greek idea of a city state, and the Colonies became separate entities, politically independent of the mother city, however closely tied to it by mutual affection. Colonies for the Greeks were fully-fledged members of that wide Hellenic community which, like the ideal of the British Commonwealth, looked upon itself as united in opposition to the barbarian world, but did not for one moment assume that all its members must live in harmony together, or that any one of them must be subject to others. The Roman Colonies were different in origin, form and function. The colonists were Roman citizens sent out deliberately to keep new conquests in order; they were primarily a military establishment, stationed for the time being in a dependency, but still citizens of Rome and proud of the fact.

The English Colonies did not conform to either model; they came somewhere between the two, but were more closely akin to the Greek than to the Roman. Like the Greek Colonies, they had their origins sometimes in discord, though religious rather than civil, and sometimes in the impression that there was a surplus population to be provided for, but generally in a desire to promote trade and commerce, or at least the wealth of individual Governors. Whatever the immediate cause, there is usually to be found somewhere in the background a great trading corporation, established by charter and backed by the City of London, a corporation such as the East India Company founded in 1600 or the Virginia Company founded in 1606. But once established, the English colony put on a character of its own. It did not break away from the mother country, as the Greek Colonies inevitably did; nor did it act merely as a military outpost in a dependency, after the Roman fashion. It managed in a way peculiar to itself to combine a measure of filial submission with a turbulent insistence on living its own life. In case after case the early history of a colony tells the same story, of power being transferred first from a private owner, whether a company or a proprietor, to the Crown, then from the Crown to the British Parliament, and finally, through varying stages, from the British Parliament to the local Assembly.

The English Colonies were founded by private enterprise, and their preoccupation with trade, their struggles for existence and their itch for self-government did not create an atmosphere favourable to the growth of empire. Indeed, the first British Empire, which Pitt is variously supposed to have created or to have saved, was not an empire in its inception, nor consciously in its growth. The early Stuarts, in whose reigns the plantations began, paid little attention to their newly-acquired possessions, and if their policy of wholesome neglect had not been interrupted, perhaps the Empire would never have come into conscious existence, perhaps the Colonies would have followed the old Greek example, becoming each a separate state without any War of Independence, without any bitterness, without any struggle. But that was not to be. The light-hearted carelessness of the early days, which combined a spirit of adventure with a hope of gain, turned to a belief that the plantations, now that they were established and likely to flourish, had been 'contrived in the special interest of home prosperity.'[1] First under Cromwell and then under Charles II, England adopted a policy of trade ascendancy which cut the wings of the Colonies, reducing them from self-sufficient communities to ready-made markets for her own manufactures, while she became the entrepôt of the Empire.[2] With the revolution of 1688 and the appearance on the throne of foreigners, the idea of selfish exploitation grew, and an ever narrower mercantile principle dominated a Whiggish Parliament.

[1] Woodward. *The Expansion of the British Empire,* p. 121.

[2] 'Instead of colonisation, the purpose of English policy, implied if not avowed, was now ascendancy.' Clark. *The Wealth of England,* p. 135.

The Empire, if it had ever been consciously alive, was now ignored and neglected. America was, on the whole, a nuisance, and like all nuisances was forgotten when out of sight and put in its place when it chanced to be noted. Walpole's political creed was to leave well alone, his practical policy to foster trade. It followed that he viewed the Colonies with complete political indifference, while tending to emphasise their commercial subjection. During practically the whole of his long premiership their administration was in the hands of the Duke of Newcastle, whose interest was slight and knowledge less. There is a well-known description of his activities in Walpole's *Memoirs*: 'it would not be credited what reams of papers, representations, memorials, petitions, from that quarter of the world lay mouldering and unopened in his office. West India Governors could not come within the sphere of his jealousy; nothing else merited or could fix his mercurial inattention. He knew as little of the geography of his province as of the state of it; when General Legonier hinted some defence to him for Annapolis, he replied with his evasive lisping hurry "Annapolis, Annapolis! Oh! yes, Annapolis must be defended; to be sure Annapolis should be defended—where is Annapolis?" When the French invasions forced him to arouse a little from this lethargy, he struggled to preserve his inactivity by ordering letters of the most abject and submissive import to be written to our Governors, who pressed for instructions, nay, for permission to defend themselves. . . . But if he sacrificed the dignity of the Crown with one hand, he thought to exalt it with the other; the prerogative was strained unwarrantably over the Assemblies.'[1] The quotation is long and amusing, and of course exaggerated, but there is sufficient truth in it to make the sarcasm bite home, and perhaps cloak unduly the difficulties with which Newcastle had to contend. There was more than ignorance and indifference to trip him up. America was, and had long been, a problem which must be faced sooner or later—a problem long overdue for solution, and already muddled beyond belief by alternate bouts of Government neglect and Government interference. Since Charles II there had been no policy beyond an unintelligent and unthinking policy of *laissez faire*. Yet the problem was pressing ever more insistently from three angles: there was the problem of securing the safety of the Colonies; there was the problem of their government;

[1] *George II*, I, 396.

and there was the problem of their relations with the home authorities—the King, the Cabinet and Parliament. Not one of these problems had been squarely faced or perhaps even realised, still less had they been solved, and after the Treaty of Aix (1748) they had been complicated by the twin facts that the boundaries between the English and French possessions had been left uncertain, and that unrest and anxiety prevailed along the whole American frontier. Whatever might be done about the other problems, the question of defence was thrusting itself more and more insistently to the front. If it seemed impossible to solve, it seemed almost more impossible to ignore. The French saw to that.

(iii)

The French! It gives food for thought, and indeed for humiliating thought, that if the present-day Englishman could be translated back to eighteenth-century America, he might easily find himself more at home in French Canada than in any of the English Colonies. The latter had each its own characteristics, but all alike conformed broadly to the same type—the turbulent, individualistic English type. In that they differed profoundly from French Canada, which was in every part of it the 'welfare state' of the socialists' dreams. To read of the rules, the regulations, the planning and the provisions which governed and controlled and guided and feather-bedded the lives of the French Canadians is like reading a modern political speech or a page of modern political propaganda. 'Perpetual intervention of Government,' says Parkman, '—regulations, restrictions, encouragements sometimes more mischievous than restrictions, a constant uncertainty what the authorities would do next, the fate of each man resting less with himself than with another, volition enfeebled, self-reliance paralysed—the condition, in short, of a child held always under the rule of a father, in the main well-meaning and kind, sometimes generous, sometimes neglectful, often capricious, and rarely very wise—such were the influences under which Canada grew up.'[1] In New France nothing was too great, nothing too small for the eye of Authority, and what Authority saw, it itched to regulate. Colbert, great and enlightened Minister as he was, wrote in the name of Louis XIV: 'As the King regards his Canadian subjects, from the highest to the lowest, almost as his

[1] Parkman. *The Old Régime in Canada*, p. 461.

own children, and wishes them to enjoy equally with the people of France, the mildness and happiness of his reign, the Sieur Talon will study to solace them in all things, and encourage them to trade and industry. And seeing that nothing can better promote this end than entering into the details of their households and of all their little affairs, it will not be amiss that he visit all their settlements one after the other in order to learn their true condition, provide as much as possible for their wants, and, performing the duty of a good head of a family, put them in the way of making some profit.'[1] Louis' intentions were admirable and his officials were zealous. In New France God was to be glorified and the King beloved; the Government was to show itself benign and the people were to be happy. Because Versailles knew best, all was arranged for the fortunate colonists; it was not for them to worry their empty heads; it was not for them to take thought for the morrow. They could relax, since Authority had decided that the programme was to be full employment and the result prosperity. To ensure it, farms were inspected and advice lavished on the farmers; factories were built for the men, light industries promoted for the women—in both cases subsidised. Then the all-providing Authorities turned to the communal necessities of life: they built roads; they planned cities; they laid out communities; they supervised buildings and controlled both sites and elevations—all the paraphernalia of town planning, on the then latest model, were put at the disposal of the young colony, and indeed clamped upon it. Nor were the private wants or the natural desires of the individual overlooked. Gifts were showered on the colonists—houses, cattle, sheep—to enable them to set up in life and become prosperous citizens. Their spiritual needs were supplied by a host of clerics and their health maintained by hospitals and dispensaries. Then because marriage was not only ordained of God and desired by man but also useful for the enlargement of the population, girls were considerately shipped from home to be the wives and mothers of the new settlements; and lest the colonists should not recognise their advantages or should be unduly picksome, marriage was embellished by bounties and the burden of children lightened by allowances, while the obstinately celibate were daunted by the curtailment of privileges. All, or most, of the blessings on which we of this century pride ourselves were lavished upon French

[1] Parkman. *The Old Régime in Canada,* p. 270.

Canada in the seventeenth and eighteenth centuries. But Nature is notoriously unwilling to conform to human expectations, and the effect of Louis' efforts in Canada was mainly a creeping paralysis.

Yet not entirely. There were three sections of the community which in their various ways flourished—the Church, the army, and those daring spirits who threw off the trammels of authority and betook themselves to the woods, the *coureurs de bois*. But the overriding fact, not sufficiently observed at the time, was that these three sections, however useful, however necessary, were essentially sterile. Monks and nuns are not as a rule sedulous to enlarge the population; the army in its professional aspect usually reduces it; and the *coureurs de bois*, by throwing in their lot with the Indians, tended to be lost to the colony and to become the fathers of half-breeds, unacceptable to paleface and redskin alike. These sterile elements were the moving spirits of Canada. All three helped to sap whatever manhood the welfare state had left—the Jesuits by their ideal of a submission which abdicates will and judgment in favour of the spiritual director; the army by providing too obviously for the safety of the colonists against the Indians; and the *coureurs de bois* by draining away the hot-blooded and mettlesome into the woods and leaving at home the tame, the meek, the lily-livered and the lazy.

Yet, if *vis-à-vis* the English Colonies Canada had the defects of the 'welfare state,' she had also its advantages. All her elements, good and bad alike, served to weld her into one homogeneous whole, and by that very fact made her formidable as an antagonist. In her soldiery she had ordered military strength; in her Jesuits she had the combustibles of a holy war; through her priests she had organisation at home, and through her missionaries close contact with the native tribes; in her *coureurs de bois* she had a hardy body of explorers and a virile army of guerillas, versed in the wiles and tricks of forest warfare; and in her inhabitants at large she had a population whose energies were not fully occupied, a population at once proud and poor, imbued from birth with a desire for military glory and brought up to give blind obedience to the seigneur or the Governor who ordered each detail of their lives. In contradistinction, her English neighbours were quarrelsome and jealous, wrapped up in themselves and bitterly opposed to standing armies or even mutual co-operation. The weighting of the dice in the event of war was obvious.

(iv)

From the first there had been constant bickering between the rival Colonies, and at no time had it been justified. The provocation generally came from the French; 'hostilities in Canada,' wrote Ponchartrain, 'have always been begun by the French,'[1] and as Louis' Colonial Minister he should have known. But the English can take no credit to themselves; they were every whit as quarrelsome, but they indulged their spleen at home, squabbling with one another and snapping at their Governors. Historians attribute the French restiveness mainly to a single deep-seated apprehension: 'the French Canadians,' they say, 'were well aware of the danger of their own position, shut in between the Hudson's Bay Company to the north and the teeming populations of the British colonies to the south. . . . Fears for their ultimate position in North America drove the French to push forward up the Great Lakes and down the Mississippi, seeking to circumvent the English who otherwise threatened to surround them.'[2] No doubt the historians know. Certainly the apprehension reflects much credit on the French Canadians, who must have been a far-sighted people; for in 1703, when Ponchartrain wrote, the teeming populations did not much exceed 250,000 souls stretched out along a thousand miles of coastal fringe, and the most northerly of the plantations was separated from Canada by 'a hundred leagues of pathless forest, prowled by her [Canada's] Indian allies.'[3] So difficult was intercourse between the two that the Canadians usually employed Indians to do their raiding, and when the English wished to retaliate they were wont to attack, not Canada which was too inaccessible, but Acadia which could be reached by sea.

There were certainly other reasons beside the French apprehensions, reasons springing from the wickedness of the human heart. Whoever began the quarrelling, both kept it going, hating each other with the bitterness of national rivalry and the profound scorn of differing modes of life. By way of further goads they had the friction of separate languages, the intolerance of diverse religions, the greed which is common to humanity, and that exclusive jealousy which dominated all colonising

[1] Parkman. *Half Century of Conflict*, I, 98.
[2] G. M. Trevelyan. *The Peace and the Protestant Succession*, p. 140.
[3] Parkman. *Half Century of Conflict*, I, 116.

countries of those days. Last, but by no means least, the French aptitude for hectoring must have been encouraged by their quasi-military organisation and that mixture of contempt and irritation which a proud and thriftless soldiery are apt to feel towards comparatively well-to-do and hard-working citizens.

There is no need to trace the rivalry in too great detail, but something must be said to explain the growth of a certain attitude of mind on both sides of the border and to some extent also in Europe. French interest in Canada began with the appearance of Breton fishermen off the Banks of Newfoundland at the end of the fifteenth century and the voyage of Jacques Cartier up the St. Lawrence in 1534. Thereafter it waned until in the second half of the seventeenth century Colbert imbued a somewhat reluctant Louis XIV with his own ideas of colonial expansion. He founded the French East India Company, encouraging it to build establishments at Surat, Chandernagore and Pondicherry; in Africa he seized Madagascar and captured Goree and Senegal from the Dutch; in America he bought a number of West Indian islands, occupied Newfoundland, and dispatched La Salle to explore the Mississippi valley and add Louisiana to the French dominions. Under his able and energetic guidance France gained a notable lead in the race for colonial empire, and if Louis XIV had not flagged, Colbert might have been able to adopt Pitt's subsequent boast that he had conquered America in Germany, for William III and Marlborough willingly allowed themselves to be 'contained' in Europe. It is true that occasional expeditions went from England to the West Indies, but in every case 'the material force given to the commander was inadequate to the work he had to do,'[1] so that the expeditions failed or at best achieved only half successes—and nobody in England seemed to care. Broadly speaking the expeditions acted merely as pinpricks—enough to remind each side how much they disliked the other, but not enough to produce a lasting decision.

Yet they roused certain definite feelings in New England hearts. The constant menace of Red Indian raids, led or inspired by the French, with all the horrors which they entailed, was beginning to have an effect. Something must be done to ensure peace and quiet, and the colonists began to think that the only certain method would be to conquer Canada and turn the French out neck and crop. The men of Massachusetts even went so far

[1] Hannay. *Short History of the Royal Navy*, II, 71-2.

in the early years of William III's war as to summon their neighbours to join with them in crushing the common enemy, but they were repulsed, and thereafter, till the Peace of Ryswick (1697), remained sunk in dejected alarm, convinced that they could not achieve their aim by themselves. With the renewal of war in Europe in 1702, the 'savage and boundless butchery' recommenced, and becoming unendurable, revived the idea of the expulsion of the French. But on this occasion the colonists did not intend to repeat the mistake of acting by themselves; they must have the support of the home country. They, or at least some of them, would help to the best of their poor ability, but the main burden must be borne by the mother country; she must succour her oppressed children; she must provide the skill, the knowledge, the funds, the arms, the ships and the men. The prime mover in the matter was a certain Captain Samuel Vetch, who towards the end of 1708—just about the time of Pitt's birth—persuaded the General Court of Massachusetts to send him to Queen Anne with a petition for help in the reduction of Acadia and Canada. He arrived in England at a favourable moment. In the early months of 1709 a Whig Ministry had imposed itself upon the Queen, and being essentially a war party were bedevilling the problem of peace, then in the ascendant, by trying to force impossible conditions on Louis. They therefore welcomed the appearance of Vetch and his demand that war should be prosecuted vigorously overseas. Without any unnecessary delay they sent him back to Boston, fully authorised to proceed with his proposals and carrying in his pocket a promise of five regiments of regular troops from England, amounting to about 4,000 men. More than that: they drew up for him the whole plan of campaign. The Colonies were to contribute their quotas; 1,200 provincials were to join the regulars in an attack on Quebec by way of the St. Lawrence, while a further 1,500 were to advance on Montreal by way of Wood Creek and Lake Champlain. Vetch returned to America in triumph and the various Colonies busied themselves with preparation for the parts they were to play. They looked with eager anticipation for the squadron from England which was due to arrive at Boston by the middle of May (1709). They looked in vain. It never came. Instead, towards the middle of October, a letter arrived to say that the promised troops had been diverted to Portugal to meet an exigency in the European war. The wrath and indignation of the colonists can be imagined.

Two points, however, are worth noting. Although Canada had not been invaded, the plan of campaign had been settled; it remained on record and—significantly—contained in its general outline the embryo of Pitt's strategy fifty years later. Secondly, there is the reflection that while Marlborough was given 120,000 men—mostly seasoned veterans—to resuscitate an exploded war in Europe, a total force of 7,000 men—nearly half of them raw colonial levies—was all and more than all that could be spared for the conquest of North America. The numbers form a striking commentary on the relative values which the Whig junta placed on the two seats of war.

Deprived of the expected help from England, the colonists were yet sufficiently in earnest to be anxious and willing to strike a blow for themselves. Nothing of course could be done on the grand scale such as they had previously contemplated, but at least they would make a descent on Port Royal, the main town of Acadia, if they could get a minimum of encouragement. They offered to besiege the town themselves if England would help with four frigates and 500 soldiers. Probably their suggestion would have been ignored, had not Peter Schuyler hit upon the idea of bringing four or five Mohawk chiefs to England and making a show of them in outlandish costumes. The savages tickled the fancy of the fashionable world, became the darlings of Society for a few months and helped materially in obtaining a promise of the modest contingent for which the colonists had asked.

Needless to say the troops did not arrive on time, but they did eventually sail into Boston harbour. The encouragement thus afforded was unconscionably small—500 men to reduce Acadia—but it was sufficient. Until the arrival of the ships the colonists had remained quiescent, half hopeful, half pessimistic; but they now sprang to life; preparations began in earnest, and on the 18th of September the expedition set sail. On the 2nd of October 1710 Port Royal surrendered and was renamed Annapolis in honour of Queen Anne and the ladylike help she had vouchsafed. As there was no other place of strength in the province, its capture meant virtually the conquest of Acadia, which was accordingly ceded to England by the Treaty of Utrecht.

The affair of Port Royal scared the French into a new watchfulness and a new frame of mind. Now, if never before, they began to think seriously of their position—not so much the danger of encirclement as of final extermination. The perennial discord with New England began to be embittered by an element of fear. Border raids were a game which could be played with a large measure of impunity; the English Colonies might be the more populous and superficially the more powerful, but they were divided and given to quarrelling amongst themselves; they were rather to be disliked than feared so long as they remained unsupported. But a confederation cemented and reinforced from England was another matter altogether. A counter-check must be found, some method of breaking up this sinister combination of mother country and daughter colonies. The French buzzed with speculation and bright ideas. Some believed in strong measures before it was too late. The best protection would be to fall suddenly upon Boston and burn it to the ground and then, while the flames were still hot, show Canada's essentially pacific intentions by offering to refrain from further hostilities if the Colonies would promise to take no share in English schemes against North America. Others, with greater subtlety, wanted to drive a wedge between England and her colonies. The easiest way would be to insinuate into colonial minds the thought that the mother country, incensed at the growing spirit of democracy in the plantations, was using the attack on Canada as a Trojan horse—an excuse for introducing strong forces into America. When once the troops had been landed, the ridiculous project of conquering Canada would be dropped and the true object would be uncovered; the plantations would be coerced into submission. Alternatively, an even surer way might be to stress in England that if once the French were ousted, the plantations would have nothing to fear and would seize the opportunity to throw off their allegiance. Here was an idea to make England's flesh creep—to conquer Canada was the surest, safest and shortest way of losing the Colonies, and any request from them for help should be rejected out of hand. None of the speculations carried any weight at the time outside Canada, but subsequent events have given this last school of thought a posthumous reputation for prophecy which was not altogether deserved.

So much for Canada. In America the victory gave enormous pleasure, but did not enlighten the colonists as to their own inherent powers. They failed to follow up their advantage and gloomily anticipated that Annapolis—their newly-acquired and gratefully-named Annapolis—would be returned to France at the peace. They could not forget that they had conquered Port Royal not once or twice, but three times (in 1654, 1690 and 1710), and on the two previous occasions a callous England had handed it back. Besides, during the summer the Queen had been ousting the Whig Ministry which had given them countenance, and even as Port Royal was surrendering, a general election was taking place which threw out the Whigs and returned to power a united Tory party. The colonists looked for no help from the Tories, who were the party of peace, and without help they were indisposed to act. They had shot their bolt, and the best they could hope was that they would be allowed to keep the bird they had brought down.

In England the repercussion differed greatly from the anticipations of the colonists. Throughout the year England had been in a turmoil which so far from ceasing when the Tories came back to power, was if anything embittered. The news therefore of Port Royal came as a great refreshment, and lured St. John into reviving the idea of an expedition against Quebec. He had many motives; it was in keeping with the Tory preference for a colonial over a continental war; it would assist in the negotiations for peace; it would be a counterweight to Marlborough's fame; and finally, but by no means least, if skilfully handled, it should provide a ladder by which St. John could climb to greater power and influence in the Cabinet. He succumbed to this mixture of patriotism and personal profit, but as he was more at home in political manœuvres than in military dispositions, his preparations were neither well conceived nor well executed. He kept his intentions shrouded in mystery, not even allowing the Admiralty to know the destination of the fleet, which he entrusted to Sir Hovenden Walker, a cipher who had never shown particular ability and now was to show undoubted incompetence. The troops—about 5,500 men—were handed over to Brigadier John Hill, whose only merit, apart from a feckless bonhomie, was the fact that he was Abigail Masham's brother. If the arrangements in England were bad, the arrangements in America were worse; no liaison had been made with the colonists before the fleet sailed, and no plan had been concerted with them when it arrived in Boston. The expedition was a fiasco; it failed ingloriously, never reaching Quebec or seeing an enemy. The loss of eight troopships and about 700 men off the Isle of Egg in the mouth of the St. Lawrence through bad seamanship so shook admiral and general alike that they retreated precipitately and thought it no small merit to regain home ports without further disaster.

But if the expedition achieved nothing material, it had its effect on England's relations with her Colonies. The unheralded arrival of the armament—not inconsiderable as numbers then went—caused the Boston authorities infinite difficulties of commissariat and billeting. Anxious not to be found wanting, they made heavy demands on the inhabitants, while the British officers, making no allowance for the strain placed on a small community, showed themselves impatient and imperious. Relations became unhappy; 'the British thought the colonists awkward, uncouth, narrow and hypocritical. The colonists thought the British haughty and incompetent.'[1] The failure of the expedition no doubt confirmed the provincials in their views and made them the less willing to accept the tutelage of the mother country. The seeds of future trouble were being sown more thickly than was to be desired.

There were other effects. Had the expedition been a success, it would have had its influence on the terms of peace, but, being a failure, it tempered the demands which England could make and stiffened the attitude of France. Louis began to think that after all he would not cede either Acadia or Cape Breton, and though he was forced to yield the former, he managed to leave the boundaries ill-defined and he clung on to the latter. More than that, his interest in America revived and he plotted how best to defend his possessions and even how best to prepare for the recovery of his lost province. Nothing was to be yielded but the bare soil; the inhabitants were to be moved elsewhere; and Cape Breton, which hitherto had been neglected as a deserted and rocky isle, was to be occupied as a bastion against further encroachment. In keeping with these decisions the harbour hitherto known as Port à l'Anglois was built into a fortress and given the name of Louisburg. The site was admirably chosen for its military possibilities and its foundation intimidated both America and England. Meanwhile the Acadians, though unwilling to leave their fat farms, remained French at heart, and, still much under the influence of their priests, were a possible fifth column in any future war. In short, although the Treaty of Utrecht

[1] Churchill. *Marlborough,* IV, 396.

(1713) gave Newfoundland, Acadia and Hudsons Bay to England, it left France in a strong position, still able to consider herself perhaps the most commanding, certainly an important, power in North America, with shadowy claims over by far the greater part of the continent, and owning the allegiance of by far the greater number of Indian tribes. There was little to show that England would, or even wished to, become paramount.

(v)

Louis XIV died in 1715, shortly after the War of the Austrian Succession had ended, but he had lived long enough to ensure that, whatever might happen in Europe, the war would sooner or later be revived in America. The train for the explosion was laid by his policy of passive resistance in Acadia, and of active defiance in Louisburg. He was succeeded by his great-grandson, Louis XV, then a boy of five, and internal politics concurred with the new King's youth to make peace desirable for France. Nor was England in any mood to renew hostilities; she had troubles enough at home to keep her occupied until Walpole began his long tenure of power. He might well have tackled the problem of America—the moment was not unpropitious—but he had no eye for the plantations over the sea. So the provisions for settling the boundaries of Acadia were ignored. Worse still, England did nothing effective to absorb the province, whatever its boundaries, into her own empire. Annapolis became the headquarters of a Governor, and was given a garrison of about 150 men, but otherwise both Annapolis and the province were left to their own devices. The garrison became more and more ragged and increasingly inadequate to keep a growing population in order. The Governor's authority was continually flouted by the inhabitants and undermined by the neighbouring French and above all by the priests, who were as much political agents as spiritual guides. No attempt was made by the English either to govern or even to tax the French peasants; no control was exercised beyond demanding from time to time an oath of allegiance, which the peasants barely understood and were unwilling to give, which meant nothing to them in the normal course of events, and which they ignored whenever its observance might have been serviceable to England. Under Walpole, England's claim to Acadia was little more than a legal fiction, and perhaps for that very reason remained a source of irritation to the French, galling to their national pride and outraging their religious feelings. It was inevitable that they should cherish dreams of recovery, and when occasion offered, hatch schemes of revenge. Openly, it was difficult for them to move, but they had other resources. The Abenaki Indians were their firm friends and full of hatred for the English. What easier than to provide them secretly with powder and guns and hound them on to burn and pillage along the borders of Maine? For forty years or more the acquisition of Acadia meant nothing but trouble for New England and a promise of wars to come.

Whilst Acadia remained as an irritant, a far deeper and more serious cause of trouble was New York's tendency to dabble in the fur trade. Compared with her compatriots to the north and east, New York had little seaboard, but she stretched along the valley of the Hudson and beside Lake Champlain which gave her easy access to the west. She and Pennsylvania alone had a direct route to the Great Lakes. She alone had a large admixture of Dutch blood, having been but lately a Dutch colony, and as Doyle says[1] 'it was certain that in any Dutch colony the interests of the farmer would give way to the interests of the merchant.' More than that, New York bordered on the territory of the Iroquois, that collection of Indian tribes who went by the name of the Five Nations, and who, fearing the French, were disposed to lean towards the English. They were willing to act as agents, to carry messages and promote trade between New York and the distant tribes in the fur-producing areas to the north-west. Everything conspired to make New York a rival of the French in the fur trade. This was a more potent threat than mere encirclement. The fur trade was the jugular vein of Canada; if that were cut, New France must perish. It was this threat which constantly haunted the French Governors and drove France, willy nilly, along the road to disaster. This was no bickering over boundaries or snapping up of unoccupied territory; this was no question of racial animosity or religious intolerance; it was a matter of life and death. The English Colonies could have grown and prospered without the fur trade; French Canada could not without altering her whole conception of colonisation. Rather than that she preferred to keep her monopoly by blocking the outlets of the English Colonies to the west, claiming the hinterland for herself,

[1] *The Middle Colonies,* p. 3.

and building forts at strategic points to bar the passage of traders. By the middle of the eighteenth century the French had got as near success as they could hope. They had built a chain of forts round the Great Lakes which went far to hamstring English trade; they had evolved a system of Indian warfare which kept the English continually on the rack; they had repelled English attempts to drive them from the country, and they had sown, or tried to sow, the seeds of discord between America and England. They had reason to hope that they had done enough, bearing in mind the English preoccupation with matters which struck the French as innocuous and futile—their constitutional development, their internal wrangles and jealousies, their suspicion of authority and their latent quarrel with their mother country. The French could observe their disunion and turbulence with a cynical satisfaction.

2

GUSTS AND FLURRIES

(i)

The Treaty of Aix (1748) restored nominal peace between France and England, not only on the Continent but in the Colonies and settlements; conquests were to be given back, including Louisburg which New Englanders had captured in 1745; and all matters in dispute, even the boundaries of Acadia, were to be finally and amicably settled. Commissioners met in Paris for the purpose and after three years of wrangling separated with nothing to show but a bundle of memoranda as large as their claims. The politicians, more interested in clearing up the debris at home, left the backwoodsmen, both English and French, to look after themselves. Which was what they tried to do; and as their interests were diametrically opposed and neither side could get adequate help from the mother country, their efforts depended on and were moulded by the initiative of a few individuals—de la Galissonière and Duquesne on the French side; Dinwiddie and Washington on the English. But their initiative led straight to the Seven Years' War.

The end of hostilities gave a fillip to trade and its accompanying rivalries, especially in the matter of furs. As French forts barred the more northerly entrance to the fur-producing districts of the west, the English looked for openings farther south. They were not difficult to find. There were many feasible routes from Maryland and Virginia into the Ohio valley, and thence along the numerous streams up to the Great Lakes. Exploring the possibilities, the English discovered not only profitable trade but fertile lands, and soon began to think of forming a company and obtaining a charter to exploit those vacant territories. Gentlemen of Virginia, including two of Washington's brothers, took so lively an interest in the matter that by 1750 the Ohio

Company was in being, and the proud possessor of a grant of 500,000 acres from the King himself.

From the French point of view this movement threatened to outflank the defences of the Canadian fur trade and undo the work of years. Counter-action was imperative and the type of action depended on the character of the Canadian Governor. At the signing of the peace he was the Marquis de la Galissonière, a naval officer who was physically a hunchback, mentally a precisian, and constitutionally a fervent patriot. He recognised that Canada, as a welfare state, had always been a burden on France and he grieved at the thought, but he was utterly and entirely convinced that France must retain her hold on her American possessions as a barrier against English ambitions. If England became mistress of all America, her trade, her naval power and her wealth would grow to such vast proportions that she would overshadow France and indeed the whole of Europe. She must be kept down. It was not merely a case of checking her trade; she must be confined to the narrow strip along the seaboard and at all costs barred from the west. Theoretically that presented no problem. France was mistress of Canada in the north and Louisiana in the south; between these two lay the valleys of the Ohio and the Mississippi which belonged to France by right of discovery and even occupation, since she had scattered a few forts over the vast territory to protect communications. All that was now necessary was to re-establish her rights openly and warn trespassers off. With this in view, Galissonière sent Céloron de Bienville with a couple of hundred troops and a band of Indians to travel down the Ohio and reassert the claims of France, which had lain dormant since the days of La Salle. Céloron did his best by affixing notices to the trees and burying lead plaques in the soil, but the tangible results of his journey were of the slightest. How far Galissonière believed that the English traders would respect, or be deterred by, his warning notices and whether he had other schemes up his sleeve must remain in doubt as he had been recalled to France before Céloron's return. But if he trusted to the gentlemanly instincts of the traders, his faith was not shared by the Governors of Virginia and Pennsylvania. Dinwiddie of Virginia called them 'a set of abandoned wretches,' and Hamilton of Pennsylvania 'a very licentious people.'[1] It may be that Dinwiddie was thinking primarily of the traders from Pennsylvania and

[1] Parkman. *Montcalm and Wolfe,* I, 42.

Hamilton of those from Virginia—for there was no love lost between them—but it comes to much the same. The traders were a rough and riotous crew, full of daring and imbued with a large and lofty indifference to moral scruples. They were not likely to be bothered by warnings against trespass.

Céloron returned at the end of 1749, leaving in his wake a feeling of resentment among the traders and not a little suspicion among the natives. He did nothing practical to advance the French cause, but he heaped up a little more tinder against the coming conflagration. The next year, possibly because of Galissonière's departure, the deep cancer of Anglo-French rivalry in the west became temporarily quiescent, and instead a surface rash broke out in the east, flaming and irritable. From the moment Louisburg was returned to them, the French had been busily strengthening it. They knew the disgust of the English colonists at having their prize snatched out of their hands, and for that very reason had been more jubilant and more ostentatious in the work of reconstruction than was altogether wise; for though Louisburg might be primarily a shield for French Canada, it was also a menace to English Acadia. Their defiant gloating aroused misgivings as well as annoyance; so much so that George II, who had never approved of the restoration of the fortress, suddenly took a hand in colonial enterprise and by royal authority founded the town of Halifax as a sentinel and makeweight on the other side. Friction promptly ensued. The French could do nothing openly, they must retain the veneer of peace unbroken, but from the King downwards they stirred up the Indian tribes to harass the new settlement, and encouraged, and almost commanded, the French peasantry to ignore their oaths of allegiance and keep Acadia in a turmoil. There was more to come. Galissonière's successor, the Marquis de la Jonquière, sent a body of troops to Beauséjour, a hill dominating the isthmus which joined Acadia to the mainland, with instructions to keep a watch on the English frontier and to aid and abet the resident French priest in his nefarious intrigues. The priest in question was the Abbé le Loutre, a fierce fanatical man, wielding his spiritual authority for temporal ends without remorse and without compunction. His flock might lose hearth and home, livelihood and life, it was all one to him provided they did his bidding and strewed the path of the English Governor, Edward Cornwallis, with thorns and boulders. His efforts were so notorious and so successful that in April 1750 Cornwallis dispatched Major Lawrence with 400 men to Beaubassin, a village a few miles south of Beauséjour and on the English side of the frontier. Hearing of his approach, le Loutre hounded on his Micmacs and Acadians to burn the village to the ground, and set the example by firing the parish church with his own hand. Lawrence thereupon built a fort named after himself, and an undeclared but very real war of raid and counter-raid began and continued—to the great suffering of the inhabitants.

(ii)

The real point of interest, however, is not the spirit of aggression shown by the French, nor yet the miserable plight of the Acadians—beaten up by le Loutre if they remained on English territory and beggared if they crossed over into Canada—but the effect which the burning of Beaubassin had upon the Ministers at home. Newcastle, after the first shock, came to think of the proceedings as 'extraordinary' but on the whole not very material, since everything would depend on the findings of the Boundary Commission. If the French claims prevailed, Nova Scotia would be of little use to us and Beaubassin none at all; while if the English claims were made good, Cape Breton would be of no great advantage to the French and we could afford to ignore the loss of a few huts. Best, in the circumstances, not to bother too much, though of course, as a matter of diplomatic form, strong representations should be made—had in fact been made already by Lord Albemarle, the British Ambassador in Paris, on his own initiative.[1] When Puysieulx, the French Foreign Secretary, told polite fibs to the effect that Jonquière had been acting without orders and offered vague promises of redress if the facts were as represented, Newcastle was ready to accept his assurances and brush the whole affair on one side. He was much too absorbed in the intricacies of European politics.[2]

Pelham was a little more agitated, a little more inclined to take some positive action. It occurred to him that what Puysieulx said in France would not alter facts in America, and that perhaps Cornwallis should be given a trifle of encouragement. What about telling him to use force in repelling French or Indians who

[1] Newcastle to Pelham, 17/23 June 1750. Add. MSS. 32,721.
[2] Newcastle to Pitt, 26 June/7 July 1750. Add. MSS. 32,721.

might presume 'to disturb the English in the uncontroverted part of Nova Scotia'—a hint that Cornwallis hardly required. What, too, about trusting him with powers to recruit 400 or 500 extra troops? Pelham's intentions were of the best, but with his ingrained infirmity of purpose he found it difficult to translate them into action.[1]

Pitt alone found matter for deep and lasting concern. The point which struck him at once was that Jonquière had been sent out as Governor after the war had ended. It followed that he could not have any excuse, as Galissonière might have had, for hostile action. He must have known—he did know—that the two countries were at peace; he must have known that the question of boundaries, if it arose at all—and Pitt denied that there was any shadow of doubt in whose territory Beaubassin lay—was *sub judice,* was being thrashed out by Commissioners and was not to be decided by force of arms or prejudiced by arson. It was too probable that he was acting under orders from the French Government. The outrage of which he had been guilty was not to be looked upon merely as an isolated incident but as the first move in a deliberate policy. 'This step,' he insisted, 'being taken under order of a governor sent out by France since the Peace has an ugly aspect and looks like a measure not slightly undertaken.'[2] The 'civil turn of M. Puysieulx's answer to the complaint' helped to reassure him, but not entirely; he was, as he said, eased of a part of his pain but was still uneasy about the probable upshot of the matter.[3] Possibly he was eased still further when news arrived later in the year that Major Lawrence had routed le Loutre and his Indians in a skirmish of respectable size, but his pleasure in the victory must have been clouded by the thought that hostilities could be in full swing in America without rousing a flicker of interest in the Ministers at home. It was the more distressing, for in spite of Newcastle's indifference, in spite of Puysieulx's denials and diplomatic fibbing, Pitt remained convinced that Jonquière's action had been premeditated, and that the French Government were consenting to it—as indeed they were. There was, however, nothing more for him to do at the moment but hope for the best and brood over the darkening panorama.

[1] Pelham to Newcastle, 2nd July 1750. Add. MSS. 32,721.
[2] Pitt to Newcastle, 19th June 1750. Add. MSS. 32,721.
[3] Pitt to Newcastle, 6th July 1750. Add MSS. 32,721.

(iii)

Meanwhile, in America, the centre of interest was swinging back again to the Ohio valley. Jonquière died in 1752 and was succeeded by the Marquis Duquesne, an abler and more vigorous man, and one, moreover, deeply imbued with the aspirations and apprehensions of Galissonière. The English must be restrained, and for that purpose the French must, as a first and indispensable step, make themselves masters of the headwaters of the Ohio. Thereafter, as opportunity allowed but with no unnecessary delay, they should push down from the north and up from the south to complete an 'iron curtain' against the English.

Duquesne lost no time. In the early spring of 1753, directly the weather permitted, he dispatched a strong expedition to occupy the Ohio country and build such forts as might be necessary. It was hard going and sickness took its toll of the troops, but the expedition arrived at last on the shores of Lake Erie, where they built Fort Presquile. Then, marching a few miles farther south, they built Fort le Bœuf on the river known as French Creek. They were now well on their way, for French Creek was a tributary of the Alleghany, which in its turn was a tributary of the Ohio. From Fort le Bœuf the French could descend by water to New Orleans in the Gulf of Mexico. Duquesne's intention had been to build a third fort at the junction of French Creek and the Alleghany, and from that vantage point send parties down the river to overawe the Indians and frighten off the English. Illness, however, among the troops and the death of their commander dashed his hopes; the best that could be done was to push forward a few miles to the old Indian town of Venango, where the French seized an English trading house and turned it into a military outpost.

News of these activities seeped through to Dinwiddie from traders and friendly Indians, and presented him with a ticklish problem. It was not difficult to guess the motives of the French, or envisage the threat to the Ohio Company. Nor was it difficult to see that prompt action was necessary. It was made the more pressing by instructions from England to build two forts near the Ohio River for the purpose of securing possession of the country and retaining the alliance of the Indians; a thoughtful Ministry were sending him thirty pieces of light cannon and eighty barrels of powder for the purpose.[1] At the same time he was

[1] Sparks' *Washington,* I, 21.

'to require any intruder who had erected a fort on the soil of Virginia to withdraw.'[1] These orders presupposed not only that the Ohio valley was part of Virginia, but also that it was effectively occupied. Both suppositions were wrong. The territory belonged neither to France nor England. Only a year or two previously, when the Ohio Company was prospecting, the real owners had made a dignified protest, which brought the true position into high relief. Where, they had asked, did the Indian lands lie, for the French claimed all the land on one side of the Ohio and the English all the land on the other—a searching question to which there was no answer. Both French and English were trespassers, and if either side had a shadow of claim, the French had the better, since they had been the first to discover and explore the rivers. Worse still from Dinwiddie's point of view, they had also been the first to occupy the land and build forts for its preservation. It was no longer a question of driving off intruders but of making good a non-existent title against an occupier. The forcible expulsion of the French could only mean war, since Dinwiddie had no Indians to use surreptitiously. His troops, mainly colonial, would have to approach openly, and there would be a head-on collision. Was he justified in risking so much? And if he did, what support could he expect? He was at loggerheads with his own Assembly, as most Governors were, and he had little ground for supposing that the other colonies would give effective or willing help. As for England, her general attitude was that the Colonies should join together for mutual protection and should bear the greater part of the expense—a view from which the Colonies profoundly dissented. Help from England, as opposed to instructions, was likely to be grudging and slow.

Bearing in mind the difficulties, financial and military, Dinwiddie adopted a mixture of protest and bluff. He wrote to the French commander, expressing his astonishment at the French invading and actually building forts on land 'so notoriously known to be the property of the crown of Great Britain,' and requiring their peaceable departure. As his messenger he chose George Washington, then a young surveyor of twenty-one and a major in the local militia. Washington's subsequent fame has lent lustre to the choice, yet in 1753 it might legitimately have seemed rash. Washington was young, inexperienced, and knew no French, and actually he was lucky to come back alive. With

[1] Doyle. *The Colonies under the House of Hanover,* p. 548.

the boldness of youth and perhaps some touch of future greatness, he pushed off impatiently into a wintry and unknown country, and in due course delivered his letter at Fort le Bœuf. The French commander, Legardeur de St. Pierre, fobbed him off with the polite observation that, being only a simple soldier, it did not lie in his province to interpret treaties; he would send Dinwiddie's letter on to Duquesne, under whose orders he was acting. Washington returned with little for his pains, but with one piece of fruitful information. In the course of his journey he had arrived at the junction of the Alleghany and Ohio rivers, and his surveyor's eye and militiaman's experience had suggested to him the importance of the site where Pittsburg now stands. Dinwiddie, who had failed to rouse much interest in his own Assembly or secure the help of neighbouring colonies, was impressed by Washington's report, and feeling that something more should be done, sent him early in 1754, with 150 'self-willed, ungovernable men'[1] to build a fort on the site he had recommended. Washington led his small force to Wills Creek, a fortified trading post on a tributary of the Potomac. Thence he dispatched a still smaller, and indeed wholly inadequate, force of forty men to the Ohio fork, 150 miles farther on, to begin the work.

His intention was to come to their support when he had himself received reinforcements. But alas! the French were more prompt. Duquesne was 'a practised soldier. . . . He had no refractory assembly to hamper him; no lack of money, for the King supplied it; and all Canada must march at his bidding.'[2] He knew the value of speed, and he was drawing deep on the two assets of his 'welfare state'—its unquestioning obedience to authority and its military preparedness. Directly the spring came, he sent Contrecœur with 500 men to rectify the position, and by the middle of April (1754) the French had appeared before the exiguous fortifications and ordered the workmen to depart. The English had no option, and as soon as they were gone, the French demolished their half-fledged efforts and set to work on a larger and stronger building which they named Fort Duquesne.

So far no lives had been lost, no blood had been shed, no prisoners taken. Nothing had been done that was irretrievable. All that had happened was that alleged trespassers had been asked

[1] Bancroft. *History of the American Revolution*, I, 131.
[2] Parkman. *Montcalm and Wolfe*, I, 143.

to leave, or shown politely but firmly off the premises. Both sides were jockeying for position, each hoping to make good their pretensions by presenting the other with a *fait accompli*. But now there was to be a change. On learning of the reverse inflicted on his men, Washington wrote to Dinwiddie for reinforcements and, without waiting for them, proceeded to march towards the French. As he believed them to be stronger than they actually were, and was in any event greatly outnumbered, and as in addition he was short of food and ammunition, it is difficult to see what advantage he hoped to gain. According to his biographer his aim was to reach the Monongahela at the mouth of Redstone Creek and there erect a fort in order to give his troops employment.[1] Whatever his motives, the inevitable happened. Long before he had reached the river, he was warned by friendly Indians of the approach of the French, and was forced to retreat to the Great Meadows, where he threw up some hastily constructed entrenchments against the expected attack. It never came. Instead, he heard that a small party had been detached from the main French body and were approaching. They were, in fact, a few men under the command of ensign Coulon de Jumonville, sent to require the English to withdraw from what they claimed to be French soil, and probably also commissioned to discover whatever they could of their opponents' numbers and movements. Washington went to find them, and coming upon their encampment just before dawn deliberately opened fire. Ten Frenchmen, including Jumonville, were killed and the rest, except for one man who escaped, made prisoners.

The affair caused a great stir in Europe, not because of its intrinsic importance—it was a trifling border incident—but because it had altered the position fundamentally. Shots had been fired; men had been killed, prisoners taken. Only one conclusion seemed possible—that negotiations were at an end, that diplomacy was bankrupt, that the only solution was war. It was a conclusion that Europe was reluctant to accept, though France did her best to whip up sympathy by pretending that Jumonville had been brutally murdered while reading out his commission.

That Washington realised the full implications of what he had done may well be doubted; he was still only twenty-two. Equally it may be doubted if Doyle was right in thinking that 'many

[1] Sparks' *Washington,* I, 44.

colonists, and perhaps even more colonial officials, must have felt profoundly thankful for an incident . . . which of necessity committed each to a policy of open and avowed war.'[1] There is little evidence to favour this view. The Colonies were certainly quarrelsome, but hardly pugnacious. Some, like Pennsylvania, were obstinately pacific; all were reluctant to vote either men or money; none was anxious to help his neighbour, and those who felt constrained for one reason or another to take active steps, instead of showing any enthusiasm, made the Governor's demands an occasion for bargaining, for claiming concessions, for curtailing the royal prerogative, for lopping the rights and perquisites of the authorities. As for the colonists individually, they could not foresee the genius of Pitt and what he would achieve. They had no reason to suppose that the new war would differ from the old either in its course or in its end. For them the prospect could only be another spell of cruel anxiety, of strained nerves, of constant fear—the loss of crops, the destruction of property, the torture and death of those they loved. It is hard to believe that they could welcome the renewal of war after so short an interval, and it is certain that they were in two minds about the prospects of help from the mother country.

Whatever Europe or the English Colonies might think, the French Canadians were certainly loth to believe that full-blooded war had come. They still preferred to put their trust in manœuvres, in their capacity for rapid action, their skill in forestalling the English, and above all in the efficacy of Indian raids. Something they had to do at once by way of counterblast, but they did as little as possible. Washington perforce retired, before a greatly superior foe, to his stockade at the Great Meadows, which he dubbed Fort Necessity. There the French found him on the 3rd of July 1754, but instead of overrunning him, as they could easily have done, they contented themselves with a distant and desultory cannonade. Even that they did not begin until Washington's sentry had first fired upon them. In the evening they summoned the English to surrender. Washington saw no alternative, and was doubtless relieved to find no hard conditions imposed. All that he was asked to do was to release his prisoners, betake himself off and promise not to build any more forts beyond the mountains for the space of a year. Indeed the French stated explicitly that they wanted to be friends—'voulant bien

[1] Doyle. *The Colonies under the House of Hanover*, p. 556.

par lâ leur prouver que nous les traitons en amis'—and on the admission of the English behaved throughout in a conciliatory manner.[1] They regarded themselves as still at peace. The outcome, however, no longer rested with them or Washington, or even with Dinwiddie and Duquesne. America had done all in her power for war and peace; the issue now lay with the authorities in Europe.

[1] Sparks, II, 466-7.

3

THE EUROPEAN OUTLOOK

The year of the Great Meadows was also the year of Pelham's death, which occurred just four months before Washington's surrender. Pelham was succeeded as First Lord of the Treasury by his brother, the Duke of Newcastle, and Newcastle's promotion created a vacancy in the office of Secretary of State. That vacancy might have been filled by Pitt, who was at the time Paymaster of the Forces. He was an obvious choice, and it is an interesting speculation what might have happened had he been in control from the first. For in 1754 America was still a separate issue, not yet confounded in the European maelstrom of the Seven Years' War. It would, undoubtedly, have been Pitt's endeavour to keep it separate—with results that are quite beyond conjecture. But, if interesting, the speculation is also idle. Pitt did not become Secretary of State. That office was bestowed on Sir Thomas Robinson, an ex-Ambassador and Master of the Great Wardrobe.

There were two main problems which that elderly ex-diplomat had to face—problems which were not so evident in the mid-eighteenth century as they are today, either in their relative importance, their urgency or their destined outcome; indeed one of them was hardly understood in England to be a problem at all. Yet each has profoundly influenced the course of history, the one beneficially, the other calamitously. They were, in brief, whether England or France should be the leading colonial power, and whether Austria or Prussia should have the pre-eminence in Germany. The answer to the first was England, and because of that answer there has grown up, and is today in process of being consolidated, a body of free nations, seeking liberty and justice, toiling painfully but hopefully towards the ideals of Christian love and fellowship, a society of free individuals in a free association. The answer to the second was Prussia, and because of that answer there has grown up in the world the doctrine of totalitarianism, demanding the sacrifice of the individual to the state, the death of freedom, the apotheosis of callous officialdom and the cult of hate.

Pitt was the representative of England's colonial interests, and Robinson, who had spent most of his working life in Vienna, not inaptly represented her interests in Europe. When Robinson became Secretary of State, what was known as the 'old system' still dominated England's foreign policy. Under that system an alliance of France and Prussia stood over against a rival alliance of England and Austria. But whatever community of interests those four nations might have had with their respective partners in the past, circumstances had changed; their interests were now divergent, and the 'old system' was not only old but obsolescent. France and England were no longer fighting in the Austrian Netherlands; their rivalry lay over the seas, in America and India. Prussia and Austria, on the other hand, were struggling for Silesia in the heart of Europe. Yet because of the alliance Austria was expected to forward England's colonial claims, and England was obliged to support Austria's continental quarrels. Both tended to hold back. The same applied to the other pair. Frederick regarded the war in America as of no more importance than the battles of the Greeks and Trojans on the banks of the Scamander; and France rated the overlordship of Silesia as not worth the shrug of Madame de Pompadour's shoulder. It was inevitable that there should be an awakening and a fresh alignment of forces. Kaunitz of Austria was the first to grasp realities and evolve new ideas. It was his object to slip out of the English Alliance and win France to a scheme for the overthrow and partition of Prussia—a scheme in which he hoped that Elizabeth of Russia might be induced to join. Kaunitz had been brooding over his plan ever since the Treaty of Aix, and was steadily gaining ground because his scheme had advantages for all the parties concerned. It held out to Maria Theresa not only the hope—the desperately cherished hope—of recovering Silesia, but the confirmation of Austrian hegemony over the German states; it attracted Elizabeth of Russia because she hated Frederick personally with all the fury of wounded pride, and would find a savage enjoyment in his downfall; it appealed to France because it relieved her from trouble on the Continent while she concentrated on the struggle in America. But while heads were thus convinced, hearts were a little reluctant; parting must always have at least its modicum of sweet sorrow, even parting between so ill-assorted a pair as the high-souled passionate Maria Theresa and the indeterminate, fussy Duke of Newcastle! One may legitimately doubt if there would have been a final break but for the intervention of that soulless genius, the King of Prussia.

In formulating her policy Maria Theresa had the advantage of Kaunitz's advice, and Kaunitz was an able statesman. Newcastle had no such help; he had only George II and Sir Thomas Robinson. Where Europe and European alliances were concerned, George II had an awkward, protean habit of changing into the Elector of Hanover and, as such, undermining Newcastle's efforts, in order to promote his own electoral satisfactions. Robinson had left Vienna before the new ideas had sprung to life; he had been brought up in the 'old system' and was too set in his ways to change; besides, he had been chosen Secretary of State, not to give Newcastle advice, but to be his colourless henchman in what was intended to be a colourless House of Commons. Newcastle had only himself to thank for the isolation in which he stood. It was due to his political manœuvres after the death of Pelham by which he secured the premiership but at the same time deeply affronted Fox and Pitt, the only two men, apart from Murray, of outstanding ability in the Commons.[1] He had therefore to rely on himself alone, for Murray was already dropping the politics which frightened him for the law which he preferred. By nature Newcastle was laborious, toilsome and meticulous, crushing himself and all subsequent historians of his times under infinite mountains of notes, letters and memoranda. In this excess of documents, his mind was stifled. He could not get away from the 'old system,' and when it began to break in his hands, became querulous rather than questioning, more ready to apportion blame than enquire into causes. His blindness and his obstinacy between them moulded his policy. The coming war with France could not induce him to make preparations overseas. All it did was to increase his anxiety to refurbish the alliance with Austria and woo her with useless gifts at a moment when she had made up her mind to jilt him.

The key to the old system was the provision that Austria should come to the assistance of England if France were the aggressor. It was essential, therefore, that France should be jockeyed into giving the first blow, or at least seeming to give it. The difficulty was that both in Europe and in America France was showing

[1] For the details of these manœuvres, see author's first volume, *Lord Chatham*, etc.

herself conciliatory to a degree. She could afford to roar as gently as any sucking dove while the skill and speed of her Canadian Governors were continually outwitting and outmanœuvring the English. Why should she seek a quarrel, why run the risk of aggression and all that it might entail, when she was getting everything she wanted by nominally peaceful means? It was becoming increasingly evident that, if she were to be checked, Newcastle would have to take vigorous steps and give obvious blows. The problem was to find a plausible explanation which would satisfy an Austria very unwilling to be convinced.

The problem was made no easier by the system of administering the Colonies which Newcastle had inherited. In dealing with them, he had to work through the Board of Trade and Plantations, which had been founded in 1643 as a special commission and had since been reconstituted in varying forms and on several occasions, but until recently had never had more than advisory powers. In November 1748, Lord Halifax had been appointed First Commissioner, and being a pushful man, had made up his mind 'to get the West Indies entirely subjected to the Board of Trade, and to be nominated a third Secretary of State for that quarter of the world.'[1] From many points of view his ambition was wise; the Colonies were too important and the problems they raised too pressing to be left as the parergon of an overburdened Newcastle. Unfortunately, Halifax's energies were greater than his abilities, and though he managed to increase his own importance, he had no new ideas to propound. His motive was mainly a love of power, to which was appended a high national pride. A few months after his own appointment he obtained a colleague after his own heart, Charles Townshend, a young man of twenty-four, starting on a career that was to be both brilliant and baneful. At a later stage much—too much—will have to be said of him. Here it is enough to note that he was as pushful as Halifax, without his honesty of purpose.

These two men set themselves cheerfully to remould the relations of the Colonies with the mother country; they wished, as Halifax assured the Governor of South Carolina, to give 'a very serious consideration on the just prerogatives of the Crown and those defects of the constitution which had spread themselves over many of the plantations and were destructive of all order

[1] Walpole. *George II*, I, 199.

and government.'[1] Reform was much needed, but progress was clogged by the attachment of the two Ministers to the royal prerogative and by the threatened approach of war. It was Halifax who, convinced that 'the country west of the great mountains was the centre of the British dominions,' persuaded Pelham to support the Ohio Company and obtain their charter from the King, thereby setting in train the events which had led to the Great Meadows. Now that war was just round the corner, he was pursuing two objects—strong military action, and a confederation of the Colonies—which were as praiseworthy in intention as they were elusive in practice.

Under his guidance, the Board prepared 'a plan of general concert to be entered into by the American colonies for their mutual protection,'[2] which in August (1754) they embodied in a circular letter to the Governors for recommendation to the several Assemblies. But before the letters arrived, the Colonies had already rejected a better scheme of federation propounded by Benjamin Franklin, and they were not likely to be attracted by a scheme which laid much more emphasis on the royal prerogative.

Their reluctance to combine led to obstacles in other directions. In support of his warlike policy Halifax never spoke of the debatable lands in America without declaring emphatically that they were part of His Majesty's possessions. It was more than the Colonies themselves were prepared to admit, partly because the majority were not interested in the Ohio valley and still more because all of them feared that the admission might involve them in duties of defence. Pennsylvania declared, perversely, that 'it would be highly presumptuous in them to pretend to judge of the undoubted limits of His Majesty's dominions,' while New York, more circumspectly, was of opinion that 'the French forts near the Ohio might, but did not by any evidence or information appear to them to, be an invasion of any of His Majesty's colonies.'[3] Nevertheless, in spite of this colonial coyness, Newcastle found some virtue in Halifax's assurance. He accepted it and drew the highly satisfactory conclusion that any action taken in America would be no more than clearing trespassers out of British territory. That was not war but police action. Of course

[1] Bancroft. *The American Revolution,* I, 44.
[2] *Journal of the Commissioners for Trade and Plantations, 1754-58.*
[3] Parkman. *Montcalm and Wolfe,* I, 166 and 168.

it might lead to developments, but if those developments were handled skilfully, they ought to result in Austrian intervention on England's side. His attitude, based, as it was, upon European politics, served to drive a further wedge between England and her Colonies. Meanwhile the stream of urgent news from America continued and Pitt remained silent.

Pitt's silence, which left Newcastle a little uneasy, requires an explanation. The death of Pelham had found Pitt at Bath physically crippled by a prolonged and exhausting fit of gout. The subsequent political gerrymandering, which overthrew all his hopes present and future, plunged him into something approaching despair. Weakness, physical and spiritual, left him prostrated, sapping his interest in Parliament and keeping him indifferent to the affairs of the great world. His apathy lasted throughout spring and summer and early autumn, only ending with his engagement to Lady Hester Grenville, which took place in mid-September at Wotton. It had an immediate effect on him, banishing despair, exploding apathy and raising ambition to new and startling heights. The engagement took the world, and possibly the happy couple, by surprise. That it was a marriage of true minds is beyond dispute, but it had taken nineteen years in the budding and why it burst into full blossom at this exact moment is one of Love's best hidden secrets. Indeed, it seems as though Fate as well as Love had a hand in the matter; for Pitt had mapped out his movements during that autumn with more than usual precision, and his plan did not include a visit to Wotton. What took him there is unknown, but when Fate intervenes in human affairs, details must needs fall into line. His engagement came at a crucial moment, coinciding almost exactly with the arrival in England of the news of Washington's defeat. That defeat made war inevitable, and war made Pitt essential—not the listless, apathetic Pitt who went down to Wotton, but the rejuvenated Pitt who came back from Wotton at the top of his powers.

Whilst Pitt was recovering poise in the stimulating role of accepted lover, the political field was left clear for others—for Newcastle and Hardwicke, for Granville and Fox, for Halifax and Murray, and in his degree for Sir Thomas Robinson. They were all rightly perturbed when news of Washington's surrender arrived, but their reactions varied. Newcastle was obsessed by the 'old system' and the fears which it bred in him. He recognised the urgency of events and indeed he invested them with more than their actual importance. 'All North America will be lost,' he wrote, 'if these practices are tolerated.' But his brave language fizzled out when it came to planning. Action must be guided, not by resentment at insults, not by the military position, not by the threat to our American Colonies, but by the need to prove France the aggressor. To use his own quaint expression, he hoped 'we shall forthwith take such measures (and some are already taken) as will, for the future, put the labouring oar and the complaint upon them [the French].' France would no doubt suggest reference of the points in dispute to a commission, but Newcastle was 'quite sick of commissaries' and hoped that we should not be 'so far amused by their conferences, as to suspend, or delay, taking the proper measures to defend ourselves or recover our lost possessions.'[1] What seemed to him the proper measures were set out in Robinson's official letter to Albemarle, our Ambassador in Paris. The French, said Robinson, are obviously bent on destroying our trade in America. We cannot be friends until they alter their conduct, and we shall not believe them to be sincere until they withdraw from their encroachments and begin in earnest to carry out the provisions of the Treaty of Aix. However, 'His Majesty does not think proper to send your Excellency any orders upon this subject, but you may, as from yourself, take an opportunity to talk, agreeably to this letter, to M. Rouillé [the French Foreign Minister].'[2] Albemarle did his best, but under such handicaps could hardly hope to impress. Rouillé was very polite; he readily agreed to accept Albemarle's remarks as 'only historical and from himself'; hoped that means would soon be found to put an end to these jealousies and disputes, and having expressed that hope went his way.[3] He was quite content with the progress France was making and had no wish to resort to war or even to commissaries—both of which struck him as in the circumstances wholly unnecessary.

Apart from this feeble effort to shift the 'labouring oar,' which seems to have been Newcastle's version of 'passing the buck,' the Ministers were very much at sixes and sevens. The majority felt that something positive must be done. Halifax, voicing the wishes of the Colonies, wanted the circle of French forts to be broken; he pressed for expeditions against Beauséjour which

[1] Newcastle to Albemarle, 5th Sept. 1754. Add MSS. 32,850.
[2] Robinson to Albemarle, 12th Sept. 1754. Add. MSS. 32,850.
[3] Albemarle to Robinson, 18th Sept. Add. MSS. 32,850.

threatened Acadia in the north-east, Crown Point at the southern end of Lake Champlain, Fort Niagara between Lakes Ontario and Erie, and Fort Duquesne which controlled the Ohio valley. Success at these four points would enable the English Colonies to breathe freely.[1] Murray also was for strong measures, ascribing the disaster of the Great Meadows to 'an interested and too ostentatious project of Dinwiddie,'[2] and assuming that English troops would soon put matters to rights. Most of the Ministers wished to send out 'the Highland regiment and to raise independent Highland companies,' but here they found themselves at variance with Granville, the Lord President of the Council, who thought the colonists should bear the brunt of their own defence and raise the necessary troops in America. It came as a shock to Newcastle to think that troops from any quarter must be employed, because, as he complained to Albemarle, if the French occupied our land and built forts in it, and we tried to push them out, 'we then began the war' and *ipso facto* lost our claim to Austrian help.[3] He seemed to think that war would not be war in French eyes if waged on a limited scale. Halifax had suggested four expeditions; it would be safer to have only two—the Ohio and Crown Point; that would hoodwink the French and incidentally be much cheaper.[4] Hardwicke supported his plea for economy, and both for that reason and to avoid the possibility of lighting up a war in Europe, was prepared to go farther and confine operations to a single object, which perhaps wisely he left unspecified.[5]

After a fortnight of discussion, a measure of agreement seemed to have been reached, and the next step was to approach the Duke of Cumberland, as Captain-General of the army. Cumberland upset all their arrangements. To send the Highland regiment was something of an insult to the victor of Culloden; it would never do; they must dispatch two Irish regiments from Cork, and also raise two colonial regiments which should be commanded respectively by Shirley, Governor of Massachusetts, and Sir William Pepperell. Further, they must adopt all four expeditions as proposed by Halifax. Newcastle, more and more frightened at the prospect of war and perhaps even more frightened at the growing importance of Cumberland, of whose influence with

[1] Williams, I, 252. [2] Murray to Newcastle, 6th Oct. 1754. Add. MSS. 32,737.
[3] Newcastle to Albemarle, 10th Oct. 1754. Add MSS. 32,851.
[4] Newcastle to Hardwicke, 2nd Oct. 1754. Add. MSS. 32,737.
[5] Hardwicke to Newcastle, 3rd Oct. 1754. Add. MSS. 32,737.

the King he was abnormally jealous, fell back on his usual chicanery. Fox, as Secretary at War, obtained the King's approval to all Cumberland's proposals, but Newcastle privately obtained the King's consent to postpone the orders for the two colonial regiments pending further consideration.[1]

It was at this point that Pitt once more appeared on the political stage. For a week or so he and Hester had kept their secret to themselves, rejoicing in their private rapture before they tempted the uncharted ocean of her family's reaction. Then Pitt dragged himself away from Wotton to seek Temple's consent to the marriage. On the 2nd of October, as he was passing through London, he called on Newcastle, who seized the opportunity to discuss American affairs with him. Bubb Dodington writing an account of the meeting from hearsay six days later says that 'the Duke would have entered with him into the American expedition, to dislodge the French from the Ohio; Mr. Pitt said, "Your Grace, I suppose, knows I have no capacity for these things (being dissatisfied that he was not made Secretary of State) and therefore I do not desire to be informed about them."'[2] For some reason this amusing but highly improbable story has been accepted as fact and even described as 'Pitt-like,'[3] but it does not tally with Newcastle's own description of the meeting or with Pitt's usual behaviour. His invective was public; in private he was courtesy itself. The legend that Pitt bullied Newcastle or was rude to him is greatly exaggerated. Even when he was most fiercely attacking Newcastle in the House, he almost invariably behaved to him with studied politeness in private, as Newcastle himself was the first to acknowledge. There is no reason to suppose that on this occasion Pitt took up a hostile or difficult attitude, though he may very easily have expressed the ignorance of events to be expected in a man who had been out of town. Indeed, that is the impression given by Newcastle. 'I then acquainted him,' the Duke wrote immediately after the conference, 'with what was designed for North America, and also with my Lord Granville's notions, which had not been followed.' The interesting point is not Pitt's intransigence, but his quick grasp of the position, his obvious interest and his decisiveness. He had no hesitations, for he was speaking on a subject over which he had long brooded; and so, as Newcastle recorded, he 'talked up the affair of North America

[1] Newcastle to Hardwicke, 2nd October 1754. Add. MSS. 32,737.
[2] Diary, p. 317. [3] Rosebery, p. 350.

very highly; that it must be supported in all events and at all risks.' He pronounced Cumberland's scheme a very good one so far as it went; but maintained that it did not go anything like far enough and that his proposals for artillery were 'infinitely too short.' Pitt was clear that the crisis in America was rapidly approaching, and insisted that we should aim at finality—'we should do it once for all.' We could not expect to make a clean sweep by troops from Europe alone; the French had greater numbers and would be too strong for us. We should certainly adopt Granville's idea of raising troops in America—not as an alternative but as an addition. We needed the help of the Colonies as much as they needed ours; we must not only support them but win their enthusiasm. His own enthusiasm was sufficient to confirm Newcastle. 'This discourse,' he told Hardwicke, 'joined with Lord Anson's opinion, has made me suspend at least the stopping the orders for the raising the two regiments etc. and for providing all the artillery proposed by the Duke.'[1] Pitt's intervention, though fortuitous, had been strong, assured, and within the limits of Newcastle's qualms, effective. The expedition was to go forward.

Cumberland chose Edward Braddock to command it—a major-general in his sixtieth year whose failure has given him an uncomfortable niche in Anglo-American history. His real character will now, presumably, never be known, but the comments of his contemporaries offer a wide choice. The King approved his selection—indeed, seemed to be more than ordinarily pleased; he had, so he said, 'a good opinion of Braddock's sense and bravery and had heard that he had become very stayed [*sic*].'[2] But after the event he changed his mind, telling Joseph Yorke (the Chancellor's third son and Ambassador at The Hague) that he had not himself chosen Braddock and had been surprised when Cumberland had recommended him.[3] Walpole reacted the other way round: whilst he believed Braddock to be still living, he spoke of him as 'a very Iroquois in disposition,' but on hearing of his death added that 'with all his brutality, he has lately been Governor of Gibraltar, where he made himself adored.'[4] Newcastle and Hardwicke expressed no opinion one way or the other, contenting themselves with oblique hints.

[1] Newcastle to Hardwicke, 2nd Oct. 1754. Add. MSS. 32,737.
[2] Robinson to Newcastle, 23rd September 1754. Add. MSS. 32,736.
[3] Yorke to Hardwicke, 13th September 1755. Yorke, II, 285.
[4] To Mann, 21st and 28th August 1755.

Their main object being to escape responsibility, they emphasised that as *civil* Ministers they did not know whom to recommend, but were sure that the *military* men would disapprove whatever they did, and so 'the present scheme, and the measures for conducting it, and for the execution of it, are entirely his royal highness's.'[1] But whilst fear made them anxious to disclaim responsibility, jealousy drove them to write in a tone of faintly irritated disapproval of the 'Great Person' who was so rudely shouldering them to one side, and presumably also of his nominee. The only factor common to all accounts is agreement that Braddock was as brave as a lion, though even that praise is marred by an occasional hint that his bravery was rooted in a want of imagination rather than in courage. In short, the contemporary portrait of Braddock is blurred.

It is a pity that more is not known of him, as he belonged to the class of generals whom Pitt discarded, and fuller knowledge of his character might throw light on the working of Pitt's mind. Certain points, however, stand out clearly. First, Braddock was nearly sixty when he was appointed, and sixty was a much greater age then than now; his faculties, whatever they were, must have grown rusty and clogged; he had no doubt 'become very stayed.' Secondly, the only active service he had seen was an unsuccessful attempt to raise the siege of Bergen-op-zoom nine years before, and few besides Cumberland would suppose that siege tactics in Holland were the best preparation for forest warfare in the Alleghanies. For the rest, his experience had been the routine duties of a regimental commander, in which he seems to have shown himself punctilious and exacting, becoming no doubt year by year more stereotyped and starched. He was by common consent a disciplinarian—brutal according to some witnesses, but probably not much more so than was required to turn the riff-raff of England's jails into indomitable English infantry. His age, his want of experience in the field, his lack of imagination, even his stubborn bravery, made him the type of general one would expect to find in a box of lead soldiers—very martial, quite brainless and utterly unbending. He was not the type to explore fresh countries or invent new methods. Literally and rather pathetically he was sent to his fate—a monument to Cumberland's shortsightedness. His end was the end of a bull surrounded by howling

[1] Coxe. *Lord Walpole,* II, 368.

picadors—bewildered, maddened, helpless, doomed. He deserves the meed of a transient tear.

But this is anticipating. The expedition was to go through many vicissitudes before it ended in disaster, and in almost every phase must have presented Pitt with a warning. Newcastle did not follow Pitt's example of 'talking up the affairs of North America very highly.' On the contrary he feared to speak of it even in a whisper: 'as I would have done it *effectually*,' he confided to Albemarle, 'I would as far as was practicable have avoided *éclat*.' His reticence worried Cumberland and Fox, who justifiably doubted his resolution, and in order to force his hand inserted an announcement dealing with certain aspects of the expedition in the *Gazette* of the 8th of October. Newcastle was horrified and wrote in a hurry to Albemarle that 'a most ill-judged advertisement from the War Office has set all the foreign ministries on fire, and made them believe that we are just going to war, which is, I hope, the furthest from our thoughts.' Worse still, the French would not only think we were going to war, but 'will know our strength, or rather our weakness, or the utmost that we intend to do, or at least send from Europe.' It was very unfortunate when we were doing nothing that was not peaceable and placable—merely 'carrying on our necessary measures for securing ourselves in North America against them [the French].' As we were being so reasonable, Newcastle hoped that Albemarle would, not officially, but as from himself—that humbugging admission that he was sailing near the wind—'give such a turn to all these necessary defensive measures as may make the French ministers ashamed to complain of them, and willing to avoid taking such notice of them as may bring on such consequences as they don't seem at present to wish.'[1] Albemarle's reputation as an Ambassador does not stand very high, but the recipient of such instructions is surely entitled to sympathy.

The Press announcement was hardly judicious, but probably told the French very little of which they had not been previously aware, and while it may have hastened their counter-measures did not jolt them out of their seemingly pacific attitude. They, too, were anxious not to begin the war. They, like Newcastle, had their eyes on European politics, and were not altogether pleased with what they saw. They were still hesitating between Prussia and Austria, and they were also acutely aware that Spain under

[1] Newcastle to Albemarle, 10th October 1754. Add. MSS. 32,851.

Ferdinand VI was not so francophile as before. Moreover, they needed time, both to make good their so-called encroachments in America, and to prepare themselves in Europe, against the pending British reaction. So they accepted Albemarle's soothing syrup, with as much sincerity as it was given. Both sides, in short, paid lip-service to peace, while they went ahead with their preparations for war.

In England the preparations were entrusted to Cumberland and Fox, and the two of them, revelling in the free hand which their technical knowledge gave them, pushed on happily with their own devices, going direct to the King and ignoring Newcastle and Hardwicke altogether. The two Ministers looked on with mixed feelings. Glad as they were to be relieved of responsibility, they were a little hurt, a little jealous, and half hoped that Fox at least and perhaps Cumberland, too, might burn his fingers, if it could be done without disaster. Their attitude boded no good, and the latent antagonism made for friction and delay.

4

SLITHERING INTO WAR

(i)

Meanwhile the country at large pursued its peaceful avocations without looking too far into the future. If Walpole is to be trusted, everything stagnated; the only ripple on the dull routine of fashionable life was the news that two regiments were actually being dispatched abroad, which roused Walpole to languid speculation on the possibility of colonial troubles leading to a European war. Too many troops were going to America, he observed, if the French did not mean mischief; too few, if they did.[1] It was a shrewd remark.

In November Parliament met. Pursuing his policy of trying to screen the blatantly obvious, Newcastle inserted only veiled references to America in the King's Speech, and for all the interest they aroused, he might just as well have left them out. The Address was voted without trouble, and thereafter Parliament turned to the innocuous but much more entrancing business of election petitions. Newcastle felt that all was well. Maybe America was a little disturbing, but it was a long way off, and largely out of his hands. Nearer home he was progressing satisfactorily with his scheme to reduce Parliament to a rubber stamp for ratifying and recording his decisions. It was his intention that there should be no Minister of weight in the Commons, no one who should have free and familiar access to the King, no one who should presume to advise. All was to pass through Newcastle's hands; all was to be settled and controlled by him. He had toiled for this end at the elections; he had manœuvred for this end ever since, and he believed he had succeeded. Murray, Fox and Pitt were all muzzled—or thought to be; Robinson, the Secretary of State, was a ponderous figurehead, and Legge, the Chancellor of the Exchequer, a mean underling. Power was to be concentrated

[1] To Mann, 6th October 1754.

where it belonged—in the House of Lords in general and in the Duke of Newcastle in particular.

His plans were overthrown by a wedding. The day after Parliament met Pitt married. Eight months earlier, in a moment of despair, he had been a self-confessed failure, craving for retreat, dreading the loss of popularity, and feeling that he had no future. The recovery of his poise had been slow and hesitating, but his engagement and marriage had swept away the final shreds of reluctance and determined him not only to renew his political activities but to give them a fresh goal. For many years he had been a quiet and loyal member of the Pelham-Newcastle Administration, buttressing the two brothers in their attempts at government and sinking his own ambitions and desires. Now he decided to break away and re-establish his own personal ascendancy, with the object of becoming Prime Minister when George II died. He returned from his honeymoon on the 25th of November (1754) and plunged straight into one of his most celebrated speeches, in which, taking advantage of a ribald harangue on an election petition, he made a devastating attack on Newcastle. He was astonished, he said, to find the House making a joke of bribery, to find them quite unconcerned at their own loss of dignity, to find them degenerating fast into 'a little assembly, serving no other purpose than to register the arbitrary edicts of one too powerful subject.' This particular phrase caught the public ear and for ever after the obvious has been underlined. The one too powerful subject, we are assured, was none other than the Duke of Newcastle, and the whole speech a direct attack upon him. So, of course, it was, but we shall stop far short of the truth if we regard it as no more. Pitt's attitude towards Newcastle, like most human relations, varied from time to time; but perhaps always, and certainly in 1754, had a hard core of genuine affection. It was tinged with a little good-humoured contempt, such as one might feel towards a child, and touched with a streak of awe springing out of Pitt's ingrained snobbery, but it was of long standing and had grown throughout the years in gratitude for benefits received. Recently both awe and affection had been waning, but they had not yet entirely vanished; Pitt still clung to the belief that Newcastle meant well by him and was fighting his battle in the Closet; he would not willingly have attacked him, certainly not out of mere wantonness or pique. If his famous invective was ever founded solely on personal dislike—which may be doubted—it was not on this occasion. The attack on Newcastle was in part a deliberate political manœuvre and in part the expression of a profound constitutional tenet. Politically, Pitt wanted to frighten Newcastle into reshuffling his Cabinet, for personal reasons; but he mingled with this personal aim another founded in broad constitutional principles. At least as much emphasis should be laid on the first part of the quotation as on the last. If Newcastle was too powerful, the House was too compliant; the mere curtailment of the former's excesses would not be enough unless at the same time the House rose to its proper height. Newcastle must be made to understand that he was a subject, but equally the House must be awakened to a sense of its pre-eminence. If Pitt was attacking Newcastle, he was attacking, not the man, but the suborner of Parliament, and the object was not merely his own advancement but also the resuscitation of the Commons.

There are many hints scattered about the records of the times which show how closely Pitt identified himself with the Commons, how intensely he believed in their rights and duties, how highly he rated their powers, how watchful he was over their dignity, how deeply he deplored anything which might tarnish their renown or entrench upon their privileges. He was 'so far from wishing to lessen the House of Commons,' he said on one occasion, 'that whatever little existence he had in this country, it was owing to the House of Commons';[1] and once, when defending the right of Parliament to order enquiries, he declared passionately that 'he would never consent to lop the bough on which he stood.'[2] His speech now, though aimed at Newcastle for political and personal reasons, was heightened both in content and significance by indignation at the feeble acquiescence of the House in their own degradation. If a sting lay in the phrase 'one too powerful subject,' so it did in the words which preceded—the little assembly, the registration of extraneous and arbitrary edicts. What stirred his resentment was not Newcastle's failure to promote him, but Newcastle's decision to make the House of Commons a mere appendage to the House of Lords, an assembly without a leader, without initiative, without a function.

His speech created a furore, ousting all other topics of conversation, including the Colonies. As Walpole put it: 'the Parliamentary campaign opening so warmly, has quite put the Ohio

[1] Walpole. *George II*, I, 9. [2] *Ibid.*, I, 60.

upon an obsolete foot.'[1] The world was much more absorbed in speculations upon Pitt's motives. Would he unite with Fox? Would Robinson fall? And how would Newcastle react? It was taken for granted that Pitt was thinking only of himself. The attack on Newcastle was the main point of interest for his contemporaries, and some of the more sanctimonious, such as George Lyttelton, blamed him. Yet, had they had eyes to see, they might have observed that, whatever the original impulse, only the first speech was aimed at Newcastle. Thereafter Pitt turned his attack on Robinson and Murray, and when within a matter of weeks the dignity of the Commons was restored by the appointment of Fox as actual, though unacknowledged, Leader of the House, Pitt gave up all semblance of opposition, until fresh happenings brought fresh problems and the need for a fresh policy.

(ii)

The fresh problems developed naturally out of the events of 1755. The Government continued their slow, reluctant slither into war. They had now dispatched troops over the seas and must expect the inevitable reaction. It was prompt in coming. Directly the French heard of Braddock's orders, they made arrangements to send 3,000 regulars to Canada—an overwhelming force when contrasted with Braddock's two regiments. It was now England's turn, and towards the end of March the King informed Parliament that he was taking measures 'to secure the just rights and possessions of his crown in America,' and Parliament voted him a million pounds for the purpose. Clearly this bandying of provocation could not go on for ever, but the problem was how to bring it to a head. France was not yet ready for war, nor very anxious for it; in America it seemed unnecessary and in Europe it did not suit the whims of Madame de Pompadour. On this side of the Channel, Newcastle had still to discover how to begin a war without being the aggressor—a difficulty which dominated all his actions, and was at bottom the reason for the more glaring absurdities of which he was guilty.

From the technical point of view he was not badly served. The British intelligence system was good and was working efficiently, giving him early information of French movements. For experts, the 'inner Cabinet,' consisting of himself, Hardwicke

[1] To Mann, 1st Dec. 1754.

and Granville, had Anson to advise on naval, and Ligonier on military, matters. But whatever intelligence was received and whatever advice was given, it was warped and twisted by Newcastle's dread of appearing to begin the war and his curious belief that fighting across the Atlantic would not be counted. The upshot was that while the fleet was put on a war footing, no attempt was made to patrol the French ports of embarkation or to intercept the French forces on their first setting out. On the contrary, Boscawen was sent across the Atlantic 'to cruise off Louisburg, with instructions to fall upon any ships of war that shall be attempting to land troops in Nova Scotia or to go to Cape Breton or through the St. Lawrence to Quebec.'[1]

This was clearly an attempt to reconcile professional advice with political expediency. It fell between the two stools. Boscawen missed the French amid the Newfoundland fogs, but on the 10th of June (1755) sighted three French stragglers and managed to capture two, the *Alcide* and the *Lys*. He was himself reasonably satisfied; it was a pity no doubt that the majority of the French fleet had slipped through his fingers, but at least he had carried out his orders and had something to show for his pains.

His report reached England on the 14th of July and delighted the populace, who were jubilant at what seemed to be a British victory.[2] But the Ministers were worried. 'We have,' said Hardwicke, 'done too much or too little,'[3] and he was right. If Boscawen had captured the whole French fleet, the check to French plans might well have delayed the outbreak of war—might even have led to fresh negotiations on a more hopeful basis—and certainly would have given England a massive preliminary advantage. As it was, England had been guilty of shedding the first blood by means of a pinprick.

There were two courses open to the Government: they could accept the facts and declare war at once, or they could promptly disown Boscawen. If they chose the former, they would have had a large public backing. The popular view was well expressed by the Princess of Wales who 'inveighed most bitterly against the not pushing the French everywhere.' She was sure the people would disapprove 'the suffering the French to bring home their

[1] Corbett, I, 43.

[2] 'Our French triumphs give [much satisfaction] to the City, where nothing is so popular as the Duke of Newcastle'—Walpole to Mann, 21st Aug. 1755.

[3] Hardwicke to Newcastle, 14th July 1755. Add MSS. 32,857.

trade and sailors,'[1] bearing in mind that this was the season when French merchantmen were returning laden with rich cargoes from the East and West Indies. What a prize was there for the taking! If, on the other hand, the Government chose to disown Boscawen, they might possibly be a little unpopular, but that would be a passing phase and in the meantime they would have escaped from a difficult situation. In fact, they chose neither, but adopted a compromise which gave them the worst of both worlds. They allowed the French to break off diplomatic relations and recall their Ambassador, Mirepoix; and on the day that he left—the 22nd of July—gave Hawke instructions to put to sea with the Channel Fleet. But he was not to make wholehearted war, he was not to interfere with trade. All he and the other commanders at sea were to do was to capture any ships of the line which they might meet, and bring them into port as securities for the redress of the French 'encroachments' in America. Not that much was expected, for Newcastle believed and even hoped that 'ships of the line will scarce come in his [Hawke's] way so soon.'[2] Here was no element of firmness, and the essential lack of resolution was emphasised when, a fortnight later, extended instructions to capture privateers and merchantmen as well as men-of-war were sent to Hawke alone, all other commanders being expressly excluded.[3]

None the less, for the next few days Newcastle felt happy and confident. 'We are all,' said Walpole, 'insolent, alert and triumphant.'[4] The various attacks in America had been launched; Boscawen had blooded the French fleet, and France, in spite of this provocation, continued 'backward and cautious and timorous.'[5] The omens were good. Nor was Newcastle's optimism based solely on American hopes. The news from the Continent seemed not unsatisfactory, while at home there was a prospect, very dear to Newcastle's heart, of putting Fox's nose a little out of joint[6] by means of an understanding with Pitt, and even of forming 'a system' which would 'disappoint the success of all these intrigues'[7] whatever these intrigues might be.

[1] Dodington, 351-2.
[2] Newcastle to Holdernesse, 22nd July 1755. Add. MSS. 32,857.
[3] Corbett, I, 70. [4] To Mann, 21st August 1755. [5] *Ibid.*
[6] 'He is no more so formidable, or so valuable.' Newcastle to Hardwicke, 22nd Aug. 1755. Add. MSS. 32,858.
[7] Newcastle to Holdernesse, 19th Aug. 1755. Add. MSS. 32,858.

(iii)

The King had left for Hanover on the 28th of April (1755), directly Parliament rose. His going was partly a matter of taste—bad taste, as the English thought—partly a matter of fear for the Electorate, which, while it sharpened the King's impatience to be off, increased the reluctance of the English to let him go. Without counting the obvious drawbacks of the King's absence and the obvious difficulties which might arise if he were caught by the war or died on the Continent, everyone knew that his impatience sprang out of his desire to negotiate alliances for the protection of Hanover. That very fact made his visit not only a renewal of the annual insult to the English nation but a formidable injury as well, since the treaties, besides involving subsidies, would sooner or later entangle England in a continental struggle and what Pitt called un-British policies. The country was reluctant, but the King had his way and went. His activities were to have speedy and unexpected results.

The European scene as it presented itself to him was sufficiently obscure, and the less easy to understand because Newcastle's diplomacy had by 1755 been reduced to something approaching chaos. His policy was governed by an implicit belief in the virtues of the 'old system,' it was bedevilled by a desire to confine the coming war to America, and overshadowed by anxiety to protect Hanover if by chance the war should spread to Europe. For some years he had been actively engaged, as he thought, in strengthening the 'old system' and binding Austria closer to England by endless negotiations, backed by the promise of subsidies, to secure the election of Maria Theresa's son as King of the Romans. Unfortunately, Maria Theresa was not interested; her object in life was to crush Frederick and recover Silesia, which the election, even if successful, would in no way forward. She would have much preferred England to spend the money on a subsidy treaty with Russia, whose aid she regarded as necessary. Newcastle ignored her suggestion, and by so doing annoyed her, offended Elizabeth of Russia, and gave a fillip to Kaunitz's schemes. His policy, in short, was founded on shifting sand and had failed.

At this stage the King suddenly intervened. His relations with his nephew, Frederick of Prussia, which had never been good, had recently been deteriorating and seemed likely to grow worse.

It became uncomfortably clear to the King that in the war which was obviously coming Frederick, partly out of resentment, partly because he was allied to France, and partly because the chance was too good to be missed, might march into the Electorate and lay it waste. Something must be done to restrain him, and the best thing seemed to be the posting of a Russian army on his eastern frontier. Here George began to see some virtue in Maria Theresa's suggestions. So much so that just before leaving England (April 1755) he appointed Hanbury-Williams to be Ambassador at St. Petersburg, with instructions to conclude a subsidy treaty with Russia as his 'chief and principal object.'[1] A definite European picture was now beginning to emerge. There was to be an equilibrium—uneasy perhaps, but effective—which was to preserve the peace in Europe and protect Hanover, while any fighting that might be necessary would be confined to America. The equilibrium would be ensured by Austrian troops brought under the 'old system' to the Netherlands to pin down France, and Russian troops hovering on the borders of Prussia to paralyse Frederick. Meanwhile the position might be strengthened by a few minor subsidy treaties with the smaller German states. The King went to Hanover to promote them but to his consternation found difficulties. The smaller German states kept glancing uneasily over their shoulders at Prussia. Only William VIII, the Landgrave of Hesse Cassel, succumbed to the King's blandishments, signing a treaty at Hanover on the 18th of June. He was however a minor potentate and all he could do was to make 8,000 troops available to the King in return for a lump sum payment of 198,000 crowns (£50,000) plus an annual subsidy of 300,000 crowns (£75,000), and promise that later on he would, if required, raise the number to 12,000 subject to a *pro rata* increase in the payment. It was expensive, and the benefits were limited by the proviso that the troops were not to be employed beyond the sea, 'excepting, always, for the defence of Great Britain and Ireland.'[2] America was pointedly omitted. This one success, for what it was worth, was more than counterbalanced by failure elsewhere, and most of all by the fact that Maria Theresa was showing herself cold and reluctant; her interest in the Netherlands seemed unaccountably small. These facts made the progress of the Russian negotiations the more important.

[1] Horn, p. 179. [2] Jenkinson, III, 51.

(iv)

The chosen Ambassador, Sir Charles Hanbury-Williams, had spent the first thirty-eight years of his life enjoying himself as a man about town, and was to spend the last two in a lunatic asylum. Between these extremes there was a period of about eleven years in which he followed the calling of amateur diplomat. In that capacity he drifted round various capitals—Dresden, Berlin, Warsaw, Vienna and Dresden again—but achieved little except a number of indiscretions and a pack of quarrels, leaving behind him, as he moved on, a trail of ruffled royalties and vexed Ministers. Why he should have been chosen for Russia is obscure; probably he owed the appointment to his friend Fox. However it came, Hanbury-Williams jumped at it, and set out for St. Petersburg to pursue with ardour his profession of lady-killer, and occupy his spare moments with flights of diplomacy, marred as ever by fits of impatient optimism and starts of incurable indiscretion. The court in which he found himself was more Asiatic than European—full of barbaric splendour, full of intrigue, profligacy and corruption. Its leading figures were the Empress Elizabeth, daughter of Peter the Great, and her Chancellor, Alexis Bestuzheff. In her youth the Empress had delighted everyone with her beauty and vivacity. She was still handsome, but had grown fat, asthmatic and indolent, though she could at times recapture some of the vigour of youth, dancing her partners off their feet and herself on to the fringes of apoplexy. Temperamentally she was cruel, superstitious and vindictive; morally she had no inhibitions and few principles. But for all her shortcomings, she had something of her father's greatness, and was ready in the interests of her country to sacrifice her own prejudices.[1] This last quality was important since Bestuzheff had for the past fourteen years been pursuing a policy at variance with every prejudice she possessed. He believed that Russia's natural enemy was France, and his ambition was to form a quadruple alliance of Russia, Austria, Great Britain and Saxony in opposition to France and Prussia. Elizabeth was reluctant to follow his advice. She had been raised to the throne by a palace revolution promoted by France and opposed by Austria, Great Britain and Saxony. It was inevitable that she should lean towards the first and feel at least some antipathy for the others. Bestuzheff

[1] Cambridge Modern History, VI, 312.

had worked doggedly to bend her to his will, but with only partial success until Frederick of Prussia had played into his hands by allowing himself the luxury of a sneer at her religion, which so angered her that 'henceforth political antagonism and private pique combined to make her his most determined adversary.'[1] Thereafter she had moved in the direction Bestuzheff wished, but had hung back from an intimate alliance with England because she had an uneasy conviction that the interests of Great Britain and Russia were fundamentally divergent, and that all Great Britain wanted was to get Russia to fight her battles. If Hanover is substituted for Great Britain, her suspicions were justified. To add to the confusion, her nephew and designated successor, the Grand Duke Peter, was heart and soul an admirer of Frederick, while the Grand Duchess, the future Catherine the Great, was strongly but secretly for the English alliance.

Some knowledge of these cross-currents is required because of their bearing on the future; otherwise the details of the Russian negotiations are unimportant. Suffice it to say that Hanbury-Williams ran true to form; he obtained a treaty but it was marred by errors and imperfections. Broadly, it provided that Russia was to station 55,000 troops on the borders of Livonia and keep forty or fifty galleys on the coast, and to put these forces in motion if Great Britain or any of her allies were attacked. In return England was to pay a yearly subsidy of £100,000 so long as peace continued, rising to £500,000 as soon as the troops were called into action. It was specifically stated that 'the dominions of his Britannic Majesty in Germany' were to be regarded as coming within the provisions. It was equally specifically agreed that 'her Imperial Majesty of all the Russias shall not be obliged to furnish the succours stipulated by this treaty for the defence of his Britannic Majesty's possessions in America, or in any part whatsoever out of Europe.'[2] Although the treaty was signed on the 15th of September 1755, Elizabeth postponed ratification; she could not rid her mind of her reluctance and her suspicions. But at last on the 1st of February 1756, Bestuzheff triumphed. Elizabeth signed—only to find within a matter of days that the treaty was waste paper. Her wrath was great, and the outcome tremendous. Yet no one was really to blame. All the nations were

[1] Cambridge Modern History, VI, 318.
[2] Jenkinson, III, 32 and 43.

manœuvring in the dark. It was not surprising that all blundered, but the result was that what began as a comedy of errors quickly took on the tragic magnificence of the Seven Years' War.

(v)

At bottom Frederick was the cause. His restless ambition, his success and his contemptuous cynicism had raised up enemies. They were beginning to close on him and he had to look to his defences. His main reliance was his treaty with France, which was due to expire in May 1756. The question of its renewal was therefore a matter of pressing interest. So was the question of France's foreign policy. She was clearly drifting into war with England, and Frederick conceived the idea of seeking safety by transforming the coming Anglo-French war into a general conflagration in which he and France would be united against their common enemies—Austria, Russia and England. To promote this end he was throughout 1755 egging France on to resent and oppose England's actions in America. But France held back for many reasons. From the military angle, she was doing very well without declaring war. Diplomatically she, like England, must avoid the first blow which would settle the question of Austrian help. From the personal angle, which was probably the most potent, Louis XV was jealous of Frederick, whose suddenness had a knack of showing up his own slowness, while Madame de Pompadour was afraid that the King would love her less if he loved warfare more. Both therefore tended to ignore Frederick's pressure, and indeed to grow weary of his alliance.

At this point it occurred to both George II and Frederick that they might be well advised to forget their mutual animosities and try to become mutually helpful. Both were driven on by the dearth of other allies, but ironically, while George was swayed by the slow progress of the Russian negotiations, Frederick was swayed by the mere fact of their existence, and a firm but erroneous belief in the extent of English influence at St. Petersburg. With both sides willing and frightened, negotiations were speedy, and the Convention of Westminster was signed on the 16th of January 1756. The preamble declared that the Anglo-French differences in America gave room to fear for the public tranquillity of Europe. And so the high contracting parties agreed not to attack each other's territories, but to 'exert their utmost efforts to prevent their respective allies from undertaking anything against the said territories in any manner whatever.' They also agreed that if any foreign power invaded Germany, they would unite to expel the intruder.[1] In a word, Frederick was to warn France against trespassing on Hanover, and England was to warn Elizabeth against marching into Prussia. Both the high contracting parties were delighted. It seemed almost too good to be true.

(vi)

It was too good to be true. The immediate result was to precipitate that general change of partners which has come to be known as the Reversal of Alliances. No one was more surprised than the two monarchs primarily responsible. George II had genuinely hoped that he was protecting Hanover. That had been the basis of all his negotiations. He had appealed to Russia because he had been on bad terms with Frederick. How much more sensible and satisfying to deal directly with a penitent nephew who had come to see the error of his ways and was prepared to behave properly. Perhaps it was a pity he had been in such a hurry to offer Russia a subsidy, but one could never tell—a second string to his bow might be useful; and anyhow as Russia would not be called upon to act, she would get only the smaller subsidy. The new arrangement might almost be called peace with economy. And there was a further bonus—France had lost her ally, if she insisted on going to war.

Frederick equally had meant to keep Europe quiet, not because he was naturally given to seeking peace and ensuing it, but because he had no ambition to challenge Russia and Austria single-handed. The apparent defection of France made it imperative for him to search for other means of curbing the two vindictive Empresses, whose enmity he had so thoughtlessly and so rashly excited. Hanbury-Williams' negotiations seemed to offer a solution. England would be able to restrain Russia, and without Russia's aid Frederick did not believe Austria would move. He could hardly hope for a better bargain. By giving up the threat to Hanover, which did him no real good beyond the satisfaction of annoying a detested uncle, he removed the menace to his eastern

[1] Jenkinson, III, 56.

frontier, immobilised Maria Theresa and gained so much more time to consolidate his position in Europe. True he had broken with France, but France involved in war with England would not be in a position to worry him. He had done well for himself.

Neither of them foresaw the reactions abroad. Elizabeth of Russia was furious, declaring with some justification that George had secured his treaty with her under utterly false pretences. It had been aimed specifically against Prussia. Troops were to be massed on Prussia's borders and were to cross the frontier at a word from George. If, after all, Frederick was not to be attacked, if, as the new convention laid down, Germany was to be regarded as inviolable, what conceivable reason was there for the troops or the treaty? Besides, Elizabeth wanted to attack Frederick; that had been her sole object, her one inducement. She had not signed out of any love for George II; she had no feeling for him, nor had ever imagined that she had any mutual interest with Great Britain beyond distrust and dislike of Frederick. England's sudden and secret change of front was infamous. Elizabeth had been tricked, and if she could hardly throw over a treaty she had just that moment signed, she would adhere to it only on the assumption that its original intention would be carried out. Meanwhile she had nothing but a cold shoulder for her new ally; her enthusiasm was transferred to Austria and the Austrian plot against Prussia. She began concocting schemes for encouraging Austria, promising the presence of Russian troops at the front and the exercise of Russian influence to keep France quiet.[1]

Not that there was any need to keep France quiet. She was deeply affronted by the offhand manner in which Frederick had been on with the new love before being off with the old. How dare he come to terms with England while his treaty with France was still in being? Louis and Madame de Pompadour felt outraged and began to entertain seriously Kaunitz's proposals with which hitherto they had been flirting only half-heartedly. On the 1st of May 1756, France and Austria signed the first Treaty of Versailles—the preliminary to a further treaty in the following year. Its main provisions were twofold—Austria promised absolute neutrality in the war between England and France, and both promised active assistance if the possessions in Europe of

[1] Butterfield, p. 33.

either were attacked, i.e. if Prussia moved. The immediate significance of the treaty was that it relieved France from the fear of striking the first blow against England. But now that Russia was assenting and all three were plotting against Prussia, the treaty bade fair to set Europe alight. So unexpected are the results of diplomacy.

5

DISMISSAL

(i)

While events in Europe were marshalling the nations for war, events in England were clearing the way for Pitt. Fox's appointment as unacknowledged Leader of the Commons suited him, because he believed that Fox could not stay the course and would fall when the old King died. Pitt would then step into his shoes, attaining power at that most favourable moment, the beginning of a new reign. With Fox's appointment he felt able to relax. But the peace between them was uneasy: they were antipathetic, and the ties connecting them began to work loose from the first. The King's visit to Hanover snapped them. His departure involved a Council of Regency, and with war so imminent, it was inevitable that Cumberland should be at its head. Fox, who was Cumberland's henchman, also became a member and thereafter, feeling himself on firmer ground, was the less disposed to cultivate his formidable rival. Pitt sensed the alteration, and by the same token was alarmed at the probable strength of Fox's position if by some unlucky chance the King should die abroad in the midst of a war. The possibilities were too serious for make-belief. Pitt felt that the time had come for what is familiarly known as a 'showdown,' and on the 8th of May, within a fortnight of the King's departure, the two had broken.

Pitt had now shaken himself free from all entanglements with the Government—except office! He was an *imperium in imperio*; in the Government but not of it—an impossible situation which could not last. That it lasted as long as it did is a tribute to the universal fear he inspired. The only person in England who would willingly have dismissed him was the King, but when George had suggested that course the previous December, Hardwicke, startled and dismayed, had entreated him to put any such idea out of his head; it would lead to too much trouble altogether.

So Pitt remained in office, rather like the skeleton at the feast, noting, perhaps with sardonic amusement, the growing malaise on the Government Front Bench. Truly, they were not a happy team. Newcastle, with a tenacity worthy of a better cause, was still hankering after the subjection of the Commons, and Fox, finding that payment for his services had not come up to his expectations, was beginning to fear that he had made a mistake. Murray was cowed and uncomfortable, looking with longing eyes towards the Courts of Justice where his preference and his genius lay. Robinson hardly counted. And meanwhile, Pitt was a moody Achilles, who might at any moment rush from his tent, not to rout the enemy, but to overthrow his colleagues.

(ii)

The war emphasised the Government's internal weakness. At the top where policy should be settled there was no unanimity. All were pulling in different directions. Newcastle, representing the ministerial view, was terrified of the war spreading to the Continent, not so much because war was horrible as because it was costly. The Treasury was a sad place for a timid Minister—full of gloomy warnings that the nation would be 'bankrupt in a year or two.' Newcastle, with sinking heart, totted up his figures—the army, the navy, America—five million pounds at least, probably six. And now Austria was throwing out dark hints of a combined attack on Prussia! If the King took up with that idea, our share of the cost would be £800,000 at least, besides the need to pay the higher rate of subsidy to the Russians. We should be saddled with an expense of seven millions 'at our first setting out,' and goodness knew now much later on. Where was the money to come from? It was impracticable! It was impossible![1] So he told Holdernesse who had gone with the King to Hanover. So he repeated in letter after letter. Holdernesse must get it into the King's head that we were inextricably entangled in America—Braddock was there already. He must convince the King that, with Vienna obstinate and Holland weak, we were quite unable to do 'anything great or effectual' on the Continent. The King should confine his activities 'to the security of his own Dominions,' perhaps arranging 'an augmentation of His Majesty's German troops,' perhaps making a more determined effort to

[1] Newcastle to Holdernesse, 18th July 1755. Add. MSS. 32,857.

conclude the treaty with Russia, perhaps renewing the old Bavarian and Saxon treaties. If only there could be 'an appearance of a stand in Flanders'! If only 'proper measures had been taken by the King's allies for His Majesty's defence'![1] Newcastle was full of doubts and hopeless wishes; but, through it all, he was clear that we could not afford to fight in America and on the Continent at the same time, and that on this occasion for better or for worse we were committed to America.

The King, enjoying the luxury of being an Elector in his own Electorate, took a more personal view of the world, freed from Newcastle's fussy cackling, from Hardwicke's laboured argumentation, and—perhaps best of all—from the irritation of Pitt's impertinence. In this calmer atmosphere he weighed America and Hanover in the balance and found, as he had expected, the American scale kicking the beam. He poured out his thoughts to Holdernesse, who retailed them in his letters home. 'I shudder at the thought of abandoning the *Continent system.*' Besides, what was the use? The defence of Hanover by itself would be very difficult and just as expensive as 'a more extended and more useful plan.' It would not do to rely on the Russians alone; they were too far away, and there ought to be some forces nearer at hand to prevent '*un coup de main.*' 'It is a melancholy consideration to be forced to make war with France and at the same time totally to abandon the continent; for I can never be brought to believe that any the greatest advantages we can have in America will counterbalance the danger of seeing France in possession of Flanders, masters of Ostend and Antwerp and perhaps even Flushing; while we should stand single without an ally to cope with the whole force of so superior an enemy.'[2] 'You need not plead with me for the Continent,' Newcastle retorted. 'Was it, at present, practicable in any shape, I think I should have found it out; and I am sure I would have laid hold of it. . . . When you have been twenty-four hours in England, you will be of our mind. In short, there is, there *can* be no reasoning upon it. *It is impossible.*'[3]

The King, however, was going his own way, which led him, as already related, to his Prussian alliance. He had not unnaturally felt a little awkward at making the first overtures and had received little encouragement from the Duke of Brunswick with whom

[1] Newcastle to Holdernesse, 11th July 1755. Add. MSS. 32,857.
[2] Holdernesse to Newcastle, 30th July 1755. Add. MSS. 32,857.
[3] Newcastle to Holdernesse, 6th Aug. 1755. Add. MSS. 32,858.

he had consulted. The Duchess, on the other hand, was enthusiastic, assuring Holdernesse 'in the most positive terms' that all would go well.[1] Her enthusiasm carried the day; reluctant Duke and hesitating King were both jollied along; the negotiations progressed smoothly; and George and his nephew signed the Convention of Westminster which was to have such unexpected results for Europe, for Pitt and for America.

So much for the divergent views on policy. There was no less divergence on matters of strategy between those who pressed for operations in America on the widest possible scale and those who were for restricting them to so narrow a front that they would never be noticed. There were differences of opinion over the troops to be employed—Scotch, Irish, English or American—disputes over preparations, hospital ships, armaments, supplies; disagreements about orders; angry reflections about publicity.

All this made for confusion, but perhaps a still more fundamental weakness was the complete severance between the army and the Government. The army was under the control of the Duke of Cumberland, the Captain-General, who was not in the Cabinet nor yet a Minister, but on the contrary was an object of dislike and suspicion, not less because he had direct access to the King. It was inevitable that Newcastle should feel himself ignored—as indeed he was—with the natural results on a touchy character. The evident lack of cohesion was bad enough; the lack of a strong guiding hand was worse. It was not altogether Newcastle's fault. True, he had not the requisite strength of character, but even Sir Robert Walpole had experienced the same difficulty without finding any solution.[2] The fault lay in the system and was not to be mended until Pitt's towering genius and forceful character had transformed the whole organisation, providing in himself the strategy, the strong hand and the administrative ability.

As it was, Braddock was dead before Cumberland and the Government had overcome their covert hostility and made up their minds what they wanted done. To the end Cumberland was playing with the idea of ordering Braddock 'to attempt Quebec and the French settlements'; Newcastle, always averse to offensives, voted for sending £10,000 towards fortifying Nova

[1] Holdernesse to Newcastle, 14th Aug. 1755. Add. MSS. 32,858.

[2] 'As I am neither general nor admiral, as I have nothing to do either with our navy or army, I am sure I am not answerable for the prosecution of the war.' Coxe's *Walpole,* IV, 202.

Scotia, and Lord Halifax, with overflowing enthusiasm, wanted fortifications everywhere—at Beauséjour, at Baye Verte and along the River St. John.[1] Hardwicke, like a cautious family solicitor, was for delaying all action until they had obtained plans and estimates, in order to check the extravagance of the military mind.[2] Not one of them had any real idea of the problem, still less of its solution; they were playing at soldiers in a land of make-belief. The only point on which all seemed to agree was that Pitt's views were wholly wrong, though even here they differed as to the weight which should be attached to them. To Newcastle they seemed weak, absurd and provoking,[3] but Hardwicke had an uneasy presentiment that they might have something in them and were gaining ground with the public.[4]

(iii)

If Newcastle had never before realised how weak a crew he commanded, he awoke suddenly to his position when, at the end of June (1755), he received the King's treaty with Hesse Cassel for ratification by Parliament. In itself the treaty delighted him, being fully in accord with the 'old system.' But who was to push it through the Commons? Of his active lieutenants, the able were unwilling and the willing were unable to stand up to Pitt, if he was determined to oppose; and oppose he certainly would, unless something were done to keep him quiet. Newcastle felt obliged to negotiate. The King gave permission but Newcastle became bogged in the slow and crab-like procedure which then distinguished parliamentary negotiations. Pitt was approached first by Charles Yorke, then by Hardwicke, and so by degrees the way was smoothed for the final meeting with Newcastle, himself. But at the last moment Newcastle postponed action. He happened to be feeling confident, and his jealousy of Pitt made him jump at any excuse to avoid bringing him into the Cabinet. Nothing, as he told Hardwicke very emphatically, nothing but 'the utmost distress' would make him do it.[5] At the moment all seemed well at home and abroad. So he postponed his interview and wrote complacently out to Hanover: 'we have

[1] Newcastle to Hardwicke, 4th Aug. 1755. Add. MSS. 32,857.
[2] Hardwicke to Newcastle, 4th Aug. 1755. Add. MSS. 32,857.
[3] Newcastle to Hardwicke, 12th Aug. 1755. Add. MSS. 32,858.
[4] Hardwicke to Newcastle, 12th Aug. 1755. Add. MSS. 32,858.
[5] Newcastle to Hardwicke, 12th Aug. 1755. Add. MSS. 32,858.

acted *honestly*. Those that know . . . flatter us with saying *ably*; and if we can secure a neutrality from Spain and Prussia, I will say *successfully*.'[1] Three days later Commodore Keppel woke him roughly to realities by arriving with a 'very bad account' of Braddock's expedition.[2]

Newcastle was accustomed to the ups and downs of life; he was for ever being disappointed at the 'improper' conduct of men and things, and had learnt to be resilient. So now, pulling himself quickly together, he summoned his 'inner cabinet,' and with their concurrence ordered unlimited commerce destruction against the French, though still without declaring war. 'This new act of vigour,' he said, 'immediately after the arrival of the bad news will shew spirit.' But the spirit was a little flat, for the news had dashed his hopes and shattered his policy. 'We must certainly now set out upon a new principle,' he wrote to Holdernesse, 'Americans must fight Americans; and regular troops must not be puffed up to their own disgrace and our miscarriage in all our operations. I hope the King will see things in this light. . . . The Indians must be engaged, if possible, and Americans must do our business.'[3]

As America faded, Europe loomed up more largely and the subsidies gained in importance. In the new circumstances Pitt and Frederick were both assuming a fresh significance. Newcastle was constrained to tell Holdernesse the whole sorry story, and he did so in the minimum of words: 'You cannot, the King cannot, my Lady Yarmouth cannot think me partial to Mr. Pitt or the King of Prussia, and yet I am forced to advise in some measure *both*.'[4] It was in this mood that he saw Pitt on the 2nd of September, and it was with these thoughts in mind that he urged Pitt to accept the subsidy treaties—not only the treaty with Hesse Cassel, but also the Russian treaty which was on the point of being signed. He tried desperately hard, for he was scared, but Pitt proved obdurate. He would not agree to the subsidies; at most he would swallow the Hessian treaty to save the King's face, but nothing else. Nor would he lead the House unless he were given full powers.

The negotiation failed. Had it started earlier or later, it might possibly have succeeded, but Newcastle unwittingly chose the

[1] Newcastle to Holdernesse, 19th Aug. 1755. Add. MSS. 32,858.
[2] Valence Jones to Newcastle, 22nd Aug. 1755. Add. MSS. 32,858.
[3] Newcastle to Holdernesse, 26th Aug. 1755. Add. MSS. 32,858.
[4] Newcastle to Holdernesse, 29th Aug. 1755. Add. MSS. 32,858.

one moment when failure was inevitable. People believed, and it seems probable, that Pitt would not have broken on the question of subsidies alone; some compromise could have been found. But Pitt also demanded the right to advise the King, which Newcastle, worried as he was, could not give him. There was a real impasse here, and its nature should be appreciated. Newcastle was loth to shed any portion of his power, but that was only half his problem; he was, at that moment, faced with another and more vital half. In foreign affairs Pitt represented the Tory tradition; his advice would be for a naval and colonial war in America. Until Keppel's arrival, that had been Newcastle's aim, but he was now convinced that 'we must set out upon a new principle.' Simultaneous war in Europe and America was, he believed, beyond our capacity; we must choose one or the other. The King's preference was well known, and now that Newcastle's temporary aberration had ended in failure, the future course was clear. We must swing back to the continental system, which we should never have abandoned. How, then, was it possible to give Pitt power to advise, when his advice would run so contrary to the Cabinet's new-old policy? If Pitt could have accepted the subsidies, if he could have joined in the continental measures which in Newcastle's eyes had now become necessary, if he had been less insistent on America, Newcastle would have welcomed him and might even have offered him the Seals. But unless Pitt accepted the subsidies and all they implied, Newcastle, however reluctantly, must let him go. The two men represented opposite principles and were right to reject each other; they could not have worked together till their points of difference had been resolved in a higher synthesis.

(iv)

So much for Newcastle. But a little more must be said in explanation of Pitt's obduracy, springing, as it did, out of his character and his political beliefs. It would be easy to recall that he had long since determined to come into power with the new King—a determination which dated back to the days when he and the Prince of Wales had been young men together, impatient of what they believed to be Walpole's pusillanimity and the King's lack of understanding. It would be easy to suggest that he had clung to that dream too long, forgetting that the Prince of Wales was now dead and that he himself was no longer a youngster serving his parliamentary apprenticeship. But it would not be convincing. No doubt his former resolution had its influence—possibly too strong an influence—but undoubtedly the events of the past few months had opened his eyes. He now knew that the path of opposition was sterile, and the policy of delay a mortification of the flesh. His engagement to Hester had not merely revived his ambition; it had punctured his prudence and fired his impatience. He was now ready to accept office—anxious to accept it—and he went to the interview with Newcastle resolved to obtain it. Yet he returned not only without the Seals, but committed to opposition up to the hilt. Why?

The obvious answer is, first that he was not offered the post of Secretary of State, and secondly that he objected to the subsidies, but the obvious answer does not entirely square with the facts. Certainly Pitt wanted to be Secretary of State and his failure to obtain the post was a disappointment. But both before and at the interview with Newcastle he maintained unswervingly that the Seals were not so important to him as the King's countenance, by which he meant the right to approach the King with advice. More than that, after the interview, when Fox had become acknowledged Leader of the House, Pitt used an expression in one of his speeches implying that he might have stood in Fox's place, had he been so minded. He was challenged at the time and has since been accused of deliberate slyness. He may have been sailing near the wind, yet in essence he was justified, for he knew, as Fox knew, that the Seals were the reward for the ratification of the treaties. Fox accepted the task and received the reward. Pitt rejected both; mainly because the Seals were no inducement unless accompanied by a mark of the royal favour. As for subsidies, it is common knowledge that when in office he was willing to pay them to much higher amounts. He rejected these particular subsidies because he disapproved the policy which underlay them.

Curiously enough, his apparent inconsistency over subsidies has been used as proof that his vagaries were all governed by personal ambition, though in fact he rejected them when they were the key to office and accepted them when they were bound to be a rod for his back. Pitt's personal ambitions were broadly those of any other politician—he wanted office. Where he differed from others was in subordinating his desire to his conception of what office involved. There were two ingredients—power and responsibility, which were by no means the same thing. It was only too possible to exercise power without responsibility—that seemed to be Newcastle's usual role—but no one could be really responsible without possessing the appropriate power. Pitt wished to be responsible; he was tired of subordinate office; he was weary of propping and shielding others. He would no longer, as he told Newcastle, 'like a lawyer, talk from a brief.' If he was to support the Government, he must do it with his heart as well as his mouth; he must be convinced, as at the moment he was not, that the Government's course was right; he must have his share in forming policy as well as expounding it. 'He could not and would not,' as he patiently explained to Newcastle, 'take an *active part* in the House of Commons without he had an *office of advice* as well as of *execution*.'[1] There were in short two things which he must, and did, steadily refuse to accept—office without responsibility, and responsibility without power. Both were repugnant to him and the second had the further drawback of being an insult to the House of Commons. As an individual 'he would very readily, in his present employment, acquiesce in measures, if he approved them';[2] but the active leadership of the House was quite another thing and must be accompanied by full responsibility. He would of course accept that responsibility, but if it were not to be given to him then Newcastle must look elsewhere. He made his views abundantly clear. Newcastle understood them and was most unwilling to accept their implications.

Yet perhaps he kept one point to himself. His determination to be no longer a subordinate, speaking from a brief, was not due solely to the workings of ambition, nor yet solely to the impatience of conscious ability. There was something more—something which the acute Hardwicke noted in part. He had hoped that Pitt might be won and had encouraged Newcastle to make the attempt, and when Newcastle failed, he commented: 'Mr. Pitt is not mended by the counsels of his friends since his interview with me. On the contrary, he is worked up to a higher pitch, and whether the miscarriage upon the Ohio, which is a subsequent event, may not have made him think himself more necessary, your Grace who saw his manner can best determine.'[3]

[1] Newcastle to Hardwicke, 3rd September 1755. Add. MSS. 32,858. [2] *Ibid.*
[3] Hardwicke to Newcastle, 4th September 1755. Add. MSS. 32,858.

'The miscarriage upon the Ohio' was certainly a contributory factor. Pitt's determination was bulwarked by his conviction that the war in America, at sea and in Europe was being grossly mishandled. He was beginning to believe that he alone could save England, and each 'miscarriage,' wherever it occurred, heightened his conviction. Compromise was becoming increasingly impossible. Either he must gather up the reins, or he must hold himself aloof. There was no third course. That he would have preferred to gather up the reins is incontestable; that he would gather them up only as a responsible Minister is equally incontestable. He had hoped so much from the interview with Newcastle that the failure must have been a bitter disappointment. But he never wavered; 'upon every point Mr. Pitt was as determined and negative as possible.'[1]

The failure to win Pitt drove Newcastle into the arms of Fox, who, making good use of his indispensability, obtained a promise of the Seals and became Leader of the House of Commons, pledged to secure the ratification of the treaties. He fulfilled his task in the early hours of the 14th of November, receiving the Seals the next day. On the 20th Pitt was dismissed. It was the final step necessary to pave the way for his Ministry. All that remained was for Newcastle to fall of his own incompetence.

[1] Newcastle to Hardwicke, 3rd Sept. 1755. Add. MSS. 32,858.

6

'THE MISCARRIAGE UPON THE OHIO'

(i)

Braddock, whose defeat so affected Newcastle, had been playing an unwilling but important part in shaping the fate of America. His two regiments—the 44th and the 48th—sailed from Cork in January 1755, at the very moment when by judicious bribery the French Chargé d'Affaires was obtaining a copy of Braddock's orders for transmission to his Government. The troops did not therefore sail under the best of auspices. Nor in the best of tempers. According to Parkman, they detested the service and deserted when they could;[1] according to Wolfe, the officers were extremely ignorant and the men full of a 'disobedient and dastardly spirit.'[2] Whether they really deserved these reproaches is a matter for speculation, bearing in mind that there is nothing like misfortune for damning character.

They arrived in due course in Chesapeake Bay and, ascending the Potomac, encamped at Alexandria. Here they were met by Braddock who had been sight-seeing, and here he summoned a council of Governors to confer with him and approve his plan of campaign. It was settled that he himself with the troops from England was to capture Fort Duquesne; Shirley, with the two new provincial regiments, was to attack Niagara; William Johnson with a force of colonists was to seize Crown Point, while Colonel Monckton, with 2,000 volunteers from New England, was to capture Beauséjour. The plan has been praised by military historians as an excellent example of 'true defensive strategy,' so designed that the defensive could 'pass into the offensive the moment the opening came.'[3] Doubtless the military historians are correct, but it is relevant to remark that, whatever its merits, the strategy was not the deliberate scheme of a master mind, but

[1] *Montcalm and Wolfe*, I, 182.
[2] Whitton. *Wolfe and North America*, p. 224.
[3] Corbett, I, 25.

the outcome of chance. It is not without significance that the operations in the Ohio valley and Acadia were under the command of regular officers, while the operations against Crown Point and Niagara were undertaken by the colonists. Braddock and Monckton were merely continuing the unco-ordinated struggles initiated by Washington and Lawrence—struggles which had attracted attention in England but in which the Colonies were not much interested, stubbornly refusing to support them in any effective fashion with either money or men. Crown Point and Niagara on the other hand loomed much larger in colonial than in home eyes. Long before Braddock arrived, Shirley had been urging an attack on Niagara, and the New England Colonies had devised and approved, on their own authority, a scheme for an advance on Crown Point.[1] After Braddock's defeat, when diffidence could be discarded, De Lancey, the Governor of New York, reporting the colonial views, ignored the Ohio valley and Acadia, not regarding them as vital, and stated categorically that there were only three ways to attack the French—by the St. Lawrence, by Crown Point, and by Niagara. Expeditions on those routes would be at once far less expensive and far more effective than an expedition from Virginia to the Ohio, which even if it resulted in the capture of Fort Duquesne would only be 'cutting off a toe,' while the capture of Niagara would 'lop off a limb from the French and greatly disable them.'[2] Whether strategically right or wrong, De Lancey wrote with a precision and certainty in vivid contrast to the vacillation and floundering of the authorities in England.

As for Braddock's special function, the colonists seem to have accepted the advance on Fort Duquesne with equanimity rather than enthusiasm. They regarded the regular troops with mingled awe and distaste, and whilst they secretly doubted the wisdom of Braddock's preparations, were disposed to believe that he knew best. Certainly the younger and more emotional were thrilled at the sight of the troops, who were, according to Washington, 'the most beautiful spectacle he had ever beheld.'[3] But taken as a whole, the colonists were not enthusiastic; rather were they full of doubts and criticisms. Braddock, in their eyes, had not chosen the best route—he should have marched through

[1] Doyle. *The Colonies under the House of Hanover*, p. 586.
[2] De Lancey to Robinson, 7 Aug. 1755. Add. MSS. 32,858.
[3] Jared Sparkes, I, 65.

Pennsylvania which had facilities for transport, instead of Virginia which was destitute of horses and wagons.[1] Nor did he properly appreciate the difficulties of the country or the requirements of forest warfare. Braddock on his side did not welcome advice, and ignored the frequent warnings that 'formal attacks and platoon firing never would answer against the savages and Canadians.'[2] Curiously enough, the one colonist whose assistance he did invoke was the colonist who had been driven out of Fort Duquesne and had failed dismally to recapture it. Why he should have chosen Washington as his aide-de-camp, why he should have 'importuned' him to make the campaign as 'a member of his family,' is a mystery not easily to be explained. The youthful Washington, who had resigned his commission and retired in a huff shortly after his defeat at Great Meadows, complacently supposed that Braddock believed 'the small knowledge I have had an opportunity of acquiring of the country and the Indians is worthy of his notice, and may be useful to him in the progress of the expedition.'[3] If so, Braddock made one more mistake.

From the first the expedition suffered as much from the aloofness of the inhabitants as from Braddock's own lack of foresight. Nothing was ready. At Alexandria Braddock had found the Governors unwilling or unable to establish the 'general fund for the service of the campaign' which he had been ordered to arrange, and at Wills Creek, now renamed Fort Cumberland, where the troops assembled for their march, he 'was disappointed, vexed and thrown into paroxysms of ill humour, at not finding in readiness the horses and wagons which had been promised.'[4] Washington was sent to Williamsburg to fetch money, and the deficiency of transport was made good by Benjamin Franklin, who had been sent to deprecate, and if possible remove from Braddock's mind, the 'violent prejudices' which he had conceived against the Pennsylvanians as being 'averse to the service.'[5] Averse they certainly were; but Franklin, seizing occasion by the forelock and displaying a considerable degree of wiliness, soothed the irate general and delighted his fellow colonists by hiring Pennsylvanian wagons on terms exceptionally favourable to the owners, thus not only satisfying Braddock's needs, but also diverting much money into Pennsylvanian pockets. Braddock

[1] B. Franklin, p. 94.
[2] Captain Adam Stephens to John Hunter, 18th July 1755. Add. MSS. 32,857.
[3] Sparkes, I, 61. [4] Sparkes, I, 62. [5] Franklin, 94.

wrote forthwith to the Ministry in praise of Franklin's action which was, he said, the only instance of address and integrity which he had seen in the province. 'Address' was perhaps the *mot juste*. Otherwise relations were, it seems, hardly cordial.

On the 10th of June Braddock began his advance, and at once experienced the difficulties of the route. He was blazing a trail rather than marching to war. Swallowed up in the trackless forest, his men fell ill, his horses died, and progress was infinitely slow. By the 18th of June the army had advanced barely thirty miles, and Braddock began to lose both heart and patience. In his need, he turned to Washington, who advised him to push on quickly towards the enemy with a small picked force, leaving the heavy baggage and the artillery to follow as best they could. It was precisely the advice which he had given to himself the previous year, and which had led him straight to defeat at the Great Meadows. It was now to lead Braddock straight to disaster on the Monongahela. Judged by results, it can hardly be called good, and so far as the artillery was concerned was completely at variance with Pitt's ideas (see p. 52). However, Braddock accepted it. He left nearly half his men and the greater part of the artillery behind under Colonel Dunbar, and marched forward himself with the remainder of the troops and such artillery and wagons as Washington thought indispensable, with the result that his advance which, up to that moment, had been thorough even if inordinately slow, now became by contrast more careless, less formidable and not much faster.

On the 9th of July (1755) he met the enemy some seven or eight miles from Fort Duquesne. The battle which ensued was, in its way, one of the decisive battles of American history because of its effect on public opinion on both sides of the Atlantic; otherwise it was a trumpery affair, Braddock having fewer than 1,500 men, and the French not more than 1,000, while the victory, although complete, led to nothing. The French had intended to lay an ambush at the ford across the Monongahela, but owing to the waywardness of their Indian allies were too late. Braddock had crossed the river before they arrived. His advance guard, numbering about 500 men, with two field pieces and a few wagons, were toiling up the thickly wooded hills a mile or so on the northern side, when they came in contact with the enemy. The British wheeled into line, as they had been taught, firing volleys with their muskets and bringing their two field pieces into action with exemplary precision. The deafening noise created a momentary panic among the Canadians and Indians, but that was the greatest extent of the British success. The panic passed and with it all hope of a British victory. Their opponents, infinitely superior in forest warfare, vanished among the trees, and the remainder of the battle was mere butchery. From behind every rock and covert and bush, an enemy twice the number of Braddock's advance guard poured a deadly fire into the ranks of their victims, so staringly visible in their scarlet uniforms, so hard to miss as they stood stiffly to attention, so bewildered as they gazed around for their invisible foes, so confounded by a method of fighting unknown to their textbooks. Flesh and blood could not endure it long, and at last the troops broke and fled.

Meanwhile Braddock, hearing the firing, had left 400 men to guard the baggage, and was hurrying up with the rest of the main body—about 500 strong—to the support of the advance guard. He met them flying headlong, their ranks broken, their nerves shattered. In the narrow confines of the forest track the two bodies became inextricably confused, and presented a bigger and better target to the enemy, still probably superior in numbers and still wholly invisible. The end could not be in doubt, nor could it be long delayed. Three hours in all were enough. With two-thirds of his forces killed or wounded, Braddock ordered a retreat. Shortly afterwards he himself was wounded fatally, and thereafter the retreat became a rout. The whole of his force might well have been annihilated but for the fact that the Indians had rarely, if ever, seen so many dead and dying, and were more than content with the scalps at their disposal. They were too busy stripping the dead to pursue the living.

Braddock, who had behaved during the battle with a mixture of berserk fury and wooden-headed stupidity, was carried off the field. After four days passed mostly in silent meditation, he murmured, 'We shall know better how to deal with them another time.' But the knowledge, so painfully acquired, was reserved for his successors. A few minutes after he had spoken, he had atoned for past follies, and—strange irony—he was buried in the road beside Washington's Fort Necessity.

The remnants of his force returned to Dunbar's camp, where they so thoroughly infected him with their own fears that he promptly destroyed the heavy baggage and artillery which had been left in his charge, and retreated precipitately over the mountains, first to Fort Cumberland and then to Philadelphia. So the last state was worse than the first. The frontiers were thrown wide open to the fire and fury of Indians flushed with victory and emboldened by contempt. The colonists were left without succour and with hopes dashed; they had seen the red-coats, from whom they had expected such great things, broken and flying before a pack of Indians; they had found Braddock to be a brave fool who had thrown away his life, and Dunbar a cowardly fool who had thrown away his honour, and from neither had they won safety or satisfaction, or indeed any return for the unwilling awe and reluctant pride with which they had received them. There was bound to be a revulsion of feelings, an upsurge of resentment which was the child of disappointment, followed by an upsurge of self-help which was the offspring of fear. The gulf of estrangement between the Colonies and the mother country had been appreciably widened.

(ii)

Compared with Braddock's failure, the fate of the other expeditions hardly seemed to matter. The limelight had been focused so entirely upon him that with his death the play seemed to have ended; the tragedy was over; the curtain should come down. 'We must certainly now set out upon a new principle,' said the inconsequent Newcastle. Even Walpole quavered: 'We pretend,' he wrote wistfully, 'to be comforted on the French deserting Fort St. John, and on the hope we have from two other expeditions which are on foot in that part of the world.'[1] By Fort St. John he meant Beauséjour and its satellites. The expedition against it had been successful, and in its minor way prepared the ground for Pitt, but it was in itself rather a shabby little affair which hardly deserved either the merit it was given at the time or the opprobrium to which it was subsequently exposed. The reduction of the place had been entrusted to Colonel Monckton with 2,000 volunteers raised in the New England Colonies. Monckton, a younger son of Lord Galway, was colonel of the second battalion of the Sixtieth Foot, commonly called the Royal Americans, and had been stationed in Acadia for some years. Previously he had seen service in the War of the Austrian Succession. He was a competent officer of

[1] To Mann, 28th Aug. 1755.

fair abilities, and a man of conciliatory temper. His present task did not call for much skill and in its aftermath can hardly have been to his taste. Unlike Braddock, he had no difficulty in approaching his objective. There was no carving a way through the forest; he and his troops sailed from Boston straight to the Bay of Fundy, where they came to anchor barely five miles from Beauséjour. He should have sailed early in April but was delayed by the non-arrival of muskets from England—another example of characteristic muddle—and did not set out till the 22nd of May. He dropped anchor on the 1st of June, landed unopposed, and on the 4th, crossing the Missaguash River without serious difficulty, encamped on the woody hill above the fort. He was in overwhelming strength. Beauséjour, which was not in a very good state of repair, was garrisoned by about 150 regulars and some 300 or 400 Acadian peasants, pressed unwillingly into the service. There were perhaps another 1,000 peasants lurking in the woods, but as they were without leaders or appetite for war, their presence could hardly be called alarming, and such attacks as they made were easily beaten off. The garrison inside the fort were not much more enthusiastic nor much better led. Their commandant, Captain Duchambon de Vergor, was a blackguard who had obtained his position by acting as pimp to François Bigot, the notorious Intendant of Canada. With him were two other scoundrels of much the same kidney, the Abbé le Loutre, a remorseless fanatic, blinded by fury and hatred, and Thomas Pichon, commissary of stores, who was a traitor in correspondence with the English. Not much could be expected under such leadership, and not much was forthcoming. There was some desultory cannonading, and on the 16th, after a cannon shot had fallen uncomfortably near Vergor, killing several of his officers, he capitulated. Monckton promptly summoned the little Fort Gaspereau, at Baye Verte, twelve miles distant, to surrender, and its commandant, Villeray, at once complied. A few days later the French burnt their post at the mouth of the River St. John and retired. All Acadia was in British hands.

There followed the well-known expulsion of the inhabitants. If we are to believe Bancroft, these peasants were an idyllic community of incredible virtue: 'They formed, as it were, one great family. Their morals were of unaffected purity.'[1] If we are to believe Longfellow, their climate was one long tranquil

[1] Bancroft. *History of the American Revolution,* I, 222

summer evening, and 'thus dwelt together in love these simple Acadian farmers.'[1] In spite of this evidence, it is possible to believe that they were much as other peasants—swayed sometimes by passions other than unaffected purity and not without the earthy cunning which often accompanies rural simplicity. Certainly they were superstitious; certainly they were misled by le Loutre; certainly by reason of his threats of damnation they refused—and had refused for years past—to take the oath of allegiance as British subjects. They had been a constant source of trouble, a running fount of disaffection; and with full-blooded war in the offing it was time to make an end. Once more they were given their chance; once more they refused. Nemesis followed and they were deported. Acadia may have reverted for the time to 'the forest primeval,' but at least it was no longer a thorn in the side of the English Colonies, nor yet a corridor for the French between Cape Breton and Quebec. The settlement of Acadia was a great step forward towards the final conquest of Canada.

(iii)

So much for Walpole's Fort St. John. There still remain the two other expeditions which he said were on foot in that part of the world. It was rather a vague description. Hostilities in America were spread over a tremendous front which stretched from the headwaters of the Ohio on the south-west to the Gulf of St. Lawrence on the north-east. Obviously there could not be a continuous line and the fighting was inevitably broken into isolated struggles. Braddock and Monckton had operated on the two extreme flanks; the two other expeditions came in between, and were aimed at gaining command of the natural thoroughfares running north and south. One, under William Johnson, was to attack Crown Point, a fort on Lake Champlain, guarding the route from New York to Quebec—the route which ran in an almost straight line up the Hudson River, across Lakes George and Champlain, and so down the River Richelieu to a point on the St. Lawrence half-way between Montreal and Quebec. The other, under Shirley, was to capture Fort Niagara which, situated between Lakes Erie and Ontario, barred the route running across the Lakes and down the St. Lawrence to Montreal. If these two forts could be secured, they would still act as a bar—

[1] Longfellow. *Evangeline.*

no longer, however, against the English, but against the French. They would also, as De Lancey pointed out and as modern military historians have endorsed, form a useful starting point for 'distressing the French in Canada,' if such a course should ever prove to be desirable.

Neither expedition was successful, though Johnson's produced an appearance of success. Shirley's attempt on Niagara can be dismissed shortly. He set out in the late summer of 1755 and on the 21st of August arrived with 1,500 men at Oswego, an English Fort on the eastern shores of Lake Ontario. Niagara was about 120 miles to the west, while some fifty miles to the north lay Fort Frontenac. When he had set out, Shirley had been under the impression that Niagara was 'but a house, almost in ruins, surrounded by a small ditch and a rotten palisade of seven or eight feet high,' with a garrison of perhaps thirty men and those poorly armed,[1] and that Frontenac was not much stronger. But the papers captured after Braddock's defeat had given the French ample warning and by the time Shirley had reached Oswego there were 1,400 regulars at Frontenac and about 1,200 Canadians and Indians at Niagara.[2] Shirley was nicely caught between the two. Whichever he attacked, the other would fall upon Oswego and cut him from his base. To add to his difficulties, his commissariat was uncertain, his stores inadequate, the weather unpropitious and his men disheartened. By the end of October Shirley had lost heart himself, and leaving 700 men to repair and garrison Oswego, returned home without attempting to strike a blow. The expedition had achieved nothing. But one point is to be noted—though the French had been fully aware of Shirley's movements, they had made no effort to molest him. They would defend themselves if attacked; but they seemed resolutely determined to refrain from provocative action.

(iv)

Johnson's campaign against Crown Point was almost as ineffectual, since, like Shirley, he never reached his objective. None the less it had many points of interest. It had been promoted by Shirley and approved by his Assembly long before it had been sanctioned or even considered by the Ministry. Unlike other projects, it had been taken up by the New England Colonies with

[1] Bancroft, I, 243. [2] Parkman. *Montcalm and Wolfe,* I, 325.

some approach to unanimity and even enthusiasm. Strictly speaking the commander should have been nominated by Braddock, but as the money had been voted and the men enlisted before his arrival, Shirley, at the request of his Assembly, took the responsibility upon himself and appointed Johnson, a choice which was subsequently confirmed. Johnson's main qualification was that he came from New York and so gave no grounds for jealousy to any of the New England Colonies supporting the expedition. Otherwise his qualifications were not very obvious. He had never seen active service and knew nothing of the science of war. In himself he was a loud-mouthed, coarse-fibred, genial soul, Irish by birth and half Indian by choice, given to high living and low thinking, but swayed by a rough sense of justice and a feeling of responsibility. His not unlikeable character had won him the confidence and even the affection of the Five Nations, which was no doubt also a qualification for his present post. But whatever his qualifications and however he came to be chosen, he fell into practically every one of the errors which have been chalked up against Braddock's memory, so that one may suppose it was good luck rather than merit which gave him his measure of success and earned him £5,000 from the English Parliament and a baronetcy from the English King instead of an unknown grave beside Fort Necessity.

Johnson had about 3,000 troops under his command, and towards the end of August (1755) arrived at the carrying-place subsequently known as Fort Edward, about fourteen miles south of Lake George. Here, in the best Washington style, he divided his forces, and left some 500 men behind to build and fortify the post. With the rest he advanced to the southern point of Lake George, where he erected a camp on the site of the future Fort William Henry, and possibly because he was still some fifty miles from Crown Point did little or nothing to secure it against surprise or to keep a watch on the movements of the French. Instead, he began in leisurely fashion to collect stores and bateaux for the final march. His dilatory methods and lack of experience produced a considerable measure of unrest among the troops, who suffered physically from a poor commissariat and psychologically from a lack of occupation. They were further irritated by the arrival of 300 or 400 Mohawks whom, in spite of all experience, they persisted in regarding as nothing but a nuisance.

Meanwhile the French had learnt the details of the expedition from the papers captured at Braddock's defeat, and had dispatched a mixed force of regulars, Canadians and Indians, about 3,500 in all, to defend Crown Point. Their commander was Baron Dieskau, a German veteran, who had served under the Maréschal de Saxe. He was both skilful in planning and daring in execution and it irked him to wait on the defensive, especially when he was equal in strength to the enemy. Accordingly he marched southward from Crown Point to Ticonderoga, where Lake George runs into Lake Champlain, and from this advanced post planned to overrun the small garrison at Fort Edward.

With this object in view he set out with 1,500 men, of whom only 200 were regulars, the remainder being Canadians and Indians, and had come within a few miles of his destination when he learnt from prisoners details both of Fort Edward and also of the camp at Lake George. At once there was trouble with his Indians. They refused to advance any farther against a position which being dubbed a fort they conceived to be strongly entrenched, but after much persuasion they agreed to attack the camp on the shores of Lake George. Dieskau realised that the change of plan, involving as it did an attack on a greatly superior force and one probably apprised of his presence, was full of peril, but he was loth to retreat without striking a blow. At first fortune favoured him. News of his whereabouts had by this time reached Johnson, who dispatched a force of 1,000 men to lay an ambush for him on his way back from Fort Edward. But they took no precautions, fewer even than Braddock had taken, with the result that they marched straight into an ambush which Dieskau had, in his turn, laid for them. Like Braddock's troops they were mown down and fled panic-stricken back to the camp. Dieskau pursued hotly and wanted to rush the place, but once more found himself thwarted by his troops; the Indians were sullen and unmanageable; the Canadians tired and apprehensive. He had therefore to rely on his small force of regulars. They advanced bravely, but were greatly outnumbered by the defenders and checked by a barricade which had been hastily thrown up. The assault was held, Dieskau was wounded and captured, and the French finally beaten off. Johnson had, against all probability, won a victory. But he failed to profit by it. Though reinforced, he contented himself with holding his position and strengthening his camp. As winter approached his troops began to desert, and towards the end of November he marched home, leaving a small garrison behind. By contrast, however, with Shirley and Braddock he had done well, and, as already related, was rewarded beyond his deserts.

(v)

It is now possible, before returning to affairs in England, to sum up the results of the year's fighting in America. Acadia had been finally settled, but as it had been ceded to England by the Treaty of Utrecht, its pacification could not be regarded as in any sense an attack on the French or as a new jumping-off ground. In all other directions, the efforts of the British, whether regulars from England or troops from the Colonies, had been uniformly unsuccessful; the routes to Canada were still held firmly by the French; the headwaters of the Ohio were still controlled by the enemy; and, perhaps worst of all, the western boundaries of the middle Colonies were dominated by the Indians who brought terror and destruction in their wake. Truly the outlook in America was poor; no wonder Newcastle was for washing his hands of the whole miserable business.

7

INTERLUDE

(i)

Dismissal gave Pitt a new sense of freedom. No longer constrained to support the opinions of others, he began to mingle with his criticisms of Government hints of his own positive views on strategy and the carrying on of the war. An opportunity came on the 21st of November—the day after his dismissal—when the Government moved for 40,000 sailors and 10,000 marines. There was no need for Pitt to intervene, but the subject was one near his heart and towards the end of a somewhat aimless debate he suddenly felt moved to speak. He not only supported the motion but declared that as English interests were at stake, he would wish to go farther. Provided unanimity could be preserved—for unanimity was essential in the face of an enemy—he would gladly move for a further 10,000 men, and 'if he could obtain it, it would be the first thing done for this country since the peace of Aix.'[1] What was needed was a strong navy and decisive action. The Government were too timid; they could bring troops over from Ireland and so do away with the need for foreign mercenaries; they could destroy the French trade which so far they had 'spared sillily.' Instead, they had sunk into a state of 'dead stagnation,' with a distorted and limited outlook. Fancy boasting that 140,000 of the best troops in Europe had been provided for the defence of Hanover, when none had been provided for England, and only 'two miserable battalions' for America—battalions which had been sent out simply to be sacrificed! He made the general trend of his thoughts clear, but as he was still smouldering under the shock of his dismissal, he soon lost the subject matter of the debate in an altercation with Fox, the main interest of which was his emphatic denial that he had struggled for power. Was he accused of it, he asked, because he had not yielded to poor and

[1] Walpole, *George II*, II, 68.

sordid measures which he saw tended to destroy his country? If he had yielded to them, he might have been given high office, but conscience and honour forbade him to concur in measures which he believed to be ruinous. It was not because he had struggled for power that he was in his present situation, but because he could not accept the subsidy treaties.[1]

A further hint of his views was given a fortnight later (2nd December) when the House debated a Bill to authorise the sale of captured French merchantmen for the benefit of the captors. There were, he declared, always sufficient seamen in the country to meet the needs of navy and merchant marine alike, provided proper use was made of them. It was a matter of wise distribution; no ship should be allowed more seamen than were sufficient for its working; the rest of the complement should be made up of marines. The difficulty was that the navy could not compete with the merchant service in the matter of wages. Hence the need for the press gang, which was often of doubtful legality and always an 'unjust and violent practice.' Nor were the results good; the courage and fidelity of a pressed man were not to be compared with the courage and fidelity of a volunteer. We ought to offer the seamen all possible inducements to join up voluntarily, and when war ended we should not be in too great a hurry to reduce the navy, for if we did there would be unemployment and the service would get a bad name.

In the same speech he dealt with France, displaying his usual repugnance to self-deception. It was no use, he argued, shutting our eyes to facts. A declaration of war might be necessary to notify neutrals and legalise the distribution of prize money; but, declaration or no declaration, we were at war with France, and should act accordingly. Wherever we could, we should seize their ships and imprison their crews, to prevent them from invading us at home or attacking us across the Atlantic. We must do more than that: 'If we do not deliver the territories of all our Indian allies, as well as our own in America, from every French fort and every French garrison, we may give up our plantations, as well as the ships we have taken.' Then roaming farther afield, he declared that his opposition to Walpole had sprung from that Minister's failure to maintain our interests in America. It was during his administration that the French had established themselves on the Mississippi and the Great Lakes—

[1] Walpole. *George II*, II, 71.

encroachments which we ought to have opposed tooth and nail and could have defeated if we had been governed by our own interests and had acted with spirit. Walpole's failure had 'brought this nation into that distressed condition every gentleman now seems to be so sensible of.' Let us avoid his humiliating example.

Pitt ended with a tribute to Walpole's memory, which was both magnanimous and genuine, but failed to do more than raise a snigger on the Government benches. 'Gentlemen may laugh,' he retorted, 'if they please, but I can perceive no joke in what I have said; it is only a proof that my opposition did not proceed from any personal resentment, nor my praise from any design to flatter'[1]—an interesting piece of self-revelation. Making speeches, as he had remarked before, was 'an instrument of action in a country like ours,' not something in which he found much pleasure.

Three days later (5th December) he turned from the navy to the army. Barrington, the new Secretary at War, in moving for 34,000 men, pointed out that this was an increase of 15,000 over the number approved the previous year; it was all that could be raised at the moment, though later on the Government intended to raise more. Pitt seconded the motion—an ironic comment on his dismissal!—and in doing so emphasised our lack of preparation. All our steps from the dispatch of Braddock onwards had 'tended to provoke a war, not to make it,' and we must expect before long to reap as we had sown. At this 'dangerous and critical conjuncture' we needed 'our whole force,' and the pity was that we had not acted a year ago when he had protested that 18,000 men were not enough. Why had Ministers shown so little foresight for England when the King had shown so much for Hanover? Did it never occur to them to picture the horrors which would follow a French occupation of London? The Ministers had displayed no 'understanding or foresight or virtue'; all their thoughts had been centred on 'the little frivolous love of power,' the 'fondness for disposal of places.' It was now time to turn to realities, and exchange futility for the wisdom needed 'to meet such rough times as these.' The increase in the army was good, but it would be better if the Government would encourage the creation of a militia to supplement the army. It was the maxims of Government, not the people, which had degenerated, and

[1] Speech, 2nd Dec. 1755. *Parliamentary History,* XV.

'he wanted to call this country out of that enervate state, that twenty thousand men from France could shake it. . . . He wished to see that breed restored which under our old principles had carried our glory so high.'[1]

Fox tried to shrug off responsibility by asking why, if Pitt had realised the danger a year ago, he had not spoken out before? Perhaps, now that he had broken silence, he would try his hand at a Militia Bill. Pitt retorted that if he had kept silent in public, he had given warnings in private. It would have been wrong to frighten the public while the Government were proclaiming their disbelief in war; but now that the facts could no longer be disguised 'we must sound the alarum in Parliament, when we have invited into our bowels a war that was the child of ignorance.'[2]

(ii)

At the moment Pitt said no more about the militia, but he had not forgotten it. If it should ever fall to his lot to conduct the war, he meant the militia to play an important part. The problem was to know where he could look for support. Men's opinions on the need and value of a militia had always been coloured by their attitude towards a standing army. At the time of the Revolution, Parliament had tended to favour a militia, on the assumption that a citizen army could scarcely be a menace to the country. The Crown, on the other hand, being involved in war after war, had always wanted a professional army. As time passed the Whigs noticed that continental armies were continually growing in size, and, realising that it was impossible to contend against their well-trained, well-equipped strength with a crowd of hastily levied, ill-armed citizens, began to change their minds; perhaps, after all, there was something to be said for a standing army; perhaps they had been a little hasty in opposing it, and a little injudicious in supporting the militia. The Tories, on the other hand, who had no hankering after a continental war and no interest in Hanover, continued to prefer the militia, though as time went on and the militia declined in effectiveness, they became less sure of its practicability and more daunted by its inconveniences. No one in short had much faith in it as a military force, and in urging its use in place of foreign mercenaries Pitt was ploughing a lonely furrow. The Whigs were contemptuous.

[1] Walpole. *George II*, II, 86-89. [2] *Ibid.* p. 92.

Wise men, sneered Fox, held back, but if Pitt thought it practicable, he would not quite despair of it. The Tories were hesitant. Pitt himself recognised that there was not much to be said for the system then in force, but saw no reason why it should not be reorganised on a different basis and made to play a material part—a part indeed which could not be filled in any other way. For support for his ideas he could look only to the Tories, and to them he made a direct appeal.

One of his small following, George Townshend, provided the occasion by moving on the 8th of December (1755) for a Committee of the whole House to consider the introduction of a Bill to establish a real militia. Without further ado, Pitt produced his scheme. 'He opened it,' said Walpole, 'with a plain precision, and went through with a masterly clearness. . . . He had never shone in this light before.'[1] Naturally, for born leaders do not shine as second strings. Pitt was a born leader and this new light which so amazed Walpole was the direct offspring of two intensely individual experiences, his marriage and his dismissal, the one giving him ballast and the other freedom.

The militia, as Pitt found it, was organised on a county basis, the landowners finding the officers and men and supplying the arms and pay. No one could be compelled to serve, though anyone standing down must provide a substitute; and no one could be called out for more than a total of twelve days in the year. Their main duty, like that of the ancient Anglo-Saxon *fyrd* from which they were descended, was to suppress 'insurrection, rebellion or invasion.'[2] It is not perhaps surprising that the Whig magnates disliked a force which entailed a good deal of trouble and expense upon themselves, and seemed unlikely ever to serve a useful purpose. Nor is it difficult to suppose that the King, as head of the armed forces, was not enamoured of so vague, so ill-trained a body, mainly controlled by persons other than himself. Pitt proposed to alter the whole character of the force. In his scheme it was to become a permanent body of a fixed size—50,000 or 60,000 men. Everyone between the ages of eighteen and fifty was to be liable for service, unless specially exempted, and in each county the actual quota was to be selected by ballot. The officers were to be members of the landed gentry and were to be unpaid. The training, which was to take place

[1] Walpole. *George II*, II, 98-9. [2] Maitland. *Constitutional History*, p. 456.

twice a week (on Sundays and one other day), was to be in the hands of sergeants, seconded from the regular army. The militia were to receive the same pay as regulars and the King was to provide both pay and arms. The period of service was to be three years. By this means a formidable body which Pitt himself described as 'a kind of half-trained Army' would be built up in a short time.

The proposal was clearly a new departure. Walpole says that Pitt 'by no means thought it feasible,' but wanted to get whatever credit might be going. It is difficult to see what credit he could expect, but it is easy to see at what he was aiming. The scheme was a mixture of the principles which in this century have produced the Territorials and the Home Guard, and was further interesting as a tentative step towards conscription on a basis other than the press gang. Pitt thought it feasible, but realised that there would be a large measure of opposition. There was, he said, no hope 'unless Government, the Army, the Law, and what in this case was most material, the Country Gentlemen, would give their assistance.'[1] It would need time to accustom all those bodies to the idea, and probably acute danger to bring them finally to the point. Hence the need to sketch the outlines at the earliest moment.

Time was certainly necessary. Pitt's first effort failed. The Commons, thanks to the Tories, passed the Bill, but the Lords threw it out. They were swayed by Hardwicke, whose views had nothing in common with those of Pitt. The Bill, he declared, was too democratic; it removed the militia out of the hands of the King into the hands of Parliament, and left the execution to officials appointed by the House of Commons, without the assistance of the peers. Worse still, the scheme would make the country military-minded, and training on a Sunday would destroy the appearance of religion.[2] Not one of those arguments could have carried the least weight with Pitt; he approved of democracy; he venerated Parliament; he wanted to rouse the country out of 'its enervate state'; and he was more interested in the fruits of religion than in its appearance. More than that, he believed the troops to be necessary and was impatient at mere negation. But the Lords accepted Hardwicke's view. Pitt was frustrated at the moment, but the seeds had been sown.

[1] Walpole. *George II*, II, 98-9. [2] Yorke's *Hardwicke*, II, 264.

(iii)

Before Parliament adjourned for the Christmas holidays, there was one more battle which Pitt had to fight, the battle on the motion to ratify the Hessian and Russian treaties. He had already made his views clear in his speech on the Address (13th November), and now could only elaborate and emphasise. He did so with consummate skill, in a series of three speeches (10th, 12th and 15th December). Walpole described the first as 'the bitterest and most insulting of all speeches'; the second as 'a very long harangue' delivered 'with little fire' by a sick man; and the third as 'a speech of most admirable and ready wit that flashed from him for the space of an hour and a half' and was 'accompanied with action that would have added reputation to Garrick.'[1] Writing to Mann nearer the time he summed up these debates by saying that 'the Opposition, though not numerous, is now composed of very determined and very great men; more united than the Ministry, and at least as able. The resistance to the treaties has been made with immense capacity. Mr. Pitt has shone beyond the greatest horizon of his former lustre.'[2]

The Government's case, in a nutshell, was that the object of the treaties was to prevent war in Europe. No one wanted war, but it would come unless we entered into alliances to preserve Hanover. Pitt could not agree. He did not believe the treaties would do anything to save Hanover; the idea was 'preposterous, absurd, and impracticable.'[3] The protection of Hanover would require a far wider continental system than we could possibly afford, so that 'we are lost *in limine*.'[4] The treaties were ineffective for defence, and provocative of war, especially the Russian treaty which was highly inflammable; it was aimed at the King of Prussia and would probably fling him into the arms of France. Everything turned upon Frederick's intentions, which were unknown: 'if he were well-disposed, this measure was not necessary; if ill-disposed it was war.'[5] He would of course like to protect Hanover if it was feasible, but he was sure the Government's method was wrong; 'he would not for any consideration have set his hand to these treaties.'[6] They must be resisted, and 'perhaps the resistance . . . might save the Administration from a

[1] Walpole. *George II*, II, 112, 132, 135.
[2] To Mann, 21st Dec. 1755. [3] Almon, I, 283. [4] Walpole. *George II*, II, 137.
[5] *Ibid.*, II, 132. [6] *Ibid.*, II, 116.

continent war.'[1] His efforts were unavailing; the treaties were approved.

(iv)

All these speeches were made within a few weeks after his dismissal, when the anger and soreness he inevitably felt were still fresh and smarting. His feelings coloured his language which was 'violent and abusive' as both Rigby[2] and Waldegrave[3] testified, whilst he himself was, in Walpole's phrase, 'like an angry wasp.'[4] It is possible, however, to read too much into these descriptions. Parliament in those days was not unlike a big family gathering, and produced the brusquerie that such gatherings often inspire. The members cherished all sorts of private quarrels and personal feuds; they indulged in 'family' jokes and bandied about phrases and expressions with special meanings. When speaking, they were inclined to show off; they liked to coin epigrams; they tried to be witty; they were fond of Latin tags; they enjoyed airing their knowledge of ancient history. 'Invective' was one of their favourite pastimes, and it had a real fascination for them. 'Debates,' said Walpole, 'where no personalities broke out, engaged too little attention.'[5] When personalities did break out, it was like watching a gladiatorial combat, spiced with the thrill of knowing that at any moment the lash might fall on one's own back. It is possible—indeed probable—that the jibes and jeers were not taken too seriously, and as it is likely enough that they would prove a little tedious in the reading today, their loss need not be unduly deplored.

The great master of invective was Pitt, who was now in open opposition, closely connected with Leicester House, and egged on by Bute. All this added an artificial stimulus to his natural wrath, and both alike must be borne in mind as the disjointed shreds of his speeches are turned over in the effort to give them a coherent meaning. They abounded in wit and irony which were too often the main attraction for onlookers such as Walpole; they were overflowing with invective which tended to veil his more serious arguments; they were loaded with much extraneous matter which has long since lost its interest and sometimes its meaning. But mingled with all this ancient lumber and shining

[1] Walpole. *George II*, II, 138.
[2] Bedford. *Correspondence*, II, 179.
[3] *Memoirs*, p. 53.
[4] To Bentley, 17th Dec. 1755.
[5] Walpole. *George II*, II, 145.

through it, there can be clearly discerned the outlines of his strategy—'our insular plan,' as he called it.[1] Broadly his view was that Hanover must be sacrificed for the time being; we had no army to defend it, nor sufficient money to buy it protection; it would have to be redeemed at the end of the war, and the exact method must be left to chance. Meanwhile our strength must be concentrated on the navy, which must defend our shores, bottle up the French and sweep away their commerce. Although the navy would keep us safe in the long run, it could not prevent occasional raids; that contingency must be met by the militia. With the country secure behind the twofold shield of a strong navy and a properly organised militia, the army could be used with impunity to conquer the French Colonies. So Pitt planned in December 1755 on the facts as he then found them. By the time he rose to power the facts had changed, and Pitt had to modify his plan accordingly, but in essence it remained. He was preparing well in advance; 'for what is the first attribute of a wise Minister, but to leave as little as possible to contingents? How do thoughtlessness, folly and ignorance differ from wisdom and knowledge, but by want of foresight?'[2] So he himself asked.

(v)

When Parliament rose, Pitt hurried down to Bath, leaving Hester behind. Partly, he was drawn by the lure of the house he was building in the Circus, but the main reason was the old reason—ill-health; Pitt felt the need of a course of Bath waters before plunging once more into the fray. Regrettable as the cause may have been, his absence had one advantage—it produced a further interchange of those letters which, for all their dullness, display so vividly the tenderness of his feelings towards his family and the thoughtfulness of Hester's protective love. 'How sweetly,' he wrote, 'was the new year ushered in to me by the sweetest letter that was ever writ. . . . I have nothing to ask of heaven but the same old year repeated to me.'[3] As usual, Pitt's style was the more spacious and rhetorical, Hester's the more detailed and practical. On this occasion her letters were much taken up with houses. There was the one in Upper Brook

[1] Grenville. *Correspondence*, I, 152.
[2] Speech of December 5th. Walpole, George II, II, 89.
[3] To Hester, 1st Jan. 1756. Public Record Office.

Street which he was anxious to acquire, and for which she had obtained a first option, at a rent of £100 a year, excluding stables and outdoor offices. It had one serious drawback—the kitchen with its smell of cooking was inside the house; it was a pity, but not an insuperable objection; 'we must,' said Hester, 'live without roast beef on Sundays.' Then there was the house at Bath, which served to emphasise the difference in their characters. Hester hinted uneasily at the expense; now that he was out of office, perhaps it ought to be given up. 'I should rejoice much more in the progress you are making . . . were it not for some objections that will intrude themselves and have their place in my mind.'[1] Pitt's profusion was to cause her much heart-searching, and this first gentle attempt to curb it bore no fruit. His answer was uncompromising; 'we are too advanced to recede.' And then, with a pun to quiet her doubts, he added that he was himself 'too far advanced in another sense ever to imagine that any plan could be long practicable for me, without a house at Bath.' His own needs were paramount and outweighed economic hesitations; the house might be expensive, but it would suit admirably for his retirement: 'I have so made up my mind to it, for the evening of my day, that I should be grieved if my dearest love were brought to disapprove or dislike it.'[2] What was poor Hester to do? She acquiesced.

If he would not let her be his conscience in money matters, he allowed her to be his memory in social affairs. She reminded him to congratulate George Grenville on the birth of another son. Pitt did so, but could not hide the pangs of envy. He felt constrained to assure her that 'Poor little Dame Hester is not less dear to me than a son and heir to our no estate could have been . . . she will not outgrow those sweet blue eyes that I have set my heart upon';[3] nor could he refrain from dubbing Mrs. Grenville 'this happy mother of males.'[4] There were times when Pitt was very transparent.

(vi)

Pitt returned from Bath when Parliament reassembled, but he came back with a feeling of savage impotence. He knew that with the ratification of the treaties he had lost his fight. It was

[1] Hester to Pitt, 3rd Jan. 1756. Public Record Office.
[2] To Hester, 5th Jan. 1756. Public Record Office.
[3] To Hester, 3th Jan. 1756.
[4] To Hester, 4th Jan. 1756.

now inevitable that the war must drift from America to Europe and he could do nothing to prevent it. For the time being he made no further effort at constructive suggestion—only a snapping at the Government. He meant to hurt, yet often enough behind his petulant irritation can be traced the outline of his deeper convictions, and it sometimes happened that a soft answer turned away his wrath.

In his first speech (23rd January 1756) he supported a complaint which Beckford lodged against Admiral Knowles, the Governor of Jamaica. As the complaint proved to have no foundation, Pitt's motive is usually supposed to have been a desire to court Beckford. It would not in itself have been an unreasonable desire since Beckford stood high in the City, had a wide knowledge of commerce and trade, and was closely connected with the West Indies, all of which made him important in Pitt's eyes. But if that swayed him, there was certainly something more. Knowles' case must be read in conjunction with the earlier case of Anstruther, in which Pitt had also intervened. In both cases a Governor was accused of tyrannical conduct, and injustice to colonials was a matter on which Pitt felt strongly. The duty to recognise them as having the same rights and privileges as Englishmen was imperative and one of his greatest contributions to the idea of empire. No accusation of tyranny ought to be ignored, and Pitt was right to take the matter up 'with great warmth and solemnity.' The pity was that his inward irritation made him 'cast reflections on Fox for endeavouring to screen the guilty,' before the guilt had been proved.[1] It is a regrettable fact that Pitt was excessively touchy at this period, and correspondingly prickly, especially towards a rival who seemed to have outdistanced him.

The same cantankerous spirit made him on the same day 'ridicule and hurt' Lyttelton, when as Chancellor of the Exchequer he opened his Budget. Unlike Fox, Lyttelton had never been a rival. He and Pitt had been friends at school and for many years thereafter; there was real affection between them, tinged on Lyttelton's side with something of awe, and on Pitt's with a dash of good-humoured contempt. But this friendship had been marred when Lyttelton, first of all the Cousinhood, had deserted their ranks. He had thereby incurred Pitt's wrath, and had suffered ever since from an uneasy conscience. At this moment

[1] Walpole. *George II*, II, 152.

his sufferings were increased by the duty laid on him to introduce the Budget. His merits, amiable though they were, did not include any of the qualities which should distinguish a Chancellor, so that he was 'strangely awkward and absent in reading the figures and distinguishing the sums.'[1] This gave Pitt an opening to be unkind, which he was not slow to seize. Lyttelton became plaintive, trying to propitiate Pitt 'with great professions of esteem,' until at last, growing tired of baiting him, Pitt allowed his natural affection some scope and 'grew into good humour.'

The good humour had vanished when on the 28th of January the Government proposed to grant £120,000 for the services of American troops in the late campaign. Under other circumstances the proposal would have appealed to Pitt, but being still in a quarrelsome mood, he used it as an excuse to disparage the Government. Seizing on a point made by Townshend, he objected that the grant was a block grant unsupported by details, and hinted at improper disbursements. From that he passed on to the lack of harmony between the Ministers who, he said, were 'united only in corrupt and arbitrary measures.' Obviously he had in mind Fox and Newcastle—the Rhone and the Saône of an earlier speech—and beyond doubt he was moved by anger and jealousy, which made him impute bad motives unnecessarily. The lack of union was a fact; the honeymoon, if there had ever been one, was over and the quarrels were beginning. The marriage had always been one of expediency; no love had ever been lost between the parties, as Newcastle had made clear from the beginning, first by his exultant remark to Lady Katherine Pelham that 'the King will not suffer Mr. Fox to do anything *even in the House of Commons,* without previously consulting me,'[2] and then by his boast to Hardwicke that he had given the King 'some strong instances' of Fox's unpopularity.'[3] Not that Pitt was showing unusual perspicacity. All the world knew that 'the Duke of Newcastle and his coadjutor Mr. Fox squabble twice for agreeing once.'[4] By the middle of the year the incompatibility had grown so great that Newcastle was constrained to ask 'Is there or can there be any means found out of having more dependence upon Mr. Fox than we had the last session?'[5]

[1] Walpole. *George II*, II, 153.
[2] Newcastle to Lady Katherine Pelham, 26th Sept. 1755. Add. MSS. 32,859.
[3] Newcastle to Hardwicke, 4th Oct. 1755. Add. MSS. 32,859.
[4] Walpole to Mann, 21st Dec. 1755.
[5] To Hardwicke, 12th June 1756. Add. MSS. 32,865.

The want of harmony was evident, was growing, and was soon to end in rupture; and one is bound to suppose that Pitt did not find the prospect unpleasing.

One further matter which arose during this interlude deserves notice as foreshadowing another of Pitt's coming innovations. A Swiss refugee, by name Prevôt, offered to raise four battalions from among the foreign colonists in America and, as they might not understand English words of command, he proposed that they should be officered by foreign Protestants with experience of active service, who were to have the same rights and privileges as provincial officers but no rank or position in England. Pitt, anxious to increase the forces in America by any and every means, approved the main proposal, merely censuring the tardiness of Government and their general lack of preparation. But he could not stomach the idea of foreigners ousting English officers, nor yet the distinction, thus emphasised, between the provincials and the regulars. He protested that 'English officers had behaved everywhere with lustre' and that to suggest that there was any lack of them came badly from Ministers who had just cashiered one (Sir Henry Erskine) 'for nothing but his vote in Parliament.'[1] Fox bristled at this charge and demanded to know by what right Pitt had brought it. There followed an aimless altercation on what was, after all, an unessential—an altercation very typical of the red herrings which were drawn across and across the debates of that period, and to which Pitt's imagery and effervescence too often gave an opening. But if his argument was lost in shallows, his attitude was clear, exemplifying once more his unshakable belief in his own countrymen and his determination that no distinction could or should be drawn between the Englishman at home and the Englishman in the Colonies.

The debates on Prevôt's proposal were spread over the greater part of February (1756) and ranged over a vast variety of subjects, relevant and irrelevant. They were followed by debates on Lyttelton's proposed taxes. Then on the 23rd of March, the King sent 'a message to both Houses to acquaint them with the advice he has received that these his Dominions are to be invaded.'[2] The lull had ended; the storm had begun.

[1] Walpole. *George II*, II, 159.

[2] Jenkinson to Miller, 23rd March 1756. Dickens and Stanton. *An Eighteenth Century Correspondence*, p. 327.

(vii)

Pitt had been right in thinking the continental treaties dangerous. The Russian treaty had touched off the train which led to the explosion; and the Convention of Westminster had completely altered the whole French strategy. France, like England, had wanted to avoid war on the Continent. They had many reasons, one of which, and perhaps the most pressing, was the shortage of money. They, like Newcastle, had no doubt that it was financially impossible to fight in Europe, in America and on the seas all at the same time.[1] That being so, they had originally intended to carry on the war in America alone and to take all possible precautions to prevent it spreading to Europe. It followed that they must spend their money and energies in rebuilding their navy, and avoid overt threats to Hanover. Hence their doubts about renewing the Prussian alliance. But it was one thing to drop the Prussian alliance temporarily, in the certainty that it could be revived if defeat elsewhere made an attack on Hanover imperative; it was quite another thing to lose that alliance altogether and with it the possibility of striking at Hanover, however great the necessity. While they were still feeling confident, they had sent an ultimatum to England (December 1755) and had prepared only half-heartedly to negotiate with Frederick. Now, when it was too late, they were jolted out of their complacency and had to find a new policy. They found one quickly—but it was perilous, and involved an abrupt reversal of strategy. Some time previously the Maréchal Belleisle had drawn up 'an extended plan of offensive war against England,'[2] which included an invasion of England, with feints against Scotland and Ireland and diversions against Minorca and Halifax. Hitherto his suggestions had been ignored, but now he was summoned from his retreat in the country to take over the command-in-chief of the whole Atlantic coast and proceed with his scheme. France had definitely moved the war into Europe, though as yet only on to its fringes.

Newcastle's secret service was still working well. His 'intelligencers' kept him fully informed of French activities. In particular they provided him with copies of the dispatches sent by Bunge,

[1] 'France is not ready for a land war nor are they rich enough to support one very long by land and sea both, without embarrassing their finances irrecoverably.' Yorke to Mitchell, 18th July 1756. Add. MSS. 6,836.

[2] Corbett, I, 88.

the Swedish Ambassador at Paris, to Höpken, Sweden's Foreign Minister. Newcastle placed great reliance on these dispatches, for Bunge was 'the most favoured minister' and Stockholm 'the most favoured court that is now connected with France';[1] they were unlikely to be deceived. From them he learnt the change of French strategy and full details of the decision to invade England. The only question for him to decide was how far the information was true. On that he had no doubt, especially as Bunge's news was confirmed by reports from all sides telling of French concentrations on their northern coasts. Newcastle, and indeed the whole Cabinet, were seriously alarmed. How was England to be saved? Clearly, by foreign troops. Their first thought was to demand the 6,000 men Holland was required to supply under her treaties, and when the Dutch refused on the ominous ground that England was the aggressor, they besought the King in something like a panic to bring over Hessians and Hanoverians.

This proposal was gall and wormwood to Pitt. It was incredible to him that we should skulk behind foreigners and mercenaries; the mere suggestion was a blot on the scutcheon, hard to be borne, and certainly to be opposed with all the vigour at his command. Not that he had much vigour, for he was greatly handicapped by illness and not a little absorbed by private affairs. Although he had recently acquired his house in Brook Street, he had forgotten his predilection for it—perhaps had been daunted by the smells from the kitchen—and had set his heart, a very fickle heart where bricks and mortar were concerned, on Mrs. Montagu's house at Hayes. In 1756 Hayes was a very small village, tucked away in the undulating country south of Bromley and east of Croydon—a country of birches and bracken and ancient oaks, of little streams in the valleys and springy turf on the downs, a country made for landscape gardeners such as Pitt and ideal for a gouty statesman fond of cantering over the hills by way of exercise. Pitt found it bewitchingly captivating, and not the less so because it was only two or three miles from 'loved Wickham.' As Mrs. Montagu's tenancy was shortly to expire, Pitt made haste to buy the property and begin schemes for enlarging the house and developing the grounds. The work, which was highly congenial, occupied much of his time in the early months of 1756. Whilst so engaged, he and Hester buried

[1] Newcastle to Hardwicke, 28th Dec. 1755. Add. MSS. 32,861.

themselves in the country and tried to forget affairs of state. 'London,' said Henry Grenville, 'sees nothing of her now and very little of him, except on busy Parliament days; Wickham possesses them entirely; but they are shortly to remove to their country residence at Hayes, which is a house of great humility indeed.'[1] Its 'humility' no doubt appealed to both of them, though for different reasons—to Hester for its promise of economy, to Pitt for the scope it offered for improvements.

But the proposal to import Hessians and Hanoverians to defend England was a summons to London which Pitt could not ignore, though it was pain and effort to go. A few days earlier he had excused himself from attending the debate on Lyttelton's plate tax because 'the pain in my face and ear is so much more troublesome that I would avoid, if I could, an unnecessary trip to town.'[2] But now necessity was laid on him, and so, putting blisters behind his ears as a counter-irritant, and muffling up his face in flannel, he struggled up to the House.[3] He was full of indignation at the pusillanimity of the Ministers, full of scorn at their reading of the military situation, full of irony at the folly of stripping Hanover of her native troops at the very moment when we were pouring out subsidies on her behalf. Here was an extravagant situation, extravagant in every sense of the word. And for what end was all this profusion? The Ministry had not begun to appreciate the military situation. The true shield for these islands was not a foreign force but our own navy. France could not hope to elude the vigilance of our ships for anything but a petty raid, and 'against what force the French could land we had certainly sufficient defence.' All history and all military experience affirmed that an invasion was 'a chimeric attempt.' By all means let us raise whatever number of new troops the Government might think desirable, but let us avoid the shame of hiding behind Hessians and Hanoverians.[4] As usual, his efforts were in vain; the Government motion was carried with ease.

The following day (30th April) the House discussed the cost of the Hessian troops, and Pitt, still suffering agonies, made what Walpole described as 'a bitter speech on the Ministers.' The amount of physical pain, generally of an acute kind, which Pitt

[1] Dickins and Stanton, p. 327-8.
[2] To Grenville, 21st March 1756. Grenville. *Papers*, I, 156.
[3] Phillimore, II, 507.
[4] Walpole. *George II*, II, 185-6.

had to endure was staggering, and the wonder is, not that he was sometimes bitter, not that he was liable to bite and snarl in Parliament, but that he was so brilliant in debate and so infinitely tenacious of his principles. The bitterness of this speech was redeemed by the earnestness of his patriotism. The Ministers were 'bubbling' the nation, squandering money on foreign troops far in excess of the cost of a similar number of English troops—and for a worse article. We should be undone, and his only consolation was that having made his protest, he would be undone 'with a clear conscience and untainted honour,' whilst those who supported these measures would be branded like Cain for murdering the hopes of fighting the battle of the colonists.

He renewed his protest a few days later when the cost of the Hanoverians came before the House. The Hanoverians, he noted, sardonically, were cheaper than the Hessians. We must be grateful to the King who, in his capacity as Elector, had accepted a lower price and so done his best to discount the extravagance of his Ministers. 'Nothing but good,' said Pitt with constitutional loyalty, 'nothing but good flowed from the King; nothing but ruin from his servants.'[1] And then, with the scorn of a patriot sure of the strength of his country and the valour of his countrymen, he compared England with France. 'Must we engage mercenaries because France does?' Think of the difference! France 'has not blood enough in her own veins for the purposes of universal Monarchy.' But we had sufficient if we would only realise our innate powers. 'This waste on Hessians would have conquered America.' It would have saved Minorca, now threatened, and indeed doomed because the Government had failed not only to use our proper strength but even to engage mercenaries before it was too late. It looked uncommonly as though the Government were riding for a fall—hoping that there would be a public demand for peace, and that 'Minorca to be regained would be a screen for compounding for America.'

So far, his bitterness, though prophetic, had been beside the mark; the Government was incompetent but not treacherous. In the remainder of his speech he touched upon a more vital weakness, deploring the fact that while we were at war, there was no central authority, no guiding hand. War, he asserted, could not be made on those terms. There were Ministers at the head of each department, but no co-ordination: 'they shift and

[1] Walpole. *George II*, II, 188.

shuffle the charge from one to another': in modern parlance, they pass the buck. And 'from such an unaccording assemblage of separate and distinct powers with no system, a nullity results.'[1]

Pitt was offering the soundest of advice, and the only use that Fox could make of it was to ask if Pitt wished to see a sole Minister—that bugbear of eighteenth-century politics, that term of reproach which Pitt himself had wielded so often and so effectively. Pitt replied, with a sigh of despair at ever making the Government understand, that 'he did not wish to see a single Minister, but a system and decision.' He added, half as a compliment to Fox, half as a back-handed hit at Newcastle, that if only Fox were sole Minister 'there would be decision enough.'[2]

The session was now drawing to an end. Pitt, largely by his unaided efforts, had pushed his Militia Bill through the Commons and it was now in the Lords moving to its death. There was little more for him to do but look with anxious eyes towards the Mediterranean and angry eyes towards Hanover. Two points alone stirred him—a vote of credit and the approval of the Prussian Convention.

On the 11th of May Lyttelton moved for a vote of credit for one million pounds. Pitt used the occasion to reiterate his fears for the country and his distrust of the Government. He did not wish to oppose the vote, he said, though he had little doubt that the money would be squandered and wasted. What could one expect from such Ministers? They 'bragged of unanimity, of activity, of spirit,' but what had they to show for it? Had the country been made safe? Or the enemy damaged? We seemed to be incapable of providing either for offence or defence. All we could do was to provoke. It was no pleasure to him to be constantly arraigning Ministers, but when he saw the old King, being as it were driven in a go-cart by a child towards a precipice, he was bound to do his best to snatch the reins out of the child's hands. Meanwhile he prayed that the King might not have Minorca written on his heart as once Mary had Calais.[3]

There was nothing, of course, in all this but words; yet it had to be said. Pitt's position was peculiarly difficult. He was bound to make his protest though he knew that, like all such protests, it could only worry and annoy. It was so hard for the Government to believe that they were courting disaster; it was so impossible

[1] Walpole. *George II*, II, 189. [2] *Ibid.*, II, 190-1. [3] *Ibid.*, II, 193-4.

for them to imagine that the junior Minister whom they had discarded six months earlier was their master in all that mattered at the moment. Why should they attend to his warnings? Especially as he was given to exaggeration and displayed an impatient acerbity which too often veiled his wisdom and led him into irrelevancies? Yet how could he keep silence when he saw calamity coming, when he noted the weakness of their measures and the poverty of their methods? He had to lift up his voice; he had to protest; otherwise he would feel guilty in his soul of the approaching ruin.

Three days later (14th May) the Prussian treaty came before the House. Here Pitt had something concrete to urge. He had pressed for an alliance with Prussia when we had been engulfed in the War of the Austrian Succession, and would no doubt find the Convention useful if by ill-luck we had to return to the Continent. But in the present period of uneasy peace he was nervous of it as tending towards a European war; and in any event some of its provisions filled him with dismay. During the previous war a dispute had arisen over certain Prussian ships which had been condemned in the Admiralty Court for carrying contraband. Frederick had disputed the judgment and demanded compensation, and when it had been refused, had recouped himself and his subjects out of the monies due to England on the Silesian loan.[1] The sore had rankled for some years but was now to be compounded. Frederick was to receive £20,000 by way of damages and was to pay the arrears of the Silesian loan, amounting to £61,000. The bargain troubled Pitt. It seemed to him that, by allowing Frederick's claim, we were giving up our right to capture and condemn neutral ships for carrying contraband of war and so were undermining the very basis of our naval power—the power of blockade. His fears were confirmed when, shortly after, Holland and Spain put forward similar claims. On this occasion he paid what seemed to him sufficient tribute to expediency when he offered to accept the Convention if only Parliament would couple with their approval 'the assertion of our rights.'[2]

The House, however, were in no mood to listen to him. They wanted Prussian protection just as they wanted Hessian and

[1] Carlyle. *Frederick the Great,* Vol. VI, pp. 296-9.
[2] Walpole. *George II*, II, 198.

Hanoverian troops, and they were ready to buy present help at the cost of possible future trouble. The Convention was approved, and four days later (18th May), confident in their treaties and buoyed up by Spain's acknowledged neutrality, the Government declared war on France. On the 27th of May Parliament was prorogued.

8

EAST AND WEST

(i)

In Europe, as opposed to America, the first actual clash had yet to come and was destined to take place in Minorca. Out of it was to arise the strange and woeful tragedy of John Byng, which shook England from one end to the other and even stirred France into pitying mockery. The story has its bearing here, for the culmination of the tragedy came at a moment when Pitt was beginning to bestride the English world, and it had a profound effect on his career.

Belleisle did not take long to discover how right Pitt had been in calling the invasion of England a 'chimeric attempt.' He abandoned the idea before January (1756) was out and instead decided to capture Minorca. By the end of February, Newcastle was fully informed of the fact—again by copies of Bunge's dispatches. This time, however, he was a little more reluctant to be convinced. If no invasion took place, how could he justify the importation of Hessians and Hanoverians? How laugh off Pitt's penetrating epithet 'chimeric'? And if Minorca was the goal of French efforts, how explain away Pitt's uneasy prognostications, his awkward references to the King's heart? Truly this denouement had its embarrassing features.

None the less Newcastle took note of the information and, with Anson's aid and without too obvious a delay, prepared countermeasures. After a week or so of gestation, Byng was ordered to fit out a squadron for the Mediterranean. He was allotted ten ships, which when joined to the three already at Gibraltar were thought to be sufficient. They were certainly not too many, nor such as to inspire confidence; about half proved to be either leaky, under-gunned or undermanned; and when Byng tried to bring up the number of his seamen he found himself hampered by orders to let other ships have priority. However, by strenuous exertions he was able to sail on the 7th of April, though still without his full complements.

Byng came of a naval family. His father had won fame and a title by defeating a much inferior Spanish force at the battle of Passaro. Both fame and title had been acquired too easily, and fate was now to redress the balance in the person of the son. At this time he was fifty-two, and by seniority stood next to Anson—for all practical purposes the second on the list of active flag officers. He was therefore the natural choice for the command, but it is to be remarked that he had attained this exalted position 'without ever once commanding a squadron or even a single ship in any important action.'[1] Both in practical experience, character and fate, he was the naval counterpart of Braddock. Temperamentally he was a martinet and a disciplinarian by no means popular with the men, physically he was brave, mentally dull, and morally fearful of responsibility. It was unfortunate for him and for Newcastle that his defects rather than his merits were to become the deciding factor in the Minorcan affair.

Ominously, wind and waves were against him on his way out, so that it was not till the 2nd of May that he arrived at Gibraltar with battered ships and sick bays uncomfortably full. There he found the Governor, General Fowke, as fearful of responsibility as himself, and the two managed to befuddle themselves with a series of councils of war in which the earnest desire to play for safety had the widest scope and the fullest success. Byng passed on to Minorca without the troops he was to have picked up and with little expectation of victory. He met the French, under the Marquis de la Galissonière, fought an indecisive engagement on the 20th of May, and then, after holding more councils of war and without attempting any further action, returned to Gibraltar to pen complacent reports to the Admiralty and wait for reinforcements. He was staggered to find himself superseded by Hawke and ordered to return home. He might not have been so surprised if it had occurred to him that he had failed to defeat the French and had done nothing to relieve the Minorcan capital, Port Mahon, now closely besieged by the Duc de Richelieu and on the eve of falling. What kept him in good heart was the mental dullness which veiled these awkward facts, combined with an integrity of intention which made him believe that he had acted for the best.

[1] Tunstall. *Admiral Byng*, p. 12.

He had better grounds for surprise than mere lack of imagination, grounds of which he was wholly unaware. The war, which had been blowing up so long and in which he was taking a transient part, was not merely colonial or maritime, let alone European. It was equally, if not more, commercial; it was bound up with that trade to America which Frederick so little understood, and the trade to India which Frederick never noticed at all; it was indeed bound up with trade wherever the commercial interests of France and England clashed. The City was well aware of Minorca as the naval base from which an eye could be kept on Toulon, and from which the merchant vessels passing to and from the Levant could be protected. The news that it was threatened cast a much deeper gloom over the City than any fears they may have had for Hanover. No one, of course, anticipated disaster, but, as the financial barometer of the country, the City experienced that feeling of nervousness which is usually described as 'bearish.' The prevalent malaise was heightened when, on the 7th of May, news came through the Spanish Embassy that Richelieu had landed on the island with 15,000 troops. Confirmation from Joseph Yorke at The Hague made anxiety querulous, and the silence which followed strained nerves already more than a little frayed. In this fretful atmosphere there came, on the 31st of May, a preliminary and disappointing report, written by Byng before the battle, dealing only with the inconsequent councils of war at Gibraltar; and two days later there came, again through the Spanish Embassy, a copy of a dispatch from Galissonière to the French Government claiming that Byng had been worsted in a naval encounter and had disappeared.

The Government were thoroughly scared. Were they to suffer the same misfortunes this year as last, merely substituting Byng for Braddock and Minorca for the Monongahela? If that were to happen, how could they face Pitt? And behind Pitt the angry City and the infuriated country? Ugly suggestions were already rife that they had been too slow to act and too niggardly of ships when they did act. If there was to be a tidal wave of popular wrath, how much better to divert it on to Byng before it could overwhelm themselves. So they argued; and so, in an access of terror, without waiting to hear from Byng himself, they accepted Galissonière's report, with all its imagined implications, and decided to make a clean sweep of Byng and Fowke and others lower down the scale. That would not only show energy on their part but also cast suspicion on to the military leaders. So much the better, for how could politicians at home be blamed for military misdemeanours in the field? Accordingly Admirals Hawke and Saunders with a bevy of generals were immediately dispatched to take over the command and order the delinquents home; Byng's preliminary report was suppressed, though its receipt was mentioned in the *Gazette*, and the pamphleteers were pressed into service to conduct a campaign of calumny.

The Government's precipitance had strong, immediate and not altogether expected results. The country accepted the implied condemnation of Byng, and while waiting for his return to England, lashed themselves into a state of frenzy against him. But at the same time they managed to retain sufficient balance to realise how monstrous it was for the Government to supersede admirals and generals wholesale on the strength of an enemy report. They mingled therefore with their anger against Byng an irritable contempt for the Government.[1] The same precipitance shook the more lukewarm members of the Government, and symptoms of a landslide appeared. Murray had long wished to escape to the judiciary, and what must have seemed to him the opportune death of Sir Dudley Rider, the Lord Chief Justice of the King's Bench, on the 25th of May, opened the door. He had already put forward his claim, which was unexceptionable, and now pressed it with inconvenient urgency, refusing to listen to Newcastle's harassed plea for delay. The extreme limit of his patience would be the first day of Parliament's next session, when he must be Lord Chief Justice and safely seated in the House of Lords.

Fox had no similar opening and was not so naturally timorous, but he, too, was disquieted, as, indeed, he had been for some time past. Hitherto he had felt uncomfortable rather than uneasy, but the Minorcan affair gave a fresh twist to his inward doubts. His latent quarrel with Newcastle was gathering volume and vehemence. He was, as he told Dodington, 'very uneasy at the posture of public affairs and, particularly, with his own situation'; nor was he reassured on finding Newcastle 'unusually light and trifling.' He and the Duke had both, it seems, been eavesdropping at the coffee-houses in the hopes of picking up some crumb of

[1] 'The consternation on the behaviour of Byng,' said Walpole, 'is extreme' (to Strafford, 6th June); people 'figured Port Mahon lost and Gibraltar agoing! agoing!' (to Chute, 8th June); none the less 'the world condemns extremely the rashness of superseding admirals on no information but from our enemies' (to Chute, 8th June).

favourable comment. The Duke was comforting himself with tattle from Garraway's to the effect that 'the City imputed nothing to him, as the sea was not his province.' Fox retorted with the gossip which he in his turn had collected, that 'the City were extremely displeased with the leaving Minorca exposed, and that, generally, it would be ever true, that those who had the chief direction in an Administration, would bear the greatest share of blame.' Fear made Fox press the point of ultimate responsibility, to the consternation of the Duke; but he was repaid in coin when Dodington, in right Job's-comforter style, agreed that 'the chief in an Administration would always be the most obnoxious . . . unless they had anyone to make a scapegoat.' At that Fox grew thoughtful![1] By June he was still more thoughtful. Honesty made him confess that Byng's culpability had not yet been proved, but fear forced him to agree with Newcastle that 'there was no staying for inquiries,' or even for facts to unfold themselves. Others, if they liked, might still cherish hopes for Minorca, Fox had none and was certain that the disappointment, when it came, would be loaded with dynamite. Byng must be the scapegoat, and Fox—well, Fox was contemplating the possibility of deserting the Government.[2]

Everything, in short, conspired to make an unscrupulous and very frightened Ministry blacken Byng's character; and everything, including Government's unscrupulous methods, contributed to inflame public opinion. It was inflamed still more by the fact that Port Mahon, or rather the citadel, Fort St. Philip, continued to hold out. Here was a contrast indeed to Byng's shuffling behaviour. All the world knew that Fort St. Philip was weakly garrisoned and that the Governor and many if not most of the officers were in England—a black mark that, against the Government who, if they had not had the foresight to strengthen the garrison, should at least have seen that its exiguous numbers were at their posts. All the world knew that the absence of the Governor had thrown the command into the hands of General Blakeney, 'a cheerful veteran of eighty-four, full of energy but afflicted with gout and generally to be found in bed.'[3] No one in England imagined that this invalid octogenarian with his tiny garrison could long withstand Richelieu and his overwhelming forces, especially now that Byng had failed them.

[1] Diary, pp. 381-4.
[2] To Duke of Bedford, 4th June 1756; Bedford. *Correspondence,* II, 195.
[3] Tunstall, p. 98.

And yet day after day passed and still they held out. It was not till the 28th of June, more than two months after the French had landed, more than one month after Byng had sailed back to Gibraltar, that Blakeney was forced to surrender. So long as he held out, England reserved final judgment, but the increasing contrast between Blakeney's spirited defiance and Byng's nerveless impotence merely heaped up fuel against the day of wrath. The delay also gave time for the country to ask why the Government had left Minorca so bare when its invasion had been so openly proclaimed and when, in any event, its *raison d'être* was to be a check on the French naval forces in the Mediterranean. The Government, as modern historians agree, had no good defence.[1] The more therefore these questions were asked, the more essential Government found it to vilify Byng. Truly he had no chance.

On the 23rd of June Byng's final dispatch arrived. The Ministers now knew the worst; they knew what Byng had done; they knew what they themselves might expect. Whatever happened to him they must at all costs save their own skins, sacrificing, if need be, honour and truth and justice. Their reaction was infamous; it can barely be explained, it cannot be justified, by assuming that they were beside themselves with terror. What they did was to publish an abstract of the report, made to appear as though it were the complete document, but carefully doctored to give a wholly false impression and one damning to Byng. They blasted their own reputation foolishly, for the truth was bound to come out; and unnecessarily, for in the existing state of public feeling the full dispatch, breathing as it did a fatuous air of complacency, would have done Byng little good. In its doctored form it became a double death warrant, against Byng and against the Ministers' reputation.

A howl of execration rose throughout the country. Byng was burnt in effigy in every town and village; his country house was invaded, and with difficulty saved from destruction; libels and lampoons appeared overnight like a virulent rash. The uproar was redoubled when, on the 4th of July, news arrived of Blakeney's surrender, and the Government, adding pettiness to villainy, issued orders to every port—and advertised the fact in the *Gazette*—that Byng was to be arrested immediately on landing.

It was in the midst of such ferment that Byng reached

[1] See Corbett, I, 134, and Tunstall, p. 46.

Portsmouth on the 26th of July. The Ministers at once made a parade of their righteous indignation. Very ostentatiously they committed him to close confinement directly he stepped off the ship; very ostentatiously they brought him up to Greenwich under an armed guard; very ostentatiously they incarcerated him in a room void of furniture and treated him like a common criminal. Their efforts were successful. The outraged country rose in its wrath. Petitions began to flow in from all quarters. In particular the City of London demanded the trial and punishment of the 'authors of our late losses and disappointments,' with a scarcely veiled threat that unless they received satisfaction, they would cut off the supply of money needed for the war. Newcastle, who thought he had already supped full of horrors, found in their threat fresh cause for despair, but on this occasion a cause which could be overcome. At his urgent entreaty, the King 'pledged his royal word that he would save no delinquent from justice.'[1] The City was satisfied and Newcastle's financial pain assuaged, but the pledge was a promise heavy with fate. Byng was as good as dead; it was only a question of time. His trial had been ordered and the verdict already pronounced by Newcastle to a deputation from the City. 'Oh! indeed he shall be tried immediately—he shall be hanged directly,' which, whether a true story or not, depicts to the life his gibbering fear.[2]

(ii)

Pitt's reaction to the whole affair was characteristic. He had been the first to express fears openly for Minorca. His views were neither brilliant inspiration, as some of his biographers seem to think, nor belated opportunism, as his detractors suggest, but the outcome of the methods which he had adumbrated in his speeches of the previous session and was shortly to exercise with such striking results. He was here displaying that foresight which, he said, differentiated wisdom from folly. His theory of blockade, the uncertainty of the destination of the Toulon fleet, the importance of Minorca for trade protection, combined with his conviction that the invasion of England was a 'chimeric attempt,' made him recognise that the information about preparations for an attack on Minorca which came flooding in from all sides could not be other than highly probable, and at least to be acted

[1] Walpole. *George II*, II, 230. [2] *Ibid.*, II, 231.

upon. He was sure that his fears were based on sound reasoning, and he therefore expressed them, not to harass the Government but to warn them. The warning passed unheeded, and to a large extent he had only himself to blame. One of the disabilities which had dogged him—perhaps from birth; certainly from Eton days—was an inhibition which prevented him from meeting others on equal terms. Some inward urge compelled him either to grovel or to be self-assertive, and in neither case did he carry proper conviction. The grovelling was deplorable, but fortunately infrequent. When not grovelling, he could lay down the law majestically as from some Olympian height, or flame into invective, but in neither case did he know how to argue or to persuade; his reasons, his hopes, remained hidden in his own breast. It was so here; Minorca was in danger because the Government's strategy was at fault, and Pitt, who recognised the fact and knew the reason, could not enlighten them. All he could do was to throw out the warning in a cloud of abuse.

His insight, however, prepared him for the blow, so that he kept his head far better than the Government when Galissonière's report arrived. Byng, he recognised, must have a chance of defending himself, but the defence, if it was to carry weight, must be good. He said he had gone back to Gibraltar, and, Pitt added, 'if his own account does not differ widely from that of the French, where he ought to go next is pretty evident.'[1] The remark foreshadows Pitt's future relations with commanding officers. He was utterly unforgiving to those who failed; they were afforded no second chance. But if he was ruthless, he was never unjust. The incompetent man must go because the risk of his retention was too great; others might suffer through him and the war might be lost. But to punish him for his incompetence would be as unreasonable as to punish him for a harelip or a crooked back. Treason must be crushed and cowardice scourged, but incompetence must simply be relegated to the obscurity from which it should never have been brought. Moreover, some share in the blame must be borne by the authorities who made the appointment. Their choice was bad, and sometimes it was not only a case of bad choice, which might be venial, but the lack of clear instructions, which was unpardonable.

This last thought was emphasised for Pitt when Fowke was brought to trial for disobeying the order to supply Byng with troops. Neither the Government nor the country were so incensed

[1] Grenville. *Papers*, I, 165.

against Fowke as they were against Byng, but he could not be allowed to escape altogether; he was therefore suspended for a year. Pitt was wrath. 'How monstrous,' he wrote, '. . . I declare that no consideration can make me find in the General wilful disobedience to a clear positive order; but at most innocent error concerning the ill-explained intentions of Government.'[1] Pitt remembered Fowke's case, and, when his own time came, spent hours polishing and repolishing his own letters in order to prevent misunderstandings.

One further reaction, even more characteristic. From the first Pitt showed how widely his outlook differed from that of the Ministry. They were concerned only with Byng and Minorca and their own skins; it did not occur to them to ponder what other effects Byng's failure might have. Pitt also was interested in Byng and Minorca and threatened skins: 'I am,' he wrote, 'in most anxious impatience to have the affair in the Mediterranean cleared up. As yet nothing is clear, but that the French are masters there, and that probably many an innocent and gallant man's honour and fortune is to be offered up as a scapegoat for the sins of the Administration.'[2] But Pitt also looked farther afield. Byng had failed; Minorca had fallen—well, the dead must bury their dead. But what of the living? 'I dread,' wrote Pitt, 'to hear from America. Asia perhaps may furnish its portion of ignominy and calamity to this degenerate, helpless country.'[3] Surely the spirit of prophecy must have descended on him, for within three weeks the Black Hole of Calcutta produced calamity in Asia, and within three months the French gained their greatest victory in America—the capture of Oswego.

(iii)

Indeed the war in America was going badly. Trading on the drop in English prestige, Dumas, the new commander at Fort Duquesne, had organised a series of Indian attacks along the western borders of Pennsylvania, Maryland and Virginia. The sufferings of the colonists were indescribable; their homes were burnt, their wives and daughters ravished, their children murdered, their young men scalped and tortured. There seemed no escape from the horror, and in despair they entreated the Assemblies for protection. But the Assemblies were too far

[1] Grenville. *Papers*, I, 171. [2] *Ibid.*, I, 168. [3] *Ibid.*, I, 165.

away to be frightened and too engrossed in politics to be interested. In Pennsylvania, the Quakers refused to stain their hands with blood, but were cynically ready to subscribe money for the victims in exchange for the right to fleece the Proprietors. The Virginian Assembly gave Washington a regiment, 1,000 strong, with which to protect 350 miles of frontier. Washington did his best with the men, who were a mutinous lot, only to find his wishes ignored and his authority flouted. The campaign offered no prospect of glory, and want of success led to abuse and disparagement. He became depressed and a little scared at the thought of being held responsible, which was a new and salutary experience for a young man hitherto praised more highly than he had deserved, though ultimately, as Sparkes said, it 'proved advantageous to him.'[1] But not at the time to the unfortunate colonists.

Meanwhile, at Boston, Shirley was preparing his plans for 1756. The mantle of Commander-in-Chief had fallen on him late in life—he was now rising sixty-three—and unexpectedly, seeing that he had never served in the armed forces. By profession he was a lawyer and had to eke out his lack of experience by a boundless enthusiasm. Because of his trained mind he showed a fair grasp of strategy, but because of his inexperience his plans went beyond his powers of execution. He proposed to renew in 1756 all the operations which had failed the year before—the attacks on Fort Duquesne, Niagara, Crown Point and Ticonderoga—and to add to the list attacks on Frontenac and Toronto. He also toyed with the idea of naval activities on Lake Ontario and a raid down the Chaudière against the Quebec settlements. It was magnificent in conception—but needed 16,000 men at least and considerable funds. The first blow was the attitude of the Colonies, most of which refused to vote either men or money.

Then followed a second and overwhelming blow. In March 1756 Fox intercepted a couple of anonymous letters, addressed to the Duc de Mirepoix, which spoke of a great body of men being raised in Pennsylvania by Shirley. Fox's nerves were at the time very much on edge, and these letters which he did not understand filled him full of suspicions. He consulted his colleagues, especially the Duke of Cumberland, and the more they consulted together, the more sinister the letters appeared. Hardwicke spoke of 'the strange dark affair' which he feared

[1] Sparkes, I, 89.

would 'be followed with great confusion in the colonies,'[1] and Fox concluded that Shirley was either a traitor or at least edging in that direction and ought to be recalled. Cumberland was for 'a rougher method'; Shirley should be brought back as a prisoner—a sort of American Byng.[2] The upshot was that Shirley was ordered home and replaced by the Earl of Loudoun. The exchange had little to commend it. Loudoun was a general, as Shirley was not, but he was to prove himself more tactless and peremptory in his dealings with the colonists, and much more laggard and unenterprising in his relations with the enemy. To add to the trouble, whatever his qualifications, his departure was too long delayed. He did not arrive in America until the 29th of July (1756), when it was too late to avert further disaster.

The Government had mishandled American affairs throughout the year. In January they had agreed to send two battalions from Ireland to replace those lost by Braddock, and to raise fresh troops in Pennsylvania and New England. But first the scare of invasion and then the threat to Minorca made them hold their hands. The two Irish battalions did not sail till towards the end of April and the recruiting in America was delayed. Shirley meanwhile continued his preparations and when Loudoun at last arrived, tactlessly told him that all was arranged and he had nothing to do but gather the laurels.[3] Loudoun was nettled; he swept aside Shirley's more ambitious schemes and decided to concentrate on Ticonderoga. His decision was probably right, for he was facing a worthy opponent.

The French, unlike the English, had been far from inactive. They had recognised 'the necessity of succouring Canada,'[4] and throughout the summer had been smuggling troops over in single ships, so as to elude the English fleet. More important, they had appointed the Marquis de Montcalm to succeed Dieskau in command of the forces. Montcalm was a very different man from Loudoun. He was a general of wide experience and quick decision, daring, impetuous and skilful. He arrived in Canada about the middle of May, and promptly set about his business. 'Everything,' he wrote, 'is in motion.' As the main attack seemed likely to fall on Ticonderoga, he massed his troops for its defence,

[1] Hardwicke to Newcastle, 28th March, 1756. Add. MSS. 32,864.
[2] Fox to Newcastle, 27th March 1756. Add. MSS. 32,864.
[3] Loudoun to Fox, 19th August 1756, quoted by Parkman, *Montcalm and Wolfe*, I, 399.
[4] Intelligence from Versailles, 24th April 1756. Add. MSS. 32,864.

but soon realising that the English were far from ready, thought there would be time for a swoop on Oswego. Assembling an expeditionary force secretly at Montreal, he set out on the 21st of July and reached Frontenac on the day of Loudoun's arrival in America. By the 4th of August Montcalm had reconnoitred the English position and satisfied himself that success was probable. On the 11th he began the attack and three days later Oswego surrendered. By this victory the French became undisputed masters of Lake Ontario and could without misgiving concentrate on the eastern approaches. Montcalm hurried back to Ticonderoga.

Loudoun, faced with this setback to English hopes—the greatest so far suffered—came to the conclusion that it was too late in the season for active operations. He took up a defensive attitude at Fort William Henry and wrote home, 'I think I shall be able to prevent the provincials doing anything very rash.'[1] It was not much of a counterweight for the loss of Oswego, nor much of a straw for the drowning Ministry.

[1] Parkman. *Montcalm and Wolfe,* I, 438.

9

NEWCASTLE FALLS

(i)

As though military disasters on every side were not sufficient, the Ministry managed to embroil themselves in a domestic quarrel. On the 4th of June the future George III came of legal age, and the fact seemed to offer an opportunity for healing the perennial breach in the royal family. Under the Hanoverian dynasty there was always friction between the Prince of Wales and the reigning monarch. Modern historians have suggested that this 'peculiarity lay not in the royal family but in the political system,' which provided heirs to the throne 'with a safe, effective and agreeable means of expressing their resentment and securing redress for their grievances by placing themselves at the head of the opposition.'[1] No doubt the historians are right; but it still remains true that the early Hanoverians were by nature bad sons and worse fathers; they had few morals, no filial affection, and apparently no capacity for training their children or winning their love. But in 1756 there was a difference. The King was growing old and mellow; he had never felt as bitterly towards his grandson as he had towards his son, and now he was disposed to hold out a grandfatherly hand with something in it that might look like a blessing. He consulted Newcastle, who suggested that the Prince should be given an allowance of £40,000 per annum, a household of his own and apartments in the royal palace. The King was delighted; he would show his generosity, and at the same time get the young boy away from his mother. She was a bad influence—narrow-minded and possessive; given to intrigue; and worst of all infatuated with the Earl of Bute. Her infatuation produced an aura of raffishness which George II would have excused if she and the earl could have changed ranks, but which, as things were, he condemned as discreditable to the lady and

[1] *Letters from George III to Lord Bute*. Ed. by R. Sedgwick, p. xii.

unwholesome for her son, who ought to be released from this degrading petticoat influence. The offer was accordingly made, but unfortunately there were sharper wits at Leicester House than at St. James's Palace. Pitt himself was taking a hand in the negotiations.[1] So was Legge. One or other of them—Legge it was thought—drafted the Prince's reply. He accepted the allowance with becoming gratitude, but begged to be allowed to remain with his mother. What was the King to do now? He could not very well withdraw the allowance; he could not, without appearing harsh, drag a callow and unwilling youth of eighteen away from his mother. George did the only thing he could think of—swear at his Ministers and order them to get him out of the tangle. To make matters worse, the Prince followed up his first letter by a second asking that when his new household was appointed, the Earl of Bute might be made his Groom of the Stole. Here was a pretty kettle of fish! The King could not abide Bute; he was the origin of all the tattle and gossip about the Princess; he was worse than her shady past, he was her very indiscreet present. The King would not acknowledge Bute's existence, still less place him deliberately in a position of confidence about the Prince. So things came to a deadlock, and so they remained until October when as the result of strenuous and prolonged efforts Newcastle persuaded the King to give way. He did so with a very bad grace.

The episode did good to nobody, but perhaps most harm to Pitt. It revived and intensified the King's ill-will towards Leicester House, and by way of reaction increased his tenderness for the Duke of Cumberland. In its first aspect it made the King more than ever reluctant to accept Pitt as Secretary of State; in its second aspect, it ensured the failure of Pitt's first Ministry.

(ii)

Military disasters and bickerings in the royal household were in a sense mere surface incidents. Far more fundamental was the breakdown of England's foreign policy. The 'old system' had gone. Its passing left Newcastle querulously angry, but at least he recognised the fact. The problem which he never solved was

[1] See Bute to Pitt, 3rd June and 20th July. Chatham. *Correspondence* I, pp. 156 and 170.

what to put in its place; as fast as he laid down fresh foundations, they crumbled into nothing.

The Russian treaty had broken in his hands. It had hardly been ratified when the Empress presented a 'declaration' which, in Newcastle's eyes, was not only 'a voidance of the treaty' but, as an additional insult, was couched in 'the very *odious* words used by the opposition in all their speeches . . . , viz. that it was only a treaty against and to provoke the King of Prussia; and could not be made use of, for any other purpose or against any other Power.' Apart from this galling use of Pitt's actual language, there was the thought—very harassing to the First Lord of the Treasury—that if this declaration held, we should have to pay £100,000 subsidy for four years and get nothing in return. Newcastle insisted that the declaration must be withdrawn and the Court of St. Petersburg taught 'to think reasonably upon the subject of our Prussian treaty.'[1] He seems to have believed that his protest would obliterate this painful episode and that henceforth England and Russia would go merrily along together; but, whatever he thought, the treaty was in fact dead. England's impotence at St. Petersburg gradually became apparent to the whole world.

The Convention of Westminster seemed to be going the same way. Frederick had been pleased enough at the time. In signing it, he had been giving up France for England and, if England really had Russia in her pocket, the exchange was marvellously good business. What was not quite certain was whether he was intent on war or peace. Probably in January 1756 he was genuinely hoping that peace would prevail. Whatever his original intentions, he soon began to have doubts. Disquieting rumours came thick and fast from St. Petersburg. Hanbury-Williams was falling into disrepute; shady characters, thought to be Jacobites or emissaries from France, were slinking up the backstairs of the Imperial Palace; troop movements of an equivocal nature were taking place. Frederick plied Mitchell[2] with urgent questions. Was England sure of Russia? Was she quite sure? 'I suspect,' wrote Mitchell, 'from the doubtful anxiety which the King of Prussia expressed in the repeated enquiries he made about the state of our affairs at the Court of Russia, that he may have received advice from that country that they are not in so favourable a

[1] Newcastle to Hanbury-Williams, 2nd April 1756. Add MSS. 32,864.
[2] Sir Andrew Mitchell, British Ambassador at Berlin.

way as I had reason to believe they were when I left England.'[1] Time merely increased Frederick's 'doubtful anxiety,' and by so doing served to emphasise the essential difference between the aims of England and Prussia.

England wanted Frederick's help in the coming war. He had promised it, but as early as May he began to hedge. Although he told Mitchell that he 'was strictly resolved to adhere to the treaty . . . and willing to fulfil every engagement,' he quietly side-stepped all Mitchell's attempts to pin him down. There was no need for plans, he declared, for nothing would happen that year (1756); he would answer for it with his head. As for the future, he had several plans in mind, from which George could pick and choose at the proper time. Meanwhile he came back to his own anxiety; 'are you sure of the Russians?' He even tried to turn the tables by asserting that 'while Russia was secured the peace of Germany was safe.' Perhaps in Newcastle's eyes he added to his sins by adopting another of Pitt's views: he regarded a French invasion of England as 'a wild and romantic scheme which can never succeed.'[2] England was therefore free to help Frederick, and the best help she could give would be by 'securing Russia,' whatever the cost; she could be frugal elsewhere and perhaps ought to be, but in Russia it was best to spend money like water.[3] Frederick's doubts grew, until towards the end of July he was convinced that 'Russia is absolutely lost to us,' and that by next spring at latest he would be attacked by Austria on one side and Russia on the other.[4] The more this view was forced upon him the less willing he became to bother about France and the more insistently he pressed England to turn her eyes and her energies eastward. He wanted a fleet in the Baltic to give Russia pause and overawe the Scandinavian countries; he thought 'auxiliary troops were necessary for the defence of Hanover in case the King of Prussia was fully occupied elsewhere and unable to defend it'; he suggested subsidies to the Elector of Cologne, the Duke of Brunswick and other minor German Princes; and did not rule out the possibility that he might need pecuniary help himself; and finally, letting his imagination loose, he talked of stirring up the Turks, promoting a revolution in Russia and starting a religious war in Hungary.[5]

[1] Mitchell to Holdernesse, 14th May 1756. Add. MSS. 6,804.
[2] Mitchell to Holdernesse, 27th May and 12th Aug. 1756. Add. MSS. 6,804.
[3] Mitchell to Holdernesse, 7th June 1756. Add. MSS. 6,804.
[4] Mitchell to Holdernesse, 23rd July 1756. Add. MSS. 6,804.
[5] Mitchell to Holdernesse, 10th June and 26th June 1756. Add. MSS. 6 804.

All this greatly troubled Newcastle, whose replies can have given Frederick little comfort. At first they were of the polite *non possumus* kind—we were doing our best with Russia; we were attempting to placate the Dutch; we would like to send a squadron to the Baltic if it were not for the navy's extensive and varied duties elsewhere. But by degrees the replies became more shrill—'France is our object, and our enmity to other Powers depends entirely on the degree of their alliance with our constant enemy. If therefore the King of Prussia means seriously to unite himself to England, he must show us that he is willing to undertake our cause against France. A camp somewhere in the neighbourhood of Wesel is the thing in the world most to be wished for at present, nor can any step of the King of Prussia gain him more friends in England. . . . We are sincere on our part, but we have a right to expect a return, and none is of consequence to us but a measure against France.'[1] When these views were propounded to him, Frederick replied briefly that 'it was impossible.'[2]

All the same, Frederick had no wish to break with England; he had nothing to gain by it. She was now his only ally, and at least she had a navy, as well as plenty of money and a stake in Hanover. Judging by the past, her maritime war, which Newcastle himself called on one occasion a 'silly notion,'[3] would soon be merged and finally swamped in a European war. She was certain to give him some help, even if unwillingly, even if unconsciously. But the help that he was going to get was not the help that he had expected nor the help that he had wanted. She had let Russia escape. That was the outstanding fact, and he had to readjust his views and plans accordingly. The readjustment did not take long. Russia, Austria and France were arming against him; together they were far too powerful. His only hope was to deal with them separately, and his main assets were his preparedness and his speed. He believed, or at least said he believed, that the Russians had intended to attack him in 1756 on one side, while Maria Theresa attacked him on the other, but as the Russians had not been ready, the plan had been deferred, but only till the next spring.[4] Now, therefore, was the time for him to strike at Austria. With luck he could knock her out before Russia was

[1] Holdernesse to Mitchell, 13th July 1756. Add. MSS. 6,832.
[2] Mitchell to Holdernesse, 30th July. 1756. Add MSS. 6,804.
[3] Newcastle to Bentinck. Add. MSS. 32,866.
[4] Mitchell to Holdernesse, 23rd July 1756. Add. MSS. 6804.

ready. As for France, he had long ago told Mitchell that 'the French Ministry was a very weak one, and we had little to fear from them,' but it might be just as well if they were given something to distract their attention. He asked therefore 'why with a fleet so superior to that of France we had hitherto remained on the defensive.' What about an attack on 'St. Domingo or some other of their possessions in the West Indies.'[1] But whether England moved or not, he must act promptly.

He was as good as his word—indeed better, for being so convinced that Russia could not move quickly, he agreed to hold 10,000 troops at George II's service to ward off a French attack on Hanover, provided George released them not later than the end of the following February (1757) in time to cope with the Russians. With the rest of his forces he prepared to march through Saxony into Bohemia, and actually crossed the border on the 29th of August. England's war with France had changed into the Seven Years' War.

(iii)

To Newcastle this seemed the final straw. Throughout the year, the weight of external events had been crushing the life out of the Ministry. One after another the failures had heaped up—the disavowal of the Russian treaty, the long-drawn-out blunder of Minorca, the Black Hole of Calcutta, the loss of Oswego, and now, to crown all, the outbreak of war in Europe. Disaster abroad was embittered by the tedious royal quarrel at home and sharpened by popular discontent. 'I never found all sorts of people,' wrote the Lord Chief Justice Willes, 'so uneasy and so dispirited.'[2] If a judge could be so stirred, it is no wonder Newcastle was alarmed. 'I am not able to bear this weight,' he wrote plaintively.[3] It was becoming daily more evident to all the world that the Government must fall, and the evidence fretted Newcastle.[4]

He was not the only Minister to feel alarm. Murray was sufficiently terrified not only to withstand Newcastle's fervid

[1] Mitchell to Holdernesse, 23rd July 1756. Add. MSS. 6,804.
[2] Willes to Duke of Newcastle, 21st August 1756. Add. MSS. 32,867.
[3] Newcastle to Hardwicke, 8th May 1756. Add. MSS. 32,864.
[4] 'I know *for certain* that some of the Dutch Ministers . . . conclude that there must be soon *a change in the Ministry in England*. . . . This language (which is *certain*) from those we thought our best friends in Holland must and ought to surprise you. What will *they* get by a change in the Administration here?' Newcastle to Sir J. Yorke, 11th June 1756. Add. MSS. 32,865.

pleas that he would give up the Bench and remain at least temporarily in office, but also the offer of ever more extravagant bribes. 'What have I done,' he demanded at last, 'to be buried under such a load of resentment by a plundered country? Chief Justiceship or nothing.'[1] Murray's defection was a staggering blow; for Murray was a good friend as well as an able advocate; he was practically the only supporter whose merits Newcastle recognised without jealousy and used without suspicion.

More staggering, but as yet unrecognised, was Fox's restlessness. Fox was indifferent to public opinion—he could never have become the Great Commoner—but he was not anxious to face public wrath and he was indignant at the treatment meted out to him by those 'two little great men,' Newcastle and Hardwicke.[2] His relations with them, never very cordial, had been made no smoother by their patent desire to load him with responsibility for the disasters abroad. Fox had no mind to carry the burden, and his distaste was increased by an uneasy conscience. He knew that he could have pressed more vigorously for stronger and earlier support for Minorca.[3] He knew that he could not explain away the deplorable military conditions at Gibraltar which Tyrawley, the new Governor, had found on his arrival. His apprehensions had sufficient foundation, and became overwhelming when, towards the end of July, Newcastle urged him to think of some 'object' to attack—it really did not matter where or what the issue[4]—for action, however aimless, would 'keep up people's spirits and divert their resentment.'[5] If Newcastle was going to dither into a panic, it was high time for Fox to think in earnest about self-preservation.

His first idea was to bring Pitt into the Government, where his presence would at once confound the Opposition and whitewash the Ministry; they could all shelter behind his back. The difficulty would be to persuade him—clearly his terms would be high. Fox was ready to barter ambition for security; after all he had not enjoyed the seat of power, and never would so long as Newcastle remained Prime Minister. He, therefore, let it be known that he was willing to give up the Seals in favour of Pitt; but seeing

[1] Quoted in Torrens, II, 324.

[2] Fox to Devonshire, 31st July 1756. Torrens, II, 299.

[3] See Dodington, p. 384, and Newcastle to Hardwicke, 19th July 1756. Add. MSS. 32,866.

[4] 'We had better fail in the attempt than attempt nothing' Newcastle to Fox, 24th July. Add. MSS. 32,866.

[5] Newcastle to Hardwicke, 19th July. Add. MSS. 32,866.

no reason why he should not make a profit out of necessity, he asked at the same time to be given 'some lucrative employment.'[1] The suggestion worried Newcastle. He could not afford to lose Fox as well as Murray. Still less could he contemplate a coalition between Fox and Pitt, which his suspicious nature at once imagined to be in the offing. The mere fact that Fox had proposed Pitt was a reason for rejecting him. Newcastle played for a moment with the idea of offering to 'enter into all proper confidence with Mr. Fox,'[2] but the idea soon evaporated. Fox thereafter concluded that there was no propping up the administration; that, in short, 'the Duke of Newcastle's reign is over.'[3] As this conviction took root, he began to see visions. The coalition with Pitt, which Newcastle dreaded and Fox had not so far contemplated, began to take shape in his mind. What was more amazing, he was confident enough to see himself as the senior partner; he would be First Lord and Pitt Secretary.

Whatever Fox might dream, the country wanted fresh blood. Petitions were pouring in from all sides, and at last Newcastle himself was convinced that there must be 'a change in the Ministry.' He also knew in his heart, though he was most reluctant to admit it, that the change must bring Pitt to the top. It would be pathetic, if it were not dull, to follow all the twists and turns of his mind, eagerly seeking an escape from the inevitable. There is only one point to his credit. He revolved many preposterous schemes, but however wistfully he may have thought of them, he recognised that they were impossible; however tightly he might shut his eyes, he saw the facts and saw them clearly. There was no alternative to Pitt. All that was left was to veil his own defeat in a decent suit of self-sacrifice, endured for the benefit of the public. 'What a figure shall we make,' he whimpered to Hardwicke, 'with Mr. Pitt coming in in conquest over us. . . . My dear Lord, pity me; alone as I am in my present distress; give me the comfort you only can, viz. a clear and determined opinion, and then I am easy.'[4] If he could have forgotten himself for one moment, posterity might have shed a tear over his anguish, but Newcastle was the one person Newcastle could never forget. Everything touched his *amour-propre*; all the troubles of the world were heaped on his innocent shoulders, all resentment levelled at his head—unjustly!

[1] Newcastle to Hardwicke, 26 July 1756. Add. MSS. 32,866. [2] Riker, II, 21.
[3] Fox to Bedford, 19th October 1756. Bedford. *Correspondence*, II, 203.
[4] Newcastle to Hardwicke, 28th Aug. 1756. Add. MSS. 32,867.

Hardwicke had no difficulty in giving a clear and determined opinion, though he knew full well that what Newcastle needed was not an opinion but resolution to take the plunge. 'I really think,' he answered, 'retiring the wisest measure.' Yet with his intimate knowledge of his colleague, he could not press the idea whilst there was the other alternative—the inclusion of Pitt in the Ministry. 'You have been told,' he wrote, 'that Mr. Pitt would not act with you. . . . One thing I am persuaded of, that, if his ambition was gratified in the point on which he has set his heart [i.e. the Seals], *that* would not stand in the way; and measures are always capable of being distinguished by some new turn to be given to them.'[1]

So wrote Hardwicke without perhaps much hope, for Pitt had made it clear over and over again that, much as he hankered after the Seals, he would not take them unless he was given at the same time the responsibility which they implied; position and wealth were of course to be desired, but they were only personal; power was a trust for the benefit of the people and was of infinitely greater import; he would not barter the one for the other. Would Newcastle yield the degree of power which Pitt demanded? Hardwicke had doubts.

When the alternatives—retirement or an attempt to win Pitt—were set squarely before him, Newcastle turned towards the latter, reluctantly and of necessity, and with reservations in his mind. 'The present great consideration,' he wrote, 'is reduced to the following questions. Can we go out? Can we go on in the House of Commons with Mr. Fox in the temper he is, and in the circumstances we are, without either Leicester House or Mr. Pitt? Can we get either or both? By what means can we get either? Should those means be tried or not, with either, with both, or with which of them?'[2]

Even as he was writing, Holdernesse was scribbling a hasty note to break the news, just arrived, of Frederick's invasion of Saxony. It was news which made Newcastle's questions infinitely more urgent. Yet still he could not take the final plunge. Instead, he chose to imagine that Leicester House was a real substitute for Pitt, and used all his powers to persuade the King to give way over Bute's appointment as Groom of the Stole. The King did give way, but, as Newcastle ought to have known, the parlia-

[1] Hardwicke to D. of N., 29th Aug. 1756. Add. MSS. 32,867.
[2] Newcastle to Hardwicke, 4th Sept. 1756. Add. MSS. 32,867.

mentary position remained unaltered. Or rather, had become worse, for the nearer the session approached, the more difficult Fox became, and the more inevitably Newcastle had to choose between his two alternatives.

(iv)

As often happens, the decision was finally brought about by what appeared to be a couple of straws. The first was the case of the Hanoverian soldier. That unfortunate man, when buying handkerchiefs at Maidstone, either deliberately or by mistake carried away more than he had bought. He was charged with theft and committed to gaol. His commanding officer demanded his release, for trial by court martial, and when the Mayor declined, complained to the King and obtained an order for it through Lord Holdernesse.[1] The 'affair' raised a furore throughout the country, which was not allayed even when the court martial ordered the miserable man 300 lashes. It has been the fashion to suggest that the matter was a trifle and Pitt's interest in it assumed, but those who have noted the problem of American airmen stationed in England will appreciate that jurisdiction over foreign troops can raise strong feelings and does involve large questions of sovereign rights as well as the lesser questions of personal safety.

The second and more proximate cause was a matter of patronage. Realising that his position was precarious, Fox had seized an opportunity to procure the earldom of Ilchester for his brother and the promise of an appointment in the Prince's new household for his nephew, Lord Digby. But as he had approached the King directly, Newcastle suffered the pangs of jealousy, and with his usual pettiness in such matters, tried to put obstacles in the way. Fox became furious, and his fury was heightened when Newcastle made several fresh parliamentary appointments without consulting or even informing him.[2]

Fox was not only feeling angry, but scared and lonely—scared because of the approaching session of Parliament and the storms which he would have to face; lonely, because every man's hand seemed to be against him. He told Stone, in a moment of candour, that 'he found himself in the most disagreeable situation imaginable: hated by the King and by the Princess of Wales on account

[1] Newcastle to Hardwicke, 18th Sept. 1756. Add. MSS. 32,867.
[2] Walpole. *George II*, II, 251.

of his attachment to the Duke [of Cumberland]; exposed to the resentment of the nation more than anybody on account of his being the principal person in the House of Commons; responsible for the House of Commons without any credit to support it,' and out of favour with the Ministers.[1] He was hardly likely to tell Stone of his dream about a coalition with Pitt, but it was perhaps significant that in the long catalogue of his woes he made no reference to his previous offer to resign the Seals or to accept a lower office. When he had previously urged Newcastle to come to terms with Pitt, he doubted if Newcastle would act, or Pitt respond, and perhaps hoped that neither would. But now he was aware of Newcastle's leanings and may even have thought that negotiations with Pitt had commenced. If so, his position was 'disagreeable' indeed: he was completely isolated and without hope. Certainly he must have felt what Hardwicke described as 'his present state of humiliation,'[2] and in the turmoil of his spirits he wrote to Newcastle, warning him, a little cryptically but quite definitely, that he intended to resign: 'The step I am going to take is not only necessary but innocent; it shall be accompanied with no complaint; it shall be followed by no resentment. I have no resentment. But it is not the less true that my situation is impracticable.'[3]

Men's motives are usually mixed, and the confusion of eighteenth-century politics makes it the more difficult to see exactly what Fox had in mind. The anger, the fear, the loneliness are confirmed by his own confession. But perhaps there was a further thought which held him back for the moment from actually leaving his post. Just before receiving Fox's letter, Newcastle had visited Lady Yarmouth. She was at once a sounding board of the King's views, and a convenient channel through which ideas could be conveyed to him. A few weeks earlier (2nd September) Lady Yarmouth had given Newcastle strong hints that he should make his peace with Pitt, and now that he was reluctantly coming round to that idea, he went to her for sympathy and support. He found to his 'great surprise and concern' that she had altered her views, and now 'said, and repeated it, that we must do the best we could with Mr. Fox; for that *we could not change him*.' Here was a fresh tangle in the skein.

[1] Newcastle to Hardwicke, 12th October 1756. Add. MSS. 32,868.
[2] Hardwicke to Newcastle, 13th October 1756. Add. MSS. 32,868.
[3] Fox to Newcastle, 13th October 1756. Add. MSS. 32,868.

If Lady Yarmouth correctly represented the King's views, then instead of starting to cobble up his Ministry by securing Pitt, Newcastle had the mortifying thought that he had disobliged Fox at a most inopportune moment, and the prospects for the coming session were of the gloomiest. It was no wonder that he offered up the heartfelt prayer to Hardwicke, 'for God's sake, my dear Lord, tell me what to do, and I will follow it. I own I am confounded with these changes.'[1] But what confounded Newcastle may possibly have been a ray of hope for Fox. The King's attitude, which Lady Yarmouth reflected accurately, was a passing phase of annoyance. He had given way over Bute's appointment and that very fact had revived his prejudice against Leicester House and anyone supposed to be connected with it. Pitt was known to be in favour there, in spite of occasional clouds, and, therefore, any slight willingness which the King might have had to accept him as Secretary was in eclipse. Newcastle had missed the boat! Royal favour was swinging back from Leicester House to the Duke of Cumberland, and Fox's stock was rising correspondingly. Fox constantly visited Lady Yarmouth; indeed, he was proposing to convey his resignation to the King through her and must therefore have been aware of the latest trend. If so, he may have hoped that Newcastle would be frightened into giving him better terms, more power and stronger support. Newcastle certainly thought so.[2] So did Walpole.[3] But if this hope was lurking somewhere in the background of Fox's mind, it is probably true to say that his intention to resign was uppermost. It soon reasserted itself.

In any event, his letter terrified Newcastle, and not the less because it was cryptic. On receipt of it, Newcastle rushed off in a panic to Granville and begged him to exchange offices, becoming himself First Lord, with Fox as his Chancellor of the Exchequer; but that shameless old reprobate replied crushingly, 'I thought I had cured you of such offers last year; I will be hanged a little before I take your place, rather than a little after.'[4]

The state to which the Government of England had been reduced was truly grotesque. The King was hinting that Fox should retain the Seals,[5] whilst Newcastle was screwing himself

[1] Newcastle to Hardwicke, 12th October 1756. Add. MSS. 32,868.

[2] See Newcastle to Hardwicke, 13th October 1756. 'If you would have my opinion . . . he makes use of this opportunity of distress to put the knife to our throats to get his own terms and all the powers he wants, which, he thinks, we cannot now refuse him.' Add. MSS. 32,868.

[3] Walpole. *George II*, II, 252. [4] *Ibid.*, II, 252. [5] *Ibid.*, II, 256-7.

up to offer them to Pitt. The King and Newcastle were both grudging, and Pitt and Fox were both unwilling. Newcastle, meanwhile, was hawking his own office round, not because he wanted to lose it, but because he was afraid of keeping it, and no one would accept it at his hands. Murray had thrown up his job and was waiting for his peerage as the door for his escape, a door at which Lyttelton, the Chancellor of the Exchequer, was also knocking. Hardwicke, looking anxiously over the scene, saw 'some hazard' in approaching Pitt; believed the Duke of Cumberland had some 'underplot' in mind; and suspected Fox and Pitt of meeting in secret and having some 'concert' together; in short, he was compact of doubts and suspicions.[1] Government was for all practical purposes at an end, and the session was at hand.

The one certainty in this welter was Fox's memorandum for the King, begging his Majesty's leave to resign.[2] Lady Yarmouth, knowing the King's views, refused to touch it, but Granville presented it to the King on the 15th of October. The effect was instantaneous. George II was stirred to wrath, and promptly authorised Newcastle to 'sound' Pitt with a promise that if he would 'support the King's affairs . . . he should meet with or have a good reception.'[3] So Newcastle's hesitations were resolved for him, and he now, as so often happens, became as eager to secure Pitt as before he had been reluctant. His chief fear was that Granville might succeed in softening the King's anger and persuading Fox to carry on, which, he wrote, 'makes it absolutely necessary not to lose a moment in applying to Mr. Pitt.' All difficulties must be brushed aside and Hardwicke must come up to Town without delay to carry on the negotiations. He should write to Pitt at once to fix an appointment: 'You see, the King wishes it; my Lady Yarmouth advises it, and if it is not done before Lord Granville returns to court tomorrow, and the Duke [of Cumberland] sees the King on Sunday, nobody can tell whether it will ever be done at all, and then it will fail, purely from a scruple or nicety in yourself.'[4] Hardwicke, though oppressed with doubts, bowed to the opinion of Lady Yarmouth and the Duke of Newcastle. He wrote to Pitt inviting him to a meeting on Tuesday, the 19th of October, at Lord Royston's

[1] Hardwicke to Newcastle, 16th Oct. 1756. Add. MSS. 32,868.
[2] Grenville. *Papers*, I, 174.
[3] Newcastle to Hardwicke, 15th Oct. 1756. Add. MSS. 32,868. [4] *Ibid.*

house in St. James's Square, 'being,' as he said, 'desirous to speak to you upon an affair of great consequence.'[1]

(v)

Hardwicke's letter reached Pitt in the seventh heaven. It is curious how often the crises of his public life coincided with the highlights of his private life. On the 10th of October, after a sharp but short labour, Hester had given birth to a son. Pitt was enraptured; at last he had an heir to his 'no-estate'; at last Hester could look her sister-in-law, that 'happy mother of males,' squarely in the face. What was public life to this exquisite joy? Pitt's whole thought was centred on Hester and the babe: 'dear Lady Hester is so happy with her offspring.' He was no less happy himself—'talking nursery,' revelling in the 'general applause' so lavishly poured out by the worshippers at the cot, admiring the young man's 'stature and strength,' his 'quality and quantity,' and listening with no small satisfaction to the nurses' assurance that 'he is without appearance of heaviness, notwithstanding his size.' Was ever a babe half a day old more fondly praised, more dotingly gloated over, more generously endowed with all the virtues?[2] Pitt for the moment had nothing further to ask of life.

But life had a good deal to ask of him, and Hardwicke's letter brought him back to earth. He did not, however, come back quite the same. Just as, two years earlier, Hester had revived his manhood in the nick of time to withstand Newcastle, so now, his eldest son added inches to his stature in the nick of time to confront Hardwicke. Pitt showed no hesitation, no wavering. He wrote post-haste to Grenville: 'Though I expect our conference will be short and final, considering the negative I go resolved to give to any plan with the Duke of Newcastle at the head of it, as well as to any proposal for covering his retreat, in case he wishes to retire from being Minister; yet, as it is impossible to be sure, in the present state of things, how far his Majesty may be brought to open his eyes, I beg of you, as I do of Lord Temple, to be in Town Tuesday evening, at my house in Brook Street, where I may receive your lights and final determinations as to any ulterior conversations with the Court, should they be

[1] Hardwicke to Pitt, 16th October 1756. Add. MSS. 32,868.
[2] Pitt to George Grenville. Grenville. *Papers*, I, 173.

proposed.' He added that he was resolved to go to the conference 'without previous participation with Lord B[ute],' to whom he would report afterwards. In short, he was going to meet Hardwicke without consulting anyone, confident in his own strength and standing upon his own principles.[1]

The conference was as final, though not as short, as Pitt had expected. It lasted from noon to three-thirty. At four o'clock, a weary and dispirited Hardwicke wrote to Newcastle: 'His answer is an absolute *final negative*, without any reserve for further deliberation. In short, there never was a more unsuccessful negotiator.'[2]

The meeting had been arranged so that Hardwicke might win Pitt over to the Ministry, but Pitt had at once taken charge of the proceedings and given them a new twist. He began by making it emphatically clear that he would not serve under Newcastle. Thereafter, the discussion centred on the conditions under which he would be willing to form a Ministry of his own. Pitt made 'strong professions of respect and duty to His Majesty and zeal for his government, and for the support of his real service,' but beyond possibly emphasising the word 'real' to indicate the profound gulf between himself and Newcastle, Pitt refused to be drawn. Though apparently saying much, he was, in fact, very reticent, confining himself exclusively to what he called 'objections,' and suggesting nothing 'affirmative as to measures of any kind.' The point is important.

The 'objections,' as given to Hardwicke, were five in number, viz.:

'1. That it was impossible for him to serve with the Duke of Newcastle.

2. That he thought enquiries into the past measures absolutely necessary; that he thought it his duty to take a considerable share in them. . . .

3. That he thought it his duty to support a militia bill, and particularly that of the last session. . . .

4. That the affair of the Hanoverian soldier he thought of great importance; that what had been done ought to be examined and he thought censured.

5. That if he came into His Majesty's service, he thought it necessary, in order to serve him and support his affairs, to have

[1] Pitt to Grenville, 17th October 1756. Grenville. *Papers*, I, 177.
[2] Hardwicke to Newcastle, 19th October 1756. Add MSS. 32,868.

such powers as belonged to his station, to be in the first concert and concoction of measures, and to be at liberty to propose to His Majesty himself anything that occurred to him for his service originally, and without going through the channel of any other minister.'[1]

The 'objections' speak for themselves, and Hardwicke summed them up in a letter to his eldest son, Lord Royston: 'The great obstacles are the Duke of Newcastle and measures; and without a change of both, 'tis impossible for him to come.'[2] Pitt's refusal did not spring out of personal feelings or pique, though possibly both had some influence; it was based on constitutional grounds which Pitt was exploring with a true instinct but an innovator's uncertainty. He was moving towards both Cabinet responsibility and party Government, which give particular significance to the reason which he assigned: it was 'that all these mistakes in the conduct of the war had been committed, and all these ill successes had happened, whilst his Grace was first Minister, and the nation was (as he said) to the last degree incensed against him. Therefore, he concluded, it was impossible for the Duke of Newcastle to keep his ground or for anybody to go on with him.'[3]

(vi)

Pitt returned to Brook Street, and with or without the advice of his friends, decided that the time was ripe for stronger action. He had told Hardwicke his 'objections,' and assumed that they would be reported. But the King had a right to know his more positive views, and Pitt perhaps a wish to divulge them—not to Hardwicke, but to the King himself. There was only one channel to the royal ear which could be regarded as at once private and unbiased—the lady who lived 'below stairs' and entertained the King of an evening, Lady Yarmouth. Whether because no occasion had hitherto arisen, or because he disapproved of her equivocal position, Pitt had never visited the lady. But the times were out of joint, and it is precisely at such times that 'every avenue must be explored.' Pitt therefore went to St. James's Palace, on the morning of the 21st of October, and asked for an interview. If Walpole is to be believed, his arrival caused a

[1] Hardwicke's Relation of my conference with Mr. Pitt, etc. Add. MSS. 35,870.
[2] Hardwicke to Royston, 21st October 1756. Add. MSS. 35,351.
[3] Hardwicke to Sir Joseph Yorke, 31st October 1756. Add. MSS. 35,357.

flurry among the Pages of the Backstairs,[1] but, if so, they were the only persons to be flurried. Lady Yarmouth received her visitor calmly, and very possibly welcomed the chance of discovering his real views; she was distressed at the political situation and most anxious to find a solution agreeable to the King. They had a long conversation. What Pitt said is not known, as the lady was discreet and the King silent, but there are sufficient hints and some facts to enable a reasonable guess to be made. One of the phrases in the jargon of the day was 'men and measures.' Hardwicke's letter to Royston had echoed it. There is no doubt that Pitt and Lady Yarmouth discussed 'men,' and some grounds for thinking that they touched upon 'measures.'

On the subject of men, Pitt emphasised the need to get rid of Newcastle: he was responsible for the misfortunes and misconduct of the war, and 'to *reassure and reanimate the people of England,* another head of the Administration was absolutely necessary.'[2] But Pitt went much farther than the First Lord. He sketched out—and the paper still exists—'his plan of a new administration,' which, said Hardwicke, after the King had shown it to him, was 'a most extraordinary one.'[3] Hardwicke found it extraordinary because it included none of the old Ministers, not even Hardwicke himself or his son-in-law, Anson, which was no doubt the reason why Pitt had preferred to discuss it with the lady rather than with Hardwicke. It must have come as a shock to the old man, though he noted, as a sign of grace, that neither he nor Anson were expressly excluded; they were simply not included, the plan making no provision for a Lord Chancellor or a Head of the Admiralty.

As for measures, Walpole states, on what authority is not known, that Pitt 'gave some civil, though obscure hints, as if, in losing his Grace [i.e. Newcastle], Hanover might not lose *all* its friends.'[4] Walpole found this a matter for cynical mirth, but the degree to which he was justified must of course depend upon what Pitt actually said. He had always agreed that 'regard' must be had to Hanover, and at this date he could have hinted at the new situation created by the alliance with Prussia, the outbreak of war, and even Frederick's semi-victory at Lobositz, news of which had just arrived. But this is speculation.

[1] Walpole. *George II*, II, 259.
[2] G. Lyttelton to W. Lyttelton, 25th Nov. 1756. Phillimore, II, 534.
[3] Hardwicke to Yorke, 31st October 1756. Add. MSS. 35,357.
[4] Walpole. *George II*, II, 259.

Whatever he said, he did not impress the King, which, all things considered, is hardly surprising. No one had any reason to anticipate Pitt's marvellous success as a War Minister, and in the meantime he was striking out an entirely new line in politics—a line which seemed to all the old practitioners 'impracticable' and almost incomprehensible. Until he was forced by lack of any alternative, George II could not be expected to accept an inexperienced Minister, personally distasteful to himself and supported only by that public opinion which the King so heartily despised, and one, moreover, proposing an 'impracticable' administration, and displaying at best only a mild interest in Hanover. Without a moment's hesitation, he ordered Hardwicke to inform Pitt that 'the King is of opinion that what has been suggested is not for his and the public service.' At the same time, he forbade Hardwicke to make any reference to Lady Yarmouth, though Pitt's visit to her was a matter of universal gossip; 'Mr. Pitt,' the King said, 'shall not go to *that channel* any more; *she* does not meddle, and shall not meddle.' Hardwicke pressed for leave to tell Pitt that the King's answer covered the 'plan' as well as the 'objections,' but the King was adamant.

Hardwicke saw Pitt again on the 24th of October and gave him the King's message. Pitt bowed in acknowledgment, and then asked if the message was 'to be considered *as an answer to the whole*.' Hardwicke, and indeed historians generally, have assumed that in asking this question Pitt was referring to his 'plan.' It may be so, but perhaps Pitt was simply wondering whether the King had been influenced by all or only some of the 'objections.' There can be little doubt that in Pitt's mind the crucial 'objections' were the first and last—the dismissal of Newcastle and his own right of access to the King. He would have been willing to drop, or at least smooth over, the enquiries into past measures and the affair of the Hanoverian soldier, if the King would have compromised on those lines. But the first and last were fundamental; granted those, the 'plan' was little more than a corollary. Whatever Pitt had in mind, Hardwicke could only reply that the answer was the King's and he could not undertake to explain it. From Pitt's point of view that was sufficient whether it applied to the 'plan' or not, and he therefore assured Hardwicke 'that he would not come into the service, in the present circumstances of affairs, upon any other terms, for the whole world.' So the conference ended and, as usual, the two parted 'with great personal civility on both sides.'[1]

(vii)

Pitt's abrupt refusal worried and puzzled the political world. Most people jumped to the conclusion that he and Fox were playing a deep game, intent on pushing Newcastle out to make way for a coalition of their own, though Hardwicke, after noting that Fox's name did not appear in the 'plan,' came to the conclusion that the coalition was not Pitt and Fox, but Pitt and Leicester House. Newcastle's friends were angry at his attitude and even the moderates were annoyed: 'Nothing,' wrote the Duke of Devonshire, 'has hurt Pitt so much as his having shown to the world that he did not value the confusion and distress that he might throw this country into, in order to gratify his resentment or satisfy his ambition, and I own it has, in some degree, altered the good opinion I had of him, for I do not think anything can justify such conduct.'[2]

The fact is that the great Whig world was more than a little frightened. Pitt was to have been their shield, and Pitt had unaccountably failed them. 'The Duchess of Hamilton,' wrote Walpole, in a sorry attempt to laugh off the crisis, 'has brought her beauty to London at the only instant when it would not make a crowd. I believe we should scarce stare at the King of Prussia, so much are we engrossed by this ministerial ferment.'[3] A week later, he could not even pretend: 'My dear Sir,' he wrote to Mann, 'what a present and future picture have I given you! . . . The crisis is most melancholy and alarming. . . . What a bold man is he who shall undertake the administration! How much shall we be obliged to him! How mad is he, whoever is ambitious of it!'[4]

Indeed the position seemed desperate. Newcastle and the King knocked fruitlessly at every door. The former even 'catched at feathers,' to use Walpole's expressive phrase;[5] he appealed in turn to Halifax, Egmont and Granville, but in vain. By the 26th of October he had come to the conclusion that hope had gone, and wrapping himself up in 'a consciousness of my own innocence'[6]

[1] Hardwicke's Relations, etc., and Hardwicke to Yorke, 31st October 1756.
[2] Devonshire to Fox, 20th October. Quoted in Torrens, II, 314-15.
[3] To Montagu, 28th October 1756 [4] To Mann, 4th Nov. 1756.
[5] Walpole. *George II*, II, 261.
[6] Newcastle to Hardwicke, 20th October 1756. Add. MSS. 35,416.

—but not, be it remarked, a consciousness of his own failure—he told the King that he must resign.

The next day (27th October) the King sent for Fox, and asked him to try his hand at forming an administration, including if possible Pitt, though the King expressed doubts if Pitt would join. The King was right. Fox met Pitt at the Prince's levee on the 28th of October, and was told firmly, finally and according to the general belief, rudely, that Pitt would not act with him. Fox certainly felt affronted, but otherwise was not quite sure whether to be pleased or sorry. He did not relish the idea of Pitt as an opponent, but equally he misliked him as a colleague, and gave vent perhaps to a feeling of relief when he told the Duke of Bedford that he could not much blame Pitt, who no doubt foresaw that 'my place would be the Treasury,' and 'in that case what would he be but paymaster again under another Pelham?'[1] The vision was bright at the moment, and perhaps Pitt's refusal added to its lustre. But, though Fox apparently hoped that he could form a Ministry without Pitt and continued his efforts, Pitt's refusal was conclusive. Fox had failed.

The next candidate was the Duke of Devonshire, whose name had figured, unknown to himself, in Pitt's 'plan' as First Lord of the Treasury, and who might therefore be expected to meet with better success. As a politician he was of a retiring nature, moderate though not altogether stable, and notable rather for commonsense that statesmanship; indeed, he was more anxious to keep the peace among jarring Ministers than to lead them. He was in many ways admirably suited as a figurehead, and would have been more so but for one drawback much to be regretted at this crisis; he was not exempt from the prejudices of his class and upbringing, so that, while recognising Pitt's ability and accepting the need to admit him to office, he looked upon him with a certain distaste which warped his judgment. At the King's invitation, he took up the task of Cabinet-making, and although both he and his friends were agreed about 'the impracticability of Mr. Pitt, who . . . seemed determined to place himself and family sole governors of everything,'[2] he busied himself to some effect; for within a week or so he had completed a new administration with Pitt as Secretary. Newcastle resigned on the 11th of November, Fox on the 13th, and Hardwicke, at Newcastle's

[1] Fox to Bedford, 30th October 1756. Bedford. *Correspondence,* II, 205.
[2] Bedford to his Duchess, 2nd Nov. 1756. Bedford. *Correspondence,* II, 207.

urgent entreaty, on the 19th. Murray and Lyttelton were promoted to the House of Lords, and Anson was dismissed.

Pitt had reached his goal; it was now for him to make good his famous claim, 'I am sure I can save this country, and nobody else can.'[1] But in this November of 1756 his position seemed instability itself. No one has summed it up better than Walpole. 'Mr. Pitt,' he told Mann, 'accedes with so little strength that his success seems very precarious. If he Hanoverizes, or checks any enquiries, he loses his popularity, and falls that way; if he humours the present rage of the people, he provokes two powerful factions. His only chance seems to depend on joining with the Duke of Newcastle, who is most offended with Fox; but after Pitt's personal exclusion of his Grace, and considering Pitt's small force, it may not be easy for him to be accepted there. I foresee nothing but confusion; the new system is composed of such discordant parts that it can produce no harmony. Though the Duke of Newcastle, the Chancellor, Lord Anson, and Fox quit, yet scarce one of their friends is discarded. The very cement seems disjunctive; I mean the Duke of Devonshire, who takes the Treasury. If he acts cordially, he disobliges his intimate friend, Mr. Fox; if he does not, he offends Pitt.'[2] Pitt cannot have been blind to circumstances so obvious to everyone else. What then were the grounds of his confidence? The answer is a long story, and must have a chapter to itself.

[1] Walpole. *George II*, III, 84.
[2] To Mann, 13th November 1756.

10

PITT ARRIVES

(i)

As a phrase, His Majesty's Opposition is of modern origin; as a fact, it goes back to Queen Anne at least. It was one of Walpole's major crimes against the constitution that he was not content with defeating his opponents but insisted on shattering the Opposition into a thousand pieces, so that for the best part of a century it ceased to exist. This murder of His Majesty's Opposition is the clue to the gerrymandering of the age; it explains the 'corruption' of Parliament; it gives significance to the interminable intrigues of the Whig oligarchy and it simplifies the involved and meaningless confusion of eighteenth-century politics.

When Walpole had worked his savage will, a few Tories still remained, but no one, not even the Tories themselves, regarded them as an alternative Government. They were not even called the Opposition—a title which the omnivorous Whigs kept as a term of reproach for the more refractory of their own rank and file. 'I stated,' said Newcastle, when reporting a conversation with Oswald (a politician who occasionally filled minor ministerial posts), 'I stated the opposition to be Pitt, Grenville, Legge and the Townshends'—all Whigs. Oswald agreed, and suggested that if they could not all be reconciled, it might be possible to 'break into them' and gain some.[1] The 'opposition' was little more than a branch of the Whig party, a sort of reserve from which substitutes could be picked, so that when Murray, for instance, dismayed Newcastle by demanding the post of Chief Justice, the Speaker pointed out consolingly that his loss could be 'made good out of the Opposition'[2]; and when Newcastle's crisis was coming to a head in October, Stone 'combined all circumstances

[1] Newcastle to Hardwicke, 10th October 1756. Add. MSS. 32,868.
[2] West to Newcastle, 29th May 1756. Add. MSS. 32,865.

to show the necessity of taking in the principal leaders of the Opposition.'[1]

The Tory party, meanwhile, 'had ceased to be a serious political factor';[2] it had become a quaint survival, a patch on the fair face of the Mother of Parliaments. Except that it was more quiescent and less arrogant, its status was not unlike that of the Liberal party at the present time. Even the best known of the Tories cut no ice at Westminster. 'Honest Shippen,' like the late Mr. Maxton, was personally popular with everyone, but politically ignored by all. There was only one party—the Whigs—and it was too large. There were not enough ministerial posts to satisfy all the claimants, and those who were unsatisfied saw no reasonable prospects in the future. It stretched out before their longing eyes as an unending Whig oligarchy in which they would share without benefit for ever and ever. Hence that curious system of 'management' in the constituencies and the House, which the Patriots called 'corruption.' The magnates were all busy collecting followers, buying up rotten boroughs and trying to influence elections—not for the good of the party, as they no doubt fondly imagined, certainly not for the good of the country, but in order to carry more weight in the House and force themselves and their adherents into office. Elections, in short, were concerned with 'men' not 'measures' and politics were generally a clash of personalities rather than of principles. The various magnates and their followers were so many factions, manœuvring against each other. Because of their numbers, they produce in the mind of the historical onlooker much the same sense of bewilderment as the many sectional interests of the French Parliament, though the central core of Whiggism gives an appearance of solidarity to eighteenth-century England which seems to be lacking in the France of today.

This crowd of candidates for office, eager and jealous, pushing and jostling, required a considerable degree of 'management.' They had to be kept loyal; they had to be kept hopeful; as far as possible, they had to be kept happy. A great deal could be done by skilful handling. The dispensers of patronage could dole out ribands and garters and peerages; they could place contracts and offer jobs; they could promise reversions and provide sinecures and pensions—especially on the Irish establish-

[1] Newcastle to Hardwicke, 10th October 1756. Add. MSS. 32,868.
[2] Sedgwick. *Letters from George III*, p. xxiv.

ment. If things became really awkward, they could always push someone in to the Great Wardrobe or kick someone upstairs into the House of Lords, and present the resultant vacancy to the most noisy of the Opposition. Let the vacancy come as it would —through death or retirement or a parliamentary wangle—an unscrupulous old broker like Newcastle was marvellously adroit in using it to the best advantage; he knew all the ropes and could drive the hardest of bargains. For one reason or another, he stirred the political pot from time to time, but it was always the same old porridge.

(ii)

Pitt had entered Parliament as a Whig; there was no feasible alternative for an ambitious young man; and he entered as a member of a faction—the Cousinhood. At the time he certainly did not think of himself as factious—he was a patriot opposing a Minister who called himself a Whig but was unworthy of the name! It was not long, however, before he began to have some inkling of his true position and the dangers it involved. Nothing, perhaps, so effectively opened his eyes as the affair of the Prince of Wales's allowance in 1737, when he helped to engineer a parliamentary crisis for the Prince's personal ends, and found the results mischievous. From that time, he grew steadily more distrustful of factious opposition, and in 1754, at the darkest hour of his career, when he was racked with doubt what course to take, he actually warned the Cousinhood against any conduct which could be called factious,[1] that is to say, founded on no principle and pursued for selfish ends.

Side by side with his distaste for faction there grew up a conviction that he was at variance with the Whig conception of foreign policy. As the principles of government laid down at the Revolution were by now the common background of all parties, and home affairs attracted little attention, foreign policy was in practice the main dividing line between Whig and Tory. When, therefore, he discovered that he disapproved of the Whig predilection for Hanover and the Continent, and was much more at home with the Tory doctrine of colonial enterprise, it would have been natural for him to join the party which claimed his spiritual allegiance, if it had not been for their political impotence. Whether the idea ever entered Pitt's head may be doubted, but

[1] Phillimore. *Lyttelton,* II, 462.

there can be no doubt that the knowledge of his disagreement with his nominal party coloured his actions and disturbed his thoughts. He showed the former by his diatribes against Hanover, and the latter by emphasising that he was a Revolution Whig as opposed to a Whig pure and simple. The logic of events was to drive him farther, and the time was not far distant when he was to proclaim openly that 'he was neither Whig or Tory, but venerated the memory of King William and would die by the principles of the Revolution.'[1] His position was paradoxical in the extreme; he was a Whig opposing his own leaders in support of Tory principles, and the main reason for his dilemma was the absence of anything which could be called His Majesty's Opposition. Truly Walpole was neatly revenged on his youthful persecutor!

The dilemma grew with the passage of time. The problem of the lost Opposition seemed insoluble. Throughout the long years of Pitt's subservience to Pelham, the fact which impressed itself most insistently on his mind was the absence of any alternative. Pelham and Newcastle, though oil and vinegar to each other and no favourites of Pitt, must, as he declared over and over again, somehow be kept in office because they were irreplaceable.

Pelham's death and Pitt's marriage gave a fresh twist to the problem. Pitt's ambitions revived and he began to see himself at the head of affairs, but it was obvious that his rise to power must bring him into direct conflict not only with Newcastle but with the whole Whig policy. What was he to do? That he gave the matter deep consideration seems clear, since it was the rock on which all the negotiations with Newcastle foundered. The breaking point had invariably been either Pitt's insistence on being given full powers or his demand for a change in the foreign policy. In his heart he must have known that Newcastle had no option but to refuse, since acquiescence meant the eclipse of himself and the end of his party. Pitt must have thought deeply about it, and he had a solution. In a sense, it was the obvious one. As he was advocating a Tory policy, the Government also should be Tory. In a word, he proposed to revive His Majesty's Opposition, and when its turn came, lead it himself. He showed the way his mind was working by starting to woo the Tories from the moment of his dismissal (20th November 1755). Within less

[1] West to Newcastle, 21st April 1760. Add. MSS. 32,905.

than three weeks, he was making his appeal to the Country Gentlemen to support his Militia Bill. Thereafter, he is continually to be found linked with the Tories in one way or another. Sometimes it is slight, such as Potter's reference to the Tory Common Councilman at Bath who embraced Pitt's interest with eagerness.[1] Sometimes it is much weightier, as the support given to Pitt's attacks on the Government for their mishandling of the war. Petitions came from all over the country, and almost always as the result of Tory inspiration. Hardwicke noted, with some indignation, that the 'Huntingdonshire Instructions' emanated from a Grand Jury which was Tory,[2] and that the City of London Address was presented by fifteen Aldermen, not one of whom was a Whig.[3] But the most conclusive evidence is Pitt's own action when he was eventually given the Seals: 'He flings himself,' said the astounded Newcastle, 'upon the people and the Tories.'[4]

But to say that Pitt intended to revive His Majesty's Opposition and lead a Tory Government is too great a simplification; it is looking at the matter through twentieth-century eyes. Pitt was feeling his way out of a morass, and it would be wrong to suppose that his ideas were cut and dried or that they were not constantly altering. A little later Legge was to speak of 'the visionary notions of Mr. Pitt,' which is perhaps a not unfair description.[5] The interesting point is that those visionary notions have to a large extent developed into the commonplaces of today, and might have developed more quickly and more surely if the difficulties which Pitt had to overcome had not been so insuperable.

(iii)

The 'notions' covered both the outgoing and the incoming Ministries. So far as Newcastle was concerned, everything turned upon Pitt's 'notions' of Cabinet responsibility and popular support. Newcastle must go because he had been First Minister in a discredited Government. His plea that he had had no share in the conduct of the war left Pitt cold: it was irrelevant: the damning fact was that the mistakes and disasters had occurred during his administration. If others had been primarily responsible

[1] Chatham. *Correspondence,* I, 162.
[2] Hardwicke to Newcastle, 26th August 1756. Add. MSS. 32,867.
[3] Hardwicke to Newcastle, 20th August 1756. Add. MSS. 32,866.
[4] Newcastle to Hardwicke, 11th December 1756. Add. MSS. 32,869.
[5] Hardwicke to Newcastle, 9th April 1757. Add. MSS. 32,870.

for wrong decisions, Newcastle as First Minister ought to have overruled them—a duty which had never entered Newcastle's head and which he now described as 'pretty great and difficult.'[1]

But Pitt did not stop at Newcastle. His Ministry had lost the confidence of the people, and without popular support it could not stand. 'He concluded it was impossible for the Duke of Newcastle to keep his ground or for anybody to go on with him.' What he seems to have wished for was 'an universal sweep of all that are at present in employment.'[2] Obviously that was past praying for; he could not have found substitutes. But failing a clean sweep, he was determined at least to get rid of the old leaders. Newcastle and Fox he had proscribed before accepting office, and if he had foreseen the difficulty of getting rid of anyone else, he might well have lengthened the list whilst he still had bargaining power. After accepting office, he marked down Holdernesse and Barrington amongst others for dismissal. The departure of Holdernesse was doubly important—trebly, if Pitt had only known his penchant for betraying Government secrets—first to get rid of a man whom Pitt regarded as incompetent and secondly because he was Secretary for the Northern Province, which Pitt coveted for himself. The departure of Barrington was desirable so that Pitt might have a congenial Secretary at War. In both cases Pitt failed to get his way, partly because he had to act through the reluctant Duke of Devonshire, partly because of the King's veto. George II had no 'visionary notions.' He was profoundly aware that he had been forced to take Pitt against his will, and he had no intention of yielding one inch more than was necessary. Newcastle and Fox might have to go—had in fact resigned—but there must be a limit to this slaughter of his old and trusted friends. He refused point-blank to turn Holdernesse out and he insisted on keeping Barrington. Indeed, the process of tying Pitt's hands had begun at once. The magnates had already discussed how to 'lay a control' upon Pitt and his party and 'confine them to that proper degree of power they had a right to expect';[3] and in the final arrangements, their reason for accepting Legge as Chancellor of the Exchequer was that he 'is not looked upon at present to be a man entirely at Mr. Pitt's disposal.'[4]

[1] Newcastle to Arundel, 30th October, 1756. Add. MSS. 32,868.
[2] Symmer to Mitchell, 2nd November 1756. Add. MSS. 6,839.
[3] Bedford to his Duchess, 2nd November 1756. Bedford. *Correspondence,* II, 207.
[4] Symmer to Mitchell, 9th November 1756. Add. MSS. 6,839.

What Pitt seems to have had in mind was to adopt the accepted division of ministerial posts into offices of business and offices of profit. The former—the Cabinet—must be reserved for himself and his friends, so that they could mould policy; the latter could be left for Newcastle's 'fellow-travellers' or whoever else might be available. On the whole he was reasonably successful; indeed, so successful that Newcastle bewailed the fact that 'amongst the many friends we have who remain at Court, we have not *one* capable of making proper representations.'[1] Hardwicke agreed.[2] It was a depressing experience for Ministers not yet accustomed to their fall, and bewildering for members of that close trade union, the Whig oligarchy.

Yet if Pitt was reasonably successful, he was not wholly so. There was inevitably a great deal of makeshift in his actions, and a good deal of chopping and changing, due to the obstacles which he met with and which it did not always lie in his power to overcome. The political ideas of the age did not allow him to form his own Ministry. The King still nominally chose his advisers, and though George II was aware that his positive powers were very circumscribed, he clung tenaciously to his powers of veto. In judging Pitt's choice of colleagues, it must always be remembered that the selection was by no means entirely his own.

Turning from the Cabinet to the rank and file of Parliament, it was universally recognised that Pitt was, in Newcastle's phrase, flinging himself upon the Tories. The news buzzed round London as a nine days' wonder. 'Their present scheme,' Hardwicke told his son, 'is to unite with the Tories,'[3] while Newcastle, chattering with his usual volubility, confided to Holdernesse that 'many of my friends, the Bishops, are now here with me. They are full, (as indeed everybody is,) that the *Tories* in a body are to support the new Administration.'[4] So strange was the fact that the whole world had to be informed: 'Pitt . . . has engaged the Torys' was how the news went to Russia;[5] and Berlin was advised that 'Mr. Pitt is the Idol of the Tories.'[6]

At first the Whigs could hardly believe their ears, but as the

[1] Newcastle to Hardwicke, 16th Nov. 1756. Add. MSS. 32,869.

[2] 'The want of a proper person capable of interposing in the closet begins to be manifest.' Hardwicke to Newcastle, 17th Nov. Add. MSS. 32,869.

[3] Hardwicke to Charles Yorke, 5th December 1756. Add. MSS. 35,353.

[4] 10th December 1756. Add. MSS. 32,869.

[5] Fox to H. Williams, 26th Dec. 1756. Stowe Papers, 263.

[6] Barrington to Mitchell, 28th Dec. 1756. Add. MSS. 6,834.

fact came home to them, they were frankly amazed: 'What will the Whig Duke of Devonshire say to it, the Whig Mr. Pitt say for it, or Mr. Legge who Mr. Pitt told me was *The Child of the Whigs*? But above all, what will this good Whig House of Commons say to it?'[1] They also became nervous; as Barrington said, 'it both alarms and provokes the Whigs, who imagine more at the bottom than I take to be there.'[2] Finally they concluded, not altogether unreasonably in view of the insignificance of the Tory party, that Pitt's scheme was 'impracticable.' That was the universal epithet, only varied by additions, such as Fox's 'arrogant, and I think dishonest, if not mad.'[3] Even officials and men of business, in their more detached and demure way, were disposed to shake their heads: 'Another inference,' Symmer wrote to Mitchell, 'that may be made, is how far the most powerful party in both Houses, that of the Whigs, will suffer a Ministry to be borne on the shoulders of the Tories.'[4] So impracticable did the scheme appear that the various Whig factions began bidding for Pitt's favour. He must, so they argued, combine with someone; why not with us?

Before dealing with their approaches, it may be as well to consider what exactly Pitt had in mind, what was his proposed course of action, and what the basis of his hopes. Nowadays, the obvious course would be to dissolve Parliament and hold a general election. It was not so obvious then, though a good many people expected it, and some even hoped for it—Fox, for instance, who thought he might capture some of the Cornish seats.[5] But Pitt rejected the idea out of hand,[6] which at first sight was strange in a man who relied so greatly on popular support. But not at second sight. Pitt knew perfectly well that the voice of the electorate was not the voice of the people. The 'structure of politics' was against him, and he could not hope to overthrow it in a moment, especially a moment of promise only, and not fulfilment. An election might alter the relative strengths of the factions, but the new House would be as predominantly Whig as the old; it might give fresh heart to Newcastle or Fox, but

[1] Newcastle to Holdernesse, 10th December. Add. MSS. 32,869.
[2] Barrington to Mitchell, 28th Dec. 1756. Add. MSS. 6,834.
[3] Fox to Sackville, 4th Nov. H.M.C. Stopford Sackville MSS., Vol. I.
[4] Symmer to Mitchell, 17th Dec. 1756. Add. MSS. 6,839.
[5] See Newcastle to Hardwicke, 8th April 1757. Add. MSS. 32,870.
[6] 'Charles talked very properly to him [Pitt], and with firmness; and upon flinging out the idea of dissolving the Parliament as a thing talked of, he disclaimed it.' Hardwicke to Newcastle, 7th Jan. 1757. Add. MSS. 32,870.

assuredly not to Pitt. Pitt had neither the money, the influence, nor the experience to 'manage' an election, and all the evidence pointed to his probable failure if he had attempted the highly technical task of wooing the wholly unrepresentative boroughs. The probability is shown by the fact that, directly there seemed to be a prospect of an election, the magnates began to put their formidable machine into operation: 'Ought not even the surmise of a possibility of dissolving the Parliament to put us upon our guard about Sheriffs, which must soon be pricked?' Hardwicke wrote to Newcastle;[1] and Fox, now breathing fire and brimstone against Pitt, used all his influence, successfully, to defeat the return of Dr. Hay, one of the new Lords of the Admiralty, as member for Stockbridge, a rotten borough which Fox had leased for ten years from Sir Robert Henley. Even Pitt himself was in something of a quandary. On his appointment as Secretary, he had to stand for re-election. As he could not decently ask Newcastle to return him once more for Aldborough, he might have been at a loss, had not Lyttelton magnanimously offered him the seat at Okehampton which he was vacating on his elevation to the peerage.

Pitt's confidence had a threefold base. First there was the adhesion of the Tories. They were now his party: he looked to them and they gave him unstinted support. They demanded neither power nor place for themselves; all they asked was that he should lift England, as he alone could, out of the abyss into which she had fallen and raise her once more to the proud position which was hers of right. They, like Pitt, were actuated by principle and patriotism—two factors which had long fallen into desuetude in the politics of the old gang. Hardwicke was frankly incredulous. He has recorded a conversation with Pitt which brings out clearly the essential difference in their attitudes, and incidentally throws light on parliamentary management. Pitt, he said, began 'to talk of *the Country Gentlemen*; how well disposed they were to support Government; how generous and candid their behaviour had been to him; and what assurances they had given him. I told him I should much rejoice to see any number of gentlemen come to the support of the King's measures; but surely it could not be quite so generous as to be without any *conditions*; and he might lose more on the one hand than he gained on the other. He said—No conditions at all; quite free and disinterested; merely to keep the

[1] Hardwicke to Newcastle, 7th Jan. 1757. Add MSS. 32,870.

ship from sinking. I smiled and asked, How long do you compute it will last on that foot? He smiled too, and said he would not pretend to foretell; but surely this session. From all his discourses upon this head I perceived that this dependence might make him imagine that he need not go very fast towards a coalition with us or any other set.'[1] Both had smiled, but Hardwicke's was the supercilious smile of the worldly-wise man, Pitt's the happy smile of unshaken confidence. He had already told the Tories that 'he desired their countenance no longer than they approved his conduct,'[2] and he was satisfied that their loyalty would be coterminous with their approval.

None the less, Pitt was realistic enough to know that the Tory party was not sufficient by itself. He needed further support, and he found it very simply in the fears of his opponents. The old administration were paralysed; they had failed; they knew that they had failed and they knew that the country was demanding a scapegoat. They had done their best to deflect the public wrath from themselves to Byng, but they knew that if Byng's case was bad, their own was no better. They dreaded the disclosures which might be made and were accordingly far more anxious to establish Byng's guilt than their own innocence; they were working feverishly to that end. Until Byng's trial was over and the enquiry which Pitt had demanded into their own conduct had been cleared out of the way, they had no intention of returning to power, even if they could. Only under the protection of Pitt himself would they resume office, and if Pitt rejected their advances, then for the time being they must sit muzzled in the wilderness. At all costs Pitt must be kept in office, for if his Ministry fell, 'anarchy must succeed.'[3] As his second line of defence, therefore, Pitt was relying on the dumbness of his opponents.

Both these factors—the Tory vote and the Whig acquiescence—rested on a third factor, the rightness and success of Pitt's policy. The third basis of his confidence was his belief in himself. All that he needed was time. His attitude of quiet optimism contrasts strongly with the confusion, flurry and self-seeking of his opponents. 'If I were to admire one quality more than another,' wrote Elliot after visiting Pitt at Hayes, 'it was to

[1] Hardwicke to Newcastle, 6th Dec. 1756. Add. MSS. 32,869.
[2] Barrington to Newcastle, 7th December 1756. Add. MSS. 32,869.
[3] Barrington to Mitchell, 28th Dec. 1756. Add. MSS. 6,834.

find him thus circumstanced, without the least impatience, his thoughts perfectly free and disengaged, and as cheerful as I ever saw him.'[1] In contrast with this quiet confidence, Fox was declaring angrily and enviously that Pitt was mad to take the whole upon himself; not even Richelieu could have succeeded;[2] Newcastle and Hardwicke were immersed in their schemes for hanging Byng and edging themselves once more unobtrusively into power; Holdernesse was bravely declaring that though he had put up with Newcastle's interference, he would not submit to any such treatment from Pitt nor be led by 'persons of my own age and less experience'[3]; and Barrington, full of surprise at being retained in office, affirmed his intention of acting with his colleagues only 'till others can be procured.'[4] None of them had eyes or ears for the needs of the country; they were tolerating Pitt only because they feared the alternative. 'Certain it is,' wrote Symmer, 'that this Ministry has nothing to depend upon but the rectitude of their measures, and their vigilance, activity and spirit in putting those measures in execution. I believe I must likewise add, as a necessary requisite, success. With those advantages, they will be able to fix, in a great measure, in their favour the spirit of popularity, almost ever fluctuating, but ever powerful in this country; and they will be able to stand their ground in Parliament against a party who, if the new administration is not supported with those advantages . . . will be able in a moment to shake it to pieces.'[5]

Time! Would Pitt have time? Whatever time he was to be given, there was plenty to pack into it.

(iv)

Parliament was due to assemble on the 2nd of December (1756). For technical reasons Pitt proposed to meet it as a private member, kissing hands as Minister only after the Address had been passed. None the less, it fell to his lot to draft the King's Speech, and the task was not easy. Apart from his inexperience, apart from the difficulty of formulating his new policy in clear terms, he had to satisfy, or at least not antagonise, several conflicting

[1] Gilbert Elliot to his wife, 13th Nov. 1756. *The Border Elliots*, p. 353.
[2] Fox to Bedford, 4th Nov. 1756. Bedford. *Correspondence*, II, 210.
[3] Holdernesse to Mitchell, 26th Nov. 1756. Add. MSS. 6,832.
[4] Barrington to Mitchell, 28th December 1756. Add. MSS. 6,834.
[5] Symmer to Mitchell, 17th December 1756. Add. MSS. 6,839.

elements. There was the King—testy, obstinate, impulsive, and most unwilling to be reconciled to his new Minister: there were his own colleagues, as yet a group of individuals, not acting by any means in unison and at least in part secretly disloyal: there was the House of Commons, elected 'in the very spirit of the Pelhams,'[1] and for the most part unsympathetic and passively hostile: there was the Tory party—hopeful, eager and expectant and so the more liable to be disappointed: there was the public, barely represented in the House, but angry and vociferous out of doors, indignant at the disasters abroad and the hardships at home, and looking to Pitt with childlike confidence for the instant cure of all their ills. Language suitable for one might easily displease another.

There was the further difficulty of adapting his views to the facts around him. He had no *tabula rasa* on which to impress his ideas. On the contrary, he found himself in a narrow field, fenced round with commitments and strewn with the ruins of his predecessors' failures. All of them had to be accepted as facts and given their due weight. For over a year now, Pitt had been making prophecies and offering suggestions: the prophecies had all come true; the suggestions had all been ignored. He had said that the invasion of England was a chimera and the loss of Minorca probable: the invasion had not taken place and Minorca had fallen. He had voiced his forebodings for India, and the Black Hole of Calcutta had given them substance. He had pressed for stronger measures and greater forces for America, and for lack of them one disaster had followed another. He had declared that the Russian treaty would lead to a European war; and the war was raging. He had protested against the admission of the Prussian views on contraband as a dangerous precedent; and Holland and Spain were demanding similar concessions. He had urged that Hessians and Hanoverians would be better employed protecting their own countries; and they were stranded in England while their own countries were being invaded. He had toiled to secure a large army and navy and a trained militia; and the lack of them was being universally deplored. Everything he had feared had come to pass: all the preparations he had demanded had been neglected. And now the sorry mess was thrown at him, ungraciously and unhelpfully, to clear up as best he could.

How much of all this could he, or should he, put into the King's

[1] Walpole. *George II*, I, 391.

Speech? How loudly should he cry 'I told you so'? How far should he go in flaunting his remedies in the face of the dispossessed Ministers? Pitt had no doubts: invective was the weapon of Opposition; it ill became a Minister, and must be dropped. His task now was to soothe and hearten and above all to push on with the work of reclamation. He had already told Devonshire that it was for the King's dignity and repose to do all he could 'to compose and reanimate the nation,'[1] and now in forwarding the Speech in its first draft, he outlined the aims uppermost in his mind. To touch on all points and to satisfy everyone was impossible, but Pitt did his best. The draft, he recognised, was longer than usual, but 'I find it quite impossible to make it shorter, and touch with any gravity and weight points indispensably necessary to be mentioned as foundations of supply and descriptive of system. I have drawn it captivating to the people, but with all regard to the King's dignity, and have avoided any word offensive or hostile to those who no longer serve his Majesty. I extremely recommend the mention of the electoral troops in the Speech. As it stands, it will go over the whole kingdom and spread a satisfaction which a subsequent message cannot do; the length is very moderate.'[2]

Nothing could well be clearer. He wanted to give a broad outline of his new policy, with the avowed object—up to then unthought of—of winning popular support for it. He wanted no less to placate George II and show him the respect due to the head of a great kingdom. Perhaps more unusual, certainly from Pitt, was the placable restraint towards the fallen Ministers—vastly different from the venom he had displayed fifteen years earlier towards Walpole. He meant to show from the outset that faction, corruption and vindictiveness were to play no part in his administration, which was to be concerned solely with the needs of the country, and the dignity of the King. For once patriotism was to rise above party, and Government was to busy itself with measures, not men.

The draft did not commend itself to the King. He found it too long; he regarded its sentiments as 'stuff and nonsense,'[3] and, worse still, he disapproved of certain trends in Pitt's foreign policy. This last fact was ominous, and not the less so because

[1] Torrens, II, 329.
[2] To Devonshire, 15th November 1756. Quoted, Torrens, II, 342.
[3] Holdernesse to Newcastle, 22nd Nov. Add. MSS. 32,869.

the grounds of disapproval were unexpected. In the past Pitt had championed America and decried Hanover. Fundamentally, his views were unaltered, and in the Speech he made the King declare that 'the succour and preservation of America cannot but constitute a main object of my attention and solicitude.' To this, apparently, the King raised no objection; it was over Hanover that he began to develop serious doubts. But not on the lines one would have expected. Since the days when Pitt had declaimed against subsidies and argued that Hanover, as an open country, could not be defended, there had come a fundamental change. England had not only promised subsidies but had entered into a firm alliance with Prussia. For months past England and Prussia had been discussing measures for mutual support. A crescendo can be traced in the official correspondence. When Mitchell first went, as Ambassador, to Berlin (May 1756), he carried with him instructions to be 'very attentive to find out what measures His Prussian Majesty will really take in conjunction with the King.'[1] He was attentive to some purpose and within two months was being authorised to promise Frederick vigorous support in ships or money or both,[2] and shortly afterwards was ordered to press for a corps of Prussian troops to be stationed on the Rhine on the understanding that at the first appearance of the French they 'would be joined by His Majesty's Hanoverian troops and by such other forces as the King might think proper to take into his pay.'[3] Thereafter there were animated discussions on the number of troops required, and the choice of the Commander—Prince Louis, Prince Ferdinand of Brunswick or the Duke of Cumberland.

These were facts which could not be overlooked. They implied at least a moral obligation and Pitt was sensitive to moral claims. Besides, they fitted in with his convictions. He had long felt and said that if England had to wage war on the Continent, Prussia was her proper ally. Possibly, too, he already had visions of 'conquering America in Germany,' and meant to use Frederick for what military historians are fond of calling 'containing operations'—that is, for keeping France occupied in Europe while he carried on his campaigns abroad. It is possible, but perhaps not probable, for Pitt at this point was as truly experimenting

[1] Some Points recommended to Mr. Mitchell for his consideration at Berlin, 11th April 1756. Add. MSS. 6,862.

[2] Holdernesse to Mitchell, 9th July 1756. Add. MSS. 6,812.

[3] Holdernesse to Mitchell, 13th July 1756. Add. MSS. 6,812.

in strategy as he was in the art of being Prime Minister. He was confident but not yet experienced and he was to learn by his mistakes.[1] What is more certain is that the alliance with Frederick and the promises made to him gave Pitt an excuse for sending the Hessians and Hanoverians back to Germany. Their presence in England had always filled him with indignation because of the slur which it cast on the courage of Englishmen, and because it gave the country a false sense of security. Let them go back—to form the nucleus of an army on the Rhine. He mentioned their return in the Speech, and, crediting the King with his own high patriotism, made him add that he had given the necessary directions 'relying with pleasure on the spirit and zeal of my people, in defence of my person and realm.' He did not however mention the army on the Rhine, at least not in the Speech as delivered. But he may possibly have mentioned it in the draft, for it was precisely the references to continental affairs which irritated the King—not, curiously enough, because they were lukewarm but because they were too ardent. The King had always disliked his nephew of Prussia; he had entered into the Convention of Westminster under a sense of compulsion rather than enthusiasm, and now that Frederick had opened the war, was beginning to repent of it heartily. He was playing with the idea of negotiating a neutrality for Hanover; he was hankering after the 'old system' and felt a nostalgic regret at the breach with Austria; in such a mood he disliked the return of the Hessians and Hanoverians and looked askance at Pitt's partiality for Prussia. It may well be that the shortening of the draft, which he demanded, was the deletion of all reference to that army of observation which was shortly to be created in Germany. This is, of course, conjecture; but it is certain, on the authority of Holdernesse, that the paragraphs on which the King animadverted were 'those which relate to foreign affairs and the faults found . . . proceed from an apprehension of going too far with the King of Prussia and from a remaining delicacy towards the House of Austria.'[2] Truly a strange *bouleversement*!

The Speech was settled at last. It promised 'resolution of vigour and despatch' in America: it foreshadowed a national militia; it spoke of the return of the electoral troops; and after

[1] 'Pitt's strategy did not develop its full qualities until he had been in office some months.' Tunstall, *William Pitt*, p. 168.

[2] Holdernesse to Newcastle, 22nd Nov. 1756. Add. MSS. 32,869.

referring to the sufferings of the poor due to the high price of corn, it recommended Parliament 'to consider of proper provisions for preventing the like mischiefs hereafter.' All were agreed that 'by its style and substance, (it) appeared to be the work of a new speech-maker.'[1]

There remained the Address: this also had to be settled by the incoming Government, and it led to a contretemps. In the Lords' Address, Devonshire agreed to the insertion of words thanking the King for having brought over his electoral troops. Temple, who was in bed with a fever, wrote to protest, and failing to obtain the deletion of the words, struggled down to the House 'at the hazard of his life' to voice his objection. The incident has been given undue prominence owing to Waldegrave's remark that Temple's motive was pique at not being consulted.[2] There were times when Waldegrave was spiteful, and this was one of them. Devonshire had thought the words a little inappropriate but had seen no great objection to what appeared to him no more than a piece of politeness.[3] On receipt of Temple's protest, he had tried to soothe him, and probably thought he had done so. Temple was by nature angular and awkward and at times very silly, but on the whole he meant well and on this occasion at least was acting out of a genuine conviction, magnified by his fever. He felt it important, as indeed it was, to start on the right foot, and feared the effect which the words might have on the public, no doubt exaggerating their possible reaction and quite overlooking the fictitious importance which his protest might give to the matter. It is worth noting that Pitt shared his views. He also was anxious to start well, and stated emphatically that if similar words were introduced into the Commons' Address, he would resign. As this was the last thing that anyone, except perhaps Fox, desired, the offending words were not moved in the lower House.

Pitt's speech on the Address was short and by common consent both moderate in tone and excellent in content. Even Lyttelton agreed that 'he spoke like a minister,' but added that he 'unsaid almost all he had said in opposition,'[4] which is interesting for the light it throws on Lyttelton's capacity for self-deception. Lyttelton is our main source of information for the contents

[1] Waldegrave, p. 88. [2] Waldegrave. *Memoirs*, p. 90.
[3] Devonshire to Temple, 2nd Dec. 1756. Grenville. *Correspondence*, I, 185.
[4] Phillimore, II, 543.

of the speech, and every point he mentions is, in fact, not the denial of Pitt's previous statements but their repetition in a 'ministerial' form. According to Lyttelton Pitt said 'he would blame nobody before an enquiry was made, nor even till it was ended,' which in no sense repudiated his previous demand for an enquiry: 'he owned the loss of the Hanoverians would make a dangerous gap in our force at home; but that gap must be supplied,' which was little more than a mild rebuke on the late Government for rejecting his Militia Bill; 'he owned we had no ships to spare, and that the French fleet was very dangerously strong,' which accorded well with his demands for more sailors. And lastly 'he poured cold water on the head of Alderman Beckford, who had vaunted in his usual style on the grand strength of England,' which was not out of keeping with Pitt's previous attitude towards lack of preparation. He believed entirely in the capacity of the country to protect itself, but he knew that the capacity had not been properly tapped. As Minister, Pitt preferred understatement to boasting, or to adapt one of his own phrases, preparation before provocation; we had neglected to recruit our own strength, but that did not mean that the strength was not there.

(v)

With the Address out of the way, Parliament adjourned to enable the new Ministers to seek re-election. Pitt was returned for Okehampton, and then promptly succumbed to a severe fit of gout, which kept him in bed for the greater part of his short first administration.

As a genius, Pitt was a giant; in constitution he was a pygmy; his body and mind alike were racked and tortured by ill-health. The physical weakness was counterbalanced by an indomitable spirit, but after every hard bout there followed the inevitable reaction—lassitude of body or mind. His illnesses were of two kinds—physical and mental. Neither can be ignored, nor should either be overstressed: the interest of both lies only in their effect on his career. His physical weakness was a continual handicap, his mental weakness an occasional but complete obstruction. Physically, his body was warped and twisted with rheumatic affections which hampered successful action more than is often realised: mentally, he was plunged from time to time into a dark and despairing melancholia. When the fit was approaching he grew restless, unhappy and childishly dependent on others; when it was actually on him, he sank into so deep a desolation that he was incapable of any useful work. Those periods, fortunately few, were simply cut out of his working life, in much the same manner as Bunyan's year of religious mania or Cowper's fits of insanity. At all other times his genius had free play and the dark cloud was as though it had never been. But the physical handicap was always with him.

On this occasion the illness was purely physical; his mental state, as Elliot testified, was calm and unruffled; but his inability to wait upon the King or to attend Cabinet meetings contributed largely to the apparent failure of his Ministry. No one can be blamed. Pitt needed time not only to entrench himself but to convince others of his capacity, and gout denied him the proper use even of such time as was allowed. Everyone grew impatient, whether it was Frederick on his battlefield or George II in his Closet, or Holdernesse in his office, and some grew antagonistic. Meanwhile Pitt struggled to deal from his bedroom at Hayes with the three main problems that faced him—at home, Byng's trial; abroad, the war in all parts of the globe; and hovering over both, the miasma of political intrigue.

II

BYNG

However one looks at it, Byng's tragedy was a shabby affair—the murder of a second-rate officer to save the face of indifferent politicians. No high principle was at stake; no great issue involved; no one came out of it well. The villains of the piece displayed no redeeming feature: the victim offered no ground for admiration, nor much for sympathy; the most that can be felt is pity. Voltaire's summary is as complete as it is scornful: 'Dans ce pays-ci il est bon de tuer de temps en temps un amiral pour encourager les autres.'[1]

Needless to say, the virulence of Newcastle and his colleagues was in no wise abated when they lost office. Byng was too intimately connected with their downfall to be forgiven, even if they had not believed his sacrifice necessary to their own preservation. If anything, the virulence increased. Pitt was now in a position to order the enquiry into their conduct which before he could only threaten. It was therefore the more imperative that Byng should be condemned as the preliminary to their own whitewashing. Besides, Byng was anathema to the people; he had been burnt in effigy in every town in England. If Pitt were foolish enough to take his part, there was the more reason for the old gang to attack him; they would thereby steal some of Pitt's popularity.

The trial, which had been hanging over Byng's head so long, opened on the 28th of December (1756). The Court, which sat at Portsmouth, consisted of thirteen naval officers, no doubt well qualified to dispense justice to seamen charged with the usual run of naval offences, but not fitted to cope, at a moment of popular excitement, with a political *cause célèbre* warped by prejudice, whipped up by propaganda, and deliberately confused by the subtlest legal minds of the day. The Courtroom was crowded with high-born spectators; private secretaries were

[1] Voltaire. *Candide.*

sending daily dispatches to London; pamphlets were pouring from the presses and the whole kingdom was in a ferment. In such an atmosphere, what wonder if the members of the Court grew bewildered? They were uncertain of the law; they were frightened of prejudicing their future promotion; some of them were antagonistic to Byng; some pitied him; all were confused or uneasy in mind.

The question they were called on to decide was whether Byng's conduct at the battle off Minorca brought him within the terms of the Twelfth Article of War which prescribed death, without alternative, for anyone who failed to do his best in action 'through cowardice, negligence or disaffection.' There was no evidence of cowardice: there was no evidence of disaffection: but there was evidence that Byng had shown little *savoir faire* and had failed, as any second-rate commander was liable to fail. Did this bring him within the four corners of the Twelfth Article? Was a lack of brains or an error of judgment really negligence? The Court professed not to know, but they were sufficiently aware of their own fallibility to be quite sure that errors of judgment did not deserve death. In an effort to wriggle out of their dilemma they asked the Admiralty whether they might impose some lesser punishment under the Twelfth Article—a foolish question, which the Admiralty had no option but to answer in the negative. In some agitation the Court then (27th January 1757) found Byng guilty of negligence, sentenced him to death in a document which no one understood and added an earnest plea for mercy.

Their action caused a good deal of bewilderment and not a little dissatisfaction, as the Court seemed to be shirking responsibility. The old Ministers, however, remained discreetly silent. Both before and during the trial they had been giving secret advice to the prosecution, supplying hints and information to the pamphleteers and hailing each point which seemed to tell against Byng with ghoulish delight. With his condemnation, the first hurdle had been cleared, for which they were profoundly thankful. The recommendation to mercy was a pity, but could no doubt be overcome.

Meanwhile the sentence went to the Board of Admiralty, whose duty it was to consider the findings and either support the recommendation to mercy or sign the warrant for execution. They were a new body, hardly yet settled in the saddle, and being divided in opinion, did, under Temple's inexpert guidance the one thing that was useless.[1] They questioned the legality of the sentence and asked the King's permission to obtain the views of the judges. Their request may have been an effort to save Byng, but otherwise had no merit. The sentence followed the findings as the day the night. What was questionable was not the sentence but the verdict. Was the verdict justified by the evidence? On this point the judges were not asked to pronounce —indeed, could not without re-hearing the whole case. And so, under the direction of Murray, now become Lord Mansfield, they put a further nail into Byng's coffin by declaring the sentence legal—rightly on the premisses. But in spite of this opinion, when, on the 16th of February, Temple presented the warrant to the Board for signature, two admirals—West and Forbes—refused to sign and tendered their resignation.

The next day (17th February) Byng's fate was reported to Parliament, of which he was a member, and the question of his expulsion before execution was raised. On this, Sir Francis Dashwood, showing a courage refreshingly bright as compared with the blackness of his morals, moved that before any action was taken, the court martial's sentence should be considered. Pitt, who was in the House for the first time since he had become Minister, spoke in favour of the motion, expressing the hope that it might lead to some revision of the Twelfth Article. Whilst by implication he appeared to be well disposed towards Byng, his advocacy lacked fervour, and he made no effort to prevent Fox from shelving the matter by calling for the Order of the Day. Dashwood, however, was not to be denied, and raised the matter again on the 23rd of February when Pitt, 'though owning how sensibly he felt the difficulty of speaking on that melancholy occasion, with true spirit avowed himself on the favourable side'—that is, favourable to Byng.[2] Fox did his best to goad Pitt into indiscretions, and what should have been a serious debate overshadowed by the wings of death degenerated into a personal wrangle, which the Speaker very properly cut short.

Having taken the plunge, Pitt warmed to his task, slowly but

[1] Cf. 'I have talked with Lord Temple upon the subject of the Admiralty, and though I found him full of apprehension of taking such a load upon him, yet, if it is His Majesty's pleasure and shall be thought by your Grace right for the whole, he will not decline, dangerous as it is, to endeavour to do his best in that most difficult department.' Pitt to Devonshire, 2nd Nov. 1756. Chatsworth Collection.

[2] Walpole. *George II*, II, 322-3.

steadily. As the execution had been fixed for Monday, the 28th of February, there was little time left. The next day therefore (Thursday, the 24th) he 'moved the King for mercy,'[1] but the King cut him short, and Pitt, who had previously owned that he had 'too much awe [of royalty] on his mind,'[2] was easily discouraged and failed to press the point.

Meanwhile three or four of Byng's judges had been making pathetic attempts to lighten their consciences by declaring that they had something which they wished to say if they could be absolved from their oath of secrecy. No one paid any attention to them, and the only one who was a member of the House, Keppel, was too frightened to lift up his voice. On Friday (25th February) Walpole, who was not a member himself, learning of Keppel's uneasiness, asked Fox to bring his scruples to the attention of the House. But Fox had no intention of doing anything to save Byng, and so after hum-ing and ha-ing and not knowing and not being quite certain, slipped furtively away. Dashwood, however, proved more sympathetic; the House was informed at the very last moment, and, in the debate which followed, Pitt promised to mention Keppel's doubts to the King, and arranged for the House to meet on the following day—Saturday, the 26th of February.

On the Saturday Pitt once more approached the King to tell him of the Commons' wish to have the admiral pardoned. The King retorted, 'Sir, *you* have taught me to look for the sense of my subjects in another place than the House of Commons.' It was a shrewd thrust, but Pitt was not to be put off so easily as before, and in the end the King agreed to a fortnight's respite to enable the Bill for which Keppel was asking to be passed. Pitt hurried to the House with the King's message, and in his impetuosity made a technical slip. He said that the King had agreed to postpone the execution after he had been informed that 'a Member of the House had in his place declared that he had something of weight to say.' In those days it was unconstitutional to inform the King of what individuals had said in Parliament. Fox, seizing with avidity on the error, taunted Pitt much in the same way as he had once taunted Robinson. But Pitt was not Robinson. The mockery so far from dashing him set him on fire, and full of indignation at the thought that anyone could play so fast and loose with the life of a man, he brushed Fox and his precedents contemptuously aside. He had done, he said, what he conceived

[1] Walpole. *George II*, II, 326. [2] *Ibid.*, II, 325.

to be his duty, he had represented the feeling of the House and 'he should have been ashamed to run away basely and timidly, and hide his head, as if he had murdered somebody under a hedge'[1]—a stinging reference to Fox's evasions of the previous evening. There seemed every prospect of another personal wrangle, but Fox, feeling himself to be on shaky ground, bit back his anger and Pitt swallowed his wrath. The Bill for absolving the members of the Court from their oaths of secrecy was introduced and passed rapidly through the Commons.

It fared differently in the Lords. Mansfield and Hardwicke had no intention of allowing it to pass, and had devised a simple expedient by which it could be shelved. They insisted that each member of the Court should be brought separately to the Bar of the House and there asked two questions—Whether they knew any matter previous to the sentence which would shew it to be unjust, or procured by any unlawful means? And whether they thought themselves restrained by their oath from disclosing such matter? Naval officers are notoriously simple-minded, and now, brought in one by one, and overawed by the solemnity of the proceedings and the greatness of their inquisitors, they were abashed and answered fumblingly or in the negative. Hardwicke thereupon 'authoritatively put an end to the Debate; said the recital to the preamble had been false; that they had sworn there had been no undue practice, and that it appeared upon what no grounds the House of Commons had proceeded; which he hoped would tend to ease the mind of his Majesty,'[2] though it obviously did nothing to ease the minds of the officers. So the Bill was strangled, and on the 14th of March Byng was shot.

One thing is clear, that in the devious ways of chicanery the impetuous Pitt was no match for the creeping Hardwicke, who had been working mole-like from beneath, unseen except for his trail. Nor was he a match for Fox, who was now his bitter enemy, anxious and willing to bring him down, and very ready to barter Byng's life for the chance of shattering Pitt's popularity. But Pitt himself was not without blame. Under other circumstances he might have remembered the ordinary Englishman's love of justice, his innate kindliness and his admiration of moral honesty, and, remembering, been true to himself and his own sympathy with the oppressed Byng. But the times were difficult and dangerous. He had come at last to a place of power where

[1] Walpole. *George II*, II, 333. [2] *Ibid.*, II, 366.

he could do what no one else could for the country's salvation. For that very purpose he had been raised up by the enthusiasm of the people in spite of the massive opposition of the Whigs and the disinclination of the King. But he had not yet had time to consolidate his position; and he knew that in adopting an unpopular role he might cut the ground from under his own feet. Was he to sacrifice everything for the sake of a failure who had forfeited the popular vote, who had been legally tried and condemned, and whom the King was unwilling to pardon? Apart from its human aspect and a fleeting effect on political intrigues, what material difference did it make whether Byng lived or died? Must Pitt risk all for a matter of such no-importance? He was sorely tempted, and wavered, and fell. At the outset he decided to keep silence, but his conscience was uneasy, as he showed by his efforts to salve it, assuring himself and others that 'the Legislature had nothing to do to advise the King on that his peculiar prerogative, mercy' which 'was more likely to flow from his Majesty, if he was left entirely free.'[1] But Fox and his followers had no intention of letting Pitt off so lightly; they combined with his conscience—though for utterly different reasons—to push him reluctantly along an unpopular road. Each step was difficult, but perhaps made the next easier. He began by 'owning how sensibly he felt the difficulty of speaking';[2] and in subsequent debates admitted that 'he had no reason to expect any tenderness to himself or his friends';[3] and that 'for himself, he should probably smart for it';[4] and finally he asked: 'How can it be for my interest to take the part I now do?';[5] but in the end he did flame out into indignation and try earnestly to save the man. It was, however, too late. Pitt had made the worst of both worlds. By his silence and lukewarmness at the outset he had played into the hands of his opponents and made it impossible to secure mercy; and by his outspoken advocacy at the end he forfeited temporarily some part of that popularity for the sake of which he had kept his lips closed at first. Some of his detractors have gone farther and have argued that he should have threatened to resign, but the argument is false. Pitt was right in stating that mercy was the prerogative of the King alone. The King might consult his Ministers if he chose, but was under no compulsion. As the constitution then stood, Pitt had no

[1] Walpole. *George II*, II, 323. [2] *Ibid.*, II, 322. [3] *Ibid.*, II, 324.
[4] *Ibid.*, II, 329. [5] *Ibid.*, II, 338.

ground for resignation, and on every other count mercy extorted at the point of the sword was neither mercy itself nor honour for the King. The gravamen of the charge against Pitt is, not that he refused to coerce the King, but that he failed until too late to show himself in earnest, and failed out of a tenderness for his own popularity. It was a pity.

12

FOREIGN AFFAIRS

(i)

Though Byng's trial absorbed so large a portion of Pitt's first administration, it was in itself of little importance, being merely one facet of the political intrigues of the times. Far more important was Pitt's handling of public affairs—particularly foreign.

He was to hold office for four months only (4th December 1756 to 6th April 1757) before being dismissed, and most of that time he was to spend in bed. But even in bed he was able to invest himself with the attributes of a statesman. He has often been called, usually in detraction, a great actor, and there is no doubt that, feeling intensely, and not seldom intolerantly, the requirements of his position, he tended to adopt the attitudes and characteristics which he regarded as suitable. But having adopted them, he also tended to make them in a real sense his own. At this time his assumption of statesmanship was of inestimable use to England. He was now no longer the firebrand in opposition, but the responsible Minister, charged with the heavy duty of raising his country out of defeat. It was now his task to create a spirit of loyalty in an age of self-seeking, of patriotism in an age of narrow interests, of endeavour in an age of indolence, of enthusiasm in an age of coolness. He set about the work deliberately. His method was the outcome of his character, and his success to a large extent the result of unconscious influence, as all true leadership is. As one of his contemporaries said, Pitt was considered as the only saviour of England; his love of power and thirst for fame were regarded as noble passions when contrasted with the normal politician's base attachment to money, and in the new atmosphere which he was diffusing, people were convinced that 'his good sense and spirit must surely discover that neither power nor fame can be permanent without the foundation of virtue.'[1]

[1] Glover. *Memoirs*, pp. 62-3.

In the country at large, Pitt exerted a magnetic force which evoked all that was good and true in the people and brought their finer qualities to blossom. In Parliament, it was different. Being at variance with the predominant party and expecting no positive help from them, he tended to hold himself aloof, intensifying the loneliness which is the penalty of genius. His unquestioned sway extended only over a small following—the representatives of the City, who appreciated his unerring eye for the needs of trade and commerce; the Cousinhood, bound to him by kinship, by memories and long association; and the Country Gentlemen, whose hearts were in the English countryside and who came to Westminster out of a sense of duty, without hope of office, but who could and did respond with sober expectation to his dreams of purer politics, and were carried away with an upsurge of patriotism by his visions of victory over France and the creation of a mightier empire across the ocean. Pitt produced an atmosphere that was quickening and ebullient, so that here and there even a Whig politician could be touched to a mood of greatness and even of self-sacrifice. It was now that George Townshend, casting away ambition, said that 'the part he had to act was to be the servant of Pitt, while Pitt served his country.'[1] The new hopefulness even leapt over the seas, and Joseph Yorke at The Hague, hearing of his appointment, was able to flatter himself that 'as he is an honest constitutional man, and has good parts . . . he will set the machine in motion again which is at present at a stand.'[2] Pitt was felt to be offering a 'new deal'; England responded eagerly to his call; Scotland stirred to a new music, and even the Colonies paused in their quarrels. It was only in high places that the response was sullen and ungracious.

His difficulties were many. Not the least of them was his ill-health which tied him to Hayes, so that he could neither wait upon the King, nor even attend council meetings. The former disability could not be overcome and contributed not a little to his downfall; the latter was mitigated by meetings in his own room. He had a constant stream of visitors—messengers, officials and Ministers—passing to and fro between London and Hayes. Nothing could stop his energy and drive; if he could not attend to legislation, he could always turn to the work of administration,

[1] Glover. *Memoirs,* p. 73.
[2] Yorke to Mitchell, 5th Dec. 1756. Add. MSS. 6,836.

using the long hours in bed to read the files,[1] to study the reports from Ambassadors and to make himself thoroughly master not only of what was happening at the moment but of what had happened in the past. It was with this background of first-hand information that he drafted his letters and issued his instructions to Whitehall officials, to colonial Governors, to Ambassadors, to admirals and generals. Not only did he study to make himself master of the facts, but he strove hard to give his correspondents an understanding of their own position, so that they might act with the firmness which comes from knowledge, and enjoy the confidence in their leader which would enable them to accept responsibility. They, too, were to share in the new deal.

(ii)

Pitt had laid down the broad outlines of his policy at the opening of Parliament, and either because of his skill in presentation or because of the obtuseness of his ill-wishers, it seemed to be Newcastle's policy without any change. 'The measures,' wrote Barrington, 'as declared and explained by Mr. Pitt the first day of the session differ in nothing from those of the last administration. Every effort in America consistent with our safety at home, every effort at sea, and whatever this country can do besides, given to the support of our allies on the Continent.'[2]

In spite of Barrington, there was a difference. It consisted in scope and emphasis; America was to come first and was to be treated with an earnestness which had hitherto been singularly lacking, while the European situation was to be regarded only in so far as it affected our imperial struggle.[3] Gradually the difference became clearer. Holdernesse who, like Barrington, had formed definite views on Pitt's supposed *volte face*, visited him at Hayes to discuss points of business. He went complacently, but the visit was an eye-opener, and he returned with the despondent conviction that upon closer examination Pitt's opinions were not what he had been given to understand, and in some essential points would not 'come up to the King's expectations.'[4]

Pitt showed his sense of urgency and the new trend of his

[1] Cf. Pitt to Sir B. Keene, 14th Dec. 1756: 'Nothing could give me more joy on my entrance into my office, than to trace in the papers of it etc. etc.' Chatham. *Correspondence*, I, 211.

[2] Barrington to Mitchell, 28th Dec. 1756. Add. MSS. 6,834.

[3] Corbett, I, 151.

[4] Holdernesse to Newcastle, 12th Dec. 1756. Add. MSS. 32,869.

policy at once. Within three days of kissing hands as Minister he had issued a circular letter to all Governors and commanders in America, telling them of his appointment and sending them copies of the King's Speech and the Addresses in the two Houses. They now had in their hands the official programme, written in that 'captivating' language which Pitt had purposely employed. A second letter soon followed, promising troops for the next campaign, which Pitt clearly visualised and as clearly outlined. All available troops, regular and colonial, were to be concentrated at Halifax where they would be reinforced by new regiments from England. The objectives of the combined force were to be first Louisburg and then Quebec. Whilst they were so employed, operations in all other fields were to be restricted to defence so that manpower should be neither wasted nor dispersed.[1] Following on the promise of troops and the plan of campaign, went letters requesting the provincial assemblies to raise as many men as possible so that they could make a substantial contribution to the main expedition as well as defend their own territories. In the arrangements Pitt included a proviso founded upon one of his basic principles of empire—the equality of all its members. The colonials were British subjects, and as such entitled to the respect due to fellow citizens; they were not to be ordered about; they were to be led; and they were to be offered the sort of inducement which would appeal to Englishmen. Though they were engaged on work which would ultimately benefit themselves, it would take them away from home and involve them in special hardships and special expenses. It would not be right to impose too heavy a burden upon them, and so they were to be assured that 'as a further encouragement . . . the raising of the men, their pay, arms and clothing will be all that will be required for this campaign on the part of the several Provinces, measures having been already taken for laying up magazines of stores, and provisions of all kinds at the expense of the Crown.'[2]

There followed a long pause, and the reason was not obstruction in America, or in the Commons, but higher up. Pitt, in planning his campaigns, left nothing to chance; 'he ascertained beforehand the force required for each successive undertaking; and he provided that force, and something over.'[3] That was his

[1] Corbett, I, 166.
[2] Pitt to the various Governors, 4th Feb. 1757. Kimball, I, 3 ff.
[3] Sir G. O. Trevelyan. *George III and Charles Fox,* I, 17.

ideal, which he was now striving to put into practice for the first time—and he found himself tied hand and foot. The army was not under his control: Cumberland as Captain-General could and did thwart Pitt's plans. 'The Duke,' so Newcastle told Hardwicke, 'will not part with more than four regiments from hence. The new Lord Lieutenant of Ireland [the Duke of Bedford] will spare only one thousand men from thence, and the old Governor of Scotland [the Duke of Argyll] cannot muster up above two thousand of his Highland friends which altogether will not amount to much above 6,000 men. Mr. Pitt insists upon 8,000.'[1] As with the army, so with the militia. Townshend's Bill was reintroduced, but it was not finally passed until the following June (1757), and then much modified by the Lords. As in England, so in Scotland, where Pitt proposed to recruit three new regiments among the clans. The design was not new; it had been tried in 1744, when Loudoun had raised a regiment which the next year had deserted with bag and baggage to the Young Pretender. Everyone had since fought shy of the idea, and Hardwicke now, in true lawyer fashion, put Pitt in mind of Loudoun's failure. But Pitt was not impressed. Any Scotsman, and Highlanders in particular, would find all the difference in the world between fighting their own Bonnie Prince Charlie in Scotland and the French in Canada. They would enlist gladly enough, and Hardwicke must comfort himself with the hope that the greater part of them would remain in North America—dead. Pitt not only believed in them, but would show his confidence by putting them under their own native chieftains—even Fraser, the son of the old rebel beheaded on Tower Green. Loyalty would never be won by half-hearted measures, and never lost by implicit trust. Hardwicke might throw up his hands in horror, but he had to admit that 'this scheme will gain the Scotch'—an unwilling tribute to a move which he feared both for itself and as adding to Pitt's popularity.[2]

Cumberland was not so apprehensive, though not for that reason the more accommodating. He approved the scheme in principle, but raised objections in detail. He was equally obstructive when Pitt wished to obtain troops from Ireland. With growing indignation, Pitt protested to the Duke of Devonshire: 'Understanding that it is intended to trust the completing the six battalions in

[1] Newcastle to Hardwicke, 4th Jan. 1757. Add. MSS. 32,870.
[2] Hardwicke to Newcastle, 6th Dec. 1756. Add. MSS. 32,869.

Ireland to the success of the Press Act, I cannot delay a moment to trouble your Grace on this interesting affair. This method of augmenting the body to 6,000 men cannot be in time, as the expedition ought to sail in February. It also tends to render indifferent corps, consisting of new men for the most part, still less fit for service. . . . I cannot, in duty to the King and to my country, acquiesce to a flat negative upon the only methods of giving effect to the expedition in due season, namely, sending another battalion, and the Americans, amounting to about 400 men. I also beg leave to observe to your Grace that the train is quite inadequate to the service; but twelve pieces, 24-pounders, and other species much too stinted. I am confident I may speak freely to your Grace because I know you love your country and are as much convinced as I am that efforts in America alone can save us. I must therefore use the plainness of a man who means right, without any particular views, and declare that I cannot acquiesce to a negative upon sending another battalion and a bigger battering train etc. to America, let that negative arise where it may. The ruin of the Kingdom shall not lie at my door but on those who obstruct and defeat a resource so obvious and ready on the spot.'[1] In spite of his efforts, he was not successful. The expedition which 'ought to sail in February' did not sail until the 16th of April—ten days after he had been dismissed, and arrived so late that the campaign which was to have captured Louisburg and Quebec in 1757, so far from achieving success ended in further disaster.

The experience of his first short administration emphasised for Pitt the need to bring the command of the army properly under control. A system which entrusted policy to the Minister in Parliament, and the means of carrying out that policy to the Duke of Cumberland outside Parliament, each supreme in his own sphere and only reconciled in the person of the King, was not a workable system in time of war; there must be a single directing mind, whether it were the mind of an individual or the joint mind of a Cabinet.

(iii)

Pitt's American strategy was linked with, and depended upon, the 'effort at sea,' to which Barrington had referred. Pitt had been

[1] Pitt to Devonshire, 30th Jan. 1757. Chatsworth Collection.

greatly dissatisfied with the handling of the navy under Newcastle. The disposition of the ships, the use made of them, and the programme for the future had all, in his view, been defective. Too large a force had been concentrated in home waters, on the assumption—unfounded as Pitt believed—that France would invade England. With such a concentration it was not possible to seize and maintain the command of the sea which Pitt regarded as essential. The navy was being wasted. Its primary function was not to be a mere static means of defence but to become the foundation for an offensive strategy. Nor had he any doubt what that strategy should be. There was only one which held out any hope of real and final victory. War on the Continent could never be decisive because England was much inferior to France in manpower. Fighting in Europe, at a distance from her own base, against superior strength, she had no prospect of success. There was not even an objective, since there was no part of France which she could hope to conquer. Continental warfare must therefore be largely purposeless, and presupposed all those alliances and subsidies which, whatever they might achieve in theory, had never been successful in practice. In place of this aimless and endless shadow-fighting, Pitt set before himself a single objective, dazzling but limited—the conquest of Canada and the French West Indian Islands—and in his strategy the navy was to ensure that England could, and France could not, concentrate an overwhelming force at the right place and at the right time. There would then be no need of alliances or subsidies; all would lie in the hands of Englishmen, who would be fighting for a rich prize which need not be shared with allies, or restored as useless, when peace returned. To achieve this end, the navy's role must be offensive. If possible, the French navy must be brought to battle and defeated; if not, it must be bottled up in its own ports by a close blockade. Hence the beginnings of that system which rose to its highest perfection under St. Vincent and Nelson in the Napoleonic wars. But before the system could be perfected, Pitt had much to learn and much to do. Fortunately, he was not faced with the difficulties which he experienced in dealing with the army. His brother-in-law, Temple, was at the head of the Admiralty and might be expected to give loyal, if not always wise, support. Moreover, Anson's choice of admirals had been more enlightened than Cumberland's choice of generals. Pitt had a number of able seamen at his command. Between them they set to work to shackle the French navy, to cripple French trade and to open the way for British forces to cross the seas in whatever direction Pitt desired. Ultimately they succeeded, but it took time.

(iv)

Command of the sea was no less essential if Pitt was in any sense to support our one ally on the Continent, Frederick of Prussia. It was necessary even for the temporary task of returning the Hanoverians and Hessians to their own country. He had promised, in the King's Speech, that they should go, and indeed they were to form the nucleus of the Army of Observation which was to protect Frederick's flank and Hanover's western frontier.

Their dispatch was a tedious affair. The King was by no means sure that he wanted them to go, for he had not yet made up his mind what his relations with Prussia were to be. The Whigs, too, were doubtful: under their system these mercenaries were the main protection of England against invasion; their departure would strip the country of its defences and was to be viewed with apprehension. Last but by no means least, there was a shortage of transports. Pitt, however, was determined that go they must; their presence in England affronted him, besides hindering the progress of the Militia Bill, while their presence in Germany would serve several purposes—they would support our ally, they would protect Hanover and they would give the French pause. Orders therefore were given at an early date for their dispatch as soon as transports were available. In the meantime they had other needs which Pitt noted, and met. Newcastle had brought them over to England without making proper provision. During the summer they had lived in camp; but they needed winter quarters. None were available, and under the law as it stood, billets could be commandeered only for men on the establishment. The conditions in which the troops were now living was a public scandal, news of which had even reached the Continent, increasing Frederick's suspicions and adding to Mitchell's worries: 'The usage the foreign troops have met with in England occasions most disagreeable reflexions,' he wrote in perplexity. 'What they are said to have suffered is so contrary to justice and the laws of humanity and hospitality that I cannot believe the facts alleged are true, unless the genius of England be entirely changed. Pray tell me what I should say, or if I should be silent.'[1] Such a state of affairs was trebly abhorrent to Pitt; it was untidy administratively, it outraged his sense of decency, and it made trouble on the Continent. Yet even in rectifying Newcastle's sins of omission, he found himself faced with dilemmas. While still in opposition, he had thundered against the importation of mercenaries, and now in power he was sending them away. How could he in the circumstances introduce general legislation to enable foreign troops to be billeted in England? The only way was to relate the Bill to the troops actually present and to limit its duration to the period of 'their *continuance here,* and *until their departure*.'[2] In this form he was sure that the Tories would be 'quite for it,' while the old gang would have to hold their tongues, recognising that the Bill was a reflection on themselves. In the event only Fox and his followers made trouble, pretending that Pitt had hidden aims and that the Bill was merely a blind to enable other troops, Dutch and the like, to be imported later on. Pitt, from his bed, warned his lieutenants, Legge and Barrington, 'to keep the words, the *said* foreign troops, and to adhere inflexibly to maintain the Bill throughout, relative only'; if they did so, 'Fox's attempt to gravel us will be baffled.'[3] The Bill was passed and the soldiers given some measure of comfort till they sailed.

(v)

Their departure was linked with the twin problems of Hanover and the Prussian alliance, which greatly exercised both the King and Frederick, and greatly complicated Pitt's task. The war was not going as Frederick had planned. He had entered Saxony partly because it was the easiest route to Austria, partly because he hoped to induce Frederick Augustus II, Elector of Saxony and King of Poland, to throw in his lot with him. He offered tempting terms, but without success. Saxony resisted, and held out long enough to disrupt Frederick's campaign. He had reckoned that if he could pass freely through Saxony, he would be able to encounter the two Austrian armies separately and defeat them in detail, so ending the war and forcing an early peace. But the Saxon resistance gave the heavy-footed Marshal Browne time to lumber up and bring him to battle in a disadvantageous terrain and when only part of his own forces were available. The battle

[1] Mitchell to Holdernesse, 2nd Jan. 1757. Add. MSS. 6,806.
[2] Pitt to Grenville, 12th Dec. 1756. Grenville. *Papers,* I, 187.
[3] Pitt to Grenville, 15th December 1756. Grenville. *Papers,* I, 188.

of Lobositz, on the 1st of October, was indecisive, though the honours perhaps rested with Frederick; but while both retired to lick their wounds, Frederick had still to deal with the small Saxon army besieged in Pirna. When they surrendered a fortnight later (16th October) the season was too far advanced for further action. The campaign had yielded Frederick nothing of real profit.

The winter added to his disappointments. Sweden and the Catholic Princes of the Empire joined the coalition against him. His military position was becoming precarious, but at least he knew where he stood. What exasperated him beyond endurance was the enigma of English politics. He and his uncle had been brought together by something not unlike a tragedy of errors. What had been the result? So far as Frederick was concerned he had long ago written off the Russian treaty. The only good he now expected from it was the use he could make of Hanbury-Williams as a link with the Grand Duke and Duchess and as a channel for bribing Russian generals. Failing any benefit from the Russian treaty, what other help could he reasonably expect? He suggested a number of things. He wanted a squadron in the Baltic to threaten Russia and keep Sweden quiet; he wanted Denmark to be won over; he wanted England to moderate the rules regarding contraband of war in Holland's favour, so that she might have some inducement to act with him; he wanted descents on the coasts of Normandy and Brittany; he thought the English might snap up Corsica in exchange for Minorca and that something—he was not sure what—might be attempted in Africa, America and Asia; he would like diplomatic action to induce the King of Sardinia to threaten France, and the Porte to threaten Austria; above all he wanted an army of German mercenaries on the Rhine, nominally to protect Hanover but actually to divert the French from Prussia.[1]

Instead of warlike preparations on these lines, all the news from England was of political turmoil as inexplicable as it was unintelligible; and out of the turmoil emerged Pitt, the well-known opponent of any action on the Continent. Frederick pressed anxiously for information, and all Mitchell could squeeze out of Holdernesse was most unsatisfying ragtags and bobtails: 'touch lightly upon the subject [of our internal dissensions] to the King; tell him something of our parties; talk of Pitt, Fox etc;

[1] Notes by Frederick, 29th Dec. 1756. Add. MSS. 6,845.

tell him what you have seen and what you know of men and manners in this country, but don't let him take any alarm at our wild, inconsiderate, precipitate way of acting.'[1] Or again, 'Mr. Pitt has got the gout and is confined. Preach a few days longer patience at Berlin. Things must, nay, they shall, clear up.'[2] No wonder that at times Frederick's irritation, and indeed his growing fear, burst out into strong language: 'Mon Dieu, il me semble que dans le moment present tout homme bien intentioné pour les interets de sa nation et pour ceux de l'Europe devroit quiter tout interet personel pour ne songer qu'a un interet devant lequel tout les autres devreroient se taire.'[3]

Pitt's assumption of office led to no immediate improvement. The King was holding back. The more he looked at the Convention of Westminster, the more it appeared to him like a dreadful mistake. Its sole object had been to preserve Hanover from invasion, and now, owing to Frederick's precipitate action, it was becoming the sole reason for Hanover's destruction. In the King's eyes Frederick had always been a most objectionable nephew, and was now once again up to his selfish tricks, without a thought for his old uncle; instead of shielding Hanover, he was turning it into a shield for himself, a highly disagreeable and quite unwarranted proceeding. Moreover, the nearer the danger approached, the more stridently the Electoral Ministers clamoured for neutrality and the more fervently George longed to lift Hanover out of the cauldron. He was full of doubts, and they were not allayed by Pitt's promotion; he not only disliked the man, but was convinced that he would not 'do my German business.'[4] How then could he face the prospect of war on the Continent with Hanover in the thick of it, like a defenceless lamb among wolves? He was tossed and racked with uncertainties, refusing to take definite action and leaning towards neutrality.

Meanwhile, what of Pitt? His views were very much in the making; he was feeling his way. Undoubtedly he had a genius for strategy, but even genius improves with practice, and there can be no denying that in 1756 Pitt was remarkably inexperienced. What is noteworthy is his willingness to learn, his capacity to grasp the ideas of others and put them into operation. Scarcely anything he did was wholly new in conception, but he brought

[1] Holdernesse to Mitchell, 3rd Nov. 1756. Add. MSS. 6,832.
[2] Holdernesse to Mitchell, 16th Nov. 1756. Add. MSS. 6,832.
[3] Frederick to Mitchell, 10th Nov. 1756. Add. MSS. 6,843.
[4] Newcastle to Hardwicke, 14th October 1756. Add. MSS. 32,868.

to everything a vigour and determination which were irresistible, and a meticulous care in preparation which ensured ultimate success. As to his strategy, there can be little doubt, if words mean anything, that until the Convention of Westminster, which he did not welcome, Pitt had visualised the coming war with France as one which should be fought solely in America; Hanover was to be left to itself for redemption at the return of peace. The position had been radically altered, first by the Convention of Westminster which tied England in some sort to Prussia, and then by the Treaty of Versailles which roped France into the coalition against Frederick. It did not require much genius to see that the more France was preoccupied with Frederick in Europe, the less attention she could pay to England in America; or that the longer Frederick could hold out, the longer Pitt would have for his own purposes. If therefore Pitt could support Frederick without weakening his own offensive, of course he would do so. He had every inducement—loyalty to an ally, a compliment to the King, and the promotion of his own ends. And fortunately he had the means in the Hanoverian and Hessian troops, if the King, as Elector, would agree.

It was on this point that the tug-of-war came. The King, and of course Pitt, was well aware that the Hanoverians and Hessians by themselves could not hope to withstand France. They needed assistance; where was it to come from? Frederick had talked of a Prussian contingent, but his offers had been vague, and the King was suspicious. The German Princes showed no great willingness to help and Holland some degree of reluctance. As for England, Pitt set his face like a flint against contributing one single British soldier; all were needed for America. Without adequate forces, was not neutrality inevitable? Pitt hoped not, but there was little he could do to settle the issue, and the struggle in the King's mind was not resolved until the end of the year. Not until the 31st of December (1756) could Holdernesse tell Mitchell of 'His Majesty's resolution upon the most material and most pressing object of your present negotiations; I mean, the assembling an army to oppose the views of France in Westphalia.' After much deliberation the King had decided that the safest method would be 'to follow as near as possible the plan laid down by the King of Prussia'; and so the Hanoverian forces, 'the small force' which His Majesty and his allies could collect, would be assembled upon the Lippe, 'there to be ready to act as occasion may require.'[1] The King had been brought to this conclusion with pain and grief. Only two days earlier, Holdernesse had found him 'more perplexed and less resolved what to do . . . but less willing than ever to enter roundly into measures with the King of Prussia';[2] and not many days later he was to be thrown into fresh perplexity on receiving 'overtures . . . tending to an accommodation' from d'Affry, the French Minister at The Hague, which cost the old King many a pang. At last, however, he was screwed up to answer firmly that he had endeavoured to avoid the war, and would not be averse to put an end to it, but 'will by no means listen to an accommodation, unless His Majesty's allies are likewise included therein, the King being determined to keep in the strictest manner the engagements His Majesty has contracted with the King of Prussia.' So the Cabinet were instructed to reply, but Pitt, who had been scared that the King might give way, persuaded them to add their humble and at first sight inconsequent advice that as this overture might have been made with insidious views, the King 'would please rather to quicken than to slacken the execution of the intended expedition to America.'[3] Inconsequent, but to Pitt the whole essence and *raison d'être* of the war. If peace was likely to supervene, America must be conquered in a hurry.

Pitt's troubles were not yet at an end. The matter of paying for the Hessians had to come before Parliament. An ironical fate decreed that it should be brought up on the first day that Pitt's gout allowed him to appear in the House. Pitt knew enough of human nature and the wiles of publicists to foresee the kind of jeer which Walpole has enshrined in his *Memoirs*, and which Fox embellished: 'Mr. Pitt had come that very day to the House of Commons for the first time since his illness, and as it was the first time since he was Minister of his acting there in office, it could not fail of being remarked, that he dated his Administration with a demand of money for Hanover.'[4] Pitt would fain have saved himself, if he could. He tried to persuade the King to accept a lump sum for war purposes and to pay the Hessians out of it. But the King refused. Pitt thereupon grasped his nettle firmly, and by being open and sincere gained a notable success. In moving the grant of £200,000 to the King of Prussia he pointed

[1] Holdernesse to Mitchell, 31st Dec. 1756. Add. MSS. 6,813.
[2] Holdernesse to Newcastle, 29th Dec. 1756. Add. MSS. 32,869.
[3] Cabinet Minute, 6th Feb. 1757. Add. MSS. 6,832.
[4] Walpole. *George II*, II, 313.

out that we should save half by stopping the subsidy to Russia. At the same time he stated his intention to increase the number of Hessians from 8,000 to 12,000—but 'this is the whole and only expense that we are to be at for Foreign Affairs,' and in return for this the King would provide 36,000 Hanoverians at his own expense. These forces, augmented by 12,000 Prussians, would form an Army of Observation in Westphalia, 60,000 strong, to act against the French if they should attempt to invade the Empire. 'You can't,' said Jenkinson, 'conceive what universal applause all these propositions met with. Mr. Fox tried to hint some objections, but he was fallen foul of by Mr. Vine among the Tories and by Mr. Beckford in the name of the City and the whole vote was universally approved of as being just the happy medium in which we ought to steer, and passed unanimously being the first subsidy vote that ever did pass so through a British House of Commons.'[1] For the moment at least Pitt seemed firmly settled in the saddle.

[1] Jenkinson to Sanderson Miller, 19th Feb. 1757. Dickins and Stanton, p. 354.

13

A COURT INTRIGUE

Appearances were deceptive; barely six weeks later Pitt's first administration had come to an end. Before asking the reason, it may be as well to consider what he had to his credit. Not much at first sight. He had failed to save Byng; he had done nothing to 'impeach the character of his predecessor'; he had not yet procured his Militia Bill; and his visible achievements were all connected with Hanover—a matter for malicious mirth to his detractors. It was a poor bag for a professed patriot. But there was much more beneath the surface. 'During this quiet course,' wrote Symmer, 'or, as some call it, remission of business in Parliament, the active part of government is said to admit of no relaxation. The Lords of the Admiralty meet early and continue their Boards till late at night. It is likewise said that Mr. Pitt is not hindered by his gout to give all due attention to the arrangements proper to be made with regard to carrying on the war successfully, especially in America.'[1] In four short months Pitt had outlined his strategy and laid the foundations. No plan was too great, no detail too small for him. All came under his own eye, whether it were the 'despairing account' of Indian affairs sent by the East India Company in December (1756) or the petition for help from Jamaica in January (1757) or the suggestion in February of a certain Mr. Cumming for attacks on the French trading settlements in West Africa, or Admiral Holburne's request in March for fishing seynes to help in the fight against scurvy. He saw to everything from his bed at Hayes—reinforcements for America, a speeded up programme of shipbuilding, the creation of the Army of Observation in Germany, the provision of a squadron for Indian waters. In all directions there was activity and the promise of things to come. Even the lukewarm Holdernesse was moved to admit that 'our unwieldy machine

[1] Symmer to Mitchell, 21st Jan. 1757. Add. MSS. 6,839.

is at last set agoing and will now roll on and move straight by its own weight.'[1] Yet on the 6th of April 1757 Pitt fell. Why?

When Pitt first took office, Walpole had prophesied that 'unless Mr. Pitt joins with either Fox or Newcastle, his ministry cannot last six months.'[2] The forecast seemed to come true and has been very generally, though not universally, accepted ever since. In modern times Lecky has expressed this view tersely enough: 'the opposition of the great Pelham interest, and the ambiguous attitude of Fox, were fatal to the Government.'[3] Yet no statement could well be less accurate. That Newcastle and his Whigs could have defeated Pitt is indubitable, though their capacity was probably on the wane; but it is no less indubitable that they did not defeat him, did not even try to defeat him, and, when he fell, refused point-blank to take office unless he would come back with them. As for Fox, the only ambiguity discernible in his conduct is the fact that twice he left London in a pet because his schemes seemed to be going awry and twice after a very small dose of rustication he returned to the fray.

Those who are not impressed by Walpole's prophecies generally regard the King or the Duke of Cumberland as the villain in the piece. George II, so their argument runs, could not abide either Pitt or Temple; they were rude and overbearing, and so he got rid of them. The argument ignores the fact that, owing to his gout, Pitt rarely saw the King; he was said to have entered the Closet only six times and then was unduly obsequious rather than rude. The theory rests upon Waldegrave's *Memoirs*. According to those *Memoirs*, the King told him in February (1757) that he was determined to dismiss both Pitt and Temple. He gave his reasons: 'the Secretary made him long speeches, which possibly might be very fine, but were greatly beyond his comprehension; and his letters were affected, formal and pedantic.' Waldegrave was a simple-minded man who really seems to have thought this a sufficient reason for dismissing a Prime Minister. Whether the King really thought so is another matter. The case against Temple was blacker. The King found him so disagreeable a fellow that there was no bearing him; he was pert and sometimes insolent when he attempted to argue, and troublesome when he meant to be civil; worse still, 'in the business of his office he was totally ignorant.'[4] This last was no doubt a good excuse in itself,

[1] Holdernesse to Mitchell, 22nd Feb. 1757. Add. MSS. 6,832.
[2] To Montagu, 6th Nov. 1756. [3] Lecky, II, 459. [4] Waldegrave, p. 95.

but one, be it noted, applicable to all new Ministers. Had Waldegrave been less simple-minded, he must surely have seen that the King was doing his best to make a case, and was whipping up personal prejudices for want of more substantial reasons. As for the Duke of Cumberland, he is supposed—and the evidence is strong—to have refused to go to Germany unless and until a new administration had been formed, apparently because of friction with Pitt on military matters. A closer examination of the evidence suggests that while all these factors played their parts, the prime mover in the plot was Fox. We are once more back in the maze of political intrigue.

When accepting office, Pitt had deliberately identified himself with the Tories and Leicester House. He had equally deliberately cut himself adrift from Newcastle and Fox. His action took them both by surprise. They had, of course, known that he was in touch with Leicester House, and probably in their hearts applauded his wisdom in seeking the support of the 'succession.' But they had believed, with Walpole, that he must approach one or other of them; since that was the typical Whig method of stirring the porridge. The world at large supposed, and Newcastle feared, that he would prefer Fox. When he held himself coldly aloof from both, they experienced a number of conflicting emotions.

In resigning, Newcastle had been playing for safety, but he had no intention of staying for ever in the wilderness, or even of retiring quietly to Claremont. He had been engaged in politics for over forty-five years and had found the toils of Government golden fetters. It was impossible for him to leave the fascinating game alone. The sense of importance was the breath of his nostrils; shadow-fighting on the Continent was better than a tonic; fitting candidates into office as absorbing as a crossword puzzle; even his tremors and continual distresses of mind gave him a sort of fearful enjoyment. Besides, he had a lifetime of experience, and if he was no heaven-born statesman, was at least a hard-working politician with an intimate knowledge of the rules. He knew that he had a strong party in the House; if he had had any doubts, they would have been resolved by Granville's jeer that he was the only 'First Minister that had ever quitted with a majority in Parliament of 150.'[1] But he was faced with something that transcended political ingenuity—the resentment of the people. That resentment had to be overcome, or provided against, before

[1] Newcastle to Hardwicke, 4th Jan. 1757. Add. MSS. 32,870.

he would return to office. The burning question for him was what attitude Pitt would adopt, and in particular whether he leaned towards Fox. Newcastle himself would have nothing further to do with Fox—he had betrayed him; he was unpopular; there was no protection under his wing—but he might use the threat of a coalition with him to frighten Pitt, with whom he wished in due course to combine.

The process of sounding Pitt began before he had kissed hands, and followed a characteristically tortuous course. On the 28th of November Hardwicke asked his son, Charles, to pay Pitt an outwardly casual visit, and while indulging in a little harmless gossip, to keep both ears cocked; for surely 'if he has a mind to approach us, he will probably drop something or other, from which some conjecture can be made.'[1] Charles seems to have been a little dilatory, for two days later Hardwicke repeated his request in more pressing terms, adding, 'I should think it would not be difficult to convey to him that it is his interest to come to us, and our inclination to come to him, rather than join with another quarter [i.e. Fox], if he will not make it impracticable.'[2]

But in the end Hardwicke did the sounding himself. On the 6th of December he paid Pitt a 'visit of ceremony on coming into his new office,' and somewhat to his surprise was invited upstairs to Pitt's bedroom, where he found Pitt 'under a thorough relapse with one leg wrapped up in flannel, and complaining of having suffered much pain in the night.' The usual civilities followed, and then the two settled down to a thoroughly eighteenth-century exhibition of verbal fencing. Hardwicke began to explain 'guardedly' that he and Newcastle had done with Fox, and gradually, as Pitt responded, spoke 'with some freedom.' He pointed out that Pitt was hardly *persona grata* at Court, and that the Whigs had more reason to feel offended with him than obliged. At the same time, he and Newcastle 'disliked insidiousness more than open hostilities, and were desirous to support the King's Government and to keep this constitution upon its true and legal balance,' by which he meant simply that he and Newcastle wanted to return to what they considered their rightful position, and in that position would rather put up with Pitt's tantrums than with Fox's double dealing. But, little as they liked the idea of a coalition with Fox, 'violence in pushing *enquiries*

[1] Hardwicke to Charles Yorke, 28th Nov. 1756. Add. MSS. 35,352.
[2] 30th Nov. 1756. Add. MSS. 35,353.

and *censures*' on Pitt's part would inevitably drive them to it. If he might speak as a friend, Pitt would do well to reflect that 'any show of violence would create and cement factions in the Parliament and intrigues in the Court, and he had foresight enough to see how that would probably end.' In all this Hardwicke was unnecessarily anxious and possibly Pitt was a trifle amused. He had moved a long way since the old days of his virulence against Walpole, and anyhow, being in office, he knew how to be magnanimous. He reminded Hardwicke that he had already shown in his speech on the Address 'his temper and moderate intentions.' Censures and an enquiry there must be, because he had promised them while still in opposition, but they would be purely formal; 'in short he treated it as a slight thing.' Much more important in his eyes was the matter of the Hanoverian soldier, because that involved a question of principle. On that point Hardwicke was able to give him a useful warning; no doubt principles were involved, but Pitt was probably unaware that Holdernesse had acted as he did on the express instructions of the King, and unless Pitt walked warily, he might find himself in deeper waters than he imagined. Pitt was obviously impressed and no doubt grateful; the matter was quietly shelved. But, after all, these were minor points. The upshot of the interview was a conviction on Hardwicke's part that Pitt did not intend to press the enquiries unduly unless he was forced to it, nor did he intend to enter into an alliance with Fox. To that extent Hardwicke was satisfied. But equally, Pitt had no intention, for the present at any rate, of forming a coalition with Newcastle; he was relying on the positive aid of the Tories, and the negative acquiescence of the Whigs. With that Newcastle must content himself as best he could. As Hardwicke said, 'I think it not an unfavourable beginning; but it must be left to him for the present, for more pressing would do no good but hurt.'[1]

Fox's reaction was very different. Originally he had been so sure of Pitt that he had spent his time wondering whether it would be safe for him to take the lead as First Lord in the new Government, or whether, owing to the popular resentment, it would be better to lie low and grow rich as Paymaster. His schemes and dreams were all alike blown sky high on the staircase of Saville House when Pitt dismissed him with a flea in his ear. (See p. 143.) From that moment his feelings towards Pitt took on a darker

[1] Hardwicke to Newcastle, 6th Dec. 1756. Add. MSS. 32,869.

and more dangerous hue. He was now, as never before, a sworn enemy, and when Pitt finally accepted office and finally barred the door against him, he determined to bring about his downfall. Who was to take his place, he did not know, nor apparently did he much care; some sort of Ministry would be botched up, in which he himself would play such part as circumstances might dictate. His intrigues were infinite. In Parliament, he carried on a single-handed opposition, seizing every opportunity to 'gravel' the new administration, but not getting very far because Newcastle's cohorts had orders to keep Pitt in office.[1] All he succeeded in doing was to irritate Pitt, who somewhat to his chagrin discovered that it was easier to indulge in invective than to endure it. Fox was so active that, before December was out, Pitt in peevish mood had told Barrington 'that things must very soon come to an explanation; that Mr. Fox had no more friends or followers in Parliament than himself, he thought not so many; that he was ready to poll the House of Commons as well as the nation against the said Mr. Fox'; that he had been entrusted with the government, and if 'factious opposers' were encouraged to thwart him, he would retire, which, as things were going, would be the happiest day of his life.[2] When Barrington reported this conversation, Newcastle looked on it as a hopeful sign; Fox was evidently driving Pitt into his arms. So thought some of Fox's friends, and it disturbed them; Granville in particular condemned 'his old friend, Mr. Fox, and the Duke of Cumberland for Fox's opposition,' and declared that Fox was 'undoing himself.'[3]

Possibly however Fox was not as blind as he seemed. In the eighteenth century there were two avenues to success—Parliament and the Court. Newcastle's tremendous staying power had rested upon the fact that he had been master of both. With neither Pitt nor Newcastle to back him, Fox had no hope of swaying the Commons. From the first therefore he made up his mind to act through the Court, where Newcastle had left something of a vacuum. It was not difficult. Cumberland was his friend—a very

[1] 'It is said that Mr. Fox goes into the country for some time, and it appears to be the resolution of all not to oppose His Majesty's measures.' Symmer to Mitchell, 7th Dec. 1756. Add. MSS. 6839. 'As yet there has been no sort of opposition to his measures, and if any should arise, it is pretended that the Duke of Newcastle will give him, or rather the government under his administration, all the support in his power. Ditto, 1st Feb. 1757. Add. MSS. 6,839.

[2] Barrington to Newcastle, 21st Dec. 1756. Add. MSS. 32,869.

[3] Newcastle to Hardwicke, 4th Jan. 1757. Add. MSS. 32,870.

staunch friend—and Cumberland's stock was rising. It had been rising ever since the King's gesture towards Leicester House had met with rebuff, and was more particularly in the ascendant now that he was going to the Continent in order to protect Hanover.

Fox used Cumberland with great skill. He was a ready-made channel to the King's ear, better even than Lady Yarmouth, and through him Fox instilled into the King's mind the idea of dismissing Pitt. The action was deliberate. Fox, as Newcastle learnt, 'had told the King or conveyed to the King that whenever it was proper to drive out these gentlemen, there should neither be wanting expedients nor courage to support his affairs.' Newcastle had no great idea of Fox's influence with the King, but was nervous at the part which Cumberland might play. 'I daresay,' he remarked, 'we shall hear no more from his Majesty about Mr. Fox, and if it was not for the Duke, I should not think it impossible but that the King would rub along with this Ministry.'[1] Certainly there were forces at work trying, not without success, to smooth the path of the new Ministry. Pitt's offer to finance the Army of Observation was said to have softened the King, and both Granville and Munchausen, the Hanoverian Minister, were eager to follow up the opportunity which this gave. But Newcastle underrated Fox's influence. The King admired his skill, and was grateful to him for his attachment to Cumberland. He began 'constantly flinging in something in favour of Mr. Fox to Lord Holdernesse,'[2] and before long had definitely promised to obtain some office for him—the post of Paymaster at least, if that was what he had set his heart upon.

Meanwhile Cumberland had reasons of his own for supporting Fox's plot. Now that the future George III had attained his majority, Cumberland's political importance was waning. In itself that was perhaps an advantage, for the role of politician did not suit him; but by way of reaction it tended to enhance in his eyes the value of his position as Captain-General. Though in no sense of the word brilliant, or even particularly capable, he was extremely conscientious in the performance of his duties. He had tried to reorganise the army and bring officers and men alike up to a certain standard of efficiency. The measure of success which he had achieved endeared his position to him and possibly gave him too high an opinion of his own abilities. He expected not only to

[1] Newcastle to Hardwicke, 4th Jan. 1757. Add. MSS. 32,870.
[2] Newcastle to Hardwicke, 9th Jan. 1757. Add. MSS. 32,870.

be consulted in all military affairs, but also to have the last word. Unfortunately his views did not coincide with Pitt's, and friction began at once. While Pitt, unable to get the troops he wanted for America out of Cumberland, was telling Devonshire 'let the negative arise where it may, the ruin of the Kingdom shall not lie at my door,' Cumberland was complaining to Loudoun 'Nothing can be worse than our situation here at home without any plan or even a desire to have one. Great numbers talked of to be sent to you, but without consideration of how, and from whence.'[1] Possibly it was because of this clash of wills that Leicester House began to think of substituting Ligonier for Cumberland, though whether immediately or when the new reign began is not clear. At all events the idea was mooted; Bute actually hinted at it to Lord George Sackville, who in some alarm 'conjured the Prince not to think of taking the command from the Duke.'[2] If, as one may suppose, rumours of this proposal reached Cumberland's ears, one can understand his suspicions of Pitt, and forgive a good deal of animosity. At all events it is certain that Cumberland seconded Fox's efforts with increasing vehemence, and finally threatened that he would not leave the country so long as Pitt remained in office.[3]

So far as inclination went, the King was ready to fall in with Cumberland's wishes. But he was more experienced than Cumberland and not so reckless as Fox; he knew that the mere dismissal of his Ministers was not the end. He must look ahead and know who was to follow. It had been difficult enough to keep going when Newcastle had resigned. What would happen now, if Pitt and his friends went? There would be nobody left but Fox, and the King very shrewdly doubted if Fox was sufficient in himself. Nevertheless, the King was ready to 'explore avenues.' In February he sent Waldegrave to appeal to Newcastle for help. But Newcastle had no intention whatever of returning to power at so inauspicious a moment. He put Waldegrave off with a number of excuses—it would be inadvisable to make any alteration till the supplies had been granted and the enquiries were over; perfect concert and harmony would have to be ensured between

[1] Cumberland to Loudoun, 23rd Dec. 1756. Charteris, p. 205.

[2] Newcastle to Hardwicke, 9th Jan. 1757. Add. MSS. 32,870.

[3] 'A decisive opportunity presented itself to the Duke; being ordered by the King to embark for Germany, and command the Army of Observation there, he made a difficulty of complying, unless he left behind him an Administration well inclined to his person and measures.' Glover, p. 83.

the principal Ministers of the new Government; the great Whig magnates would have to reach mutual agreement 'cheerfully to support the Administration and each other *contra quoscunque*'; Hardwicke and Fox must be reconciled, and if Fox was to be Paymaster and therefore in no responsible office, terms must be agreed with 'all the considerable speakers and gentlemen in the House of Commons'; and even if all these conditions were satisfied 'the Duke of Newcastle is far from being able to say whether such a plan of Ministry can be formed, and therefore can only declare his readiness to act in concert with *anybody* whom the King shall desire, if a proper and solid plan of Ministry can be formed.' So he declared in a Memorandum dated the 1st of March (1757) which he asked Waldegrave to present to the King. The King read it attentively, and 'approved every article in it.'[1] The King's approval, if it was more than mere politeness, must have meant acquiescence in Newcastle's refusal. But the King was not to be left in peace. Fox was noting with anxious eyes the various straws which showed that Pitt was gaining ground—the Government constituencies were turning towards him; foreign powers were snubbing Newcastle; members of Parliament were being won over; the King was softening; the City's attitude made finance certain. He told Dodington in some agitation that 'if these gentlemen remain two months, they are conquerors and Leicester House masters,'[2] and he pressed Cumberland harder than ever.

Cumberland acted promptly, and on the 4th of March Waldegrave returned to Newcastle by the King's order, given him, very significantly, by the Duke. The King wished him to consult Fox and in conjunction with him draw up a scheme 'with regard to the future administration, which the King would have gone about forthwith.' Newcastle was in a quandary. It distressed him to disoblige the King, but it distressed him still more to think of running the risks inherent in his return to power. He followed his usual timorous course of shielding himself behind his friends, whom he found, to his comfort, unanimously opposed to any such scheme. Mansfield called it 'laying my head down upon a table to be struck at';[3] Halifax thought it 'the wildest scheme imaginable'[4]; and Newcastle himself, with unaccustomed brevity,

[1] Newcastle's Memo. dated 1st March 1757. Add. MSS. 32,870.
[2] Newcastle to Hardwicke, 13th March 1757. Add. MSS. 32,870.
[3] Newcastle to Hardwicke, 5th March 1757. Add. MSS. 32,870.
[4] Newcastle to Hardwicke, 13th March 1757. Add. MSS. 32,870.

dubbed it 'madness.'[1] All combined to urge the King to be patient, assuring him that, whether he wished to keep his present Ministers or not, this was not the moment to get rid of them. If he did, chaos would supervene.

The King was only too well aware that no one could produce a decent alternative. Indeed the only plan put before him was one concocted by Fox and Cumberland which the King regarded as useless and which proved to be abortive.[2] It can hardly be doubted that, left to himself, he would have 'rubbed along' with Pitt. But he was not left to himself. Fox and Cumberland increased the pressure, and the King grew seriously worried. His main hope was that the obnoxious Ministers might resign, in which case he might reasonably expect help from Newcastle. He feared, however, that he would have to dismiss them, and in that event had grave doubts if Newcastle would move. 'What,' he asked plaintively, 'must be done, if, after all this delay, the Duke of Newcastle should at last fail me?'[3] No one could give him an answer, and the more he pestered Newcastle, the more determined that wary politician became to decline. It seemed to him so essential to restrain the King from giving in to Fox's schemes that on the 25th of March, in response to yet one more, almost despairing, appeal, he drew up a short memorandum, in conjunction with Hardwicke, Mansfield and Stone, in which he stated bluntly that he did not believe Pitt and Temple meant to resign, but if they did, the only expedient would be to carry on to the end of the session, without filling their places, in the hope that time would provide a solution. If, on the other hand, they were dismissed, Newcastle could only say that he was 'extremely apprehensive that such a measure at this time may be turned greatly to the prejudice of his Majesty's service.'[4]

Waldegrave presented the document to the King, who read it through carefully and then, without showing surprise or anger, complained in general terms that 'everybody thought of themselves and did not enough consider what he was obliged to go through'—a remark which is usually supposed to have been aimed at Newcastle and Hardwicke, but could equally and perhaps more legitimately have been aimed at Fox and Cumberland. What, however, is most significant is that 'Lord Waldegrave thought the

[1] Newcastle to Mansfield, 5th March 1757. Add. MSS. 32,870.
[2] Waldegrave, pp. 102-5. [3] Waldegrave, pp. 99-100.
[4] Memo. for the King, 25th March 1757. Add. MSS. 32,870.

King seemed rather dispirited and low when first he went into the Closet, and that he continued so during the whole audience but without any emotion or passion of any kind.'[1]

The fact is, the King was being bludgeoned into action against his better judgment.[2] Cumberland was on the point of sailing, and 'the immediate necessity of the Duke's journey has been made the pretence for accelerating this change.'[3] Delay until after Cumberland had sailed would deprive Fox of his lever and probably of his prize. So the date of Cumberland's departure was made a matter of uncertainty while the final twist was being given to the screw. The King succumbed; on the 4th of April with much foreboding he dismissed Temple and ordered Winchilsea to take over the Admiralty. Winchilsea had no desire for the office, but he was no friend of the politicians and rather enjoyed flouting men who, as he said, when they 'had for so many years received favours from the King and had got immense estates for themselves and their families, would not come to the King's assistance when his Majesty was in distress.'[4] So the first hurdle was overcome. The King hoped against hope that Pitt would follow Temple voluntarily, but as Temple wrote to his brother, 'we were wiser, to the great surprise and concern of our antagonists.'[5] Pitt remained stolidly on, and the King had no option but to take the unpopular step of dismissing him, which he did on the 6th of April.

So Pitt fell—not because he had failed, not because he had been defeated in Parliament, but because of a Court intrigue. Three days later Cumberland sailed, not knowing that he was on his way to disaster and disgrace.

[1] Stone to Newcastle, 26th March 1757. Add. MSS. 32,870.
[2] See especially Hardwicke to Newcastle, 9th April. Add. MSS. 32,870.
[3] Hardwicke to Anson, 9th April 1757. Add. MSS. 15,956.
[4] Newcastle to Hardwicke, 8th April 1757. Add. MSS. 32,870.
[5] Grenville. *Papers*, I, 192.

14

THE INTERMINISTERIUM

Pitt's fall had little effect on the administrative world; the plans which he had prepared moved forward of their own momentum, though much of the life had gone out of them. But chaos came down on the political world. Legge and the two Grenvilles followed their leader into the wilderness, and Devonshire's Ministry became a mere ghost of itself. No one imagined that it could last, but no man knew how to replace it. The King had created the perfect deadlock.

He himself wanted to fulfil his promise to Fox and set up what Newcastle called 'the Duke of Cumberland's Administration carried on by Fox,'[1] but he found himself unable. The 'expedients' of which Fox had boasted proved illusory. At least six different schemes were projected, and all came to grief. Others would certainly go the same way because the chief characters were all at loggerheads.

Pitt was the key to the position; his courage was needed to face external disasters and his popularity to calm internal ferment. The King was forced to deny this obvious fact because he could not restore Pitt without stultifying himself, but the political world was acutely aware of it. Pitt, for his part, was not willing to work with either Fox or Newcastle. He and his Tories had been dismissed, unreasonably, and certainly against the popular wish. He did not quarrel with the King's decision; he had never liked the idea of coercing the King; if he was not wanted, he was content to wait, but he saw no point in supporting his rivals. If the King preferred the Whigs, let them come back and do the King's business. In his 'visionary' manner, he believed in the responsibility of Cabinets, and if he was regarded as undesirable or inefficient, then he and his Ministry must go, just as Newcastle and his Ministry had gone. Pitt, in short, sat back in an attitude

[1] Newcastle to Hardwicke, 8th April 1757. Add. MSS. 32,870.

of quiet expectancy. For the moment he regarded himself as out of the running.

Fox, on the other hand, believed that his chance had come. He had ousted Pitt; he held the King's promise; and he was ready and willing to accept any office—he would be First Lord, Chancellor of the Exchequer, or Paymaster, just as the King or his colleagues thought best; he would even serve with Pitt, so greathearted was he, and forgiving! But the political world had other ideas. No one would work with him. He was the most unpopular man in England, disliked by the Commons and distrusted by the people. Even the King was growing weary of him, and Cumberland was in Germany. Fox could project Ministries but utterly failed to create them.

There remained Newcastle. The King saw no reason why he should not return as First Lord; he still had a large majority in Parliament and could easily collect a Cabinet; all that was wrong with him was timidity; he must get over that, relying on the King's favour and protection.[1] But Newcastle saw the matter differently. He had no faith in his own ability to conduct a war; disasters seemed inevitable and never-ending, and with such a burden on his shoulders he dared not face the resentment of the people. Pitt was his only sure shield, and until he could win Pitt, his majority in Parliament was a mockery. He could hardly be expected to admit this openly to the King, but his hints and excuses were clear enough, especially the way in which he harped on the need to lie low until the Enquiries were over. The King attached no importance to them, but he thoroughly appreciated Newcastle's position, and it placed him in a quandary. He could not take Pitt back without offending Cumberland, and he could not have Newcastle unless he did. There was a sense of impotence as well as irritation in his grumbles—to Waldegrave, to Barrington, to Holdernesse, to all who came near him—that Newcastle was playing for his own hand, approaching Pitt without authority, and driving everybody else out of the royal service. 'I shall see,' he fumed, 'which is King of this country, the Duke of Newcastle or myself.'[2] All of which was a brave show and displayed a certain perspicacity, but did not make Newcastle's task the easier or provide a solution to the deadlock which the King had himself created.

[1] Waldegrave, p. 96.
[2] Newcastle to Hardwicke, 8th April 1757. Add. MSS. 32,870.

When every effort had failed, Newcastle's suggestion of carrying on without filling the vacancies had to be adopted. There was no proper Ministry from the 6th of April to the 29th of June (1757), twelve weeks in all. The interest of this period does not lie in the war, which languished when it did not go from bad to worse, nor in the abortive efforts of the King and Fox to provide a new administration, but in the manœuvres which ultimately led to the Newcastle-Pitt coalition. They display, as nothing else can, the chicanery and intrigue which riddled the Whig magnates and made the politics of the period at once so revolting and so unintelligible. They also show the violence which was done to Pitt's 'visionary notions' by those who should have supported him.

Pitt, as already explained, had been prevented from choosing his own Cabinet. Ministers had been forced upon him, partly because in Walpole's phrase he had not 'cousins enough,'[1] partly in order to act as a brake. He was surrounded by spies, whose actions were rarely loyal and were often discreditable.[2] So long as Pitt was in office, these doubtful friends kept up a decent pretence, contenting themselves with private grumbling and simple betrayal of official secrets. They did not actually intrigue against their leader. But directly it was clear that Pitt was falling, their attitude changed. They had now no hesitation in throwing over that part of his theories which did not suit their ends. Not that they were completely disloyal, but that they knew better what was good for him!

The prime mover in this new development was Legge, whom the Whigs, it will be remembered, had accepted as Chancellor of the Exchequer because he was 'not looked upon to be a man entirely at Mr. Pitt's disposal.' He was seconded by Potter, an enthusiastic but not very wise adherent who was apt to jump to conclusions; and possibly by Temple, who was notoriously awkward, self-centred and unpredictable. These three, or at least Legge, made up their minds that their only chance of

[1] To Montagu, 6th Nov. 1756.

[2] Sir Thomas Robinson, for instance, receiving official reports from New York, addressed to him while he was still Secretary, sent them straight to Newcastle with a covering letter in which he admitted that 'I am under no doubt but that it is my duty to send them to the office . . . they are in reality Mr. Pitt's property not mine. But out of a peculiar regard to your Grace I thought it necessary you should see them.' He hoped Newcastle would send them back quickly so that the delay might not be noticed, and concluded 'Your Grace will be pleased to believe that I shall be careful to keep this incident an entire secret.' Robinson to Newcastle, 10th February 1757. Add. MSS. 32,870.

returning to office was to enter into a coalition with Newcastle. The problem, from their point of view, was first to get into touch with their proposed partner and then, if he proved willing, to persuade Pitt. Neither design was easy. To accomplish the first, Legge adopted mass tactics. Newcastle was approached from every side. Legge told Halifax that he would like to see Newcastle 'any night in private, provided the intercourse be never disclosed.'[1] A few days later he went to Anson with a similar message; he wished to see Newcastle 'but it must be contrived so as by no means to transpire,' and by way of hinting at the purport he said that 'there had been a *great mistake committed* in the beginning of this winter by his friends and allies in not joining with the Duke of Newcastle, and insinuated that this was principally owing to the visionary notions of Mr. Pitt.'[2] The next morning he told Dupplin that 'people must now unite upon principle,' that he had been teased to join Fox but had refused emphatically, and now 'depended upon the honour, integrity and discernment of Lord Dupplin's friend.'[3] Meanwhile, on Potter's instructions, Dr. Warburton was telling Charles Yorke that Newcastle and Pitt ought to meet,[4] and Temple was sending vague messages which were meant to be encouraging, through Coventry, Ashburnham and Holdernesse.[5] A little later Legge was trying to interest Oswald,[6] and Granby was in touch with Robinson.[7] Later still George Grenville approached Newcastle through Lord Egmont.[8]

They could not be altogether blamed. Fox, Cumberland and the King had, between them, produced a crisis as irrational as it was insoluble; 'It is an amazing scene,' said Hardwicke, 'precipitated without reason or common sense.'[9] No one knew where he stood or what might be evolved. In the scramble there was an inevitable tendency among Pitt's more doubtful followers to discard new ideas which Pitt alone could interpret for old methods which seemed to have stood the test of time.

Newcastle and Hardwicke received these overtures with carefully concealed satisfaction. Besides tending in the direction they

[1] Halifax to Newcastle, 7th April. Add. MSS. 32,870.
[2] Hardwicke to Newcastle, 9th April 1757. Add. MSS. 32,870.
[3] Newcastle to Hardwicke, 8th April 1757. Add. MSS. 32,870.
[4] Hardwicke to Anson, 9th April. Add. MSS. 15,956.
[5] Newcastle to Hardwicke, 8th April.
[6] Newcastle to Mansfield, 13th April 1757. Add. MSS. 32,870.
[7] Note, 22 April 1757. Add. MSS. 32,870.
[8] Memo. from Lord Egmont, 29th April. Add. MSS. 32,870.
[9] Hardwicke to Newcastle, 9th April. Add. MSS. 32,870.

desired, it was a salve to their wounded pride. Though they hesitated to respond openly, Newcastle arranged to see Legge at Dupplin's house, which lent itself to clandestine meetings because it had 'a back door to the park.'[1]

Apart from the Whigs' ingrained delight in backstair methods, what was the reason for all this secrecy? The answer is twofold—Newcastle was afraid of the King, and Legge was afraid of Pitt.[2] George II was sure that Newcastle was negotiating with Pitt; why else was he so unwilling to join with Fox or even to set up a Ministry of his own? Had not the King offered him any terms he liked to ask? What explanation then could there be of his backwardness but an understanding actual or incipient with Pitt? Newcastle denied the charge on his honour, but Newcastle's honour failed to impress the King, who remained suspicious. It was hard on Newcastle because in fact he had not yet approached Pitt, nor did he think the time was ripe. He poured out his woes to Devonshire and asked him to disabuse the King's mind. The result was one of those comedies in which innocent simplicity routs the dissembler. Devonshire was sympathy itself; of course he would tell the King that Newcastle was not in negotiation with Pitt, and would add that he never had been and never would be. 'To that,' said Newcastle, realising that he had overreached himself, 'I absolutely objected.' He would give no promise about the future; so long, however, as the King remained under the influence of Cumberland, so long as 'the Master of the family was absolutely resigned to one person,'[3] he would do nothing without the King's knowledge; so much he had promised. And now came this feeler from Legge. It looked hopeful; Legge's anxiety to keep the transaction dark suggested a scheme that could be carried on 'without making Mr. Pitt the principal figure in it' and 'without introducing *immediately* into the King's presence any of those who have very justly given him offence.'[4] Such an opportunity was surely not to be lost for a mere promise. Whatever twinges of conscience Newcastle may have had, they were assuaged by Hardwicke. 'If,' that legal luminary remarked, 'you had actually engaged not to enter into a negotiation with any of those gentlemen without the King's privity, I should have thought that would not have laid you under any obligation not *to hear*.'[5] It was a

[1] Torrens, II, 373. [2] Halifax to Newcastle, 10th April 1757. Add. MSS. 32,870.
[3] Hardwicke to Newcastle, 9th April 1757. Add. MSS. 32,870.
[4] Newcastle to Hardwicke, 8th April. Add. MSS. 32,870.
[5] Hardwicke to Newcastle, 9th April. Add. MSS. 32,870.

distinction which did more credit to Hardwicke's finesse than to his honesty, but it amply sufficed for Newcastle, and it explains his desire for secrecy.

Legge's desire rested on a different foundation. He had made no promise. On the contrary it is probable that he and Pitt had often discussed the possibility of a coalition. What stood in the light was Pitt's visionary notions. His reactions were not favourable, and he was now being subjected to pressure. It came from others besides his colleagues, for, as Glover told him, 'all orders and conditions of men were now united in one cry for a coalition between him and the Duke of Newcastle.' Glover thought such a coalition would be disastrous, and Pitt agreed on the ground that 'all our public misfortunes were more imputable to him [Newcastle] than any other man.' But the pressure was intense and Pitt evidently felt that he might have to give way. He had clearly turned the matter over in his mind, for he told Glover, 'Do not imagine that I can be induced to unite with him, unless sure of power; I mean power over public measures; the disposition of offices, except the few efficient ones of Administration, the creating Deans and Bishops, and every placeman besides, is quite out of my plan, and which I willingly would relinquish to the Duke of Newcastle.'[1] One must suppose from this that Pitt was gradually hammering out the conditions which he would demand. The question was how far he was prepared to go. At the date of his meeting with Glover (9th April), he was determined to keep control of policy in his own hands while Newcastle was to be a sort of establishment officer. Was that his last word? It seemed to be, from the way in which he summed up his position as he and Glover parted: 'let me assure you that I have drawn a line, which I will not pass; so far perhaps, I may be driven, but beyond it—never.'[2] Legge was proposing to drive him up to, and if necessary beyond, that line by negotiating with Newcastle behind his back. One can appreciate his desire for secrecy.

Meanwhile Pitt's stock was rising. His dismissal swept aside any little irritations which his defence of Byng had created, and brought home to the country at large how badly they needed his help. They could not force him on the King, but at least they could show their feelings. London paved the way by presenting him with the freedom of the City in a gold box worth £100, and the example was followed by one town after another; in Walpole's

[1] Glover's *Memoirs*, p. 86. [2] *Ibid.*, p. 88.

well-known phrase, 'for some weeks it rained gold boxes.'[1] Exeter preferred oak, much to the dismay of some of the Whiggish citizens who, recalling Pitt's connection with the Tories and the famous Cocoa Tree Club, thought his enemies might 'frame the complex idea of *Royal* Oak, and so misinterpret the poor intention of this compliment.'[2] The correspondent who voiced this doubt had enquired the price of gold boxes and found that a plain one engraved with the City's arms could be got for as little as £25. But Exeter 'with singular affectation' and perhaps with one eye on the rates, stuck to oak.

These presentations must have solaced Pitt for his rough dismissal, but there was one fly in the ointment. Legge equally received gold boxes. It was ironical that the one member of his Cabinet who was leading the secret revolt and pushing Pitt along a path he was reluctant to tread, should have been chosen to stand beside him on the pedestal of the country's homage. Pitt was beginning to suspect, if he did not already know of, Legge's overtures to Newcastle, and was correspondingly cool, speaking of him, as Glover noticed, 'with some indifference.'[3]

The devotion shown to Pitt by the outside world had no counterpart in the House. There everything was confusion, which Fox thought an admirable background for the Enquiries. He had contrived the matter with some skill. On the 22nd of March George Townshend had moved for papers, and Fox knowing that the fall of Pitt's Ministry was at hand, had promptly proposed that they should be considered on the 19th of April. Dodington declared that this was 'evidently throwing it [the enquiry] into contempt,'[4] but in fact it was something much more subtle; it was a method of ensuring that the enquiry should be conducted when Fox, as he hoped, would himself be in power. He had been disappointed of that hope, but the dismissal of Pitt was the next best thing, and provided him with an opportunity for white-washing himself and the old Ministers. Temporarily assuming the vacant leadership of the House, he managed very adroitly to perplex and bemuse the whole question. The debates continued on and off till the 2nd of May, when fifteen resolutions were passed absolving everyone from blame. There was to have been a sixteenth—'a vote of acquittal or approbation'—but this was

[1] Walpole. *George II*, III, 5.
[2] W. Davy to the Town Clerk, 28th April 1757. H.M.C. Report on the Records of the City of Exeter.
[3] Glover. *Memoirs*, p. 95. [4] Diary, p. 394.

hurriedly dropped when, on one of the motions, Fox's normal majority fell by nearly one-half.[1]

Pitt, true to his promise, took part in the debates, and at times showed something of his old fire, but managed on the whole to be 'gentle and civil to politeness.'[2] To some extent he was playing a part, as he had warned Hardwicke he would be forced to do. People expected him to live up to his denunciations and act the prosecutor with vigour, if not with venom. He must put up a show, but he had no wish to press his charges home, still less to dole out punishments. One of his 'visionary notions' was a belief in Cabinet responsibility, and here he avowed that he meant to charge the loss of Minorca on the Government as a whole. But how could a whole Government be punished? Dismissal, that form of parliamentary death, was the proper wages of sin, and erring Ministers could and should be left to repent their shortcomings in the wilderness.

Walpole could make neither head nor tail of this doctrine, and being out of his depth, exercised his journalistic acumen by devoting most of his space to a description of Pitt's clothes—the coat and waistcoat of beaver laced with gold, the red surtout lined with fur, the crape sling for his arm and the riding stockings on his legs. He sensed that Pitt was hardly his normal self, but having no idea of the reason, merely noted that the drop in Fox's majority showed 'what Mr. Pitt had in his power, had he exerted himself.'[3] Many explanations of Pitt's attitude have since been given, the most common being that he wished to avoid antagonising Newcastle because he was aiming at a coalition. But this hardly seems to fit the facts. Pitt at the moment was resisting coalition and was following a line of conduct which he had adumbrated the previous December when, notoriously, he was refusing coalition. Moreover, as Walpole points out, the conclusion of the Enquiries, so far from producing a new administration, 'facilitated nothing.' Except for his statements to Hardwicke in the previous December, there is no indication of Pitt's motives, but there is no reason for rejecting those statements. He was once more perplexing historians by his lack of duplicity.

Nevertheless, the conclusion of the Enquiries did create a fresh atmosphere. Newcastle began to take heart of grace and adopt a more positive tone, almost wooing Pitt and almost

[1] Walpole to Mann, 5th May 1757.
[2] Fox to Devonshire, 26th April, quoted in Ilchester, II, 32.
[3] Walpole. *George II*, III, 10.

flouting the King, and exercising his parliamentary influence in secret opposition to both. Fox, equally, held his head a trifle higher. Pitt no longer had things entirely his own way. The Lords made a number of amendments in the Militia Bill, amongst others one slashing the numbers by almost a half. In the Commons Pitt's intervention in the debate on a vote of credit for £1,000,000 cut no ice. He observed that the amount was large, that no indication had been given of the use to which it was to be put, and that there was no Ministry whose policy might throw light on the matter. Until Government had been set going again, and it was known if the Minister could be trusted, it would be as well to impose restrictions. He would gladly consent if the money was to go on objects in Great Britain and America; but if it was to be spent on Hanoverian troops, he would feel differently. Even if it was all to go to Europe, there were distinctions to be drawn. That morning (20th May) news had arrived of Frederick's victory at Prague; Frederick was a King 'who saw all, did all, knew all.' He had never asked for a subsidy, and yet 'had raised the spirits of everybody who hoped for a decent end of the war.' It would be worth while giving £100,000 or £200,000 to the King of Prussia at the head of 170,000 men, but it would be greatly to be deplored if 'a conciliabulum of Ministers' had the power to settle over their port wine 'another subsidiary plan, at once minute and extravagant,' going to market in the summer to buy up small German Princes who would prove to be a burden in the winter. Were he Minister himself, he would deprecate this measure in its present form, which he could only call 'a surreptitious vote of credit.'[1] But Pitt's efforts to guide the course of the war and keep some control over the disposal of funds left Newcastle's cohorts unmoved. The vote was passed without a division.

Meanwhile the dreary round of intrigue for ministerial power had begun again—the whispering in corners, the scuttling up backstairs, the furtive exchange of letters, the compilation of ever-changing lists of proposed appointments. The details are of no interest; all the schemes were shipwrecked on one or other of three rocks—Fox's unpopularity, Newcastle's failure to find a leader in the Commons, and the King's whims and fancies. There were, however, certain trends which were becoming pronounced. Fox's practical ostracism was binding him more

[1] Walpole. *George II*, III, 16-19.

closely to Cumberland, and Frederick's victory at Prague (6th May) was boosting Cumberland's influence. Leicester House grew alarmed and began to take a more active interest in Pitt's fate. They could no longer afford to sit back whilst he fought it out with Newcastle. There was always the chance that Cumberland might return in triumph to impose Fox upon the King and the country; there was also the chance that Newcastle, despairing of Pitt and fearful of Cumberland, might voluntarily unite with Fox. The whole weight therefore of Leicester House was suddenly thrown into the scale on behalf of a Pitt-Newcastle coalition. Bute, that sinister figure, was moving in the background and enlisting Chesterfield's aid. Meanwhile Pitt's Whiggish colleagues, hungering for the fleshpots of office, were clamouring for him to throw over the Tories, those country gentlemen who were so confoundedly independent, and swap their disinterested favour for the mechanical votes of Newcastle's well-drilled automatons; he must be 'reasonable.'

The role of Athanasius can never be easy, and it was hard for Pitt to resist the combined threats and entreaties of practically all England. Yet he stuck firmly at the line he had drawn. If they were to be co-chefs, Newcastle might do what he liked with the garnishing, but the meat was to be Pitt's. The problem was how to ensure this division of labour. In theory the answer was easy; Pitt had already given it to Glover; he must have power over public measures, and the disposal of 'the few efficient offices of Administration'; Newcastle might have the rest. If that meant anything at all, it meant that Pitt and his principal Ministers were to be restored to office unconditionally, and while he would still have the Tories as his chief adherents, the Whigs must progress from mere negative acquiescence to positive support. In return for these concessions, he would leave Newcastle to dole out the minor offices and work his will with the whole genus of Deans, Bishops, Tidewaiters and the like. Pitt was asking a great deal, but equally he had much to offer. He had the whole of England behind him; he and Legge were 'not only the most, but perhaps the only two popular men now in the kingdom.'[1] That popularity he would bring with him, and, far more important, he was ready and willing to accept responsibility. All the trouble, all the worry, all the anxiety were to be taken off Newcastle's shoulders, who would henceforth be free to exercise

[1] Chesterfield to Dayrolles, 26th April 1757. Bradshaw III, 1168.

that lower form of power which made his spirit swell with pride unalloyed and conscious delight.

So much for theory. It presented no serious difficulty to either party. The waves of popular wrath, which had passed over Newcastle's head, had left him deeply appreciative of the narrow haven of immunity. He would gladly leave the wider responsibilities to Pitt. In the Whig system of politics, at least as represented by their correspondence, wars and rumours of wars were of far less note than appointments and petitions for appointments. In the impasse to which things had come, Newcastle agreed that for Pitt to be Secretary of State 'with full power in his Department' was a proposition 'such as must be complied with.'[1] Indeed, he was prepared to go much farther and accept Pitt's views, once so repugnant to him, on the need for a leader in the House of Commons, and on the proper method of conducting the war. In one of the numerous memoranda in which at this period he recorded his thoughts, he admitted that 'the King's Ministers in the House of Commons should be the Secretary of State and the Chancellor of the Exchequer'; he admitted that 'the measures relative to the operations of the army and navy should be previously concerted and agreed with His Majesty's Ministers' and he even admitted that the King should tell the Lords of the Cabinet that he expected them to give his Ministers their wholehearted support.[2]

The theory was easy; the difficulties arose when the theory had to be put into practice. They sprang to light directly the King, after failing in all other directions, was forced to let Newcastle negotiate with Pitt. What were 'the few efficient offices of Administration'? And when they had been taken out, what would be left for Newcastle? What sort of a figure would he cut? After all, he had his feelings. He was fifteen years older than Pitt, and till these last days had been infinitely his superior not only in the social scale, but also in the political hierarchy. It is never pleasant to yield to one's junior, especially a junior hitherto considered as a mere underling.

Pitt, true to his visionary notions, wanted his own Admiralty, his own Secretary at War, his own Chancellor of the Exchequer. So much was necessary to give him the power over policy which

[1] Memo. dated 12th May 1757. Add. MSS. 32,871.

[2] Considerations for the Duke of Newcastle's conduct, 18th May 1757. Add. MSS. 32,997.

he required. But he wanted something more. As Temple was barred from the Admiralty by the King, he must be given some other Cabinet rank, and the 'cousins' must be restored to their former posts as a matter of justice. Pitt was clear that he and they had been unjustly dismissed; he knew that his personal return was the only hope for a stable Ministry, and not only his theory of Cabinet responsibility, but every instinct which he possessed, demanded that his Cabinet should be restored with him.

To Newcastle these demands seemed woeful indeed. There were two points at which the shoe pinched, and pinched excruciatingly. In the first place, if Pitt came back with his whole Ministry, and especially if he insisted on nominating the Chancellor of the Exchequer, Newcastle would become 'the dependent of Mr. Pitt.'[1] It was a galling thought, and was not the less galling because it seemed unreasonable. Newcastle felt that if he agreed to hand over to Pitt the office of Secretary of State, lock, stock and barrel, he was entitled to have the Treasury 'entirely for himself.'[2] There was much to be said for that view; in any compromise there must be give as well as take, and Newcastle was only asking for a fair share. The trouble, of course, was that Pitt did not see any need for compromise. He knew that the full burden of Government would fall on him; he knew that his popularity was essential; he knew that he had not been defeated in Parliament and believed that he could carry on unaided, provided the King would support him. What need, then, was there for compromise, or for Newcastle's intervention? Was it not a fact that while he was prepared to return to office at any moment the King wished, no one else either could or would take his place? It is not surprising that he was reluctant to compromise, especially on any point which seemed to him important. The weakness of his position, *vis-à-vis* Newcastle, was that his Chancellor had been Legge, and his confidence in Legge was waning. What he wanted to do was to push Legge into the Lords as head of the Admiralty and put George Grenville in his place as Chancellor.[3] This, however, was not returning with his old Ministry, and if there was to be a change, Newcastle's claim to be master of his own department was strengthened.

There was a second point at which the shoe pinched. Newcastle was worried at the accession of power which Pitt would receive

[1] Memo. dated 12th May 1757. Add. MSS. 32,871.
[2] *Ibid.* [3] Glover, p. 99.

by having at his disposal one or two 'great offices' for Temple and the like. Still more distressing would be his right to fill up 'the inferior places in the Admiralty,' for that would 'stand like a barrier in the way of all the Duke of Newcastle's friends,' and the places still lower down the scale would 'lose their value, being no longer steps to rise by'; there would be perpetual friction between 'those whom the Duke may desire to promote' and those 'whose pretensions Mr. Pitt will certainly push.'[1] This was not giving Newcastle authority over minor offices; it was cutting him out altogether; his occupation would be gone. There is little doubt that Newcastle's estimate was right. Pitt had no intention of coming back unless he was in complete control. He did not regard himself as entering into a coalition with Newcastle in the ordinary sense; he was not following the Whiggish practice or the Whiggish system of bargaining for posts, but adopting a new method of his own. He was, in short, borrowing Newcastle's majority, and offering as security nothing but his own inherent genius.

The clash was complete. Pitt stuck to his point and such was his firmness, combined with his indispensability, that Newcastle felt obliged to put the plan before the King. The King rejected it flatly; he had no option if he was to keep faith with Cumberland and Fox; and he rejected it the more willingly because he was relying on a promise which he had previously extracted from Newcastle, that if Pitt proved 'unreasonable,' he would take office without him. The King, however, was too confiding, or Newcastle too timid. Everyone apparently agreed that Pitt was 'unreasonable,' that his views were impracticable and his demands exorbitant. It is surprising in the circumstances how sure they were that he was indispensable. At any rate Newcastle went back on his word. Without Pitt he would not take office. His distress was pathetic: 'I can't come in,' he wrote in a Memorandum for the King, 'without bringing in my enemy, Mr. Pitt. He turned me out. But I can't serve without my enemy. He will be unreasonable. He is, Sir. Beat him as low as I can, if your Majesty won't approve it, I can't come in alone.'[2]

The deadlock had returned. The King, in despair, tried to cut the Gordian knot by insisting on Waldegrave becoming First Lord and, in conjunction with Fox, scrambling together whatever

[1] Memo. of 12th May 1757. Add. MSS. 32,871.
[2] Memo. for the King, 6th June 1757. Add. MSS. 32,871.

Ministry they could. Waldegrave, who had never dabbled in politics, knew that he had no aptitude for the job, but had not sufficient strength of mind to resist the King's entreaties. He set about his impossible task with spirit, but was saved from inevitable disaster partly by Fox, who having no confidence in him began promptly to hedge, and partly by Newcastle, who adroitly compelled Holdernesse and a number of placemen to resign or threaten resignation. The scheme fell through. All that came of it was the Garter for Waldegrave as a token of the King's gratitude for his attempt. At long last, the King, angry and discomfited, was reduced to sending for Hardwicke and ordering him by hook or by crook to produce a Newcastle-Pitt coalition.

Hardwicke undertook the job not unwillingly; he had his own axe to grind, which was to bring back his son-in-law, Anson. But he was aware of the difficulties and that he had three awkward people to cope with. George II was not in a good humour, which made Hardwicke's audiences 'most uneasy and painful.'[1] He had much to vex him. He knew that the coalition for which he was asking meant the overthrow of Cumberland and the victory of Leicester House. It irked him to let Cumberland down; it irked him, as it had once irked Henry IV, to see his successor trying on the Crown. But what was he to do? When no one would take office without Pitt, he was faced with the unpalatable alternatives of restoring Pitt or accepting a coalition of which Pitt would be the leading member. As the first alternative was unthinkable, the second was inevitable. In either case Pitt would come back and, as he represented Leicester House, the 'succession' must needs be endured. All that the King could do was to be testy and fretful, and save as much as possible out of the wreck. He would claim his royal prerogative, and accept Pitt and his friends only 'under certain restrictions, from which His Majesty declared he would never depart.'[2] He would do nothing for the pestilential Temple; if the man must be given Cabinet rank, it must be in a position in which he would not come into contact with the King. Nor would he make Legge a peer as well as First Lord of the Admiralty; he was 'determined not to do two great things for one man at the same time.' The Admiralty must remain in the hands of Winchilsea who had come so chivalrously to his aid. Barrington, who was his friend, must remain Secretary at War,

[1] Hardwicke to Anson, 18th June 1757. Add. MSS. 15,956. [2] *Ibid.*

and his honour required that Fox, to whom he had made a promise, should be appointed Paymaster.

Here was a load of trouble. How was Hardwicke to persuade Pitt to give up so much of what seemed to him essential? Yet probably these demands of the King, unfortunate as they were, had better chance of being accepted than Hardwicke thought. Pitt was generally supposed to be 'haughty and arrogant,' and certainly was unyielding on points of principle, but his hard-faced attitude was largely a façade, disguising his inferiority complex. There was another and more yielding side which showed itself, amongst other things, in a reverence for royalty that can only be described as obsequious, and would have been degrading if it had not been so patently sincere. The King's wish carried enormous weight with Pitt.

Newcastle, the second of the trio, was as unstable as water, blown hither and thither by his hopes and fears, querulous, unhappy, hurt to the quick, and yet unable to resist the flame that so attracted him. Symmer described his position with a feeling of wonder. Pitt's demands, he said, 'were undoubtedly sufficient to constitute Mr. Pitt the Minister, so that he only graciously condescended to allow the Duke of Newcastle to take a subordinate rank in his administration. Could one imagine it possible for his Grace to remain in suspence, or to waste so much time, in such a treaty? And yet there are who say that if Mr. Pitt would still abate of his high demands, he would find that the doors of favour are not shut against him and his friends.'[1] Indeed they were not; Newcastle was only too anxious to win Pitt as the one means of returning to power; but his pitiful and pathetic pride must be saved. It was bad enough to be beholden to Pitt; it would be intolerable to be under the thumb of George Grenville. He must therefore have a say at least in the choice of the Chancellor.

And lastly there was Pitt. Hardwicke had always been on good terms with him. In the various battles behind the scenes, he had always supported him against Newcastle's predilection for Fox, and in any negotiations he had always been employed to break the ground. But Hardwicke was a little nervous of him; he never felt entirely at ease; was never quite sure if Pitt's compliments were sincere; and never entered into discussions with him with any certainty of success. He knew Pitt's demands; he knew that

[1] Symmer to Mitchell, 3rd June 1757. Add. MSS. 6,839.

Pitt always made a point of the restitution of his friends, so that 'there was no possibility of altering that.'[1] Pitt, for all the suavity of his manners, was unbending steel within. There was bound to be a clash and Hardwicke had, by way of background, the memory of that interview eight months earlier, when 'there never was a more unsuccessful negotiator.'

As an old campaigner, well versed in wiles, he left as little as possible to chance. Pitt was likely to be more stubborn if he were alone than if he were accompanied. Hardwicke therefore brought Bute into the picture. It was an astute move. Leicester House was more nervous than Pitt, more anxious for finality, more ready to compromise. It neither shared nor cared for Pitt's visionary notions; its only object was to get the better of Cumberland. It would think more of expediency than principle, and Bute would therefore be more malleable as well as less experienced than Pitt. Hardwicke had every reason to desire his presence at the conference table. He was accordingly introduced and contributed much to the conclusion.

Yet, in the upshot, chance played the first and biggest part—chance and Hardwicke's skill in seizing an opportunity. At one of his audiences, the King inveighed angrily against the attempt to force his hand by the threat of resignations, and in that connection happened to remark that Winchilsea was in the next room waiting to resign. Hardwicke noted the fact, and when the King's indignation had had time to cool, insinuated that Anson might very well take his place. The King jumped at the idea—'I shall like it extremely,' he said. That was enough for Hardwicke. At the four party conference that evening—himself, Newcastle, Pitt and Bute—he blandly declared that Anson's appointment as First Lord of the Admiralty was a *sine qua non* laid down by the King himself. Newcastle was of course delighted and after Bute had agreed, Pitt acquiesced. In such fashion did Hardwicke grind his own particular axe.[2]

He did something more, for Anson's appointment left Legge in the air. Hardwicke cleverly suggested that he should return to his old position as Chancellor of the Exchequer. Recognising that it was difficult for him to object, Pitt was coldly non-committal; he had already been persuaded by Bute not to insist on his choice of Grenville, and he now washed his hands of the

[1] Hardwicke to Anson, 18th June 1757. Add. MSS. 15,956.
[2] *Ibid.*

matter, declaring that it was not for him to interfere in the Treasury; Newcastle must decide. Newcastle, hiding eagerness under a veil of condescension, said that 'if it was agreeable to Mr. Legge, to make everything easy, he would consent to his restitution.' So that difficulty was overcome.[1]

There remained only Fox and Barrington. As for the former, on hearing that the King felt that his personal honour was involved, Pitt gave way; he might be Paymaster. As for the latter, Bute provided the solution by persuading Lord George Sackville, Pitt's choice for the post of Secretary at War, to decline the offer. With his own candidate gone, Pitt had little option but to bow to the King's wishes and confirm Barrington in his old post, and perhaps did so with the less reluctance as Barrington had been showing signs of closer attachment to him.[2]

So the coalition Ministry was completed. Hardwicke hurried round to the King with the news. 'I never,' he wrote, 'saw such a change in man. He said at once with a gracious smile "Then the thing is done; and, my Lord, I thank you heartily." He is in haste to carry it into execution.' The King was not alone in his delight. 'When I look back,' said Hardwicke, 'I stand amazed at the sudden change. All our friends are in raptures with it, the Court in general pleased, and the Town more. It is looked upon as the strongest administration that has been formed many years.'[3] What was the cause of this universal joy? Was it Newcastle's return? Was it the coalition? Was it the resumption of Government? No doubt all these points played their part, but surely the main reason lay in the fact that Pitt had returned. Pitt without whom nothing could be done. With Pitt at the helm, nothing else mattered.

For all that, the joy was not universal. Some of Pitt's followers were indignant at the turn of events, and some even deserted him, amongst others the two Townshends, who expressed astonishment at 'the ridiculous and dishonest arrangement of men which is now to take place.'[4] But perhaps the Townshends, who had been described only the previous November as 'a couple of profligate creatures, who will stick at nothing to serve their own purposes of interest or revenge,'[5] should not be taken as

[1] Newcastle to Stone, 20th Aug. 1757. Add. MSS. 32,873.
[2] See West to Newcastle, 2nd May 1757. Add. MSS. 32,871.
[3] Hardwicke to Anson, 18th June 1757. Add. MSS. 15,956.
[4] H.M.C. Townshend MSS., 20th June 1757.
[5] Pyle to Kerrich, 13th Nov. 1756. *Memoirs of a Royal Chaplain,* p. 270.

representative. More important, Pitt himself was by no means pleased. From the first he had been reluctant and doubtful. Whilst the negotiations for a new Ministry had been in spate, he had 'maintained his dignity and would be sued to, not sue.'[1] When at last he had been forced by Leicester House and his eager adherents to go down into the market place and chaffer, he had made large demands, in the interests of his 'visionary notions'; and though he had been beaten down on many points, to the end he was fighting hard to retain what he called 'the essential and indispensable parts of a mutilated, enfeebled and half-formed system.'[2] It had been hard going, for nothing had been given to him voluntarily, even down to his last demand, which was that his old and trusted friend, Charles Pratt, should be his Attorney-General. On this he had insisted, so that he might have a staunch ally to confront Mansfield on matters of law. To contrive the necessary vacancy, the King had to be induced, much against his will, to promote the existing holder—the bibulous and negligible Henley—to the post of Lord Keeper; and even then, Hardwicke had toyed with the idea of pushing his favourite son, Charles, into Henley's vacated post, and had taken credit to himself for resisting the temptation. Given this last demand, Pitt had agreed to play his part 'whatever foreboding of mind I carry about me,'[3] but he suffered all the irritation natural to a man driven to accept a plan which he found 'every hour growing more distasteful and yet every hour becoming more necessary for the King and kingdom.'[4]

Had he been left to himself and especially had he foreseen the near future, he must surely have held out for all his terms, and Cumberland's fate and Frederick's approaching disaster must have restored him to power without the coalition; for the King could not have stood up to the one, or Newcastle to the other. But fate and his followers were against him. Leicester House was frightened by Frederick's victory at Prague into pushing him into the coalition prematurely, while a presentiment of Cumberland's approaching debacle made the King anxious 'to expedite the settlement of an administration at home.'[5] Impatience to be again in office sharpened Newcastle's apprehensions and made him urge Hardwicke 'for God's sake to conclude tomorrow,'[6]

[1] Walpole to Mann, 5th May 1757.
[2] Pitt to Hardwicke, 22nd June 1757. Add. MSS. 35,423.
[3] Pitt to Hardwicke, 26th June 1757. Add. MSS. 35,423. [4] *Ibid.*
[5] Hardwicke to Newcastle, 25th June 1757. Add. MSS. 32,871.
[6] Newcastle to Hardwicke, 26th June 1757. Add. MSS. 32,871.

and Hardwicke admitted, when all was over, that 'the fear of some bad success was one material ingredient with me to hasten to a conclusion.'[1] With everyone sitting on thorns, there could hardly be much delay, but the resultant coalition could not be said to start under the best of auspices. In spite of the feeling of relief, no one was really satisfied, and the general embarrassment became obvious when the new Ministers kissed hands. Pitt and his party behaved with becoming decency; 'they had neither the insolence of men who had gained a victory, nor were they awkward and disconcerted, like those who come to a place where they know they are not welcome';[2] but for all their brave bearing, they knew they were no favourites, and the King emphasised the fact by giving them the briefest of audiences; some were 'not in the Closet long enough for the door to be shut,' and even Pitt remained for only about five minutes.[3] Nor were Newcastle and his friends any more cordially received; they were snubbed and displayed 'a mixture of fear and of shame'; which turned them into 'real objects of compassion.'[4]

[1] Hardwicke to Lyttelton, 4th July 1757. Phillimore, II, 595.
[2] Waldegrave, p. 138.
[3] Rigby to Bedford, 29th June 1757. Bedford. *Correspondence,* II, 259.
[4] Waldegrave, p. 138.

15

THE ROCHEFORT EXPEDITION

Whatever the feelings of the incoming Ministers, events abroad soon presented them with problems in plenty. On the very day that they kissed hands, news came of Frederick's stunning disaster at Kolin (18th June), where he lost over a third of his army and, worse still, the military initiative. For the next five months he was little more than a fugitive, standing desperately on his guard. From the first he had realised that unless he could beat his enemies in detail, or force a peace as the result of a single overwhelming victory, he was doomed. That thought was always present, not only when he was dejected in defeat, but also when he was confident in victory. It was shortly after Prague, when all was *couleur de rose*, that Mitchell wrote home: 'the King of Prussia certainly sees that at last he must succumb before the united powers of Austria, France and Russia.'[1] His object in 1756 and again in 1757 was to defeat Austria before France and Russia could reach the scene of action, and his original hope had been that England could give France and Russia pause until he was free to deal with them himself. He did not at that time want an English army on the Continent; it would be too small to be effective and would weaken England's efforts in other and better directions. His views therefore, though reached by a different route, corresponded closely with Pitt's, whose policy he had noted and welcomed during his first Ministry.[2] Had Pitt remained in office, the atmosphere might have continued bright, in spite of George II's reluctance and the urge of his Hanoverian Ministers towards neutrality. But when Pitt fell on the 6th of April and all energy seemed to forsake England's councils, when Cumberland not long after began to show himself inefficient as

[1] Mitchell to Holdernesse, 17th May 1757. Add. MSS. 6,806.

[2] 'Since my return from Brunswick,' Mitchell had written at Frederick's request, 'the King of Prussia told me he had had such accounts of your behaviour in the House of Commons that he thought himself much obliged to you, and he desired me to acquaint you with it, and in his name return you thanks.' Mitchell to Pitt, 12th March 1757. Add. MSS. 6,806.

well as clumsy, and when Hanover developed and extended her lukewarmness, Frederick grew increasingly suspicious. What was he to expect from his spineless ally, who could not even produce a Government? And what, in the circumstances, was his best policy? It is not surprising that he began to think seriously of seeking a separate peace. Mitchell threw out a warning hint. 'His Prussian Majesty,' he wrote, 'is at present thoroughly well-intentioned to his Majesty and I am persuaded will hearken to no terms of accommodation that do not comprehend the King, his most faithful and generous ally, but the law of self-preservation is stronger than any other tie.'[1] Mutual distrust was growing and as things began to go wrong Frederick tended to become shrill and censorious. 'I see,' he told Mitchell, 'I have nothing to expect from England. . . . Your want of union and steadiness has dissipated the natural strength of your nation, and if the same conduct is continued, England will no longer be considered of that great importance in Europe. Your marine is certainly superior to that of France, and yet for want of spirit to exert yourselves that of France still triumphs. It is in your power to distress France many ways, but you have acted hitherto with the cool indifference of auxiliaries and not with that ardour of spirit which would become your nation.' 'Here,' added Mitchell, whose nerves were being flicked on the raw, 'I was very glad the conversation ended.'[2]

Six days later Frederick's hope of giving Austria the *coup de grâce* vanished at Kolin; his gamble had failed; nothing was left but tears for the holocaust of his Lifeguard of Foot.[3] Mitchell, with diplomatic meiosis, remarked that Frederick 'unaccustomed to disappointment, was a good deal dejected immediately after the battle.'[4] So he undoubtedly was, admitting gloomily that he was now entirely on the defensive, unable to help himself or his ally, unable even to angle for peace, but humbly hopeful that if George could come to terms 'I shall not be forgot.' And then —crowning humiliation!—he faltered out that, hemmed in as he was on all sides, his territories invaded, his revenues reduced, he would be grateful to learn whether in case of absolute necessity he could expect a subsidy. 'I must observe,' commented Mitchell, 'that it is the first time I ever saw his Prussian Majesty abashed.'[5]

[1] Mitchell to Holdernesse, 17th May 1757. Add. MSS. 6,806.
[2] Mitchell to Holdernesse, 12th June 1757. Add. MSS. 6,806.
[3] Carlyle. *Frederick the Great,* VII, 164.
[4] Mitchell to Holdernesse, 29th June 1757. Add. MSS. 6,806. [5] *Ibid.*

When the first despair had softened into bitterness of heart, he renewed his demand for a fleet in the Baltic, and revived his suggestion that we might 'alarm the coasts of France by means of our fleet.'[1] His demands grew more querulous as he contemplated the number of his enemies and the attacks threatening from so many directions, and rose almost to hysteria when news arrived of a Russian fleet blockading Memel. The fury and indignation which he poured on Mitchell's head were such that Mitchell felt he could bear it no longer. He asked to be recalled; 'the period,' he wrote, 'is now come that I can be of no more use.'[2] He was wrong; the period had now come when both he and Frederick were to learn that England is never so formidable and never so capable of producing the right man as when she appears to be beaten; the period had come when they were to learn that a new and powerful hand was on the helm, and that, while they had been recriminating, Pitt had been preparing such help as could be given at a moment's notice.

Three days before news of Kolin reached England, Newcastle had written; 'Mr. Pitt must seriously think of foreign affairs, in a different manner from what he has hitherto done, or the King of Prussia will make his separate peace; and we shall lose the Electorate this year, and God knows *what* the next.'[3] Kolin gave point to his remark and Maria Theresa underlined it by choosing this moment to break with England and hand over Nieuport and Ostend to the French, as pistols aimed at England's heart. The Continent was not the only source of anxiety. The first week of June brought the horrifying story of the Black Hole of Calcutta; hard upon its heels came news that the French had managed to elude the blockade and win the race across the Atlantic, and, to crown all, commerce destruction was rising to unbearable heights.[4]

It was indeed necessary for Pitt to think seriously of foreign affairs. As he could do nothing about America until he knew the result of the plans he had set in motion, his thoughts turned first to the Continent, but only because it was nearer and more immediately pressing, not because he regarded it as more

[1] Mitchell to Holdernesse, 2nd July 1757. Add. MSS. 6,806.

[2] Mitchell to Holdernesse, 11th July 1757. Add. MSS. 6,806.

[3] Newcastle to Hardwicke, 26th of June 1757. Add MSS. 32,871.

[4] 'Our trade suffers much by the depredations of the French. . . . Scarce a post comes from the seaport towns but brings an account of some merchantmen taken.' Symmer to Mitchell, 19th April 1757. Add. MSS. 6,839.

important. On the contrary, he went out of his way to emphasise, especially to Frederick, his view of its secondary significance. 'The distant operations in America are of at least as much consequence to what ought to be the King of Prussia's ultimate end in the measures he has pursued, viz. a safe and honourable peace. There is no answering for success, but at least it will be a comfort for his Prussian Majesty to know that the utmost vigilance and care has been used by the King, as far as circumstances would allow, not to be baffled in that point, which is the primary cause of all the present disturbances; and notwithstanding other intervening circumstances you will agree with me that it is the result of the great struggle between England and France that will determine the conditions of the future peace.'[1] So Pitt made Holdernesse write. Frederick must have opened his eyes, for hitherto he had undoubtedly regarded himself as the main person in the war, his army as the most important weapon, and his strategy as the only one that mattered. Perhaps he had been justified, for hitherto England had done little or nothing. But Pitt was now proposing to play a decisive part, and he wanted Frederick to understand what England was aiming at, what she could do, and what prevented her from doing more. There must be no misunderstandings, no grounds for recrimination, which could only slow up the machine.

He set out the position in two masterly letters. The first cleared the ground, dealing solely with the question of a fleet in the Baltic. Frederick must believe that it was only impossibility which prevented Pitt from complying with his wishes. He must also appreciate the general situation in Scandinavia. Russia was not the only country concerned. For many years Denmark had claimed the right to cover contraband of war under her own neutral flag, but had never pressed the point until recently. Now within the last few months she had come to an understanding with Sweden; the two countries had issued a declaration setting out their pretensions, and—more ominous—had fitted out a squadron of fourteen sail of the line and were threatening reprisals against England. Any fleet therefore which England might send to the Baltic must be sufficiently large to overawe not merely Russia but Denmark and Sweden as well, or we should merely add to the number of our enemies. Nor must it be forgotten that the entrance to the Baltic lay through the Sound and was

[1] Holdernesse to Mitchell, 17th July 1757. Add. MSS. 6,815

commanded by batteries on the Danish shore, which could not be passed unless they were first silenced. Lastly, a fleet in the Baltic would not help Frederick as much as he thought, for there was so much shoal water along the southern shores that men-of-war would not hope to get in near enough to intercept 'prams and gallies,' carrying troops for a descent upon the Prussian coast. The political background and the physical obstacles, serious as they were, did not stand alone. There was a further and conclusive reason, which Pitt recorded with reluctance and only because of his 'earnest desire of convincing the King of Prussia.' The fact, the damning fact, was that the navy was not as strong as Frederick supposed. England must keep a squadron in the Mediterranean equal at least to the Toulon fleet; one in the Channel to keep an eye on Brest and Rochefort; one in North America; another in the West Indies; and one in Indian waters. At all those vital points the French were almost as strong as the English, and there were no further ships that could be spared for the Baltic. The shortage was mainly one of crews and Pitt was doing his best to make good the 'deficiency of men from whence our weakness chiefly arises,' but he could not do it at once. In the meantime he was trying, though admittedly without great hope, to come to terms with Denmark and Holland. Frederick must rest content with that.[1]

Pitt could add nothing positive in this first letter because his strategy had not yet been approved. There was a tussle going on in the Cabinet. Pitt, in keeping with the Tory conception of the war, proposed 'to alarm the coasts of France' by an expedition against Rochefort. It was a new and startling idea from which his older colleagues recoiled with a very human dislike of innovation and the natural timidity of old men. On the other hand, Fox, as an exponent of the Whig conception, clamoured for English troops to be sent to Germany in support of the Duke of Cumberland and the Hanoverian army. Whatever merit there was in Fox's demand, he had no good grounds for making it at that moment. The Duke was not asking for it; on the contrary, at setting out for Europe he had expressly denied any thought of taking 'so unreasonable or improper a step,'[2] and within the last few weeks had written that "tis not the smallness of our forces that I complain of; but it is the unfortunate situation of these

[1] Holdernesse to Mitchell, 5th July 1757. Add. MSS. 6,815.
[2] Rigby to Bedford, 21st March 1757. Bedford. *Correspondence,* II, 241.

countries without any provision of any sort. . . . I fear we should not be able to subsist, if much greater bodies were to be assembled.'[1] Nor was Frederick anxious for English troops. He never mentioned them to Mitchell until, as a result of Kolin, he proposed to withdraw his own contingent from Cumberland's command, when he suggested that England might make good this loss.[2] But this suggestion did not reach England until after the Rochefort expedition had been settled. Fox's only grounds were loyalty to Cumberland and the lure of the 'old system.' In the end Pitt prevailed, obtaining the concurrence of his Cabinet on the 14th of July.[3] Mitchell was at once informed in a letter which had its startling as well as its pleasing aspect. 'I am convinced,' it said, 'you will agree with me in one principle, that we must be merchants while we are soldiers; that our trade depends upon a proper exertion of our marine strength; that trade and maritime force depend upon each other; and that the riches, which are the true resources of this country, depend chiefly upon its commerce.' It was by that principle that the efforts of England must be weighed and settled. We could not produce armies on the continental scale; 'the truth is, men are not to be furnished from hence.' But if we maintained our trade, if we used the natural strength of the country, we might be able 'to furnish gold as our contingent in the alliance,' and so 'at a critical moment, enable his Prussian Majesty to supply what is wanting on our part.' Meanwhile there was one point where principle, policy and power united. Our Channel Fleet, besides defending the British Dominions and protecting the trade, could at the same time be used 'to cover a number of land forces considerable enough to alarm the coasts of France.' What could be done in this direction to give Frederick relief would be done, and he would gain much more from the consternation and confusion in France than from 'the uncertain and precarious efforts of a Baltic squadron.' But—and here once more Pitt returned to first principles—Frederick must believe that neither the coasts of France nor even Germany were decisive; America was at least of equal consequence. Peace would spring, not out of the European cockpit, but out of 'the great struggle between England and France' on the seas and over the seas. What happened else-

[1] Cumberland to Mitchell, 6th May. Add. MSS. 6,835.
[2] Mitchell to Holdernesse, 9th July 1757. Add. MSS. 6,806.
[3] Cabinet Minute, 14th July 1757. Add. MSS. 6,832.

where was transitory and passing; and could never be conclusive in itself.[1] The principle here laid down so clearly and emphatically guided Pitt's policy from beginning to end, and was the influence moulding his attitude at a later date towards the question of peace.

Not unnaturally, Frederick received the first letter without enthusiasm. He was not to be shaken in his belief that the English navy stood supreme, and ascribed the refusal of a Baltic squadron wholly to commercial and political reasons. Such conduct, he protested, was hard on an ally in desperate straits, and if it was symptomatic of the way in which England meant to interpret her treaties, he should have been warned beforehand. He was an embittered man and he felt the apparent betrayal bitterly. The second letter, which had nearly caught up on its predecessor, arrived two days later. A radiant Mitchell hurried to communicate 'His Majesty's noble, generous and just sentiments' to Frederick, who received them 'with a flow of gratitude not to be described.'[2] Pitt had set Frederick on his feet again; he could look his world of enemies in the face once more, confident that at last there were steadfast and powerful forces working for him in England.

It is ironical to turn from him to the source of his new-found hope. The steadfastness and power emanated from a single valetudinarian who stood like a rock amid the vacillations of his unwelcome colleagues. Pitt and the Whig magnates ran uneasily in double harness. If Pitt endured them, it was not of choice, but because of external pressure. Being still without the authority of success, he had to borrow their majority, but he could not absorb it into himself or regard it as his own. They, for their part, were to a man against him on both principle and method. They had acquiesced in his proposals sullenly and of necessity and had hardly done so before they wanted to recant. 'Surely,' Devonshire wrote to Newcastle, 'this war must have convinced every thinking man of the folly and absurdity of a maritime war.' By hook or by crook Pitt must be prevented from allowing 'either the love of gaining or the fear of losing popularity' to deter him from 'entering far enough into continent measures.'[3]

What Devonshire thought, the King had come to believe, probably at the instigation of Fox; 'I found the Closet,' Newcastle

[1] Holdernesse to Mitchell, 17th July 1757. Add. MSS. 6,815.
[2] Mitchell to Holdernesse, 28th July 1757. Add. MSS. 6,806.
[3] Devonshire to Newcastle, 20th July 1757. Add. MSS. 32,872.

wrote, 'as much for sending the troops [to reinforce Cumberland] as it has ever been against it.' Newcastle himself had always thought the measure right; it was only the possibility which he had doubted. He now lingered fondly over the arguments in favour: 'such a reinforcement might certainly enable the Duke to do more than I am afraid we should do by any attempt on the French coasts. It would give spirit to the Protestant cause, to the Princes of the Empire and to the Dutch, and it would shew we were in earnest, and not altogether deserving the reproaches the King of Prussia makes us from abroad and I daily hear at home.' Much as he would have liked to support the King's view which coincided so entirely with his own, he foresaw trouble with Pitt and all he dared suggest was that the admirals and generals should be induced to pronounce against the Rochefort expedition, when the alternative of troops for Cumberland might be more favourably received. As a nominally loyal colleague he dissembled his satisfaction at finding the King 'very severe upon Mr. Pitt, both with regard to his abilities and his intentions,' but did not balk at suggesting insidiously that while it was inopportune to oppose the expedition, the time would doubtless come when Pitt's arrangements could be scrapped.[1]

With the possible exception of Mansfield, there was only one Whig magnate whose opinion Pitt regarded. He had always some respect for Hardwicke's brains, though the use he made of them was rather as a support against Newcastle's babblings than as a guide for himself. Hardwicke was as much against him as the rest. 'I find the situation abroad,' he wrote, 'as bad as possible and tremble for the next news that shall come.' Now that Austria had given Ostend and Nieuport to France, now that forty battalions had been sent from the Lower Rhine to canton along the Belgian coast, invasion would, he feared, be but 'an easy trip over,' if our fleet was absent off the mouth of the Charente. It would be well to think twice before dispatching the expedition, and in the meantime 'God send us better news than there is reason to augur from all these circumstances.'[2] Truly Pitt stood alone.

According to the Cabinet Minute, Pitt expected the expedition to do two things—alarm the coasts of France, and create a powerful diversion. But he was also swayed by something more

[1] Newcastle to Hardwicke, 25th July 1757. Add. MSS. 32,872.
[2] Hardwicke to Newcastle, 2nd July 1757. Add. MSS. 32,872.

fundamental. Writing after the event, when failure had sharpened criticism, Potter, as Pitt's mouthpiece, asked whether it was really 'so very absurd and romantic, that when their [i.e. the French] maritime force was drawn away to America and their land forces engaged in Germany, the reserved strength of this country should be exerted in attempting a blow so very decisive as the taking of Rochefort would have been?'[1] The question throws a flood of light on Pitt's outlook. He combined in himself the dual, and usually separate, gifts of strategy and tactics, fusing the steadfastness of the one with the opportunism of the other. His avowed object was not the defeat of France as such, but her defeat in America and on the seas. To face her on the Continent was beyond the power of England alone, or even England aided by Hanover. Hence his repugnance to the 'old system,' which he regarded as a bankrupt policy. But Fate had given him Frederick as an ally, and while he appreciated from the first the moral obligation which this involved, he began before long to appreciate also the possibilities which it offered for containing operations. Frederick's campaign was in itself a containing operation of gigantic proportions. His disasters and his urgent demands for help gave Pitt an opening for a minor containing operation of his own, which had the double advantage of benefiting Frederick and England alike. Frederick's enemies were closing in on him. The Russian army was on the move, in spite of innumerable delays which their general, Apraxin, invented in return for the bribery lavished upon him; they were coming down upon East Prussia, while their fleets, in conjunction with the Swedes, were already ravaging Pomerania; the Austrians were lumbering up from the south-east, and the French pressing in from the west. If they crushed Frederick, there would be an end of the major containing operations. He must therefore be helped, and had himself suggested two methods—a fleet in the Baltic and descents on the French coasts. Pitt saw no advantage in the former; but a descent on the French coast was another thing altogether. It would throw France on the defensive, and force her to retain on and around her coasts troops who would otherwise have been free for action elsewhere—possibly in Westphalia. Better still, if the descent were upon a naval harbour and the ships and arsenals of France could be damaged or destroyed, it would also assist the English navy. In that respect it

[1] *The Expedition against Rochefort*, p. 35.

was the exact converse of a fleet in the Baltic. The course of events made the moment propitious and the task feasible. Pitt wanted to seize the fleeting opportunity.

Every sort of obstacle was placed in his way. As Newcastle had hoped and probably engineered, the admirals and generals were unfavourable. Pitt ignored them. Then there was wrangling over the choice of commanders. Pitt held strong views on the type of leader he required. He wanted to get away from the stubborn martinets of the Cumberland school and the wooden-headed blusterers of the Mathews type; he was looking round for younger and more vigorous men—men of initiative and imagination, ready to face risks and able to inspire confidence. As yet, he had not had time to discover them but he was probing, and the expedition would prove a valuable testing ground. For the fleet, Hawke was the only man available, and could hardly be bettered. For the army, Pitt's choice fell upon Lord George Sackville, whom he had wanted to make Secretary at War. Judging by the future, the choice was bad, and perhaps not less to judging by the present, for Sackville refused to go on what he contemptuously called buccaneering. Pitt's second choice—also a bad one—was Conway, a personal friend, an amiable, well-meaning man and a conscientious soldier, but hesitating and over-cautious. The King refused to accept him, declaring that he was too young, and brusquely appointed Sir John Mordaunt to the chief command, with Conway as second, and Cornwallis third. Mordaunt, like Braddock, was about sixty; in his youth he had won a reputation for daring, but with advancing years had lost his nerve, and was now in bad health, a slow-witted man afraid of responsibility. Cornwallis had done good work as Governor of Acadia, and was described by Walpole as 'a brave, sensible young man, of great temper and good nature,' but he had become suspect by being implicated in the Minorcan affair, and acquiescing in the feeble Councils of War which had endorsed Byng's laggard behaviour. Mordaunt and Conway expressed themselves as 'full of apprehension that the intended expedition may be hazardous in the greatest degree,'[1] which was emphatically not the attitude Pitt desired. The omens were dubious, the only bright spot being Pitt's appointment of Wolfe as Quartermaster-General.

[1] Newcastle to Hardwicke, 21st July 1757. Add. MSS. 32,872.

The next hitch was over ships. Pitt ordered transports for ten battalions of infantry, and a covering fleet of sixteen ships of the line, to be assembled at Spithead by the middle of August. Anson protested that it was impossible. The story goes that Pitt retorted with a threat to impeach him if the ships were not forthcoming by the appointed date. No doubt the story is apocryphal or at least exaggerated, but it illustrates the restless energy which Pitt displayed in himself and demanded from everyone else. His threat, whatever form it took, was only partially successful; the men-of-war were assembled in plenty of time, but not the transports. Perhaps through carelessness, perhaps through the difficulty of securing enough ships, the Admiralty miscalculated the required tonnage. On hearing of the shortage, Pitt sent peremptory orders to Hawke to take on board the battleships any troops who could not be accommodated elsewhere.[1] Hawke was not best pleased.

Adverse winds delayed the sailing and at the same time blew up Pitt's impatience as he reflected that the disasters on the Continent were multiplying and the season for action was passing. By the 5th of September his patience had gone; he wrote with barely suppressed fury to Hawke that 'the King expects to hear, by the return of this messenger, that the fleet under your command, with the troops on board, have proceeded to sea,' and told the messenger to wait until he could come back with news that the fleet had sailed.[2] Hawke's displeasure grew, and he replied huffily, 'I should have expected that before yours was sent His Majesty would have been fully satisfied that I needed no spur in the execution of his orders.'[3] None the less the spur struck home. He sailed next morning.

After a slow and tedious voyage, the armament arrived off the coast of France on the 20th, and was then, by a change of wind, promptly blown out to sea again. Not until the 22nd did it come to anchor between the islands of Rhé and Oléron which stand sentinel at the mouth of the Charente, some few miles from Rochefort. The next day (23rd September) Captain Howe in the *Magnanime* bombarded and captured the fortified Ile d'Aix nearer inshore.[4] It took him precisely thirty-five minutes. In spite of this encouragement, the whole higher command lapsed into a fit of indecision and acrimony. Possibly the generals were all sea-sick—

[1] Burrow's *Hawke*, p. 126. [2] *Ibid.*, p. 128. [3] *Ibid.*, p. 129.
[4] Rodney to Grenville. Grenville. *Papers*, I, 208.

Wolfe wrote that he had not been well one hour since embarkation[1]—but certainly the success at Aix for all the good it did them might have been a defeat. They were paralysed by doubts or fears or ineptitude, and the admirals showed no desire to help them. Hawke, testy and abrupt, said he would land the troops wherever they liked, but ostentatiously washed his hands of all responsibility thereafter, not even promising to take them off again. As for advice, he would give none. Wolfe, who alone of the commanders seems to have thought more of his orders than of his state of mind, went on shore at Aix, reconnoitred the adjacent mainland and returned with a possible plan; troops could, he believed, be safely and easily landed at Châtelaillon, a promontory between Rochefort and La Rochelle, from which place either city could be attacked with a reasonable prospect of success. The generals and admirals 'heard him' in the lawyer's phrase, and then returned to their spleen, their sea-sickness and their councils of war, varying these activities by gazing aimlessly at France through telescopes.[2] At midnight on the 27th they made their grand effort. There was a stir and movement; the troops were bundled into boats and kept there for three or four hours, after which, as the generals changed their minds, they were taken on board again, cold, disheartened, and more seasick than ever. The next morning, friction broke out once more and to avoid a complete breakdown, admirals and generals alike decided to adopt the lowest common factor, which was to sail for home at once. They arrived at Spithead on the 7th of October. 'The public,' wrote Wolfe, 'couldn't do better than dismiss six or eight of us from their service.'[3]

The return of the expedition empty-handed was a terrible blow to Pitt. He had hoped so much from it and it had done nothing. It had not even properly failed, but like some nautical Duke of York, had sailed to France with ten thousand men, and then sailed back again. So Pitt thought at the time, though not altogether correctly. News of the intended expedition had spread alarm not only in France itself, but in the hearts of the French Marshals who were invading Germany. They paused, irresolute and uncertain, while 'everyone of the generals who held commands along the coasts of the Channel or the North Sea felt himself threatened.'[4] But of this Pitt knew nothing.

[1] Waugh. *James Wolfe,* p. 134. [2] *Ibid.*, p. 135. [3] *Ibid.*, p. 137.
[4] Waddington, quoted in Corbett, I, 194.

His mortification had many roots. The expedition was essentially his; he had not only proposed and supported it against the reiterated wishes of the King and the magnates, he had forced his views on reluctant generals and admirals who for weeks past had been talking the whole project down as the fantastic conception of an amateur strategist. They could now preen themselves on their foresight. And yet, it could have been so successful. It was, said Rodney, 'wise, prudent and well-timed.'[1] The French were caught unawares, with their defences unorganised and their garrison inadequate and untrained; they themselves agreed that if there had been an immediate attack 'it would have been all over with the port of Rochefort.'[2] Instead we lost, as Wolfe said, the lucky moment.[3] There was nothing here for Pitt but the fretful agony of the might-have-been.

No glimmer of success in other directions came to counter-balance this failure. On the contrary, disappointment was piled on disaster. Pitt's plans were snapping like rotten sticks, even in England itself. In June his Militia Bill had become law, but the attempt to enforce it led to widespread riots. The fault lay not so much in the common people as in the lack of honesty shown by Newcastle's former Ministry. The previous year men had been secured for the forces on an absolute promise that they should not be sent abroad; but no sooner had they enlisted than they had been shipped off to America. This want of faith had struck deep and was now bearing fruit. The men were running no risks. It was in vain that the authorities pointed to the express provisions of the Act. For the countryman, who probably could not read and to whom royalty meant much more than parchment, the fact that the King's word had been broken the previous year was the overriding consideration. What had happened before could happen again. Their suspicious minds jumped to the conclusion that they were being conscripted for service abroad. Indeed, now that the threat of invasion seemed to have vanished, they could see no other reason, and being full of 'terror and apprehension'[4] resisted forcibly. 'The tumults and riots,' so we are told, 'made Mr. Pitt uneasy'[5] but worse still, they frustrated for the time

[1] Grenville. *Papers*, I, 209.
[2] Sommaire, etc., quoted Corbett, I, 215. [3] Waugh, p. 135.
[4] Potter to Pitt, 11th Sept. 1757. Chatham. *Correspondence*, I, 258.
[5] Jones to Hardwicke, 6th September 1757. Add. MSS. 35,417.

being his cherished schemes. Yet facts had to be faced, and Pitt decreed that if the trouble was merely local, the Riot Act should be read and some examples made; but if the resistance was universal, the scheme should not be pushed.[1]

[1] Notes. Claremont, 7th Sept. 1757. Add. MSS. 32,997.

16

NADIR

(i)

If the alarm on the coast of France was evanescent, the diversion was too late to help even Cumberland's Army of Observation. Everything about Cumberland became sooner or later distorted. His appointment was a mistake. Frederick had pressed for it, not because he thought him a good general, but in the hope that he would prevent the Hanoverian Ministers from proclaiming neutrality.[1] Whatever good he did in that direction—and it is doubtful if he did any—was more than counterbalanced by his insistence on Pitt's dismissal before he would take up his command. He arrived in Germany with preconceived ideas which proved to be altogether wrong. He was convinced that the war would be very short; all that he had to do was to 'weather the storm for *five* or *six* weeks' after which Frederick would take sufficient measures for his relief.[2] He believed that there was no connection between the war in Europe and the war in America. George II was needlessly 'venturing the welfare of his German Dominions' on Frederick's behalf; they would never have been attacked because of quarrels in the Colonies and were being invaded solely 'en haine de l'alliance avec le Roi de Prusse.'[3] His attitude of mind affected his conduct. His views on the cause of the European war made him anxious to spare Hanover, and his belief that his own services were temporary attuned him to surrender when the stipulated time had elapsed. From the first he was lackadaisical and uninterested, making no effort to outwit or outmanœuvre, still less to defeat the enemy. Even when he advanced over the Weser, it was, on his own admission, 'rather to stop the incursions of the enemy's advanced bodies,

[1]Mitchell to Holdernesse, 31st March 1757. Add. MSS. 6,806.
[2]Cumberland to Mitchell, 17th April 1757. Add. MSS. 6,835.
[3]Cumberland to Mitchell, 23rd April 1757. Add. MSS. 6,835.

than from hoping to strike any great blow.'[1] Though he was at a loss to know what to do with his troops, he liked to have them about him, and protested vigorously when, after Kolin, Frederick wanted to withdraw the three regiments he had put at Cumberland's disposal. The protest had nothing to do with the military situation. He told Mitchell that he foresaw the worst consequences but 'not from the fear of weakening this army so much as from the very bad appearance it will carry with it.'[2] It was typical of the spit-and-polish Cumberland to stress appearances, and it was typical of the bellicose Frederick to reply that if Cumberland meant 'to defend the passage of the Weser and to fight the French, he could keep the Prussian battalions.'[3] Cumberland kept them, though he had no intention of fighting. His five or six weeks were up, and he now preferred to retire.

His opponent, D'Estrées, followed on his heels. D'Estrées was not young, and was noted more for caution than brilliance, but he was thorough, hard-working and not easily diverted. He liked to be sure of each step before he took the next, and so while Cumberland was falling back, he looked to his own flanks, capturing Emden on the left and Cassel on the right. Emden was a serious loss, being not only a port but the nearest connecting link between Cumberland and England. Recognising its importance, Pitt had ordered a squadron to sail to its defence, but he could not make up the time lost through the 'interministerium.' Nine days before he kissed hands, D'Estrées had dispatched a flying column to surprise it, and three days after Pitt had returned to office, it surrendered. With his flanks thus protected, D'Estrées advanced towards the Weser, to find that Cumberland had already retreated to Hastenbeck where he had taken up a strong position covering Hanover. No doubt he thought himself safely entrenched, but on the 26th of July D'Estrées had no difficulty in attacking and beating him soundly. Cumberland fell back towards Stade, on the Elbe, leaving Hanover wide open to the French, who proceeded to occupy it.

While the prospect of battle was drawing nearer, George II had struggled vehemently to deflect Pitt's expedition from Rochefort to Germany and was supported by the whole Whig interest. Pitt was hard put to it to hold his own, and the more

[1] Cumberland to Mitchell, 6th May 1757. Add. MSS. 6,835.
[2] Cumberland to Mitchell, 10th July 1757. Add. MSS. 6,835.
[3] Mitchell to Holdernesse, 16th July 1757. Add. MSS. 6,806.

determined he showed himself the more loudly the King complained that he was neglecting his German business. England, he said, was abandoning him, and Newcastle, who could not see the King suffer without a pang, declared with more sincerity than usual that Pitt 'was extremely in the wrong.'[1] When on the 3rd of August news came of Cumberland's defeat, the King broke down completely. Hanover must be saved; she must have peace; negotiations must begin at once; Maria Theresa must be told that George would disband the Army of Observation, dismiss his auxiliaries, send back his own troops to Hanover and give a guarantee that as Elector he would take no further part in the German war.

He poured out these heartbroken intentions to Newcastle, who hurried to inform his colleagues. The 'conciliabulum' on that occasion consisted of Newcastle, Granville, Holdernesse and Pitt. All agreed that they had no right to advise the King in his Electoral capacity; if he intended to make peace for Hanover, they could not stop him. All agreed, though apparently after some argument, that now at any rate it would be useless to divert the expedition to Germany. For the rest, Newcastle, rather surprisingly, took the military disaster calmly, having a suspicion that the King might welcome an excuse for declaring Hanover's neutrality.[2] What mainly preoccupied him was how to exculpate himself. It was, he declared, precisely to avoid such a denouement that he had wanted to reinforce Cumberland, and it was some comfort to him to think 'that no part of this misfortune, or of any that may happen in America' could be imputed to him.[3] Hardwicke, when he heard the news, fell headlong into despair; he supposed the expedition against Rochefort must proceed though it would do no good; and he was sure the troops must return by the end of September at the latest, since France, when she had 'done her business in Germany,' would infallibly invade England. 'Is there no way,' he asked plaintively, 'of making tentatives discreetly towards a general peace?'[4] Bute, on behalf of Leicester House, felt it incumbent on him to add to the general gloom by writing Pitt a lugubrious letter, the only positive element of which was a reliance on Pitt to get them out of the mess,[5] while Chesterfield thought it self-evident that 'neither we, nor our

[1] To Dupplin, 2nd Aug. 1757. Add. MSS. 32,872.
[2] To Hardwicke, 3rd Aug. 1757. Add. MSS. 32,872. [3] *Idem.*
[4] Hardwicke to Newcastle, 4th Aug. 1757. Add. MSS. 32,872.
[5] Bute to Pitt, 5th Aug. 1757. Chatham. *Correspondence,* I, 240.

only ally, the King of Prussia, can carry it on three months longer.'[1]

In the midst of so much despondency, Pitt had need of all his resolution. It was not difficult for him to show what Newcastle called 'a proper feeling of the King's distress,' since he was neither heartless nor insensible to the divinity which hedges a King. Otherwise, he probably regarded the loss of Hanover without much misgiving; it was something he had taken for granted in the old days before the alliance with Prussia. Cumberland's defeat was a matter for regret, but not for heart-searching. What should be considered seriously was the effect which the King's reaction might have upon Frederick. It would be a thousand pities if Frederick gave up the struggle at this moment, and it would be still worse if he gave as the reason that he had been abandoned by England. The tender spot on which to apply the salve was Berlin rather than St. James's or Hanover. Looking round for the opportunity, Pitt recalled Frederick's hint that he might need a subsidy. Hitherto Pitt had wished to postpone the grant till the next campaign, but now he 'declared his opinion that we should forthwith send him most large offers of money in order to engage him to continue in his present system.'[2] His next thought was to boost the King's morale, so that he might retain the Army of Observation in being. At the moment the danger was that it might dissolve. If it was to be kept going when Hanover had been occupied, England would have to find the necessary funds and Pitt was prepared to be liberal. He was also eager to be prompt so that he could keep a jump ahead of the King, and he asked Lady Yarmouth to salt the ground for an audience. When she had done her best, Pitt saw the King and offered an immediate grant of £100,000 for Cumberland's needs and £20,000 as a solatium for the Landgrave of Hesse. George was touched at this unexpected offer and accepted it, whereupon to clinch matters, Pitt at once ordered warrants to be drawn against the vote of credit for the services of the year, and then proceeded to inform George Grenville: 'I trust,' he wrote, 'that you and Lord Temple will be of opinion, upon fully weighing the whole extensive consideration, that I have not done wrong. My own lights, such as they are, assure me I have made the only

[1] To Dayrolle, 15th Aug. 1757. Bradshaw, III. 1172.
[2] Newcastle to Hardwicke, 3rd Aug. 1757. Add. MSS. 32,872.

tolerable option in so violent and urgent a crisis.'[1] Grenville's reply was a grudging acquiescence; no doubt Pitt's action had been necessary, 'but it certainly was very much to be wished that that expence should, if possible, be defrayed for the present from *some other quarter*' (i.e. from Hanoverian sources).[2] It is a sad reflection that this exchange of letters marks another step in the break-up of the Cousinhood. There was no reason why Pitt should consult a junior Minister when Newcastle had agreed. He wrote because he was trying to keep the Cousinhood in being as the solid core of his only party, which the coalition was killing without offering anything in exchange. The Whig magnates were taking the posts, but not the place, of the Cousinhood, and Pitt, effectually separated from his friends, was becoming steadily more lonely and more isolated. The result was twofold; Pitt in unconscious self-defence became autocratic and overbearing towards colleagues with whom he had nothing in common, while the Cousinhood, no longer fully in his confidence, drifted away from him. So far as Grenville was concerned, the process was hastened by jealousy.

(ii)

Whilst Pitt believed that he had made sure of both Army of Observation and Frederick, he had to prepare for the worst. They might be lost, and what then would become of the containing operations? Vague talks had been proceeding for some time with Denmark and Holland, but Pitt had no real hopes of assistance from either. He had nothing with which to bargain, and he knew that small states are shy of provoking big neighbours on whose standards victory seems to be sitting. The net must be cast more widely. As he told Newcastle, 'since we could do nothing in the north, we must see what could be done in the south.'[3] Everything pointed to Spain. She was seemingly powerful; her interests in Italy were threatened by Austria; her King was well disposed and her Prime Minister a personal friend of Pitt's. Best of all, both she and we had something to offer. She could help us to recover Minorca, and we could restore Gibraltar. Pitt proposed to negotiate on these lines. To the Englishman of today, the suggestion would be unendurable. It was not so then. 'Your Lordship

[1] Pitt to Grenville, 11th August 1757. Grenville. *Papers*, I, 206.
[2] Grenville to Pitt, 14th August 1757. Chatham. *Correspondence*, I, 244.
[3] Newcastle to Hardwicke, 9th August 1757. Add. MSS. 32,872.

knows,' Newcastle wrote to Hardwicke, 'that this exchange for Gibraltar is not a new thought. . . . I own I always liked it.'[1] Minorca had always been regarded as more important; it had greater naval facilities; and it offered a much nearer base for blockading Toulon. Its possession ensured the protection of England's trade in the Mediterranean in a way that Gibraltar could never do. Hence the fury when Richelieu captured it. Probably no one in England, certainly no one in the City, would grudge the exchange of Gibraltar for Minorca.

Pitt had a further reason. Since Tyrawly had succeeded Fowke as Governor he had sent home one report after another, first to Cumberland, then to Fox and finally to Pitt himself, full of alarming accounts of the sorry conditions he had found and the great expense that would be required to put matters right. 'I take it,' he affirmed, 'to be a matter of great indifference to our neighbours, by sea or land, whether we are at Gibraltar, or settled upon the Eddystone, in respect of the use this place is of to us, or hurt to them.'[2] Tyrawly obviously did not regard Gibraltar as any substitute for Minorca nor, by his account, did the French. In point of fact Gibraltar was to remain a liability rather than an asset for the next fifty years, until it was developed at the end of the century by Lord St. Vincent.

For all these reasons Pitt asked for and obtained consent to approach Spain. On the 25th of August he sent instructions to Sir Benjamin Keene, our Ambassador at Madrid, to broach the subject to Wall, adding that he was prepared not only to cede Gibraltar, but also to compound the ancient dispute over the English settlements in the Bay of Honduras, provided the bargain were reciprocal. Keene was to watch his language like a lynx, 'so as to put it beyond the possibility of the most captious and sophistical interpretation, to wrest and torture' the offer into anything but what it was; for under no circumstances would Gibraltar be restored until, by the aid of Spain, England had recovered 'the island of Minorca, with all its fortresses and harbours.'[3] The instructions reflect Pitt's own methods. He took infinite pains to forestall 'captious and sophistical interpretations,' driving Holdernesse half crazy with his meticulous drafting; he took no less pains in preparing his strategical plans and his

[1] Newcastle to Hardwicke, 9th August 1757. Add. MSS. 32,872.
[2] Tyrawly to Pitt, 1st Feb. 1757. Chatham. *Correspondence,* I, 219.
[3] Pitt to Keene, 23rd Aug. 1757. Chatham. *Correspondence,* I, 255.

expeditionary forces. If an infinite capacity for taking pains is a sign of genius, Pitt displayed it to a remarkable degree.

In spite of his care, the overture bore no fruit. Once more he was frustrated by the legacy of the past. Spain had once been friendly, but her attitude was changing; she had been irritated by the failure of Pitt's predecessors to punish English privateers who, she complained, 'for two years had lorded it over her coasts and subjects, neither sparing their properties nor their lives.' Wall, when Keene sounded him, held out no hope of a favourable answer, though he showed 'something of a regret either that this proposition should come too late, or in circumstances when he would not, or dared not, make use of it.'[1] So hard was it for Pitt to catch up on the tardiness of his own admission to power.

(iii)

The sky grew steadily darker. In Europe Cumberland was not only a defeated general, he was a man without hope. He declared that we had 'lost the means of restoring the affairs in Germany,' and then adopting the role of seer foretold a melancholy future: 'Thus far I will venture to prophesy, that before it is long we shall feel the weight of our unhappy separation from the Continent.'[2] He was in this fatalistic mood when he was told of the King's resolve to snatch Hanover out of the war, and was thus fortified in his conviction that it was useless 'to attempt to support this unequal struggle any longer.'[3]

Meanwhile the French were giving him no peace. D'Estrées had been superseded by Richelieu, who, making the most of his predecessor's victory, hustled Cumberland back to within twenty miles of the Elbe. There the impetus of his attack fizzled out. All might yet have gone well if Cumberland had been made of sterner stuff and had entrenched himself at Stade, relying on the fleet for his supplies. But Cumberland was in no mood to fight back. On top of the news that the Hanoverian Ministers had been ordered to treat, he had himself received very full powers from the King to come to terms, and was in every way disposed to use them. With the help of Denmark, and acting, as he said, 'in compliance with His Majesty's intentions and orders,'[4] he

[1] Keene to Pitt, 26th Sept. 1757. Chatham. *Correspondence,* I, 263.
[2] Cumberland to Mitchell, 17th August 1757. Add. MSS. 6,835.
[3] Cumberland to Mitchell, 20th August 1757. Add. MSS. 6,835.
[4] Cumberland to Mitchell, 30th Sept. 1757. Add. MSS. 6,835.

negotiated and signed the notorious Convention of Closterseven, under which he agreed to disband his army, dismiss his auxiliaries and send away the greater part of the Hanoverians, but failed or forgot to secure any concessions for Hanover itself. Richelieu, who was in a hurry, swallowed the Convention hastily. It was no part of French strategy to keep an army idling on the extreme left of their front. Their main line of attack was 200 miles away on their extreme right near the borders of Saxony, where the Prince de Soubise was operating against Frederick. Richelieu's business was to finish off Cumberland without delay, and join hands with Soubise. He was, therefore, only too ready to leave points of dispute in the air, and sign the document without looking at it too closely. He did so on the 9th of September.

Whilst Cumberland had been tumbling from gloom to pessimism and finally to surrender, the King had been rising steadily from despondency to hope and even to pugnacity. Strong representations from the Prussian Ambassador, coupled with the fervent entreaties of Lady Yarmouth and Pitt's gilded persuasions, so far worked upon him that by the middle of September he was writing to Cumberland in quite a new strain. Frederick, he said, had pointed out how useless the Army of Observation would be if they were cooped up at Stade, and that it would be better for them to make their way to Magdeburg 'where there are great magazines for subsisting the troops and an asylum under the cannon of that fortress.' The King had been impressed and now told Cumberland to turn the matter over in his mind and to omit no opportunity of annoying the enemy. He would, he said, be very impatient to hear what Cumberland might be able to do.[1]

He had not long to wait. Two days later came news of the signing of the Convention. Once more Pitt had been foiled by the wasted weeks of the interministerium. All was again in confusion; all had yet to be done.

(iv)

After Closterseven, America. The plans which Pitt had made in his first administration had never been cancelled. Loudoun and Holburne were to join forces at Halifax, capture Louisburg by June at latest, and then attempt Quebec before winter put an end

[1] Holdernesse to Cumberland, 16th Sept. 1757. Add. MSS. 6,815.

to the fighting. Meanwhile, in Europe, a close blockade would prevent French reinforcements from reaching Canada.

But planning and performance are two different things. Pitt had found it hard enough to push on with the preparations when he was in power, and with his dismissal his erstwhile colleagues had found it still harder. Holburne was smothered in red tape so that he was late in starting; and the blockade was left so loose and untied that French troops and provisions got across to Canada. At New York Loudoun sank ever deeper into difficulties. Never remarkable for tact, he irritated the colonists by his brusque manner and high-handed actions. Relations, bad to start with, became embittered when he laid an embargo upon shipping. All he had meant to do was to prevent news of his movements reaching French ears, and his action might have been tolerated if the embargo had been of short duration. But Holburne's non-arrival meant its indefinite prolongation. It soon became unbearable, not only to the colonists who refused to submit to it, but even to the home Government, who found that it affected their imports of grain.[1] It was first ignored and then raised, so that the French, sufficiently informed of Loudoun's intentions, were able to make plans for all eventualities.[2] Loudoun might reasonably have been either daring or patient, but in fact was neither. He might have proceeded by himself; he might have waited for Holburne; actually he dallied until the 20th of June and then, as Holburne had still not arrived, sailed for Halifax without him. It was too late if Loudoun meant to act alone, too early if he intended to co-operate; and as it happened it was extremely risky, for on the day that he sailed unescorted a French fleet under de la Motte arrived in American waters. Fortunately for him they did not meet and he reached Halifax safely at the end of the month.

Holburne arrived on the 9th of July, and as it was now too late in the year to capture both Louisburg and Quebec, the question arose which to attack first. Whilst they were making up their minds, they heard of de la Motte's presence, whereupon Loudoun, thinking discretion the better part of valour, promptly returned to New York. Holburne, with more spirit, cruised off Louisburg in the hope of tempting de la Motte to battle, but had the misfortune to encounter a hurricane of unprecedented fury which dispersed and shattered his fleet. Whilst he was collecting the remnants, de la Motte slipped safely back to France.

[1] Kimball, I, 19. [2] *Ibid.*, I, 72. See also Parkman. *Montcalm and Wolfe,* I, 469.

The tale of discomfiture is not yet told. On reaching New York, Loudoun was faced with news of a fresh disaster. His enforced delay and his move to Halifax had given Montcalm the chance for which he had been looking. Knowing better than Loudoun that Quebec was safe for that year, he collected a force of 7,000 or 8,000 men, some quarter of whom were Indians, and made a sudden descent on Fort William Henry at the end of Lake George. It fell on the 9th of August. The Red Indians, beside themselves with rum and insolence, celebrated its fall by a massacre of the English, which Montcalm tried without much avail to prevent. His regrets were no doubt solaced by the knowledge that the key to the Hudson route now lay in his hands and New York was open to attack whenever the time should be ripe.

(v)

Official reports of these various defeats reached Pitt in driblets. On the 2nd of September he heard that Loudoun was retiring.[1] On the 16th came news of Closterseven. The Rochefort expedition returned empty-handed on the 7th of October. The 11th brought Keene's admission of failure in Spain[2] and news of the loss of Fort William Henry.[3] At the end of October Pitt learnt the fate of Holburne's fleet. With that, his cup of bitterness overflowed. 'I fear,' he wrote to Hester, 'we do not stand in the smile of heaven.'[4]

The strain of repeated disappointment was telling on him. His health was wretched, and in order to struggle up from Hayes to the house in St. James's Square which he had taken for his official residence, he was indulging in violent remedies, which no doubt had violent reactions. Looking, in this overwrought state, at this series of failures, one point stood out starkly—none of the leaders seemed to be trying; all were blenching at shadows, all were daunted by phantoms. Inevitably a measure of suspicion grew up in his mind. He was beginning to link together various incidents and draw dangerous conclusions. He had not forgotten Cumberland's anxiety to drive him from office, or the King's eagerness for Hanover's neutrality. They had played into each other's hands, and between them had corrupted the admirals

[1] Walpole to Mann, 3rd Sept. 1757.
[2] Pitt to Newcastle, 11th Oct. 1757. Add. MSS. 32,875.
[3] Walpole to Mann, 12th Oct. 1757.
[4] Pitt to Hester. Half-past 4 o'clock. Public Record office.

and generals. So Pitt came to think, and was encouraged in his suspicions by the rumours spreading up and down the country, that neither King nor Duke wanted the Rochefort expedition to succeed, and were trusting to miscarriages elsewhere to drive Pitt into a full-blooded German war.[1] At times Pitt's vexation found vent in high and passionate language, which terrified Newcastle, and once at least—on the 14th of December—he poured out his bottled wrath in Parliament. Catching at a remark by Beckford during the debate on the Army Estimates, that he did not know in what hands we were, Pitt plunged into the whirlpool of his indignation. 'Nothing,' he declared, 'could be well till the Army was subjected to the civil power'; their duty was to obey, not to reason; instead they had laughed at his expedition, jeering at it openly in their messes. As with Rochefort, so with America. What had he received from Loudoun? Nothing but one small scrap of paper containing a few lines of no moment. He believed that all might have been well, if Loudoun had not shilly-shallied for a month, poking and probing to find out whether the French outnumbered him or not. If a scheme involved the least appearance of danger, no one, it seemed, was ready to carry it out. He could no longer indulge in hope. Nothing was done, nothing was attempted. Neglect and indolence prevailed everywhere. We had lost control of the Great Lakes—not a single English boat was to be seen on them; the corridors between Canada and America were all in French hands. 'Our ill-success had hurt his quiet and tainted his health.' The more so because it was not inevitable. How different had been our fortunes in the East! There Watson, with a few crazy ships, without waiting to repair this or condemn that, had sailed boldly up the Ganges and supported by Clive, 'that man not born for a desk, that heaven-born General,' had recaptured Calcutta and avenged the Black Hole.[2]

Yet the thunder and lightning of his ill-humour did not blast his sense of justice or cloud his discernment. If he could not excuse Mordaunt or Cumberland or Loudoun, he was not prepared to damn them unheard.[3] When Mordaunt returned, the public, with vivid recollections of Byng, were athirst for his blood. They went farther. 'They will not be persuaded,' Potter wrote after a tour

[1] Newcastle to Hardwicke, 8th Oct. 1757. Add. MSS. 32,874.
[2] Walpole. *George II,* III, 89. Almon, I, 332.
[3] Pitt to Sackville, 15th Oct. 1757. H.M.C. Stopford Sackville MSS., Vol. I.

of the whole west country, 'that this pacific disposition was not a preliminary for the Convention of Stade'; on the contrary, they believed that 'the same pacific orders' had been sent to Holburne as well. They hinted darkly at the King's connivance and were trembling on the verge of high treason. Potter, thoroughly frightened, urged that 'proper measures may be taken to obviate what may be attended with such dreadful consequences.'[1] Nor was he alone in his views. Newcastle came to much the same conclusion. 'It is certain,' he said, 'that even Port Mahon did not occasion a greater run than this miscarriage has done.' But on this occasion Pitt stood as a buffer between him and the popular fury, and he was therefore able to take a calmer view, and indeed to weigh up the position with some acumen. There were, he noticed, two distinct trends of opinion. Most people imagined that the retreats at Rochefort and Closterseven were put-up jobs to propitiate the French and persuade them to spare Hanover. Pitt's official statements would, he hoped, put an end to such a ridiculous idea. The other opinion, propagated with great industry, was 'that the expedition was chimerical and impracticable and the production of a *hot-headed Minister*.' This, Newcastle noted with relief, was 'levelled directly against Mr. Pitt,' who would undoubtedly combat it. Newcastle could take a detached interest in such a controversy. What mainly bothered him was that while an enquiry into Mordaunt's behaviour seemed inevitable, 'the King and all of us' were at a loss what line to take.[2]

Pitt, unlike Newcastle, had no doubts whatever. He had no intention of turning Mordaunt into another Byng. What he had in mind was something quite different and much more important. The canker eating the heart out of all his plans was his inability to choose his own generals and his lack of authority over the army. As he had said in Parliament, 'nothing could be well till the Army was subjected to the civil power.' He proposed to use both Rochefort and Stade to secure that subjection. The object therefore of an enquiry into Mordaunt's actions should be, not to impose punishment, but 'to vindicate and establish the practicability and great advantage of his project, and in order thereto to lay before the officers, the grounds and evidence upon which it went.'[3] This was a new and surprising idea to Newcastle, who

[1] Potter to Pitt, 11th Oct. 1757, Chatham. *Correspondence*, I, 277.
[2] Newcastle to Hardwicke, 15th Oct. 1757. Add. MSS. 32,875.
[3] Newcastle to Hardwicke, 23rd Oct. 1757. Add. MSS. 32,875.

could find nothing to say about it except to deplore Pitt's habit of insisting from time to time upon what Newcastle called 'improper points and improper conclusions.' It was also new to Mansfield, who at Newcastle's urgent entreaty had been co-opted into the Cabinet. He objected that an enquiry on those lines would be 'submitting the King's measures and ministers to the judgment of a Board of General Officers and publishing the reasons for their conduct.'[1] As such it was thoroughly undesirable. There was no doubt something in Mansfield's argument, but it struck Pitt as typical of that quirk of the legal mind which so exasperated him. In his view such a trumpery slap at the *amour propre* of Ministers was a very small price to pay for control of the army. By being 'violent,' he had his own way, but only within limits. Mordaunt's court martial was, by contrast with Byng's, a tame affair, ending in whitewash. What distinguished it was the intervention of Pitt himself, who appeared nominally to authenticate his orders, but in fact to make what Walpole described as 'an imperious speech'[2] in support of his plans—a speech cut short by the tribunal, who clearly failed to understand his motives and were not interested in his policy.

(vi)

His comparative failure in the case of Mordaunt was forgotten in his success in the case of Cumberland. The King had been shocked by Closterseven; it had come too rapidly and had achieved too little. The first news left him dumb; neither he nor his favourite advisers knew what to say or what to do. To Pitt, on the contrary, it presented at once a problem and a possibility. As a problem, he had to consider how best to check Richelieu while Frederick was dealing with Soubise. His lively imagination conceived two methods. The first was simplicity itself; the Convention must be ignored, Cumberland recalled and the command handed over to the Hanoverian General Spörcken with instructions to attack Richelieu at once. The second was more subtle; the forces at Rochefort, which had not yet returned and which were supposed to be prospering, must seize and occupy the island of Rhé, which would act, not as a temporary diversion, but as a running sore, draining away the French troops and distracting the higher command.

[1] Newcastle to Hardwicke, 23rd Oct. 1757. Add. MSS. 32,875.
[2] Walpole. *George II*, III, 78.

Pitt summoned the Cabinet to consider both proposals. They agreed to the Rhé project, though they did not like it, and were probably not displeased when the return of the expedition two days later upset the plan. But Pitt, foiled once more, flared into sudden wrath, becoming, in Newcastle's phrase, 'outrageous upon it,' and declared roundly that fleet and army must be sent back at once with peremptory orders to capture the island. Ligonier was on his side; so, unexpectedly, was Holdernesse. But Ligonier was an old man and no politician, and Holdernesse was becoming 'a greater cypher than ever.'[1] They cut little ice, and as the great body of the Whig magnates were opposed, 'the thought was dropped very readily.'[2] As yet there was no smallest cheep of victory, and without it Pitt must perforce suffocate beneath the blanket of Whig prejudice and Newcastelian timidity. To free himself was a labour of Hercules. There was, after all, no very good reason as yet for anyone to trust his strategic ability.

There remained the proposed breaking of the Convention. Pitt was 'most violent for it';[3] the Whigs backboneless and fearful. Fortunately the King, as he recovered from the first shock, felt touched in his honour. He was not insensible to the clamour outside, and a guilty conscience made him anxious to cover his tracks, and forget his first infirmity of purpose. The bolder instructions, which he had sent to Cumberland too late, assumed a new importance. He insisted on them; he made a parade of them. Pitt read the workings of his mind and saw his chance; a very little push, but a prompt push, would topple the King over the edge; 'the present moment,' he told Newcastle, 'is *decisive*, and that *moment, so seldom seized*, is *rarely offered twice*'; in his agony of suspense he underlined the words.[4] The Cabinet were swept off their feet by his urgency, and told the King that if he would regard the Convention as broken and annulled, then, as the Electoral revenues were entirely cut off, England would finance the Army of Observation—but only 'from the day that they shall recommence the operations of war against the forces of France, in concert with the King of Prussia.'[5] The mind of Pitt may surely be seen in this adroit turning of the screw.[6] The offer was psycholo-

[1] Newcastle to Hardwicke, 23rd Oct. 1757. Add. MSS. 32,875.
[2] Newcastle to Hardwicke, 8th Oct. 1757. Add. MSS. 32,874. [3] *Ibid.*
[4] Pitt to Newcastle, 11th Oct. 1757. Add. MSS. 32,875.
[5] Cabinet Minutes, 7th Oct. Add. MSS. 32,874.
[6] See Newcastle to Hardwicke, 23rd Oct. Add. MSS. 32,875.

gically wise and well timed. The imperfect drafting of the Convention had led to difficulties, and Richelieu, agitated by disapproving dispatches from the French Government who wanted peace with Hanover to be conditional on peace with England, had contravened its provisions by threatening to disarm the Hessians. This fact enabled the King to lay the blame for repudiation elsewhere, and Pitt's provisional offer of money gave him an incentive to renew the war. He accepted the position; the Convention was repudiated and the Army of Observation reconstructed under the command of Prince Ferdinand of Brunswick.

So much for the problem. The possibility which sprang out of Closterseven was that Cumberland's recall might give Pitt the control of the army. As Cumberland did not arrive in England till the 10th of October, the King had plenty of time in which to nourish an indignation, simulated to start with, but by the normal process of self-deception becoming steadily more real. His feeling of guilt made him anxious to justify himself, which he did by abusing his son. Each day the abuse became more extravagant. The Duke's head was turned; he had lost his courage; he was a rascally son; his blood was tainted. Finally he declared that Cumberland had exceeded his orders, and sent Munchausen to a Cabinet meeting with copies of the correspondence to prove it. 'They proved,' Pitt observed dryly, 'the direct contrary,' and when later the King insisted that he had given Cumberland no orders, Pitt was able to reply with conviction, 'But full powers, Sir; very full powers.'[1] It was ironical that Pitt should be the one person to defend the Duke, on whom incidentally the irony was not lost; from that moment—all too late—his attitude towards Pitt altered. The King, meanwhile, plunged deeper into that self-justification which condemns itself. Everything had to be twisted to the Duke's disgrace. Even the news that the Russians, after winning the battle of Gross-Jägendorf, had been forced by the failure of their commissariat to retire, merely produced the comment, 'And now, if my son had not made this Convention, what a good situation we should have been in.'[2] When Cumberland arrived at the palace, the King was playing cards. He paused in his play to greet him with the words, 'Here is my son who has ruined me and disgraced himself,' and after four minutes' conver-

[1] Walpole. *George II*, III, 60; Bedford. *Correspondence*, II, 278.
[2] Devonshire to Fox, 29th Sept. 1757; Charteris, p. 309.

sation—mostly abuse—dismissed him. Cumberland felt he had no option but to resign.

Here was Pitt's chance. But again speed was necessary, lest the King, having vented his ill-humour beyond reason, might in remorse wish for a reconciliation. Indeed, the day after his outburst, he talked of inviting his son to breakfast and dilated on the trouble which his resignation would cause.[1] There was also the possibility that the Duke might regret his retirement and try to return; Newcastle thought he had some such idea at the back of his mind.[2] Pitt, therefore, pressed for immediate action, suggesting that Ligonier, now Lieut.-General of Ordnance, should be promoted to the rank of Field-Marshal, given a peerage and appointed Captain-General, and should be succeeded in the Ordnance by Sackville. Inevitably he found obstacles. To Newcastle the proposal seemed 'ridiculous.' Obviously the King must be his own Captain-General; Ligonier as chief adviser might perhaps be made a Field-Marshal, if Pitt insisted, but a peerage was out of the question; it was also doubtful if Sackville would be acceptable as his successor. The sad truth is that any promotions which did not emanate from Newcastle himself were suspect; they trenched too much on the field of patronage which was at once his pleasure and his strength. Without patronage his power was gone—a fact which Pitt overlooked in his scornful distaste for 'corruption.' On this occasion Newcastle made haste to push his own nominee; he proposed that Granby should be given command of the Blues—a supplement to Pitt's plan which Pitt accepted with demur, and which Newcastle, with stupid conceit, claimed to be 'the best part of it.'[3] Storms seemed inevitable over the main proposals, but fortunately Hardwicke appreciated Pitt's purpose, and disposed of Newcastle's objections by the one argument likely to touch him. He pointed out that sooner or later Cumberland would regain his influence, and if the King were head of the army would be able to control it behind the curtain without incurring responsibility and without being called to book.[4] That anyone beside himself should be able to exercise hidden influence in the Closet was anathema to Newcastle, who accordingly swung round to Pitt's views. It remained to convince a reluctant King. All the usual methods of persuasion

[1] Newcastle to Hardwicke, 15th Oct. 1757. Add. MSS. 32,875.
[2] *Ibid.* [3] *Ibid.*
[4] Hardwicke to Newcastle, 16th Oct. 1757. Add. MSS. 32,875.

had to be employed and at long last he gave way. Pitt was delighted. 'I never,' said Newcastle, 'saw a man more pleased.' He had reason to be. It was the first real victory he had won—wresting the tools from the hands of incompetents and getting them into his own. Now he had grounds for hope—if he failed hereafter, the fault would be his. Having gained his point, he was willing to give Newcastle the credit, but he was not to get anything easily and there was one last brush. Newcastle, supported by Mansfield, thought it absurd and dangerous to refer to America in Ligonier's commission; Ligonier could not be responsible at such a distance, nor could anyone predict in the present ticklish situation what the Colonies would think 'if an officer in England, and residing constantly here, was to have the supreme command over them.' He pressed the argument, only to find, to his chagrin, that Pitt resumed 'his usual fierté, and all good humour was over.' But the storm was a passing one; Pitt was able to convince Mansfield that Ligonier's authority in America would be no more and no less than Cumberland's had been, and did not imply 'a power in the Commander-in-Chief in England to send orders to America independently of the civil ministers here.'[1] Indeed, Pitt's object was precisely to avoid any such possibility. With Mansfield convinced, Newcastle was perforce satisfied. 'I have too many proofs,' he said, 'of the uncertainty of his [Pitt's] temper. . . . But as I have bore it, and he comes round again, I shall endeavour to bear it, or at least I will make no complaint.'[2] One can legitimately feel sorry for both—impatient genius and fussy pride are very unequally yoked together.

[1] Newcastle to Hardwicke, 23rd October 1757. Add. MSS. 32,875. [2] *Ibid.*

17

DISJUNCTIVE COALESCENCE

Pitt obtained control of the army only just in time, for his position was more precarious than he thought. The coalition, which so many people had hailed as 'the strongest administration in years,' did not produce coalescence; friction was constant and tempers short. Hardwicke's initial rapture soon evaporated, and was so far forgotten that barely nine months later he was writing: 'I always feared it would be bad. . . . I don't, however, pretend to have foreseen the *manner* and *extent* of the disagreeableness.'[1] Instead of giving strength and stability to Pitt, the coalition began at once that process of attrition which ultimately caused his downfall. Its significant feature was not the return of Pitt—that was inevitable in any case—but of Newcastle. He came back a chastened, but not an essentially different man; the basis of his character remained self-satisfaction unsupported by self-reliance. Now, as before, he was jealous and frightened of his superiors, and was for ever scheming to get and keep them in subjection. Now, as before, his method was persistent intrigue. Absence of any alternative had made him accept Pitt as a colleague, but he felt towards him much as he had once felt towards Bedford. Indeed, the antagonism was the stronger when he reflected that Bedford had merely thrust himself into office while Pitt had thrust Newcastle out, coming in as a 'conqueror,' with policies which in Newcastle's eyes were 'wild notions,' 'ridiculous,' 'absurd' and 'improper.' It could not be long before Newcastle would begin to formulate the old slogans; at the first favourable opportunity the whispering campaign would begin—Pitt must go—and the coalition brought the opportunity nearer. There was balm for him in Lady Yarmouth's advice to 'keep Mr. Pitt till we have peace and then do what you will with him.'[2] Her advice chimed in with his hopes. Pitt, no doubt, was essential so long as the

[1] Hardwicke to Newcastle, 6th April 1758. Add. MSS. 32,879.
[2] Newcastle to Hardwicke, 16th May 1758. Add. MSS. 32,880.

war continued, but with peace what rosy prospects would unfold!

The malaise was not solely personal. Beside the deep cleavage in temperament there still remained the fundamental difference in policy. It was, in the main, still as true as it had been in 1756 that 'the two great parties in this Kingdom consisted properly in the Court Party under the Duke of Newcastle and the Opposition under Mr. Pitt and his friends,' the former composed of Whigs and the latter embracing 'the Leicester House people, the remains of the old opposition, and the Tories.'[1] Their foreign policies were diametrically opposed; the one looking to the Continent, the other overseas. Newcastle did not dare to defy Pitt on broad questions of strategy, but he was for ever pushing the claims of Europe, and in his usual fashion treating any concession, or even appearance of concession, as a justification for further demands. There was here the material for eternal squabbles.

But differences of policy gave rise only to limited troubles. More serious in the long run was the effect which the coalition had on Pitt's prospects. He had come to power in his first Ministry as leader of the Tory Opposition, and had banked upon the grudging acquiescence of the Whig majority for so long as might be needed to consolidate his position. It had been no part of his policy to seek a general election before victory abroad had made victory at home probable, but he had hoped and believed that in the meantime the force of popularity and the prestige of power would gradually bring him adherents. The leaven was beginning to work with every sign of success, when the King had wantonly dismissed him. Now all was altered. With the coalition he had to give up hope of securing Parliament: he could not intrigue against his own partners. Newcastle was in control and he himself was leader only on sufferance. He recognised the fact; and with his unfailing sense of realities, told the startled West that he would not sign the usual circular letters to members because 'this was not *his* Parliament but the Duke of Newcastle's Parliament.'[2] The coalition, in short, effectively isolated Pitt; in the new circumstances the Whigs merely tolerated him as a temporary inconvenience, while the Tories, though still loyal, felt disappointed, depressed and a little bewildered. His prospects for the future were correspondingly

[1] Holdernesse to Mitchell, 5th December 1757. Add. MSS. 6,832.
[2] West to Newcastle, 2 Nov. 1757. Add. MSS. 32,875.

diminished, and even for the present he could rely on no one but himself.

Parliament was due to meet on the 25th of November (1757), but Pitt was anxious to postpone it until news had been received from Germany. News there must evidently be before long, and Pitt hoped that it would be favourable. He wanted something besides failures for the King's Speech. He wanted, in particular, to be able to say that the Army of Observation was once more in being, under the command of Prince Ferdinand. Unless something of the sort could be said, he feared there would be a thorny debate on Closterseven, and a slippery tightrope to walk if he was to do justice to Cumberland without reflecting upon the King. Needless to say, he got no help from Newcastle, who, now that he could shelter behind Pitt, looked upon postponement as a 'wild notion,' and dismissed debates on the Convention with a shrug as 'our sore place.' Nor did he get much help from the King, who, because he wanted to forget Closterseven, was disinclined to mention it; he would much prefer to dilate on the corn riots, the depredations of the privateers and the lawlessness of the mob, all of which he insisted on including in his speech.[1] Clearly he thought offence was the best defence, and was not imaginative or sympathetic enough to worry about the debates after his own speech was over.

Possibly Pitt hoped that news might also come from Frederick, who for some months now had been slowly recovering from the disaster of Kolin, and with infinite pains striving to recapture the initiative. Though Pitt could only guess at his progress, his plans were in fact coming to fruition towards the end of October. The Austrians were advancing with their usual slow deliberateness to the siege of Leipzic, and Frederick planned to meet them there and bring them to battle—a desperate throw at the fag-end of the campaigning season for a victory to carry him through the winter. He contrived a sudden concentration on the spot, coming himself from Torgau, while other troops marched from Magdeburg and Berlin. They had all arrived, keyed up to battle, by the 26th of October, only to learn that the enemy had heard of their approach and were retiring. Frederick was 'most sensibly affected with the sudden disappointment, having taken so much true pains to give them battle.'[2] None the less he had saved

[1] Newcastle to Hardwicke, 5th Nov. 1757. Add. MSS. 32,875.
[2] Mitchell to Holdernesse, 29th Oct. 1757. Add. MSS. 6,806.

Leipzic and checked the Austrians; and as the Russians had fallen back and the Swedes in Pomerania were a nuisance rather than a menace, he was now free to turn his thoughts to France. He suggested, apparently at Yorke's instigation, that in the coming year, the troops lately returned from Rochefort should be landed in the Elbe and assist the reconstituted Army of Observation to dislodge the French from Hanover. If that were agreed, Frederick would contribute a substantial force under one of his Marshals,[1] and between them they could deal with France's northern army under Richelieu.

There still remained her southern army under Soubise. Frederick meant to deal with that himself, partly because he was too restless and too hard-pressed to put faith in schemes, which were to be implemented by unreliable Hanoverians and the English whom he regarded as 'triflers,'[2] and partly because peace negotiations which he had been pursuing had come to nothing. He had recently been sounding the French, only to discover that they had secretly undertaken to help Austria to reconquer Silesia in return for compensation in the Netherlands.[3] The discovery angered him, and by way of retaliation he made up his mind to give France a buffet she would remember. Breaking up his camp at Leipzic on the 30th of October, he crossed the Saale, and on the 5th of November (1757) at Rossbach utterly routed Soubise. Mitchell, delighted with this happy event, urged him to advance on Richelieu, but Frederick was in no mood to do anything for his allies; enough for him to have gratified his own revenge. He answered sourly that he had to take some care of his own country, since no one else would help him. 'From your nation,' he added tartly and not altogether untruly, 'I have had nothing but good words.'[4] He intended to hurry back to Silesia and he chose well, for at Leuthen, on the 5th of December, he won 'the most complete of all his victories,'[5] routing 80,000 Austrians with an army not much over one-third of the size.

Pitt was content. When the news of Rossbach arrived he wrote post-haste to Grenville, 'Heaven be praised for this great event. And now to dinner with a better appetite.'[6] He no longer had any

[1] Mitchell to Holdernesse, 30th Oct. 1757. Add. MSS. 6,806.
[2] Mitchell to Holdernesse, 1st Nov. 1757. Add. MSS. 6,831.
[3] Eichel to Mitchell, 6th Nov. 1757. Add. MSS. 6,847.
[4] Mitchell to Holdernesse, 11th Nov. 1757. Add. MSS. 6,806.
[5] Carlyle, VII, 285.
[6] Pitt to Grenville, 15th Nov. 1757. Grenville. *Papers*, I. 230.

need to worry about Parliament. When it met on the 1st of December 'there was not the least appearance of opposition in either House.'[1]

Much as Pitt rejoiced in Frederick's victories and greatly as they relieved his gloom, they also added to his difficulties. The time had come to prepare for next year's campaigns and he found consideration of them overshadowed by the glories, and over-weighted by the needs, of the 'Protestant Hero.' Everyone, including the Protestant Hero himself, wanted to cash in on his successes. Frederick hastened, through his Ministers, Podewils and Finkenstein, to impress upon Mitchell that, if he allowed Prince Ferdinand to take command of the Army of Observation, he had a right to insist on its reinforcement by English troops; such a demand was not only founded in justice, but was in accord with England's true interests; indeed 'les affaires du Continent meritent dans les circonstances epineuses ou elles se trouvent, toute l'attention de la Nation Angloise.'[2] This imperiousness was new, and one can understand that his victories may have gone a little to his head. There is no doubt, however, that these demands coincided with the views of the preponderating Whig element in Pitt's Ministry, and with the views which seemed to be sweeping the country. 'Thus,' said Symmer, epitomising the new trend, 'we have at last got into the sound path of politics, and I hope we shall persist in it.'[3]

Pitt was not blind to Frederick's needs, nor unwilling to help, but he was determined that he must himself decide the measure of that help, and in coming to a decision must be guided by his own views of England's overriding requirements. He was satisfied that the reconstituted Army of Observation, or Execution as Newcastle now dubbed it, was 'fully adequate to the great object of clearing the Electorate and finishing the French armies and French insolence and rapine in that suffering country, provided the King's army begins in time, and goes roundly to work.'[4] The safety of Hanover was, in his eyes, the full extent of England's true interest on the Continent; all else was at best loyalty to an ally and the price to be paid for 'containing operations.' He did not propose to waste a single English soldier—that precious commodity in such short supply—on Frederick's schemes; all

[1] Symmer to Mitchell, 2nd Dec. 1757. Add. MSS. 6,839.
[2] Podewils to Mitchell, 24th November 1757. Add. MSS. 6,848.
[3] Symmer to Mitchell, 2nd Dec. 1757. Add. MSS. 6,839.
[4] Pitt to Newcastle, 27th Nov. 1757. Add. MSS. 32,876.

that Frederick could expect, certainly all that he would get till circumstances had changed, was money, and of that, within reasonable limits, he could have as much as he could spend. Pitt was prepared to give a subsidy of four million crowns (£670,000) —up to then an unheard-of sum—and Parliament at his instigation was prepared to foot the bill.

For the moment Pitt had his way, but the ferment beneath was very visible. Whilst Holdernesse told Mitchell that 'distraction and new dissensions would be the sure consequence of sending English troops,'[1] Newcastle told him with equal emphasis that he saw 'no salvation for this country, or Europe, but by some proper system on the Continent.'[2] What Mitchell was expected to make of these conflicting views, received by the same post, and how he was to interpret them to Frederick was not very clear. His position was particularly difficult, for he had to deal with an exasperated man for whom he felt not only the deepest respect but also the profoundest sympathy. Newcastle's view chimed in with his own wishes, and in the circumstances he could hardly be blamed for remembering that Newcastle was a man of weight and experience and also the First Lord of the Treasury. Inclination and some appearance of authority joined to justify him in his own eyes in supporting Frederick's demands. How far he misled Frederick it is impossible to say, but Frederick chose this moment to show himself more than usually difficult. He thought he could force Pitt's hand, and by way of bringing pressure to bear refused to sign a Convention, proposed by England, under which, in return for his subsidy, he would undertake not to make peace except 'in concert and by mutual agreement' with Great Britain.

Pitt's irritation overflowed and was vented on Mitchell. It was bad enough to have continual struggles with his own colleagues; it was intolerable if our Ambassadors in foreign capitals were to join in the opposition. Mitchell was an old friend and should have known Pitt's mind; he was admittedly no fool and yet, as Pitt pointed out, his letters were constantly urging the dispatch of English troops to Germany, and 'his chief and favourite object' seemed to be 'to nourish the King of Prussia's mind with the fitness and practicability of that impossible measure.' Being well aware that Newcastle, as of old, was corresponding secretly with

[1] Holdernesse to Mitchell, 21st Dec. 1757. Add. MSS. 6,832.
[2] Newcastle to Mitchell, 23rd Dec. 1757. Add. MSS. 6,832.

all our representatives abroad, Pitt suspected that Mitchell's attitude was at least encouraged by, if not wholly due to, Newcastle's machinations. Determined to bring matters to a head, he sent a strong remonstrance, ostensibly aimed at Mitchell, but both in reality and in fact addressed to Newcastle himself. 'As,' he wrote, 'I cannot suffer myself to suppose that ignorance of all that passed last year, and is passing this, can have any share in Mr. Mitchell's conduct, it is evident to whom he belongs and whose work he is doing. Thus it is, my Lord, in every part of Government; the tools of another system are perpetually marring every hopeful measure of the present administration. In a word, if your Grace is not able to eradicate this lurking, diffusive poison a little more out of the mass of Government, especially from the vitals, I think it better for us to have done.'[1] The letter was too near the truth to leave Newcastle unmoved. In some perturbation he tried appeasement; he showed himself particularly gracious, making personal enquiries about Pitt's health, which Pitt answered with 'a thousand thanks' and something suspiciously like a snort; but he betrayed himself to posterity by writing at the same time to Hardwicke, 'Though I imagined Mr. Pitt would be still negative upon the point of sending troops from hence, I did not think he would have thought the present attempts for that purpose material enough to enter his *protest* in writing. . . . I am sorry this point is stirred *so soon*, and at present *so mal à propos*.'[2] It was of course disconcerting that Pitt should have penetrated his schemes so quickly and reacted so promptly; Newcastle was accustomed to more leisurely procedure.

Hardwicke could appreciate Pitt's feelings rather better, even if he could not enter fully into his hopes. He thought it as well to visit him about this time and has left an account that is not without its pathos. Pitt was 'wrapt up, in his easy chair, but low in spirits, possibly fatigued by being taken out of his bed.' Racked with pain, 'much affected' by the intrigues of the Hanoverian Ministers, still more affected by the intrigues of his colleagues, uncertain of Frederick's intentions and doubtful of the King's constancy, he had yet to bear on his shoulders the whole weight of responsibility. He was isolated and alone, thwarted by those who should support him, and for ever forced to battle with the whims of royalty. In his moment of depression he forgot even his innate awe of Kings,

[1] Pitt to Newcastle, 28th Jan. 1758. Add. MSS. 32,877.
[2] Newcastle to Hardwicke, 29th January 1758. Add. MSS. 32,877.

and confessed to Hardwicke that 'he saw a certain *great person* [George II] so apt to spoil his own business, that he pitied those who had served him formerly, whom possibly he had been forward to blame'—a recantation of previous tirades to which his detractors are welcome.[1]

None the less he was still conscious that he alone could save England, and he was still determined to raise her out of the trough of failure. Weak and ailing as he was, his spirit enabled him to outdistance others in physical effort no less than in genius. At the moment his main object was to come to an understanding with Frederick, for complete confidence between them must be the preliminary to success. He insisted that Mitchell must be recalled and his place taken by Sir Joseph Yorke, as the one hope of securing Frederick's signature to the Convention. In the meantime Mitchell must be given instructions which it was impossible for him to overlook or to misinterpret. Pitt's colleagues demurred, but he was on his high horse and simply overrode them. Holdernesse was instructed to prepare the draft. He brought it to Pitt, who proceeded to revise it. At three in the morning an exhausted Holdernesse, 'worn out with fatigue and *ennui*,' complained that for over five hours Pitt had been 'weighing words more than matter' and mutilating the draft 'so as to be scarce legible' without in any way altering the substance. 'I would not pass such another evening,' he declared, 'for the King's revenue or for what is perhaps more valuable, Mr. Pitt's abilities. Whatever objections he may for the future have to my performances, he will please to set down in writing, for I neither can nor will be detained for hours upon the introduction of a monosyllable.'[2] Newcastle soothed him in a kindly paternal fashion, but to Hardwicke he was forced to admit that Pitt knew what he was doing, and that a great deal more than monosyllables was at stake. 'The letter,' he said, 'is quite altered, and plainly is not from the same hand. In many parts it is better; and in the whole contains a justification of the present measure of denying the English troops, and is wrote for that purpose.'[3]

The letter, as altered, was masterly. Frederick, so its purport ran, must look at more than Europe; he must look at the whole field of war. If he did so, he would appreciate that however true

[1] Hardwicke to Newcastle, 19th Feb. 1758. Add. MSS. 32,877.
[2] Holdernesse to Newcastle, 25th Feb. 1758. Add. MSS. 32,878.
[3] Newcastle to Hardwicke, 26th Feb. 1758. Add. MSS. 32,878.

his arguments might be, their application was limited, while their converse was equally true and more far-reaching. In pressing for English reinforcements he had surely forgotten that Prince Ferdinand's army—'so very large a body of excellent Protestant troops'—was in fact an English army, not indeed composed of English troops but maintained by English money. He had forgotten, too, the enormous subsidy which had been offered to him and out of which other armies could be financed. One way or another England had allotted two millions sterling for the continental war, which could not be called neglect nor brushed aside as trifling. No doubt operations on the Continent would assist the campaigns in America, but it was no less true that 'the war in America will contribute considerably to bring France to reason.' France, as their latest treaty with Austria showed, were bent upon 'lowering the House of Brandenburg.' Prussia and England were thus thrown inevitably together; their fortunes were interwoven; they must stand side by side, each labouring in the field most suited to their respective abilities. England would do her part, but must first be assured that Frederick was in earnest; the subsidy would be paid as soon as the Convention had been signed, not before.[1]

Whether Pitt really doubted Mitchell, or was simply using him as a lever, is not altogether clear; there is some reason for thinking the latter. In either case his treatment proved efficacious; it gave a check to Newcastle and it brought Frederick to heel. The latter growled but gave way, authorising the signing of the Convention before Yorke arrived, and doing his best to retain Mitchell. It was his first direct experience of Pitt, and it drew him up with a jerk. Hitherto he had had a poor opinion of English Ministers; they were a weak and incompetent crew, and he believed that if he pressed them hard enough they would do as he bade them. Their trouble was lack of courage and he was playing with the idea of making up their minds for them by threatening to recall his own Ambassador, who was in fact joined shortly afterwards by a special envoy, Baron Knyphausen.[2] When therefore he heard that Pitt had forestalled him, the news came as a shock, both because he liked Mitchell and because this turning of the tables was an experience which he did not relish. The result was that he indulged in a little bluster, telling Mitchell that he had

[1] Holdernesse to Mitchell, 25th Feb. 1758. Add. MSS. 6,816.
[2] Mitchell to Holdernesse, 9th Feb. 1758. Add. MSS. 6,831

refused to be governed by Kings and would not be governed by Pitt. But he knew that Pitt had won, and after the bluster, he signed. With that Pitt relented and allowed Mitchell to remain.

Frederick's dawning respect for Pitt was no doubt increased by what he heard from Yorke. Pitt, so Yorke declared, insisted on Mitchell's recall, not only against the wishes of all the other Ministers but even of the King. Indeed, the King was helpless in his hands; all he could do was to protest that Pitt 'did not know mankind, much less how to deal with Kings,' before proving in his own person that at least Pitt knew how to deal with him. Pitt, in short, 'was now everything in England'; he was 'the sole man,' and being supported by Leicester House would 'govern absolutely' when the new reign began.[1] All of which was interesting but not by any means wholly correct.

Pitt had still to deal with America. Here, the problem was not so much how to coerce his colleagues as to win their attention. For them, America was still an annoying side-show, where the rapacity of France was only equalled by the boorishness of the colonists; they would be thankful if both could be forgotten. Yet here, in their unwilling admissions no less than in Pitt's reiterated belief, lay the key to victory and peace. To Pitt it seemed of the utmost importance that the plans of campaign should be settled at the earliest moment, and that the whole Cabinet should contribute whatever they had of wisdom and experience. But Christmas was coming, and Newcastle had guests at Claremont, that stately home in which he entertained his friends with the regal opulence of the eighteenth century. He slipped off to it quietly, sending excuses by Barrington. Pitt was not a master of irony for nothing. He replied through Barrington, which gave the letter a deliberately impersonal touch, expressing his sorrow at interrupting Newcastle's pleasure and business, which he recognised were one and the same, but declaring none the less that he could not take upon himself to direct the whole plan of American affairs without the assistance of a Cabinet, and particularly of his Grace; he must therefore ask him to attend a meeting in two days' time.[2] Newcastle was forced to write a personal apology, which incidentally underlined the contrast between his own superficial interest and Pitt's burning eagerness. He begged to be excused for the sole reason that the Bishop of

[1] Mitchell's *Journals*, April 1758. Add. MSS. 6,867.
[2] Barrington to Newcastle, 26th December 1757. Add. MSS. 32,876.

Durham was to be his guest for a few days. He thought he knew what was proposed for America, approved everything he had been told, and was sure he would concur in anything Pitt might do. He supposed that few of the Cabinet would attend as most were out of town for the holidays, and he hoped that in the circumstances there was no necessity for him to be present.[1]

Pitt's reply was dignified and should have crushed Newcastle had he not been so volatile. 'I hope,' he said, 'your Grace will not think me unreasonable or improper in wishing to have the sanction of a meeting of the Cabinet and particularly of your Grace present there, concerning so important and extensive a scene as the campaign in America, where England and Europe are to be fought for, and where all the data on which we are to ground any plan are so loose and precarious that, I confess, I do not see my way as clearly as I wish to do in matters where I make myself responsible. I cannot, however, after the desire your Grace has expressed not to break the agreeable engagements of Claremont, press any further your Grace's taking the trouble to come to Town.'[2] So much for the dignified façade. What it concealed appears from a letter written the same day to his cousin John. He had been waiting, he said, for a moment of leisure in which to write. But leisure was a rare commodity and as it seemed unlikely to come, he had set business on one side for a moment, to dream delicious dreams of his cousin walking through 'the solitudes of verdant Dorsetshire, amidst warm leases, heavy ewes and bounding lambs.' But the dreams faded, and he found himself once more in his office, 'worn with constant fatigue, and broken-hearted with the wretched interior of our condition, worse than all the foreign ills that threaten us. But I will not grow morose if I can help it, or utterly despair of better days.'[3]

Deserted by Newcastle and the usual Lords of the Cabinet, he set to work on what no one could now deny was his own plan. His determination was to recall the dawdling Loudoun, and to make a thrust at the gates of Canada with fresh troops under fresh leaders. In its broad outline there was nothing new in his strategy; he could only play variations on the original tune composed for Vetch in 1708 (see p. 25), displaying his mastery

[1] Newcastle to Pitt, 27th Dec. 1757. Add. MSS. 32,876.
[2] Pitt to Newcastle, 27th Dec. 1757. Add. MSS. 32,876.
[3] Pitt to J. Pitt, 27th Dec. 1757.

not so much in the choice of theme as in its development and execution. During his first Ministry he had concentrated on one single object—the capture of Louisburg—as the preliminary to an advance on Quebec by way of the St. Lawrence. To become master of Quebec was the heart of all his schemes; without it, Canada could never be conquered; with it, the conquest was for practical purposes complete. Shortly after his return to office he had learnt of Loudoun's failure. Angry as that had made him, what he regretted most was not the absence of victory but the loss of time. If Loudoun had tried and failed, he might have been forgiven; but he had wasted a year, which was unforgivable. To Pitt speed meant everything when his plans might be frustrated and his hopes cut off at a moment's notice by the doubting men around him, and the hazards of the European war. Peace might supervene, and as one, Murdoch, remarked about this very time: 'peace, in my simple conceit, might be the worst thing that could happen to us for these two years to come. We should lose all our past expence (with our honour) and it would still remain undecided who was master at sea.'[1] Pitt needed a couple of years at least to decide not only the mastery of the sea but the future of America, and Loudoun had thrown away twelve precious months.

In order to catch up some part of the lost time, Pitt no sooner heard of Loudoun's failure than he dispatched orders to Holburne not to bring his whole fleet back to England but to leave at least eight ships of the line to winter at Halifax, 'taking care to choose such as shall be in best condition and fittest for that service.'[2] With this dispatch Pitt laid the foundation for a new system of naval strategy, which was not only sounder in conception but swifter in action. Hitherto the main fleet had been used to convoy the transports across the Atlantic, a system which involved intolerable delays while the transports were being collected, cramped the activities of the fleet during the voyage, and left the ocean largely unguarded for the passage of French troops. To Pitt it seemed evident that transports ran very little risk while they were at large on the high seas; they were most open to attack and most in need of defence near the ports of embarkation and arrival, where their routes were well known and defined. The home fleet could protect the transports at the beginning of

[1] Murdoch to Mitchell, 29th Nov. 1757. Add. MSS. 6,840.
[2] Pitt to Holburne, 21st Sept. 1757. Kimball, I, 110.

their voyage and keep a watch over the French ports. Across the Atlantic, the fleet destined for American affairs, if sent out in advance, could see the transports safe into harbour and cut off any French troopships that might slip over. Thus distributed, both fleets would have the benefit of greater flexibility, whilst the troops would be safer, and operations could begin at an earlier date. It was a momentous development.

The actual operations contemplated by Pitt were simple in conception. Abercromby was to take Loudoun's place, and with 6,000 regulars and 9,000 provincials was to advance by the Hudson route for 'an attempt on either Montreal or Quebec, or both of the said places successively.'[1] Meanwhile Amherst with 14,000 regulars was to renew the attack on Louisburg and then, if time allowed, follow on to Quebec by way of the St. Lawrence. A third force of 4,000 men under Forbes was to deal with Fort Duquesne and recover the control of the Ohio valley. Such was the strategy, which, if simple in its broad outline, involved a multitude of details. Pitt wasted no time; by the end of the year the necessary orders had been issued.

[1] Kimball, I, 144.

18

TROUBLES AT HOME

(i)

Whilst Pitt was waiting for his plans to fructify abroad, there was plenty to occupy him at home. First in importance, because most entirely characteristic, was his fight to extend the Habeas Corpus Act.

Someone had been illegally taken by the press gang, and on applying for a writ of habeas corpus, had been unable to obtain it because writs could not be issued in civil cases during the vacation. Here was a challenge which Pitt could not ignore, the more so as the man's treatment not only drew attention to this defect in the Act but also to a new procedure which the judges had introduced on their own authority. Owing to the increase in the size of the forces, the Courts were being overwhelmed with cases of alleged wrongful impressment, and the judges had privately decided that, instead of issuing the writ automatically, they would first give the military authorities an opportunity to show cause why it should not be issued. Their object was to speed up legal procedure, but their action horrified Pitt. He had always mistrusted lawyers. Law was the safeguard of liberty, but the abuse of law was the end of liberty. In their thin-spun arguments and maze of subtle distinctions, the lawyers were apt to overlook the great principles of life; they could too easily degenerate into petty tyrants without even realising the fact, and for that reason arbitrary power was more to be feared in their hands than in the hands of the military. Here was a case very much in point: the judges were taking upon themselves to alter an Act of Parliament; it was their business to declare the law and apply it to the individual case, never to make it. Above all they must not meddle, even with the best of intentions, in anything that pertained to the liberty of the subject.[1] Pitt, with the help of Pratt,

[1] C. Yorke to Hardwicke, 11th March, 1758. Add. MSS. 35,353.

his Attorney-General, drafted a Bill to put this matter right.

His proposals were bitterly opposed by Hardwicke, Mansfield and Newcastle. The first two were no doubt honest objectors but, according to the general belief, were acting out of pique at not being consulted in advance—a view which receives some support from Hardwicke's acidulous remark: 'I do not believe there ever was, from the beginning of time, an instance of a point of this nature so taken up, and so pushed. A mere question of law; two lawyers in the King's Cabinet Council, and not one word of consultation or communication with either of them; but entirely cooked up between himself and his new Attorney-General, who must be entirely unexperienced in constitutional or parliamentary measures.'[1] Newcastle had no views on the matter and was simply following Hardwicke's lead; he was not concerned with the merits of the case, but welcomed any chance to trip up Pitt and blacken him in the King's eyes, short of driving him to resign. It was with obvious relish that he wrote: 'His Majesty is more zealous than ever against the Bill. . . . He expressed the greatest dissatisfaction with Mr. Pitt, and I could find, though there was nothing dropt directly, that the King entertained a hope that somehow or other he should get rid of him.'[2] Nor were Newcastle and the King alone in looking forward to the time when they could turn to rend the greatest of their Ministers. It was about this same Bill that Lyttelton wrote with bitter venom: 'these things will be treasured up against the *day of wrath*, which will come sooner or later, according to the success we meet with in the war.'[3] Whatever their motives, the Whig magnates took infinite pains to secure the rejection of the Bill;[4] they rallied their followers in Parliament; they primed Lady Yarmouth with arguments and they persuaded the King that his prerogative was involved. In the circumstances it was highly significant that the Bill passed through the Commons with ease. Pitt was gaining the ascendancy even in Newcastle's Parliament.

None the less the political world was expecting trouble; so much so that Fox, who had sunk into obscurity at the Pay Office, pricked up his ears, and thought it as well to ingratiate himself with Newcastle by opposing Pitt. A breach in the ranks of

[1] Hardwicke to Newcastle, 17th May 1758. Add. MSS. 32,880.
[2] Newcastle to Hardwicke, 16th May 1758. Add. MSS. 32,880.
[3] Phillimore, p. 609.
[4] 'The King and myself are taking measures every day to make our majority as great as possible.' Newcastle to Hardwicke, 16th May 1758. Add. MSS. 32,880.

coalition seemed certain, and the defeat of the Bill in the Lords, where Pitt had little influence, was taken for granted.[1] There were ominous growls in the Press, where it was suggested that public meetings should be called to support the Bill of 'the three monosyllables.' (Pitt, Legge and Pratt.) Newcastle took fright. 'Mr. Pitt,' he told Hardwicke, 'should certainly be spoken to, by some person of great weight and consideration, and shewed the consequences to government which must arise from letting the mob loose in this manner.'[2] It did not apparently occur to Newcastle to consider the consequences to the mob which might arise from the failure to amend the law.

If Newcastle was alarmed and Hardwicke hurt, Pitt was not growing more amenable. No doubt he would have been wise to take Hardwicke and Mansfield into his confidence before embarking on the Bill, but perhaps the omission was due to their own conduct. Pitt had tried to secure Cabinet help in matters of moment where the responsibility pressed heavily on him, and he had been fobbed off with trivial excuses, learning without enthusiasm that dinner parties must be allowed precedence over the war in America. Why court similar repulses in a matter where he felt no weight of responsibility and had no doubt of the proper course? At the same time, he was earnestly anxious that the Bill should become law, because he was convinced that it was necessary and just. When therefore he realised the strength of opposition in the Lords, he took considerable pains to overcome it. He descended suddenly on Newcastle, found him entertaining guests at dinner, outstayed the company, and after a little forced conversation, plunged headlong into his subject. He spoke in the manner customary to him when in earnest, the manner which had so often dismayed the King—as though he were addressing a large meeting—and overwhelmed Newcastle in a spate of arguments and eloquence. Newcastle had never responded to either and was not likely to respond now. He neither knew nor cared about the rights and wrongs of the subject; his mind had been long made up and the only result of Pitt's efforts was that he became mulishly obstinate. As he explained afterwards: 'I saw I was to be bullied and I determined to stick to my point.' Pitt grew exasperated, and giving up argument, took a high line: 'those who supported my Lord Mansfield,' he declared, 'must

[1] Walpole to Mann, 31st May 1758.
[2] Newcastle to Hardwicke, 27th March 1758. Add. MSS. 32,878.

take my Lord Mansfield's fate.' Upon which Newcastle spoke reproachfully of his conscience and of doing what he thought right; and when Pitt went on to complain, in a heightened tone, that in entering into the coalition he had thought he was connecting himself with those who were friends to liberty, Newcastle asseverated, quite untruthfully, that he was very indifferent to what people might think of him. 'In short,' Newcastle summed up, 'a greater rhapsody of violence and virulence could not be flung out'—from which one may assume that Pitt had gone the wrong way to work and had failed, and that failure was widening the breach between them.[1] The assumption is confirmed by Newcastle's querulous complaint a few days later: 'For my own part I am determined not to continue in business upon the present foot; obliged every day to be teazing and proposing disagreeable things to the King, and instead of being thanked for it, to meet with constant reproaches, jealousies and an overbearing superiority; and (what is still worse) laid under the greatest difficulties every day, from proceedings in Parliament without concert, or any management whatever for myself or my friends, with whom no measures are kept, or of whom no *good* notice is ever taken.'[2] His complaint can fitly stand beside an extract from a letter by Pitt which shows that feelings in the other camp were not unruffled: 'my heart is too full not to say, what a happy scene of harmony and strength to governments is thrown away for the glory of the Robe. Are they determined to involve all in confusion?'[3]

Having failed with Newcastle, Pitt tried Lady Yarmouth. But in negotiations of this type he was no match for his opponents. Lady Yarmouth had already been primed. Hardwicke's method for securing the rejection of the Bill was to refer the matter to the judges in a series of carefully prepared questions, leaving Mansfield to give them 'right hints' on the answers expected.[4] The propriety of this suggestion had been impressed upon the lady. She, in turn, urged it upon Pitt and had the privilege of striking out of him one of his better known and more picturesque remarks: 'Madam,' he said, 'if all the Bishops on the Bench should be of opinion that the people should not have the use of the Bible, would the people part with their Bible?' His point

[1] Newcastle to Hardwicke, 14th April 1758. Add. MSS. 32,879.
[2] Newcastle to Hardwicke, 26th April 1758. Add. MSS. 32,879.
[3] Pitt to Newcastle, 11th May 1758. Add. MSS. 32,880.
[4] Hardwicke to Newcastle, 17th May 1758. Add. MSS. 32,880.

was sound. Judges should not be introduced into the arena of legislation. By all means let them expound the law, but let them be silent on proposed alterations or extensions. When the matter came before them, the judges proved to be wiser and more constitutional than Hardwicke. They answered those of the questions put to them which merely asked for a statement of the existing law, but excused themselves from answering any others.

In spite of their silence, Hardwicke had his way: the Bill was rejected. But in the long run Pitt was justified. The defects of the Act, says a great constitutional authority, 'notwithstanding a serious attempt in 1757 to render the habeas corpus at Common Law more efficient, subsisted down to the year 1816, when they were at length removed.'[1]

(ii)

From law, Pitt turned to finance. It is commonly supposed that in prosecuting his wars, he was financially reckless. The supposition is misleading. He preferred not to interfere in the more prosaic details of ways and means, possibly because he had no flair for such matters, and certainly because they lay within Newcastle's department. None the less he was deeply interested in finance. His motive in waging war was not merely conquest. In a sense conquest was immaterial; its virtue lay in promoting and safeguarding trade. Pitt's ultimate aim was to make war pay by removing rivals and securing markets. He knew, however, that success could not be bought without its price in money as well as in men. If wealth was the end of war, it was also the means; capital must be risked in order to be increased. In Pitt's strategy economic pressure was one of the weapons of war and by no means the least important; its claims for men and material must be weighed against the competing claims of the services. The workings of his mind appear with startling clearness in the instructions given to Mitchell, who was directed to tell the incredulous Frederick that in the allocation of England's manpower, the needs of England's manufacturers must take precedence over continental expeditions.[2]

[1] Taswell-Langmead, pp. 491-2.

[2] 'It would be equally improper to think of sending a body of national troops into Germany. . . . By the numbers that are now in arms our manufacturers lose a number of hands formerly employed in the most useful manner to that which makes the strength of this country, its trade.' Holdernesse to Mitchell, 12th Dec. 1757. Add. MSS. 6,815.

Pitt kept a careful watch over trade and commerce, and saw nothing in their progress, after his own rise to power, to cause him alarm. It is significant that 1756 'marked the lowest point of the depression of commerce, whence it gradually rose';[1] it is no less significant that 'the prosperity of our foreign traffic, during the war of 1755, at least from the year 1758, is a fact, in our commercial annals, which has excited the amazement of the world.'[2] So long as income was rising faster than expenditure, Pitt could feel that he was justified. But not even the justification of the end could excuse extravagance on the way, and from time to time Pitt chafed at evidence of carelessness and waste.

At this particular period, the quarrel over the Habeas Corpus Act made him look with a jaundiced eye at any signs of extravagance. He was also influenced by his distrust of the Chancellor of the Exchequer. Early in January, Legge showed signs of restiveness. He complained that Pitt was treating him without regard and was obviously avoiding meetings. He professed a desire to support Pitt, but protested that 'he did not like to remain under the harrow,' and therefore wished either to be sent as Keene's successor to Madrid, or, preferably, to be given a peerage so that he could take refuge in the House of Lords. It is certain that Pitt had been suspicious of Legge for some time past and probably doubted his abilities as well as his honesty. But Legge's feelings are not so clear. He was ambitious without any real capacity, and wanted a peerage for its own sake, and not merely as a refuge from Pitt's tyranny. When therefore he said that Pitt was jealous of him and wanted to get him out of the House of Commons, it may well be that he was purposely exaggerating.[3] Yet the presence of friction can hardly be denied, and it added to Pitt's responsibilities and increased his sense of loneliness.

In this mood he undertook the task of getting the House to pass a vote of credit for the Army of Observation. He approached the subject in a grudging spirit, impelled to condone the expense because of the failures in other directions—in America, where nothing had been done; at Rochefort, where nothing had been attempted; in Europe, where Closterseven had nearly annihilated an army. That army, he stressed, needed instant succour, which the vote would enable him to give. The cost would be great; it would be enormous; but the time had come when the country

[1] Chalmers' *Estimate*, p. 115. [2] *Ibid,* p. 142.
[3] Newcastle to Hardwicke, 7th Jan. 1758. Add. MSS. 32,877.

must exert its whole force to secure victory. Not to follow up Frederick's unparalleled success at Rossbach, not to make use of Ferdinand's 50,000 Protestant troops, would be the greatest folly, especially when commerce destruction was beginning to constrict the power of France. Her resources were dwindling, ours were great; and great expenses were now the best economy.[1] The House passed the Vote, to Newcastle's satisfaction.[2]

But a Vote of Credit was one thing; the actual expenses another. When Pitt came to examine the estimates he was, or professed to be, shocked. The total, he declared, was so prodigious that he could not rest at ease. The figures were inflated, the numbers were excessive, the demands were 'preposterous and enough to revolt all the world.' 'I would to God,' he continued, 'I could see my way through this mountain of expense, but I confess I cannot, unless your Grace can prevail to reduce things to a reasonable bulk.'[3]

In making these protests there can be little doubt that he was not actuated solely by the desire to keep costs down. One of his most lively fears had been that the King would accept the money for Ferdinand's army without handing over the control, and would continue to use the troops for Hanoverian purposes, under the directions of his Hanoverian Ministers. Pitt considered that as England had now taken over the expense, the army should be regarded as part of the English forces, should be used for English purposes and should be subject to the orders of the Cabinet—that is to say, of Pitt. At an early stage, he had hinted this to Hardwicke, who had clearly not understood him.[4] Now, he pressed the point again. Newcastle, who was worried over the popular attitude towards the Habeas Corpus Bill, and frightened at Pitt's fulmination against extravagance, was only too thankful to find something which seemed to him trifling and could be conceded by way of a sop. Accordingly he persuaded the King to meet Pitt's wishes, and having done so, wrote with 'great satisfaction' to tell him that the King had most readily agreed that 'all the correspondence with Prince Ferdinand relating to the motives and operations of the Army should be carried on with the English Secretary of State.'[5] It was—*pace* Newcastle—an

[1] West to Newcastle, 20th Jan. 1758. Add. MSS. 32,877.
[2] Newcastle to Hardwicke, 21st Jan. 1758. Add. MSS. 32,877.
[3] Pitt to Newcastle, 6th March 1758. Add. MSS. 32,878.
[4] Hardwicke to Newcastle, 19th Feb. 1758. Add. MSS. 32,877.
[5] Newcastle to Pitt, 24th March 1758. Add. MSS. 32,878.

important concession, for with it Pitt obtained direct control of all the forces which England could bring into the field. There remained only the need to make sure of Frederick, who had not yet signed the Convention. Until Pitt had obtained his signature, he continued irritable and restive, and greatly troubled his colleagues by allowing his restiveness to appear. In particular he dismayed Holdernesse by telling him that, as he was not greatly edified by the nature or tone of Frederick's latest instructions to his Ambassador, he was in no hurry to see Michel, who must wait 'till the ordinary round of weekly labours' began again on Monday, when Pitt would hear him as patiently as he could.[1] Pitt was creating an atmosphere which he hoped would produce results in Berlin. Actually, and perhaps unexpectedly, it produced a stronger reaction in London. Shocked to the core at such cavalier treatment of an Ambassador and searching for the possible cause, Newcastle recalled with a feeling of guilt that he had ignored a modest request from Pitt and augured the worst from Pitt's ominous silence. 'I suppose,' he said, 'the disposition of the Bishoprics don't please him,'[2] but he knew perfectly well that the Bishops were not the real cause of Pitt's displeasure. If he had any doubt, Pitt made it plain in a letter too delicious to be omitted: 'I had not time today, in the multitude of other matters, to renew an affair I have extremely at heart, and which I mentioned to your Grace some time since. It is a Prebend of Westminster, Canterbury or Windsor, for the Chaplain of the House of Commons. Mr. Speaker has again strongly recommended him to his Majesty's favour; and I, knowing my entire inability to *do this mighty matter*, beg leave to rest it with your Grace, upon the justice and decency of the pretension. As I have not had one word to say concerning Hierarchys or Powers, I would fain hope that I might be indulged an humble prebend in the name of the Commons of England.'[3] Perhaps it is needless to say that the steam-hammer successfully cracked the nut.

But this by-play was not allowed to obliterate the question of finance, nor was compliance in the matter of prebends taken as excuse for non-compliance in the matter of pounds. Newcastle's efforts to reduce the estimate for Ferdinand's troops produced a total which still left Pitt 'astonished and overwhelmed with its

[1] Pitt to Holdernesse, 26th March 1758. Add. MSS. 32,878.
[2] Newcastle to Hardwicke, 27th March 1758. Add. MSS. 32,878.
[3] Pitt to Newcastle, 29th March 1758. Add. MSS. 32,878.

exorbitance,' and as Newcastle was being difficult over a number of matters Pitt was determined to show his displeasure. He gave vent to his feelings in a brief but exceedingly pungent letter. 'Permit me to observe, that every discussion this insatiable service has undergone, your Grace has suffered the demand to swell in a manner beyond all decency. I must beg to *disclaim* any part in the controlling and reducing this expence: the work, such as it is, must stand upon the authority of the Treasury, and I fear the public will think that the necessary monosyllable *NO* has been forgot between your Grace and M. Munchhausen. Pardon this freedom, but I owe it to your Grace, to my self and to an ill-requited Country.'[1]

If Pitt was acrimonious and tart, it is only right to remember that he was also ill, overworked, lonely and up to the present unsuccessful. Nor must it be forgotten that he had been forced into a coalition with men whom he distrusted and despised, knowing that they had the cohorts with which to overwhelm him, if they dared, whilst he had nothing to oppose to them except the fickle popularity of the mob and the lash of his tongue. He felt himself 'cabined, cribbed and confined,' and he rebelled against the undignified and unnecessary frustration which he had to endure.

The only effect of his tartness was to confirm Newcastle in his determination to run no risks. If Pitt disliked the estimates, if he thought they would rouse the ire of the nation, then Newcastle would have nothing to do with them until they had been countersigned by Pitt. 'I do not,' he replied, 'look upon the fixing this estimate to belong to the Treasury. . . . I know too well my own situation to think it either for the service of the King, or the public, or for my own credit, to bring any such demand before Parliament which has not your entire concurrence, approbation and support.'[2] In parliamentary finesse there is not the slightest doubt that Newcastle was Pitt's superior. He knew that Pitt could not afford to lose the money. He was quite safe, therefore, in throwing the onus, and whatever unpopularity there might be, on to Pitt. Pitt accepted the burden; he had no alternative; but it only served to emphasise his loneliness and to inflame his irritation.

[1] Pitt to Newcastle, 4th April 1758. Add. MSS. 32,879.
[2] Newcastle to Pitt, 5th April 1758. Add. MSS. 32,879.

19

MINOR OPERATIONS

(i)

By November 1757, Ferdinand had taken over command of the reconstituted Army of Observation. That part of Germany in which he had to operate is cut into a number of oblongs by rivers running roughly parallel with one another—the Elbe; the Weser with its tributary the Aller; the Ems and the Rhine. The opening phases of the new campaign took place between the Elbe and the Weser, where Ferdinand and Richelieu alternately advanced and retired. Ferdinand's policy was clear. There was no necessity to risk a pitched battle; he could, if he were skilful, manœuvre the French backwards as far as the Rhine by cutting off their sources of supply. Those supplies were coming from East Friesland down the Ems and the Weser. There was no other source nearer than the Rhine towns, and the country between the Rhine and the Weser was not fit for road transport in the spring. Ferdinand's object therefore was to gain control of the river estuaries. He was already master of the Elbe, and shortly after the campaign opened in February (1758) he was able, by pouncing on Verden near the junction of the Aller and the Weser, to drive the French behind those rivers. His next objective was the Ems, and, as further advance was becoming difficult, he wanted Pitt to help by blockading, and if possible seizing, Emden at the river's mouth.

Pitt was in high spirits at Ferdinand's initial successes. He declared that they had cured the gout in his hand, and he must use his recovered limb 'to express the true joy of my heart at these favourable openings of a plan worthy of his Majesty.' His glee, as too often, bubbled up into quaintness of style which tended to hide his real feelings under a veneer of artificiality. 'May the sword of Prince Ferdinand,' he prayed on this occasion, 'confound the insidious friendship of the French Pensioner Bernstorff, and the Collegiate cunning of the Pedants of Stade!', Bernstorff being the Danish Minister who was frustrating Pitt's attempts to secure an agreement with Denmark, and the Pedants of Stade being presumably the Hanoverian Ministers who had approved the Convention of Closterseven.[1] Pitt, in short, was disposed in Ferdinand's favour, though he was not disposed to alter his policy in any fundamental aspect.

As the English fleet had by this time gained an ascendancy over the French, it was possible, without departing from any principle, to bring naval pressure to bear on the coasts of Germany facing the North Sea. Accordingly Pitt sent Commodore Holmes with a tiny squadron of two frigates, a bomb-ketch and an armed cutter to operate off the estuary of the Ems. In a brilliant little campaign, Holmes entered the river, captured a number of vessels, and by threatening Emden from an unexpected quarter, either forced, or at least hastened, the evacuation of the town. The French, under Clermont, who had succeeded Richelieu, retired behind the Rhine, whereupon Ferdinand urged Pitt to send a garrison of English troops to occupy Emden. This request, involving, as it did, military as opposed to naval intervention, raised a new and thorny problem.

It came whilst Pitt was still fencing with Frederick over the matter of the Convention, and was very much in his mind on that Monday morning (27th March 1758) when he received Michel and 'heard him as patiently as he could.' The meeting was not as uncomfortable as Holdernesse and Newcastle had feared. Pitt was reasonable, calm and firm. He told Michel that he could not comply with Frederick's request for a fleet in the Baltic, and went on to make the penetrating remark that, by asking for a small force, Frederick showed that his real object was not military but political; he was clearly doubtful of England's intentions and wished to compromise her. There were, however, other and better ways in which England's sincerity could be proved, and Pitt would adopt them. Meanwhile he would soon be obliged to bring before Parliament the estimates for the Army of Observation, and it would both help him and be for the honour and interest of Frederick, if those estimates could be 'founded upon and blended with the Prussian Convention.' The conversation ended with a reference to Emden. Michel hoped that Pitt would send a small English garrison to occupy the town. Pitt was

[1] Pitt to Newcastle, 28th Feb. 1758. Add. MSS. 32,878.

discreetly silent. He recognised 'in its full extent the utility of that measure,' but he also recognised its implications. As an offshoot of the Convention with Frederick it might be acceptable because it could be limited, but without the Convention it would be regarded by political friends and foes alike as something more than the mere defence of Emden, as, in short, the thin end of the wedge which would lead to a continental war pure and simple. 'If,' he told Holdernesse, 'proper assurances were given him that no future demand in relation to English troops would be founded on his compliance in this article, he would see—he would try—how far the measure of sending a small force to Emden could be complied with.' But, above all, the concession, if made, must be made in such a way as to forward the negotiations with Frederick. Pitt had sensed that they had taken 'a favourable turn,' and he was willing to make this small concession in order to clinch matters.[1] He was right in his hopes and his methods. Frederick, as already explained, signed the Convention, whereupon George II, in a Declaration no doubt drafted by Pitt, stated that, as a fresh proof of his sincere friendship, he had 'ordered one of his battalions to march, without loss of time, to Emden.'[2]

(ii)

Holmes' small squadron and the Emden garrison did not exhaust the forces available to Pitt for minor but profitable operations. There was one project which he had long had in mind, both for its own sake and for its possibilities. As far back as the early months of 1756 Thomas Cumming, a Quaker merchant, had tried to interest the Government in the French trading posts at Senegal and Goree on the West African coast; he thought they could be captured easily and perhaps without bloodshed, and would more than repay the cost by the trade in gums and slaves which they would promote. He had put his plans before Fox, Halifax, Anson and the Duke of Cumberland, and had been received with the bored politeness of sceptical authority, which had no intention of doing anything. When Pitt became Secretary of State, Cumming tried again, and was received in a very different spirit. Pitt appreciated the many possibilities.

[1] Holdernesse to Newcastle, 27th March 1758. Add. MSS. 32,878.
[2] Jenkinson, III, 66.

Success would mean that the French navy would be further extended; the French army burdened with more objects to defend; a port of call for the French East India-bound ships closed; and lying behind all these military advantages, French trade would *pro tanto* decline and English trade improve, and there would open up the prospect of exploring the unknown hinterland with its promise of untapped riches. Pitt took immediate steps to prepare an expedition, but his plans were shelved when he was dismissed. He had not, however, forgotten them and they were revived on his return to power. They fitted in very well with his desire to distract French attention from Germany in the early months of 1758; they offered the prospect of a minor success with which to cheer the nation; they were in keeping with Frederick's suggestion that expeditions should be undertaken in other continents; and, perhaps best of all, they required very small forces. In March (1758) Pitt dispatched a squadron of three men-of-war, a sloop and two busses under Captain Marsh to see what could be done. Cumming went with the expedition, which was strengthened by the addition of Major Mason and 200 marines.

It arrived off the mouth of the Senegal River on the 24th of April, and a week later captured Fort Louis which protected the French settlement. There was a rich haul of booty—230 prisoners, 92 cannon, 500 slaves, 400 tons of gum, a quantity of gold dust and dollars, together with goods for barter, stores and provisions.[1] Pitt received the happy news on the 10th of June. He promptly appointed Mason Governor of the new conquest and diverted four companies, who were on the point of sailing for Jamaica, to Senegal as reinforcements, because, as he said, 'the preservation and defence of the Forts and Settlements . . . are of high importance to the trade of these kingdoms.'[2] Mason, meanwhile, was told to discover 'the nature of the trade carried on up the said river Senegal, and also the various productions and sources of the riches of those countries.'[3] Pitt was determined to promote trade whilst he prosecuted the war.

Mason's first attempt on Goree failed, but, later in the year (see p. 296), Pitt sent a further expedition under Keppel, which after a stormy and eventful voyage arrived off Goree on the 28th of December (1758) and captured the island the next day.[4] France

[1] Hotblack, p. 36.
[2] Pitt to Mason, 15th June 1758. Hotblack, p. 196.
[3] Hotblack, p. 37.
[4] Keppel, I, 273.

had been driven from the west coast of Africa, and her trade there absorbed by England.

(iii)

Useful as these operations were, Pitt had another object nearer his heart—the renewal of descents on the French coast. He was convinced that such small forces as could be spared, whilst the American war was still undecided, would be employed far more effectively in spreading alarm and uncertainty along the coasts of France than in forming a trifling addition to European armies. He was supported in his views by Frederick, who at this very moment was telling Mitchell that a descent at Boulogne, Calais or l'Orient would throw the French into confusion, as their troops at home were few in number and very scattered.[1]

But if these descents were to produce their full effect, they must be made at the proper time as well as the proper place. They should as far as possible coincide with the movements of the allies in Germany. Ferdinand's early successes pointed to the probability of a pitched battle in the course of the summer and, if Frederick did not throw up the sponge, he too might produce another of his unexpected encounters. Pitt studied the possibilities and, directly he saw a prospect of Frederick's signature to the Convention, called a meeting of the Cabinet to consider and approve his tentative arrangements. Truth to tell, he indulged in a little *suppressio veri.* He played down his real intentions and played up to his reluctant colleagues by declaring that nothing could be more satisfactory to the King of Prussia than an assurance that England's forces were 'actually in readiness to act offensively' when the proper moment arrived, for which purpose he intended to collect troops on the Isle of Wight with sufficient transports to carry them wherever necessary. Such a concentration, he added with a hint of *suggestio falsi,* would be 'equally useful in regard to defensive as well as offensive measures.'[2] His advocacy was successful; Cabinet and King gave their approval; and troops and transports were collected and a fleet assembled. The choice of commanders came next and was not easy. The troops were placed under the Duke of Marlborough and Lord George Sackville. Marlborough was fifty-two and Master-General of the Ordnance, but had little experience of field operations and has

[1] Mitchell to Holdernesse, 9th Feb. 1758. Add. MSS. 6,831.

[2] Holdernesse to Newcastle, 27th March 1758. Add. MSS. 32,878.

been described as 'a man with a great name but small ability.'[1] Sackville enjoyed at the time a high repute with Pitt, but his subsequent behaviour belied it. The omens therefore were not good from the military point of view. On the naval side, the difficulties were of another sort. Pitt had decided on an innovation. He was always willing to learn from mistakes and had come to the conclusion that the expedition against Rochefort had failed mainly because the wrong type of ship had been chosen; there had been too many large vessels which could not approach inshore, and too few boats to make the landing swift and successful. He had consequently determined that on this occasion the main fleet should cover the operations from a distance, while a flotilla of smaller vessels under a separate command should be responsible for the disembarkation. Hawke was to command the covering fleet, while Richard Howe was to have charge of the smaller vessels. Howe was an officer of outstanding ability, but he was low on the list of post captains, and his appointment in this way to an independent command so outraged Hawke's sense of propriety that he instantly struck his flag. His explosive and impetuous reaction created a difficult situation, which was not overcome until Anson agreed to take the command of the covering fleet himself, appointing Hawke as his second.[2] One other alteration Pitt made: the miscarriage at Rochefort had depreciated the word 'expedition,' and Pitt substituted the word 'enterprize.'[3]

When the preparations were nearing completion, the occasion had to be created. As the descent was to coincide with active operations on the Continent, Pitt encouraged Ferdinand to advance across the Rhine, and then, after allowing sufficient time for him to receive and act on his instructions, set the diversionary 'enterprize' in motion. It was no easy task, especially as Pitt was ill and worried. At home, Hester had recently given birth to their third child, Harriot (18th April), and had gone down to Stowe to recuperate, leaving him lonely and anxious. In Parliament there was no peace for him. The wrangle over the estimates was barely subsiding; the storm over the Habeas Corpus Bill was steadily mounting; and his colleagues were angry and obstructive. He himself was depressed and discouraged, inclined to be sulky and unwilling to see Ministers or even the King. His general

[1] Tunstall. *William Pitt*, p. 208.
[2] Burrows, pp. 176 ff.
[3] *A Journal of the Campaign*, etc., p. 2.

theme was that if he was to be thwarted, others should bear the burden; he could do no more in view of 'the fatal difficulties thrown on me in carrying forward the King's business.'[1] The difficulties were, of course, simply his inability to get his own way, coupled, perhaps, with his colleagues' complete sterility of ideas; but he felt them acutely and they aggravated his mental dyspepsia. 'My condition,' he wrote to Newcastle, 'still disables me from having the honour to attend his Majesty's presence and my health requires country air,' which he proposed to get at Hayes. At the same time, as the season was advancing, some decision must be reached on the expedition. He therefore begged Newcastle to get the King's consent to the plans and his authority for the drafting of Marlborough's instructions.[2]

A week later Pitt was back in Town, and with or without the King's authority had Marlborough's instructions in his pocket. Still feeling peevish, he sent a peremptory summons to Newcastle and Holdernesse to attend a meeting the next evening so that Marlborough could be dispatched to his command at once. Newcastle was sufficiently overawed to obey, though he did so reluctantly as he was taking his ease at Claremont and had 'engaged a great deal of company to dine.' However, he now knew better than to delay any service which Pitt regarded as important,[3] but he complained privately that the meeting was unnecessary, that little passed at it which was material and that the instructions contained nothing new.[4]

In spite of the bickering between the Ministers, the expedition sailed on the 1st of June and came to anchor two days later in Cancale Bay, near St. Malo. The troops were landed without loss and with very little opposition; they burnt a number of vessels at St. Servan, and apparently indulged in an orgy of plunder and destruction 'to the reproach of discipline, and disgrace of humanity.' Shortly afterwards they were re-embarked as, on nearer view, the generals considered St. Malo too strong to be taken. They then reconnoitred along the coast, looking in at Granville, Le Havre, Harfleur and Cherbourg, but the weather becoming unfavourable, provisions running short and hay for the horses being almost exhausted, they decided to return to England and reached St. Helen's on the 30th of June. 'Such,' said a member

[1] Pitt to Holdernesse, 11th May 1758. Add. MSS. 32,880.
[2] Pitt to Newcastle, 11th May 1758. Add. MSS. 32,880.
[3] Pitt to Newcastle and Newcastle to Pitt, 18th May 1758. Add. MSS. 32,880.
[4] Newcastle to Hardwicke, 21st May 1758. Add. MSS. 32,880.

of the expedition, 'was the issue of our first enterprize; an enterprize achieved with considerable success, if we consider the damage done to the enemy's shipping, and the object which the Ministry had in view, namely, to secure the navigation of the English Channel; to alarm the French King in such a manner as would oblige him to employ a great number of troops for the defence of his coast; to hamper him in the prosecution of his designs upon Germany; and to screen the kingdoms of Great Britain from all apprehension of invasion and insult.'[1]

If the writer's conclusion must be regarded as exuberant, it is still pertinent to remark that the enterprize coincided very closely with Ferdinand's operations on the Rhine culminating in his victory at Crevelt (23rd June 1758), and was clearly intended by Pitt to do so. He wanted a specific operation to draw away French forces, and when news arrived of the failure at St. Malo, he emphasised that a desultory cruise along the coast of Normandy would produce no result, and that an attempt should be made on a definite object—'Brest, Rochefort or somewhere in the Bay.'[2]

Meanwhile as Ferdinand was advancing over the Rhine and was short of cavalry, Pitt came to the conclusion—a little hesitantly—that English troops might safely be sent to support him in an arm not much required either in America or for descents on the coast. Such hesitations as he had were resolved by the news of Crevelt, when he wrote jubilantly to Grenville, 'we are sending twelve squadrons of English cavalry to this glorious school of war, and I hope to share a sprig of Germanic laurel very soon.'[3] The decision filled Newcastle with triumph. Counting the garrison at Emden there would be nearly 6,000 men in Germany. 'That,' he told Joseph Yorke, 'is a good reinforcement *for the Continent* and will shew our friends that we mean to do something in this war.'[4]

(iv)

Pitt was in a highly nervous state, sorely missing the calming influence of Hester who was still on her visit to Wotton and Stowe. 'Expectation,' he told her, 'grows every hour into more anxiety—the fate of Louisburgh and of Olmutz [besieged by Frederick] probably decided, though the event unknown—

[1] *Journal*, etc., p. 53.
[2] Newcastle to Hardwicke, 16th June. Add. MSS. 32,880.
[3] Pitt to Grenville, 27th June 1758. Grenville. *Papers*, I, 244.
[4] Newcastle to J. Yorke, 30th June 1758. Add. MSS. 32,881.

the enterprize crowned with success or baffled, at this moment—and indications of a second battle towards the Rhine. I trust, my life, in the same favouring Providence that all will be well, and that this almost degenerate England may learn from the disgrace and ruin it shall have escaped, and the consideration and security it may enjoy, to be more deserving of the blessing.'[1] But Providence was not yet inclined towards favour. Whilst Pitt was writing, Frederick was listening to a tale of captured convoys which made it necessary for him to raise the siege of Olmutz, and three days later Pitt was to hear that the 'enterprize' had returned baffled and unheroic. He could find 'delight and consolation' nowhere but in Hester's letters.

Indeed, conundrums were pressing him on every side. The uncertainties of the Continent convinced him that now was the time, above all others, when attacks on the coast of France would pay a handsome dividend, and should be redoubled. In spite therefore of his disappointment, he summoned the commanders up to town to discuss fresh attempts. But the commanders were not co-operative. When they heard that troops were to be sent to Germany, Marlborough and Sackville promptly demanded transference to that command, refusing to indulge any more in what they contemptuously called buccaneering. Worse still, no one seemed inclined to step into their shoes. The service was not popular: 'Frequent murmurs issued from the mouths of many officers,' and even the more tractable spoke of it as 'not extremely honourable.'[2] If the army and the navy disliked descents on the French coast, the City frowned on the dispatch of troops to Germany; and while Newcastle could barely be restrained from urging greater reinforcements for Ferdinand,[3] the King was promulgating a plan of his own to surprise Nieuport.[4] Pitt, it seemed, was the last person in England who could be left to run the war.

It was not in the circumstances surprising that he was apt to flare into sudden wrath. His 'violence' was only partially successful; it sufficed to quash the King's project against Nieuport, but it failed to suppress Newcastle's hankerings. Unable to face Pitt directly, he fell back on intrigue, trying to make catspaws of Holdernesse, Hardwicke and indeed anyone he

[1] Pitt to Hester, 1st July 1758. Public Record Office. [2] *Journal*, etc., p. 72.
[3] Hardwicke to Newcastle, 4th July 1758. Add. MSS. 32,881.
[4] Newcastle to Hardwicke, 15th July. Add. MSS. 32,881.

could influence. 'I am very cautious,' he wrote to Holdernesse, 'of making any proposal that would not go down. There can be no good in that, nothing but altercation and ill humour, which must ruin everything.' Nevertheless he heartily wished that more troops could be sent to Ferdinand, and 'flung out' the idea to Holdernesse, adding 'I don't desire you to make any use of it, and beg in all events that my name may not be mentioned. If it strikes you as it does me, you will fling it out where you may think proper.'[1] Being in a flinging mood, he 'flung out' the same idea to Hardwicke. But Holdernesse was reluctant to beard Pitt, and Hardwicke was not more than lukewarm—'I wish as much as your Grace can do that not only ten, but twenty, thousand men could be sent; but we must look at what is practicable.' Newcastle, however, was undeterred, and was next to be found assuring his friend, John White, that 'except we can divert the power and force of France by measures upon the Continent, all our other attempts, by expeditions on their coasts, and most expensive operations in both Indies and in North America, will turn upon us and signify nothing, and prove a most useless expence.' The clash of opinion could hardly be stated more clearly; Pitt and Newcastle were as far apart as the poles. In spite of the common belief that Newcastle left the conduct of the war to Pitt, it is evident that he did nothing of the sort, but was for ever interfering or attempting to interfere in the hope of deflecting Pitt's strategy. The bias of his mind is shown by his satisfaction at any event which placed obstacles in Pitt's path. 'I am sure,' he told White, 'you are not sorry to see that the militia goes down in very few counties; so I hope we shall soon have an end of that chimera,'[2] though it is difficult to see what advantage would accrue to either Newcastle or the country by the failure of the militia.

If Newcastle was underhand, Pitt was determined. He pointed out that Ferdinand was doing all that was required of him, and that Frederick's repulse at Olmutz was no more than 'an echec.' If by ill chance the position on the Continent grew worse, the dispatch of a few troops from England would not remedy the evil and would upset the arrangements elsewhere.[3] How right he was appeared almost at once; no sooner did Frederick hear

[1] Newcastle to Holdernesse, 22nd July 1758. Add. MSS. 32,882.
[2] Newcastle to White, 29th July 1758. Add. MSS. 32,882.
[3] Holdernesse to Newcastle, 25th July 1758. Add. MSS. 32,882.

that English cavalry was to join Ferdinand than he recalled his own light horse—'very unseasonably,' said Pitt[1]—leaving Ferdinand no better off than before. Pitt had great faith in Ferdinand, whom he described as a man 'apprehending without timidity, and hoping without visionary confidence,' but this very faith added to his irritation at Newcastle's antics. 'In this anxious state of affairs,' he said with more than a touch of resentment, 'the Duke of Newcastle has according to his Grace's wonted nobleness of proceeding, begun to make his court at my expense, and proposed what I never could consent to, viz, to send some battalions from hence to Stade, and thinks two thousand men taken from the expedition would be well employed in this service. The chief objects too of these battalions would be to guard seven thousand French prisoners which embarrass the Electorate, and which his Grace thought, on a silly suggestion of Yorke's, both proper and practicable to be secured on board English ships in the rivers Weser and Elbe. These were the arduous and wise deliberations of Council yesterday. . . . When we parted, he [Newcastle] immediately set out for the more urgent affairs of Sussex races.'[2]

Pitt would have none of Newcastle's nonsense which was based, not on military necessities but on politics and opportunism. In contradistinction Pitt claimed to be acting 'upon system.' If he could not command success, at least he could dispose of his forces on a settled plan, knowing what risks he ran, what benefits he hoped to gain, and what ultimate objects he had in view. He did not grudge Ferdinand or Frederick troops, provided he was not asked to supply them. If they could be hired on the Continent, he would not shrink from the expense; but for the moment English troops could not be spared in sufficient numbers and so would be better employed in minor operations on the coast. There is little doubt that he had high hopes of the diversionary effect of these expeditions, but it is also possible, indeed probable, that he favoured them because they ensured that troops who might be needed for America should not be engulfed too early or too entirely on the Continent.

Whatever the reason, he declared that there was 'a returned expedition to get out again,' and confided to Hester that 'out it will go, if I am alive and retain the honour I now bear.'[3] His first problem was to find a successor to Marlborough from among

[1] Pitt to (?) Temple, 3rd August 1758. Add. MSS. 37,232. [2] *Ibid.*
[3] Pitt to Hester, 13th July 1758. Public Record Office.

the reluctant and mediocre generals at his command. Dury was thought of first—'a most sad commander,' according to Newcastle. Then Lord Ancram was appointed but made ill-health an excuse to resign. The final choice—Bligh—was not a happy one. He was a veteran of seventy-three who had been selected for Germany, only to be superseded by Marlborough. He felt his supersession as a humiliation, and was consequently a disappointed and even an embittered man; he took up this new command unwillingly and with no heart in the business.

The expedition sailed on the 30th of July, coming to anchor off Cherbourg on the 8th of August. Here they discovered the practical effect of the previous expedition. The French had been so jolted out of complacency that they had dug some four or five miles of trenches along the coast. However, with the aid of the guns from the covering fleet, the landing was made good, and the French, who were present in some numbers, retired. Under other and more energetic commanders the initial success might have been followed up, but Bligh was cautious and dilatory; he moved slowly, unskilfully and without proper control of his men. Cherbourg, which was then an open town, was occupied, a few small ships burnt and some half-completed fortifications dismantled, though the demolition proceeded very slowly owing to 'the sloth and drunkenness of the men, who had discovered some magazines of wine, and became extremely dissolute.'[1] Meanwhile news arrived from every quarter that the enemy were assembling in considerable force. As soon therefore as the demolition was complete, the troops were re-embarked—without incident, though it was noted by some of the more thoughtful officers that as no proper arrangements had been made, a sudden attack by the enemy might have had awkward results.[2] They returned to Weymouth, bringing a few brass cannon as evidence of their prowess. Pitt made the most of their very minor success, by parading the captures, but his main object was to get them out again, so that they might do something more effective. He suggested an attack on Morlaix, one of the more considerable towns of West Brittany, but when they sailed on the 26th of August, for some reason best known to themselves they ignored his wishes and without informing him[3] steered direct to St. Malo. Their action was the more strange as

[1] *Journal,* p. 81. [2] *Journal,* p. 83.
[3] See Newcastle to Hardwicke, 5th Oct. Add. MSS. 32,884.

the previous attempt must have put the French on their guard and 'every person of judgment acquainted with the situation and state of St. Maloes, believed it was above insult, either from our land forces or our shipping.'[1]

Again, thanks to Howe's skilful handling, the troops were landed without mishap and burnt a few small vessels at St. Briac. But there Bligh's initiative dried up. After wasting three days in 'deliberating what could be done for the annoyance of the enemy,' he decided to scrap whatever designs he may have cherished against St. Malo, and 'to penetrate further into the country, moving, however, in such a manner as to be near the fleet, in case it should be necessary to re-embark.' When the objective was so vague, little could be expected. The troops marched a few miles aimlessly along the coast, and then, hearing that strong French forces were approaching under the Duc d'Aiguillon, held a council of war at which it was agreed to re-embark forthwith off the beach of St. Cas. The operation was carried out with incredible lack of skill, and an attack by the French, which might easily have been avoided, resulted in the loss of about 1,000 men. 'It was a humiliating and unhappy blow, if only because it was so unnecessary, and because it went far to condemn for ever a policy which above all others was suited to the British resources.'[2] But there were other and perhaps more serious results. With the threat to the French coast gone, the scales were tipped against Ferdinand, who was forced to retire across the Rhine. Nor did the Prussian troops which had been taken from him suffice to give Frederick victory over the Russians in the bloody and indecisive battle of Zorndorf (25th August 1758), or save him from defeat by the Austrians at Hochkirch (14th October 1758).

The last of the expeditions returned with ignominy, confirming in Whiggish eyes the truth of Fox's jibe that they were only breaking windows with guineas. None the less, if they had not done a tithe of what Pitt had hoped and might have obtained with better generals, they had served a twofold purpose, alarming the French at a critical moment and preserving the English forces for America whilst the issue there was still unknown.

[1] *Journal*, etc., p. 93.   [2] Corbett, I, 300.

20

NEWS FROM AMERICA

(i)

In the midst of the hopes and disappointments of the expeditions, news came from America. The long pause since the armament had sailed had been doubly anxious. Beside the normal fret of expectation, there was the ever-present fear that a setback, however temporary, or even the mere lack of news, when thrown into Newcastle's scales, might tip the whole balance of the war irretrievably into Europe. If that happened, if Newcastle's continental policy won the day, Pitt recognised that he himself would be a failure. Victory might be gained, but it would be a sterile victory, restoring the *status quo*; the prize would be lost and all would be still to do. But if the campaign in America—'this great, and it is hoped, decisive campaign'[1]—were successful, how easy it would be to clinch matters in Europe—far easier than Pitt originally expected. He had always supposed that there would be some lost territory in Germany to be redeemed at the peace, but now Frederick and Ferdinand were reducing that loss to a minimum. If success could come quickly in America, if Frederick and Ferdinand could hold out a few months longer, the war could surely be brought to a triumphant conclusion, perhaps that very winter.

As the days went by the nagging suspense grew. Rumours came trickling in—rumours and partial news—but nothing substantial, nothing conclusive. It was more to relieve his own anxieties than to enlighten Amherst that Pitt, reversing the desired roles, sent news instead of receiving it—news of the landing at Cancale, and Ferdinand's passage of the Rhine—adding his own wishful hopes that 'this fortunate coincidence of events will not fail to have the best effects in disconcerting and distracting the views of the enemy, and distressing the French in such distant parts.'[2]

[1] Pitt to Abercromby, 10th June 1758. Kimball, I, 268.
[2] Pitt to Amherst, 10th June 1758. Kimball, I, 266.

But he still had long to wait. Not till towards the end of July was it known that the troops destined for the siege of Louisburg had landed at Cape Breton.[1] The news, though only hearsay from France, at once stirred Pitt to action. The first step had apparently been successful and now, when hope was first kindled, was the time to be thinking about following up the advantage and parrying possible rebuffs. He summoned a Cabinet meeting to settle the number of ships which should remain in America throughout the winter, and on the 28th of July dispatched their decision to Boscawen. Ten ships of the line with the appropriate number of frigates were to remain at Halifax and there be refitted for service 'very early in the spring'; the Admiralty would send out 'stores, provisions, ammunition, with whatever else may be requisite.' So much by way of instructions. He ended wistfully: 'His Majesty waits with great impatience for some news from you.'[2]

On Friday, the 18th of August, the news came. Here was the American scene with all its light and shade.

(ii)

Pitt's plans for 1758 envisaged an offensive against the whole French position in America. Forbes was to attack Fort Duquesne; Abercromby was to advance along the Hudson route; and Amherst was to sail direct to Louisburg, and after its capture proceed up the St. Lawrence to meet Abercromby at Quebec.

The most immediately important of the three objectives was Louisburg, which in the eyes of eighteenth-century strategists was the key to Canada, a place strong by nature and artifice and easily reinforced by sea, besides being an admirable base for privateers and the centre of a flourishing fish trade. For the other objectives Pitt relied on a mixed force of regulars and colonials, but for Louisburg nothing must be left to chance and none but regulars would do. Some 14,000 royal troops were to be collected at Halifax and were to be accompanied and supported by a powerful fleet under Boscawen. Pitt hoped the campaign would open on or about the 20th of April.

In choosing the commander Pitt broke with tradition. He selected a comparatively unknown man of forty-one, Jeffrey

[1] Holdernesse to Mitchell, 1st August 1758. Add. MSS. 6,816.
[2] Pitt to Boscawen, 28th July 1758. Kimball, I, 309.

Amherst. Perhaps he was influenced by the fact that Amherst had entered the Guards in 1731, the year in which Pitt had received his own commission. At least he must have noticed that since that date Amherst had seen much active service, not without distinction. His rank was that of colonel, but Pitt proposed that with his new appointment he should receive immediate promotion to the rank of major-general. His selection and his promotion were both alike highly distasteful to the King, who believed that generals, like wine, improved with age and that promotion went better with long service than with merit; he had to be alternately bullied and cajoled into giving his consent.

These preliminaries took so long that Amherst did not set out from Portsmouth till the 16th of March. He sailed in the *Dublin*, whose captain, Rodney, was not best pleased at the service. There was, he observed, a junior captain in American waters with a superior command, and if by ill-chance he and Rodney should meet, Rodney knew of but one alternative—'either his broad pendant being struck, or my being in honour bound to resign,'[1] truly an awkward choice. In such a frame of mind he sighted a French East Indiaman off Ushant, and could not resist the temptation to defer any untoward meeting across the Atlantic by giving chase. No doubt he thought himself justified when, to his infinite satisfaction, he found himself master of the *Marmontel* from Nantes, loaded with coffee, timber and private merchandise. But the chase, the capture and the subsequent search for a cruiser to escort the prize home occupied the best part of a fortnight, and still further delayed Amherst's tardy progress. It was an example of the lax discipline throughout the services which put private advantage before public service, and personal wishes before duty; it was to be found in all ranks from the drunken private to the picksome admiral or general.[2] Pitt was greatly hampered by it in the early days of his Ministry, but was steadily creating a new spirit of disciplined patriotism, which was permeating all classes. Walpole observed it with wonder, and in the midst of mockery at the failure before St. Malo paused to confess that 'the difference in our situation is miraculous.'[3]

On the 1st of February, while Pitt was still struggling to secure Amherst's appointment, Boscawen sailed with five men-

[1] Rodney to Grenville, 15th March 1758. Grenville. *Papers*, I, 231.

[2] 'Unfortunately the point of profit weighs more than the point of honour with our military gentlemen of honour.' Chesterfield's *Letters*, III, 1,205.

[3] To Mann, 11th June 1758.

of-war and some smaller ships, carrying with him additional troops and also James Wolfe who had been nominated one of Amherst's three brigadiers, the others being Charles Lawrence and Edward Whitmore. The voyage was far from prosperous, and it was not until the 9th of May that the fleet arrived at Halifax with crews 'very sickly' after so long a passage. Boscawen's instructions were to pick up the transports and proceed at once to Louisburg without waiting for Amherst, but he was held up by bad weather. Whilst thus detained, he and Wolfe and the other brigadiers spent their time discussing the best method of landing on Cape Breton. They produced a carefully considered plan, generally supposed to be Wolfe's, for disembarking at Miré Bay, ten miles to the north-east of Louisburg, under cover of feints nearer the town, and a demonstration by the fleet at the harbour mouth. The virtue of the plan was that it took into account all the known facts, made the most of the flexibility derived from mastery of the sea, and avoided the dangers and loss of a frontal attack.[1]

Amherst arrived as Boscawen was leaving Halifax and on the 2nd of June the whole expedition came to anchor in Gabarus Bay, where Amherst, after inspecting the shore from the ships, scrapped, or at least ignored, Wolfe's plan with all its tactical advantages, and instead made fresh dispositions for a landing directly in face of the enemy. The attempt—a head-on collision —was made on the 8th of June and was within an ace of failing. The French held their fire until the boats were close inshore and then unmasked their guns. The effect was so devastating that Wolfe, to whom the task had been entrusted, is said to have given orders for retreat, when fortunately two young subalterns, Hopkins and Brown, discovered a small cove, screened from the French view, where they made good their landing. Wolfe followed hard on their heels, jumping through the surf and scrambling over the rocks, and then, forming his troops rapidly into order, routed a detachment of French grenadiers sent to oppose him. A footing had been effected.

From that moment, in view of Amherst's vastly superior power, the fate of Louisburg was sealed, but the operation was slow, and all initiative left to Wolfe. Amherst proved himself to be precise, businesslike and soldierly, as soldierliness was then understood, but at the same time cautious, correct and chary

[1] Corbett, I, 318.

of innovation. He was not to be hurried, and his leisurely movements were not assisted by the weather. Nor was Boscawen more enterprising. Pitt, anxious that the business should be completed at the earliest moment so as to leave plenty of time for the advance on Quebec, had hoped that the fleet would make a powerful contribution by forcing the harbour.[1] To give them every chance, he had sent Hawke and Osborne to shut the exits from the Atlantic and Mediterranean ports of France, and had left Hardy all the winter in Halifax to seal the entrance to Louisburg.

Yet in spite of all precautions, a few French ships had slipped through, and their presence seemed to paralyse Boscawen. He held his hand on the seaward side, though eager and willing to support Amherst and Wolfe on the landward side with guns and marines and the smooth delivery of stores.

The siege pursued a leisurely course till a lucky shot on the 21st of July set fire to three French ships. Their destruction roused Boscawen. Four days later, under his orders, the boats of the fleet captured or burnt two further French ships in a brilliant cutting-out expedition. It was the last straw. The town, battered by five weeks of constant bombardment, was in no condition to face a new menace from the now defenceless harbour. On the 26th of July (1758) Louisburg surrendered.

(iii)

Though Pitt had been grudgingly allowed his way in the choice of Amherst, he had not been so successful in the case of the commander-in-chief. The King is supposed to have insisted on Abercromby's appointment and Pitt to have acquiesced rather than approved. Probably Pitt had little option. Service in America was almost as distasteful to the higher command as 'buccaneering' on the French coast. The generals one and all panted for Germany, where war was conducted in a manner they understood and where glory was to be won. Even Wolfe, with the laurels of Louisburg fresh on his brow, could write, and mean, 'it is my fortune to be cursed with American service.'[2] To this universal reluctance, which Pitt could not overcome, and which severely limited his choice, there was added the weighty fact that Abercromby was Loudoun's second-in-command and already on the spot. He was fifty-two and therefore old enough to satisfy the

[1] Pitt to Boscawen, 3rd Feb. 1758. Kimball, I, 180. [2] Waugh, p. 185.

King, and perhaps not too old to repel Pitt who, knowing nothing to his disadvantage, was disposed to think well of him. It was at once his passport to high office and his misfortune to be, in Walpole's disparaging comment, 'a man who signalized himself neither before nor after his advancement.'[1] In short he was colourless. *Faute de mieux*, he was named as Loudoun's successor and entrusted with the second prong of Pitt's threefold offensive —the advance up the Hudson route.

His commission reached him at Albany on the 7th of March, and with it came detailed instructions of what was required of him. He was to make the necessary arrangements for setting Amherst and Forbes on their respective ways; he was to leave his brigadier, Stanwix, behind in order to protect the frontiers; and was himself to 'attempt an invasion of Canada, by the way of Crown Point, in order to proceed, if practicable, to an attempt on either Montreal or Quebec, or both of the said places, successively.'[2] As a preliminary he was to raise 20,000 provincials and provide a number of boats and vessels for use on Lake George. His instructions were minute, specific and all inclusive. It seems clear that though acquiescing in his appointment, Pitt regarded him rather as an instrument to carry out a prearranged plan than as a general to be left to his own devices. The weakness of such an appointment lay in Pitt's inability to foresee the conditions which might arise on the field of battle, and the possibility that too much spoonfeeding might promote bewilderment in an unexpected situation. To provide as far as possible against such contingencies, Pitt gave him Lord Howe as his second-in-command, a young, energetic man of thirty-two, highly adaptable in himself, reputed to be the brightest of the rising generation of officers, and perhaps not least, most acceptable to the colonists.[3]

Abercromby busied himself to some purpose. The colonial Assemblies, stirred by their Governors and responding to Pitt's manner of approach, produced the men with reasonable dispatch. Amherst and Forbes were sent on their ways, and on the 7th of June (1758) Abercromby set out with 15,000 men for Fort Edward, which he reached two days later, and thence proceeded to a camp on the site of the old Fort William Henry at the foot of

[1] Walpole. *Geo. II*, III, 91.
[2] Pitt to Abercromby, 30th December 1757. Kimball, I, 144.
[3] See Chesterfield to his son, 8th Feb. 1758. Bradshaw III, 1,208.

Lake George. The artillery, stores and provisions were loaded on to boats with exemplary precision, the troops were embarked with bands playing, the whole expedition launched out on to the lake, and on the 6th of July landed without incident at its northern end. Here Abercromby's luck deserted him. A reconnoitring party fell in with the French advanced guard as it was withdrawing and in the ensuing skirmish gained a minor success. But the victory was far more than counterbalanced by the death of Howe, who was leading the English detachment and was the first man to fall. Abercromby, too well aware of his own loss, reported that 'as he was very deservedly, universally beloved and respected throughout the whole army, it is easy to conceive the grief and consternation his untimely fall occasioned; for my part, I cannot help owning that I felt it most heavily, and lament as sincerely.'[1] Lacking Howe's guidance, Abercromby stumbled on to Ticonderoga and, after a perfunctory reconnaissance, decided to storm the enemy's position at once, without a preliminary bombardment. The whole body of infantry advanced, only to find 'the entrenchments not only much stronger than had been represented, and the breastwork at least eight or nine feet high, but likewise the ground before it covered with felled trees, the branches pointed outwards.' Abercromby, a mile and a half to the rear, and forgetful of his artillery still lying by the side of the lake, ordered one assault after another, keeping the troops at their impossible task, as he reported himself, 'for upwards of four hours under the most disadvantageous circumstances.' Then, suddenly overcome by a belated fear of 'total defeat,' he retired precipitately to the camp at the foot of Lake George. Here he decided that it was 'impracticable, at this time, to reattempt the reduction of Ticonderoga and Crown Point,' and that his best course was to strengthen Stanwix 'in order, if possible, to prevent the enemy from putting into execution their designs against the Mohawk river and coming down to Albany.'[2]

Montcalm must have heaved a deep sigh of relief. He had faced Abercromby with under 4,000 men, and had to the last been in two minds whether he should make his final stand at Ticonderoga, where defeat seemed inevitable, or retreat to safety. At the end of the attack, he had lost 400 men to Abercromby's 2,000. The odds against him were still four to one. It had been all he could do to withstand the fury of the English

[1] Kimball, I, 298. [2] *Ibid.*, I, 300-1.

when they had made their frontal attack against barricades impassable by unaided infantry. There was little prospect that he could repeat his success if Abercromby advanced again with the merest soupçon of skill and supported by his guns. Truly the deliverance had been great, and not without reason did Montcalm, a devout Catholic, erect a great cross on the battlefield ascribing the victory to God. He wrote excited letters home, but no 'designs against the Mohawk river' crossed his mind, still less thoughts of invading Albany. He was more than content to settle himself in at Ticonderoga and harass Abercromby's now disorderly troops by sudden forays.[1]

Abercromby, looking back from the gloomy standpoint of defeat, sent a dejected report to Pitt. At the same time he besought Amherst to come to his aid when he had finished with Louisburg, in the hope that thus reinforced he might be able to make a second and more successful attempt.[2] His letter exploded Amherst's prospects of an advance on Quebec. Leaving Wolfe to reduce the various French settlements in the Bay of Fundy and at the mouth of the St. Lawrence, he set out with six battalions to add them to Abercromby's already overwhelming numbers, arriving just in time to join in Abercromby's withdrawal to winter quarters.

The campaign in America was not working out according to plan.

(iv)

Yet there were to be further successes, small in themselves but pregnant with hope. In Abercromby's original instructions Pitt had told him to employ Lieut.-Colonel Bradstreet as Deputy Quartermaster-General in the southern colonies,[3] but by an inspired piece of disobedience Abercromby had substituted Sir John St. Clair, thus leaving Bradstreet free for a greater achievement. He explained that, when Pitt's instructions arrived, Bradstreet was busily engaged in building the boats which would be needed on Lake George, and wanted to finish the job. 'To which,' said Abercromby fatuously, 'I yielded the readier, as he declared himself by far better qualified for this business, than that of Deputy Quarter Master General.'[4] When the boats were com-

[1] Parkman. *Montcalm and Wolfe,* II, 112.
[2] Abercromby to Pitt, 19th August 1758. Kimball, I, 327.
[3] Kimball, I, 146. [4] *Ibid* I., 252.

pleted, Bradstreet was put in charge of the Batteau Men, because, as Abercromby explained, he knew best how to deal with them, they being 'an unwieldy and unruly set.'[1] It seems clear that Bradstreet was a man of some decision of character. He knew his own mind and was both forceful and tenacious. The previous winter, while still only a captain, he had tried to make a bargain with Loudoun, under which he proposed to raise a force at his own expense and attack Fort Frontenac, on the understanding that if he succeeded he was to be repaid his expenses and 'recommended to the King's Ministers for their favour and such reward as they may think his services deserve.'[2] Doubtless his adventurous spirit had appealed to Pitt so that the mere offer had won him promotion and the post of Deputy Quartermaster-General. Now in the hope that failure might make Abercromby compliant, Bradstreet returned to the attack. He still believed in his proposition and there were now troops to spare. A chastened Abercromby gave him 3,600 men.

When reporting these arrangements to Pitt, Abercromby had ventured to hope that Bradstreet might be successful. But Abercromby was a fearful man, and had become more timid with defeat. He augured the worst when, a month later, he heard from Bradstreet that desertion and sickness had made great havoc with his force, and felt no stirring of the heart at Bradstreet's resolute assertion that, even if he could muster no more than a thousand men, he would do his best. Though he had reason to think that Bradstreet would meet with little opposition, and wrote to tell him so, he could not refrain from adding that he 'did not mean to encourage the undertaking.'[3]

Bradstreet, however, had no qualms. He made his way up the Mohawk and down the Onondaga to the site of the dismantled Fort Oswego. There he embarked on the waters of Lake Ontario and on the 25th of August (1758) landed near Fort Frontenac. The French garrison proved to be only 110 strong; their position was hopeless, and two days later they surrendered, giving up at the same time the nine armed vessels which formed their whole naval force on the lake. The fort was razed to the ground, the vessels destroyed, and the stores, provisions and other booty burnt or carried off. Thanks to Bradstreet, the French had lost

[1] Kimball, I, 255. [2] Loudoun to Pitt, 14th Feb. 1758. Kimball, I, 194.
[3] Abercromby to Pitt, 19th August 1758. Kimball, I, 324.

control of Lake Ontario, and with it the passage to the Ohio and Louisiana. It was a shrewd blow.

(v)

For the third prong of his offensive Pitt's instructions were far less precise. All that Forbes was required to do was to 'proceed without loss of time to Pennsylvania' and there concert 'any such offensive operations as may be judged by him most expedient for annoying the enemy, and most efficacious towards removing and repelling the dangers that threaten the frontiers of any of the southern colonies.'[1] The lack of precision may have been due—and one hopes was—to confidence in Forbes. At the time of his appointment he was a colonel, forty-eight years of age, who had grown grey in the service, without much chance of distinction. He was also a man with something of a grievance for though, with the appointment, he received a commission as brigadier-general, he had been placed below Amherst, who had hitherto been his junior, not only in age, but also in the list of lieutenant-colonels. Yet in choosing him Pitt had chosen wisely. Forbes, unlike so many of his contemporaries, was a conscientious as well as an experienced soldier, endowed with a strong sense of duty and upheld by a selfless spirit of patriotism. Neither danger nor difficulty was likely to daunt him and reverses would spur him to greater effort. His main drawback was his health, which was in no way suited to forest warfare, nor yet calculated to promote the patience required in dealing with provincial Assemblies. He was in almost constant pain from inflammation of the stomach, which he regretted mainly as being a handicap to his work. Truly a worthy disciple of the gout-ridden Pitt.

On the 14th of April (1758) he received his orders from Abercromby, and at once proceeded to Philadelphia, where he entered on the thankless task of trying to raise money and men from the colonial Assemblies. The Southern provinces, being far removed from the main seat of war, were disinclined to bestir themselves. 'Everything,' he reported sadly, 'except fresh disputes which arise every day, goes on very slowly.' Pennsylvania was absorbed in local politics; Maryland was 'extremely dilatory in their proceedings'; Virginia's effort was feeble and faltering; 'nothing was to be expected from the Carolinas.' The Indians were his one

[1] Pitt to Abercromby, 30th Dec. 1757. Kimball, I, 146.

bright spot, a number of Cherokees and Cataubas having rallied to him; yet even they presented a problem, for they came to him 'almost naked and without arms,' and as they were 'capable of being led away upon any caprice or whim that seizes them,' Forbes was hard put to it to find them sufficient occupation to keep them from returning home.[1] In the event not many accompanied the army, but by his skilful handling of them he managed to win over most of the neighbouring tribes to friendship or, what was nearly as good, neutrality.

His plan was to capture Fort Duquesne, which, with the pacification of the Indians, would result in peace along the borders and give England the command of the Ohio valley. By the end of June his preparations were complete, and he set out at the head of 1,500 regulars and 4,500 provincials. The difficulties were immense, but at least he could learn from Braddock's failure. Washington, who commanded the Virginian contingent, gave him the same unhappy advice that he had given to Braddock, urging a speedy advance along the old road. But Forbes thought differently. He chose a new and shorter route through Pennsylvania, much to the disgust of the Virginians, and insisted on a methodical advance. He told Pitt that owing to the vast distances, the badness of the roads, and the absence of inhabitants, the only safe method was to build blockhouses and stores for provisions every forty miles, 'by which means although I advance but gradually, yet I shall go more surely.' 'I need not point out to you, Sir,' he added, 'my reasons for these precautions, when you consider that had our last attempt upon Fort Duquesne succeeded, we must have retired directly, for want of provisions.'[2]

His choice of a new road had other advantages. The French had heard of his intended advance, and assuming that he would follow in Braddock's footsteps, spent their time 'securing the strong passes and fords of the rivers' on that route. It was not until Forbes was about forty miles from Fort Duquesne that they discovered their mistake.[3] He needed any advantage he could gain for he had disadvantages in plenty. The Pennsylvanians were up to their old tricks of hiring out at exorbitant rates their worst horses and most rickety wagons, so that Forbes was hard put to it to maintain the commissariat. His soldiers, too, were

[1] Forbes to Pitt, 1st May 1758. Kimball, I, 235.
[2] Forbes to Pitt, 17th June 1758. Kimball, I, 280.
[3] Forbes to Pitt, 6th Sept. 1758. Kimball, I, 339.

none of the best. The Colonies had made up their contingents from the lowest classes. The provincial officers were, with a few exceptions, 'an extreme bad collection of broken innkeepers, horse jockeys, and Indian traders,' and the men under them were 'a gathering from the scum of the worst of people.'[1] Nor was he helped by Abercromby's substitution of St. Clair for Bradstreet as Quartermaster-General. Forbes described St. Clair, with exemplary moderation, as 'a very odd man, and I am sorry it has been my fate to have any concern with him.'[2] Yet amidst all these difficulties and in spite of his ill-health, Forbes kept a stout heart. The thought of failure never entered his head. What worried him was what to do with his prize when he had won it. 'If it should please God,' he confided to Pitt, 'to grant success to his Majesty's arms, in their attempts upon the Ohio, and which I think can't well fail, I shall be greatly at a loss how to dispose of Fort Duquesne, whether to blow it up, and destroy it and the whole settlements thereabouts, or to keep it and leave a garrison there for the winter. The execution of the first is as easy as the second appears to be attended with many difficulties,' for the Governors of Pennsylvania and Virginia would not or could not tell him whether they would provide the necessary troops and provisions.[3]

To all his other troubles were added first bad weather, which brought transport almost to a standstill, and then a minor defeat. When Fort Duquesne was nearly reached Major Grant obtained permission from Colonel Bouquet, Forbes' second-in-command, to carry out a reconnoitring expedition in order, as he said, to see whether he could strike a blow which would animate the English and depress the French. He took 800 men with him, woefully mismanaged the whole affair, and returned in disorder with the loss of nearly 300 in killed, wounded and prisoners. 'Your letter of the 17th,' Forbes wrote in remonstrance to Bouquet, 'I read with no less surprise than concern, as I could not believe that such an attempt would have been made without my knowledge and concurrence. The breaking in upon our fair and flattering hopes of success touches me most sensibly. . . . My friend Grant most certainly lost his wits, and by his thirst of fame brought on his own perdition and ran great risk of ours.'[4]

[1] Kimball, I, 342. [2] Parkman. *Montcalm and Wolfe,* II, 137.
[3] Forbes to Pitt, 6th September 1758. Kimball, I, 342.
[4] Parkman. *Montcalm and Wolfe,* II, 155.

Success, however, was nearer than he thought. He was advancing steadily and irresistibly. The French realised that hope had gone and, as Forbes drew near, blew up the fortifications, burnt the barracks, destroyed the provisions, and retreated. On the 25th of November 1758 Forbes and his men took over the ruins. He had now to make up his mind what he should do. In spite of repeated applications to Abercromby and the various Governors, no one had given him advice, still less instructions. There was one exception; the Lieut.-Governor of Virginia had written to say that whilst 'his Assembly and Council would not venture to give any opinion,' the Virginian troops would be recalled by the 1st of December. In this plentiful dearth of views, Forbes decided to leave a small garrison, and report the position to Pitt. He ended his report with words which have had a significance from that day to this: 'I have used the freedom of giving your name to Fort Duquesne, as I hope it was in some measure the being actuated by your spirits that now makes us masters of the place.' He addressed the letter from 'Pittsburgh.'[1]

His duty done, Forbes returned painfully to Philadelphia, carried in a litter. The news of his success reached England in January 1759 before his own report was received. Pitt at once wrote a letter of congratulation referring to the 'high consequence' of Fort Duquesne, and hoping that Forbes would soon recover his health and live long 'to enjoy the great honour you have acquired, as well as to finish the arduous work you have so happily begun.'[2] In March, on receipt of Forbes' own report, Pitt wrote again, repeating his own and the King's 'approbation of your zeal and conduct,' granting him sick leave, and 'adding my particular acknowledgments for the very great and undeserved honour you have done my name.'[3]

It is possible that Forbes read and found comfort in Pitt's first letter. It is certain that before the second was written Forbes was dead.

(vi)

News of the capture of Louisburg reached London on Friday, the 18th of August. The effect was instantaneous. The country, as countries will, celebrated the victory with bonfires and beer, compounding for Saturday's headache with thanksgiving on

[1] Forbes to Pitt, 27th November 1758. Kimball, I, 409.
[2] Pitt to Forbes, 23rd Jan. 1759. Kimball, II, 16.
[3] Pitt to Forbes, 15th March. Kimball, II, 68.

Sunday. They were right; it was the first golden ray of Pitt's mounting sun, and with prophetic intuition they saw in it the future course of the war.

But if the result was instantaneous, it was also varied. The King was like a schoolboy granted an unexpected holiday. His Majesty, so we are told, exclaimed excitedly 'we must keep Cape Breton, take Canada, drive the French out of America, have two armies in Germany consisting together of 80,000 men'; and then we should be a great nation. His exuberance shocked Newcastle, who begged him to consider how we should raise the men and money, the latter at least being to his knowledge impracticable.[1]

Newcastle himself, true to his nature, was more concerned with the effect on the Duke of Newcastle than on the country. 'This,' he told Hardwicke, 'is the greatest and most glorious event that ever was, and if proper use be made of it, must do our business,'[2] our business being to secure peace, when Pitt would no longer be required and Newcastle might return to his pristine eminence. It was easy and natural for Newcastle, troubled over many things, particularly finance, to see in any advantage an opening for peace. The war, to use a common phrase, left him cold; he had slithered into it, he hardly knew how or why, and having no objective, was willing and anxious to slither out of it again. Louisburg was a godsend; it could be exchanged for Minorca or Hanover; it was a bargaining point of the highest importance. The only problem was whether it should be restored with the fortifications demolished or intact. Good as demolition would no doubt be for the security of the Colonies, might it not reduce the exchange value? On a balance of profits, Newcastle was against demolition, especially bearing in mind the popular clamour for the retention of the place. His mentor, Hardwicke, was for it: 'I will venture to prophesy,' he argued, 'that it will be given up on some terms or other at a peace, which must come sooner or later, and it had better be restored demolished than otherwise.' Newcastle should pay no attention to popular clamour. 'The addresses for annexing proceed from mob-politics and tend to entangle administration. Ministers should never encourage such things. . . . What the Yorkshire manufacturers may think of it, is not the question. It is a question of a higher kind of politics.'[3] Hardwicke's argument would have carried

[1] Newcastle to Hardwicke, 26th August 1758. Add. MSS. 32,883.
[2] Newcastle to Hardwicke, 18th August 1758. Add. MSS. 32,882.
[3] Hardwicke to Newcastle, 21st September 1758. Add. MSS. 32,884.

more weight if he and Newcastle had been aiming at any fixed end, but their only motive was a natural yearning for peace.

There is no direct evidence of Pitt's immediate reaction, but Hester, as most conversant with his mind, may fitly speak for him. Her words are redolent of patriotism and humble piety. 'Happy and glorious,' she wrote, 'for my loved England, happy and glorious for my most loved and admired husband . . . every various, happy, pleasing sentiment inspired by this great success is accompanied with the devoutest gratitude and most unfeigned praise to the Almighty Disposer of every event.'[1]

Her words reflect what might have been expected from Pitt himself. But whatever his immediate reaction, however great his joy, however deep his gratitude, four days later news of Ticonderoga gave him reason for fresh misgiving. It altered the whole situation, and altered it far more fundamentally for him than for anyone else. To the country at large Ticonderoga meant little. England was accustomed to reverses, and was not disposed to let Abercromby's failure blight her joy at Amherst's success.[2] To Newcastle and Hardwicke its main significance lay in the fact that it might be expected to draw off troops to America from the expeditions on the coast of France, which in the obscure workings of their minds would be a beneficial result.[3] But Pitt saw the matter differently. He had hoped that the campaign in America would be decisive. He had so carefully and so completely laid the foundations that he not only had a right to expect results but had looked forward to them with some confidence. He had widened the plans of campaign since the previous year; he had sealed the French ports; he had dispatched ample and even overwhelming forces to each of his three generals; he had provided supplies with a lavish hand; and he had appointed young and forceful leaders. What more could he have done? Even genius could not provide against the stray shot which killed Howe. So confident had he been that he had allowed his hopes to affect his policy elsewhere. No sooner had he heard that Wolfe had landed on Cape Breton than he stiffened in his attitude towards Spain. Lord Bristol, our Ambassador in succession to Keene, was instructed to take a stronger line over the

[1] Hester to Pitt, 18th Aug. 1758. Public Record Office.

[2] See Symmer to Mitchell, 12th Sept. 1758. 'The success that has attended Mr. Pitt's measures in the taking of Louisburg, and in our descent on the coast of France at Cherbourg shuts the mouths of his opponents and opens those of his friends and the multitude in his favour.' Add. MSS. 6,839.

[3] See Newcastle to Legge, 22nd August 1758. Add. MSS. 32,883.

points in perennial dispute—the cutting of logwood in Honduras Bay and the rights of fishing on the Newfoundland banks—and more especially to consider the proposal to restore Gibraltar 'as totally at an end'; he was not to mention it or even to admit knowledge of its existence.[1] Spain's help was no longer so necessary. Equally Pitt had taken a more lenient view of the Dutch contraband trade with the French Colonies, thinking it no longer a matter of immediate importance and one that might well be sacrificed to secure the good will of Holland, which Frederick regarded as so important.[2] Last, but by no means least, he had allowed English troops in small numbers to be sent to Ferdinand. Success in America, fancied or real, was turning his thoughts to Europe and its needs.

Ticonderoga drew him up with a jerk. 'I own,' he told Grenville, 'this news has sunk my spirits, and left very painful impressions upon my mind.'[3] He had to readjust himself. Instead of a complete victory, he had won only a partial victory, which might well be more dangerous than a total defeat. No one had supposed that the war could end when Braddock had been annihilated, but this mixture of success and failure might well produce a revulsion of feelings, especially as Frederick was openly acknowledging that he 'was heartily tired of war and wished very sincerely for peace.'[4] Something must be done to distract attention; fresh plans must be produced in a hurry. Pitt at once gave up all idea of reinforcing Bligh on the Continent, and instead decided to send 1,000 Highlanders and 2,000 regulars to America to make good the losses.[5] He also determined to strike elsewhere, in order to secure bargaining counters in case peace parleys should be forced upon him. For Louisburg he would not restore; nor Canada if he were given time to conquer it.

As he thought over possibilities, his sanguine temper revived. 'Providence,' he told Temple, 'which has so greatly favoured us, will I think guide this shattered country to a safe harbour, and without any loss of her cargo, either in possessions or in honour. Europe may be again unfettered; France taught her vulnerability and England her power to wound. All this, I trust, will come to

[1] Pitt to Bristol, 1st Aug. 1758. Add. MSS. 32,882.
[2] See Sir J. Yorke to Holdernesse, 14th June 1758. Yorke, III, 213.
[3] Pitt to Grenville, 22nd Aug. 1758. Grenville. *Papers*, I, 262.
[4] Mitchell to Holdernesse, 31st July 1758. Add. MSS. 6,807
[5] Newcastle to Legge, 22nd Aug. 1758. Add. MSS. 32,883.

pass; but much yet remains unfinished of this arduous task. I am endeavouring to push some offensive plans of operation but instruments do not abound. Martinique appears to me the most sensible part to France in South America. . . . The other object is the island of Goree on the coast of Africa where the attempt was lately made but faintly.'[1]

For Goree Pitt required very few troops—700 in all; he proposed to get them from Ireland. It was, perhaps, to be expected that Bedford, the Lord Lieutenant, should protest at a measure which would, in his opinion, 'still further weaken Ireland,' and tempt the French to make a descent 'in the wild parts of Munster and Connaught.'[2] None the less Pitt had his way, riding roughshod over Bedford, and when Keppel, who was chosen as the naval commander, wrote of difficulties in getting to sea, Pitt, in a fever of impatience, told him to be gone at any sacrifice. His urgency bore fruit for, as already related (see p. 270), the expedition was entirely successful.

Martinique was a more serious affair. Pitt originally settled on 3,500 men for the work, but as he delved into the proposal and realised the part which it could play in his wider strategy, he successively raised the numbers, first to 4,500 and then to 6,000. Newcastle, when he learnt of the idea, rather surprisingly fancied it and at the outset even showed a measure of enthusiasm. 'If practicable,' he wrote, '(and many knowing people think it is) it will be the coup de grace to all the French trade.'[3] The King also came into the scheme, definitely earmarking Martinique as a *quid pro quo* for Minorca.[4] With no one to oppose, preparations progressed rapidly. The main difficulty, as ever, was the choice of commanders—'instruments' did not abound. Again, it was comparatively easy to settle the naval side. Commodore Moore was already in the West Indies; he was a man of forty with a good reputation; there was no need to look further. For the army, Pitt was at a greater loss, and more under the King's thumb. His original idea had been 'Elliott with Clarke Q.M.G.,' but the royal veto worked, and the final choice fell on General Hopson. Pitt appointed Brigadier Barrington, the Secretary-at-War's younger brother, as his second-in-command. The expedition sailed in the middle of November.

1. Pitt to Temple (?), Monday night (? 4th Sept.) 1758. Add. MSS. 37,232.
2. Bedford to Pitt, 29th Aug. 1758. Bedford. *Correspondence,* II, 360.
3. Newcastle to Hardwicke, 4th Sept. 1758. Add. MSS. 32,883.
4. Newcastle to Hardwicke, 19th Oct. 1758. Add. MSS. 32,884.

21

ENTER BUTE

(i)

Pitt's rapid readjustment of his plans was only just in time. Newcastle was becoming more and more convinced that the war must be brought to an end; and the more he thought of Louisburg, the more he itched to make use of it. 'Now,' he wrote to Mitchell, 'is our time to push, in order to make a safe and honourable end.'[1] His eagerness was the greater because he was faced with problems difficult in themselves and aggravated by the wide divergence between his views and Pitt's. There were three main problems to distract him—the cost of the Army of Observation, the subsidy to the Landgrave of Hesse, and 'dédommagement' for both Landgrave and King at the end of the war. All three involved much money, which Newcastle believed could never be raised. His doubts and his inclinations alike induced him at this moment of semi-victory to try to force on peace by the threat of financial stringency; and to make the threat more effective by exaggerating the expenses. Pitt resented both the exaggeration and the threat, which he felt sprang out of weakness: Newcastle wanted peace for the sake of peace, which however right in the abstract, was wrong in the circumstances. The war must be fought to a finish, or it would merely be postponed, and Pitt had strong and perhaps expanding views of what the finish should be. The very least he would accept was safety for England's Colonies and England's trade. What constituted safety was no doubt open to discussion and would be influenced by facts, but Pitt either started with the idea, or soon came to it, that the only sure safety was the expulsion of France from America combined with the defeat and decay of her navy. Neither object had yet been attained and therefore the war must go on. His outlook on Newcastle's problems, as Newcastle himself

[1] Newcastle to Mitchell, 12th Sept. 1758. Add. MSS. 6,832.

appreciated, was coloured by this conviction, and his exasperation at Newcastle's attitude was the greater because he did not admit or believe that England could not out-finance France. If we were in a bad way, France must be in a worse, and it the more behoved us to 'stick it.'

Conscious of their different standpoints, Newcastle dreaded the approach of the estimates. Pitt, with his bias towards America and against Hanover, was bound to quarrel with the provision for Prince Ferdinand, and might refuse to renew the Hessian subsidy. Both points affected the King as Elector. If in that capacity he were thwarted by Pitt, friction would abound and Newcastle would be helpless to deprecate wrath. He might plead for peace as the perfect solution of all troubles, financial and political alike, but he was uncomfortably aware that neither Pitt nor the King would listen to him. On that point they would concur, however fundamentally they might differ on all others. The King was too intoxicated by victory, and Pitt could always threaten to economise by 'lopping off from the continent.' Even if the first two hurdles were safely negotiated, there remained the third and possibly the highest hurdle—the problem of 'dédommagement.' The King was pressing for a promise of compensation to the Landgrave for his losses in the war, in the belief that any concession to Hesse would strengthen his own claim as Elector. Pitt, on the other hand, had made it clear that he would sanction no claim from anyone; it was too dangerous and could have too serious an effect on present efforts; if damages must be taken into account, they must be met by larger subsidies in return for immediate help. Newcastle saw no comfort in either suggestion; whether the payment took the form of present subsidies or future compensation, he would be expected to find the money.

His fears of trouble were justified. When it came to a discussion, Pitt was in an unyielding, an almost impish, mood; his revised plans were well advanced and the immediate crisis had passed. When therefore Newcastle urged the necessity for peace, Pitt, anticipating the hard-won knowledge of the twentieth century, replied briefly that 'the only way to have peace was to prepare for war.' When Newcastle expatiated on the cost of the Army of Observation, Pitt declined 'giving one farthing more for the electoral troops' than had been given the year before. When Newcastle spoke of the financial difficulties of the King, as

Elector, Pitt 'treated all that as the greatest joke,' and when Newcastle pressed the point, remarked blandly that if Newcastle was serious then 'we must have done with the continent, recall our troops, make a naval war and employ our troops in expeditions.' Pitt was adamant and Newcastle helpless and full of forebodings. 'This,' he confided to Hardwicke, 'does not look well for next session. The two parties are at present widely different from each other. Mr. Pitt won't go, at present, one step farther; and the King expects great additions, next campaign, from hence. . . . But the worst of all is the little inclination in any quarter for peace.'[1]

Parliament was to meet on the 23rd of November (1758), and the first explosion took place the day before, when Pitt received from Munchausen a copy of the estimates for the King's German troops. They amounted to nearly £2,000,000. Pitt was startled and angry. He dashed off a couple of furious notes to Newcastle—he had never seen anything like it in his life; he was astonished at the enormity of the demand; he noted that the figures included the cost of several thousand men over the agreed number—'in the name of God, my Lord, how comes such an idea on paper? Has your Grace ever encouraged a hope that England could vote more troops than the fifty thousand, including Hessians, voted last year? Or is it your Grace's opinion that the Electorate can be defended without some effort on its own account?' Newcastle's reply in effect disclaimed responsibility, which merely increased Pitt's fury. 'As you are pleased,' he replied in his haughtiest tone of rebuke, 'to decline favouring me with your opinion . . . I will not trouble your Grace again on that matter; but beg leave to express my wonder and concern that your Grace has now, the very eve of the Parliament, only to tell me that a plan of expence, *just double* that of last year, new in mode, and one part *quite additional* (of which *addition* I had never received either from your Grace or any person that lives the most remote intimation whatever), I say that I should only have the honour of learning this night that things are *open to deliberation*. Allow me, my Lord Duke, to confess extreme astonishment, to find that things such as a new corps of troops should slip into consideration, your Grace at the head of the Treasury neither countenancing yourself, nor apprizing me of such a measure; and that you should still think it a matter

[1] Newcastle to Hardwicke, 19th Oct. 1758. Add. MSS. 32,884.

of deliberation. I will take up no more of your Grace's time.'[1]

The involved grammar betrays Pitt's hurry and indignation, and indeed he had reasons enough for wrath. There was first his normal revolt against extravagance at the public expense. Newcastle was supposed to be the watchdog of the Treasury and he was not doing his duty. Worse still, he was allowing money to be squandered on Hanoverian troops who should by rights be paid by the Elector. It always irritated Pitt to think that Hanover should make a profit out of self-defence, and it irritated him the more when he thought the subsidy was in fact going into the Elector's private pocket. Pitt grudged the money no less because he wanted to spend it in other ways. His eager mind was always one leap ahead, and now that Louisburg, Duquesne and Frontenac had marked the turning of the tide, he was beginning to think more seriously of Europe. Victory in America would release a number of troops who might be used there, and even without English troops, there were other forces which might be hired if the money was available. Lastly, Pitt realised that both Bute and the City would be unsympathetic towards his European leanings, and he had no wish to antagonise them prematurely by doling out excessive funds to Hanover. For all these reasons he wanted the estimates pared. That he was justified seems evident from the fact that, after further examination, they were reduced by nearly one-third.[2]

Pitt was still simmering the next day (23rd November), when the debate on the Address took place. In his speech he very pointedly stressed the responsibility of Newcastle and Legge for examining details of cost, which, he emphasised, lay outside his own department, adding, with a hint of menace, that 'at a proper time an estimate would be laid before the House and every member would judge and vote as he thought proper.' All the same, he had no wish to create unnecessary difficulties, and his speech as a whole was couched in proud and encouraging language. The Address had been moved by Lord Middleton, a Whig, and seconded by Sir Richard Grosvenor, a Tory, and Pitt therefore began by congratulating the House on its perfect

[1] Pitt to Newcastle, 22nd Nov. 1758. Add. MSS. 32,885.

[2] Barrington to Newcastle, 6th Dec. 1758. Add. MSS. 32,886. See also Tunstall, *William Pitt*, pp. 249-50.

unanimity. He went on to describe 'in lively colours the success of His Majesty's arms in North America, the distress of the French and the vast importance of our conquests there; then took a view of the affairs on the continent; represented the King of Prussia as great in prosperity, greater still in distress, and emerging, he hoped, from every danger; while our enemy, the King of France, like a proud and imperious vessel, was drove in a tempest of ambition upon the rock of Germany, where he hoped it would stick till the waves of perdition went over it.'[1]

The House was stirred to enthusiasm. A happy unanimity reigned in Parliament, and Pitt added to it by a notable speech on a motion of thanks to Boscawen, Amherst and Osborne on the 6th of December. 'I was at a loss,' said Barrington with unusual warmth, 'which to admire most, the prudence, the good sense or the manliness of it.'[2] Yet in spite of the unanimity, the House was losing its attraction for Pitt. He no longer identified himself so closely with it, nor regarded it as the instrument on which he had to play. In part, this was because his time and thoughts were taken up with administrative work; in part, because he knew that if he went to the House, he would meet with no serious opposition. Curiously enough, he found no pleasure in the thought; he did not ascribe his ascendancy to himself; on the contrary he said and felt that he was living on sufferance. In the first days of the coalition he had declared that it was Newcastle's Parliament, not his; and in this coming year of victories (1759) he repeated the same thought twice at least, first when he said that, whatever he might have desired, he had left the management of the House of Commons to Newcastle,[3] and secondly and more bitterly when he told Devonshire that he knew all Newcastle's friends 'railed at him, and upon any ill-success would have been ready to have torn him to pieces.'[4] It was perhaps as well that the House was so quiescent, for beneath the smooth surface there was turmoil in plenty. The Ministry's whole horizon was overcast by the worthless ambitions of two unnecessary men—Temple and Bute. Their wishes and intrigues are smears of mud on the flashing scutcheon of Pitt's fame.

[1] Symmer to Mitchell, 24th Nov. 1758. Add. MSS. 6,839.
[2] Barrington to Newcastle, 6th Dec. 1758. Add. MSS. 32,886.
[3] Newcastle to Hardwicke, 22nd Sept. 1759. Add MSS. 32,896.
[4] Devonshire's Diary, 14th Nov. 1759. Chatsworth Collection.

(ii)

Temple had long realised that he deserved the Garter. He had mentioned as much to the world, and had been affronted to find that the world went on its way unheeding.[1] At last he complained to Pitt. His deserts, as he saw them, were undoubted. He had been a loyal friend to Pitt; he had stood by him in the dark days, giving him his sister to wife and a handsome income to boot; he was still standing by him in these brighter days, and had worked hard for some eighteen months in high office; he was a man of boundless wealth, who could afford the robes financially, even if physically he could not fill them out; and anyhow he wanted the pretty thing and would not be happy till he got it. Privately, Pitt owned that he might not approve of what Temple was pushing him to do,[2] but, with even greater loyalty than Temple's, he acknowledged his debt, and, doing violence to his commonsense, put forward Temple's pretensions and pressed them.

The King gave a blunt refusal, whereupon Pitt, like another Achilles, stalked to his tent and began to unbuckle his armour. His action left the political world aghast. Nothing had ever shown them more clearly how completely Pitt dominated the English scene, what pygmies they all were compared with him, and how essential it was that his hand should remain on the helm, if America was to be won and Hanover saved. Newcastle has drawn, with a fidelity which almost amounts to genius and certainly betrays his terror, a minutely detailed picture of the confusion and consternation which reigned. Everyone joined in urging the King to yield, and one by one, as they failed, expressed their dismay in their own fashion. Newcastle declared that 'if Mr. Pitt went now, I should think myself a traitor to the King if I pretended to undertake the carrying on his affairs'; Holdernesse was less vocal, but 'lifting up his eyes with astonishment' murmured that 'he never saw anything so bad in his life.' Lady Yarmouth was 'in the utmost distress and concern'; she was appalled at the fact that Pitt had absented himself from the Court and 'she knew of no means to bring him back'; all she did know was that the King was infinitely in the wrong and Pitt wholly

[1] His first application, through Newcastle, was on 18th September 1758. Grenville. *Papers*, I, 267.
[2] Devonshire's Diary, 11th Sept. 1759. Chatsworth Collection.

justified in whatever he might do. Devonshire returned to the attack time after time, assuring the King that nobody wished the honour to be given on Temple's account, but everybody thought it absolutely necessary for the country's sake. The King, in high dudgeon at being so bothered and badgered, showed extreme displeasure with Pitt, refusing to give him any orders and answering all questions with an angry 'Do as you please, do as you please.' Even when he had grown a little calmer, he would say no more than 'that he was out of humour the other day; that he had been plagued; why might not he be out of humour when he was so?'[1] But if he was a little shamefaced, he was no less resolute. His resistance had justification in plenty, for the only reason which Temple could find for his demand was that it would efface the reproach of the continual slights which the King had put upon him. Had that been all, the matter might have dissolved in jeers and laughter. But Pitt gave it substance by asking for the honour as a reward for his own services: 'he thought he might without vanity say that he had done more than anybody had or could do' for the King;[2] he desired no return beyond a mark of the King's approbation and 'he thought he could not do it in any way more easy or more unexceptionable than by this Garter for my Lord Temple.'[3] Here was the crux of the matter, which kept the King in a temper and the world on tenterhooks.

At last, on the 14th of November 1759, Temple resigned in spite of the King's strenuous efforts to dissuade him. Full of alarm at what might follow, the King sent for Devonshire, poured out the story to him and asked him to see Pitt and come to some arrangement. With great difficulty Devonshire extracted a promise that if Temple would return the King would give him the Garter at the end of the session and in the meantime treat him with civility. For the moment this contented Temple, but it soon became evident that he was growing impatient again. Devonshire therefore kept up the pressure until on the 31st of January 1760, Lady Yarmouth told him, to his relief, that the King had yielded and would give the Garter at once. He hurried round to Pitt with the glad tidings.[4] So ended the affair of Temple's Garter. In itself it was a farce, but in its repercussions it was a tragedy. For well over a year it was a source of constant

[1] Newcastle to Hardwicke, 19th Sept. 1759. Add. MSS. 32,895.
[2] Devonshire's Diary, 11th Sept. 1759. Chatsworth Collection.
[3] Newcastle to Hardwicke, 22nd Sept. 1759. Add. MSS. 32,896.
[4] Devonshire's Diary, 31st January 1760. Chatsworth Collection.

irritation, which was not to be mollified even by the balm of continual victories; it strained Pitt's relations with most of his colleagues, driving him into greater isolation, and, most pernicious of all, it gave Bute a handle for mischief. Its importance is not to be judged by its bad taste but by the altogether excessive space which it occupies in Devonshire's political diary and Newcastle's correspondence. In dealing with the events of this year of victories it must never be forgotten; for as Newcastle said 'The Garter operates in everything.'[1]

(iii)

It was towards the end of 1758, just about the time when Temple was first appreciating how good was his claim for the Garter, that Bute, a dark and baffling character, began to loom large on the horizon. His influence came at first in patches, uncertain and unexpected, like wisps and streaks of fog, but it was to grow and finally envelop the whole kingdom.

Bute was an impecunious Scottish peer, possessed of good features and a store of miscellaneous erudition, but without much interest in, or training for, the world of politics. Coming to London in 1746, when thirty-three years of age, he managed to attract the notice of the Prince of Wales, who admired his figure and made him welcome at Leicester House. There he was looked upon as a sort of poor relation, useful to make a fourth at cards or to act as stage manager at private theatricals, but beneath an obsequious exterior he concealed both cunning and shrewdness. After the Prince's death he won his way into the Princess's confidence, becoming her intimate adviser and possibly, as many people thought, her paramour. More important, he was in due course entrusted with the education of the young Prince destined to become George III, whose head he filled, out of his own abundant ignorance, with vague and cloudy ideas of government and the duties of a King, in which 'true piety and virtue' played a conspicuous, if not very practical, part. Still more important, he gained a complete ascendancy over the young man, who felt towards him the sort of adoring attachment which immature girls sometimes feel towards their schoolmistress. His attitude therefore towards the political world became a matter of great and increasing importance.

[1] Newcastle to Kinnoull, 26th October 1759. Add. MSS. 32,897.

The little community at Leicester House, very largely cut off from the world and a prey to its own imaginings, had persuaded itself that Cumberland intended, on the death of the King, to oust, or at least overshadow, his young nephew and seize the reins of power. This belief led to intense hostility not only towards Cumberland himself but also towards Cumberland's friends and adherents. When, therefore, after Pelham's death, Fox and Pitt quarrelled, Leicester House turned naturally towards the latter as their champion. He had once been intimate at Leicester House, and Bute found an occasion to renew the intercourse. More than that, he supported Pitt, discreetly and in the background, through Pitt's first Ministry, and subsequently played a decisive part in jockeying him into the coalition with Newcastle.

Bute's influence grew from both ends. As it was evident that the Prince intended to make him Minister when he came to the throne, the friends of the 'succession' were eager to stand well with him. Concurrently, Bute himself, having played a minor part in the affair of the coalition, began to fancy his own abilities. The idea of becoming a Minister at once fascinated and frightened him, so that he wavered between a pompous self-satisfaction and a very real conviction that he needed guidance. In the latter mood he regarded Pitt as his natural prop; 'indeed,' he wrote to him, 'the entire confidence I place in you, dear Pitt, the perfect knowledge I have of your sentiments, supports me, though surrounded by the most threatening symptoms.'[1] The tone of pseudo-regal condescension discernible in this otherwise slightly abject praise explains how in his more self-confident moments he could press his views on Pitt and expect them to be accepted.

It was, in the circumstances, unfortunate that his opinions were mostly secondhand and based on prejudice. He disapproved of Hanover and the continental war, not because he had any strategical skill or military knowledge, but because Leicester House was at variance with the King and Cumberland. He approved of the Newcastle-Pitt coalition only on the understanding that Newcastle would be a sleeping partner—a view in which he was echoing Pitt's wishes rather than the facts. It was not therefore altogether surprising that when at the end of June (1758) Pitt agreed to send cavalry to Ferdinand, Bute should feel uneasy. Pitt seemed to be leaning unduly towards the Continent, to be too much under Newcastle's thumb, to be ignorant of what

[1] Bute to Pitt, 4th June 1758. Chatham. *Correspondence,* I, 316.

was going on around him, and in short to be losing grip. Bute began to listen to the popular rumours that the King had ordered the generals to play down the raids on the coast of France so that the troops might be sent to Germany, and he came to believe that Pitt's hands were being forced, perhaps not without his own consent. He retailed these doubts to the Prince, who dutifully reflected them back; he was sure the King would send the troops to Germany, and could not help 'fearing your wavering friend (Pitt) would not be against it.'[1] So they fanned each other's fires, and Bute went so far as to tell Viry—the Sardinian Ambassador and a voluntary tale-bearer and father confessor to most of the Cabinet—that 'Mr. Pitt was a very good man and a very able man, but that he had not the fermeté that he imagined he had had.'[2] Bute had a further and more fundamental grievance; Pitt had actually told him that Newcastle was necessary, and that, if he were driven out, they would find they could not do without him. Pitt may have been thinking only of the fact, which rankled in his mind, that 'the Parliament was Newcastle's,' but Bute undoubtedly took it as a snub to his own future pretensions. Friction was growing between them, and was fomented by Holdernesse and Legge who, with their usual self-seeking, were turning towards the rising sun. They kept Bute posted with news of all that took place in the Cabinet and regaled him with tit-bits of ministerial scandal and back-biting. His uneasiness, thus augmented, led to intrigue. Before long, Pitt discovered that Dodington, another time-server, had been sent as 'a missionary to the Tories, to blow them up against the English troops being sent to Germany,' using as his slogan that 'Pitt was Hanoverian under the name of Prussian.'[3] Though the Tories remained loyal to their adopted leader, the position was sufficiently serious to make Pitt seek out Bute and try to come to an understanding.

The meeting took place in December (1758), and after the minor causes of friction had been smoothed over, Bute raised the point which he had at heart. What was going to happen when the King died? Pitt had no doubt; 'everything should be done in concert with the Duke of Newcastle.' To which Bute replied, flatly, that 'to be Minister of this country hereafter was what the Duke of Newcastle could not be.'[4]

[1] Geo. III to Bute, 2nd July 1758. Sedgwick, p. 11.
[2] Newcastle to Hardwicke, 5th Oct. 1758. Add. MSS. 32,884.
[3] Newcastle's note, 10th Oct. 1758. Add. MSS. 32,884.
[4] Note. Newcastle House, 20th December 1758. Add. MSS. 32,886.

In spite of this brave bearing, Bute was in something of a quandary. When in 1756 George III had reached his legal majority, Bute had promised to take the Treasury in the coming reign,[1] but being nervous, was anxious to be pressed, and was still not quite sure if he dared accept. Pitt's bland assumption that Newcastle was to continue came as a cold douche, and perhaps by a natural reaction made him for the moment the more keen. But on reflection, his keenness waned. If Newcastle and Pitt were opposed to him, could he possibly make good? He became diffident, and finally drew back, telling the Prince that he had not got the ability himself, and that his supporters, Legge and Holdernesse, could not hold their own against Newcastle and Pitt.[2] The Prince was genuinely disturbed. He recognised his own inexperience and, while he had unlimited confidence in Bute, he had been taught to distrust the others. He therefore begged Bute to reconsider his decision, expressing with obvious conviction his admiration of Bute's capacities, his unbounded trust in him, and his very real need of his support.[3]

All this was balm to Bute's soul and helped to restore his self-confidence. By degrees he was even able to let his dislike of Pitt overcome his fear of him. By February (1759) he had so far recovered that he could declare, in private, that 'Pitt was not contented to be Secretary of State, but he must direct the Treasury too, which he ought not to do,' and spoke bitterly of his 'temper and overbearing.'[4] By March he was trying to interfere with ministerial appointments and finding fault with Pitt for his animosity against Legge, whom Bute had taken under his own wing. By April he had gone a stage farther and was deliberately courting Newcastle as a counterpoise to Pitt, probably with some vague idea of taking Pitt's place instead of Newcastle's in the coming reign. Newcastle, succumbing to his flattery, had the pleasure of informing the King that 'Pitt is quite beat out at Leicester House,'[5] and a fortnight later was actually urging Hardwicke to discuss ways of forcing Pitt out of office. 'I cannot but hope,' he wrote, 'that you will see my Lord Bute. The impossibility of going on with this gentleman (Pitt) and bearing his usage will, I hope, put us all upon thinking how to get out of it.'[6]

[1] Sedgwick, p. 20. [2] Geo. III to Bute, December 1758. Sedgwick, p. 19.
[3] Geo. III to Bute, Dec. 1758. Sedgwick, pp. 19-22.
[4] Note. Newcastle House, 21st Feb. 1759. Add. MSS. 32,888.
[5] Memo. for the King, 1st May 1759. Add. MSS. 32,890.
[6] Newcastle to Hardwicke, 12th May 1759. Add. MSS. 32,891.

There can be little doubt that Temple's Garter was at the bottom of this outburst, which had no immediate effect; Newcastle would have been horrified if Pitt had gone with the war in its then condition. Nor had Bute any intention of overthrowing Pitt at once, but he now knew how easy it was to widen the breach between the two parties to the coalition, and how surely by dividing he could rule. He was becoming set in his hitherto tentative belief that he was capable of governing. A *tertium quid* had been thrown into the political arena.

22

THE ROOT OF ALL EVIL

(i)

In his own way, Pitt gave as good as he got. He had no confidence in his colleagues. From time to time he let slip his opinion of them, and some of his descriptions have survived. Newcastle, he declared, did not understand Treasury business and being aware of his ignorance, abandoned any proposal the moment it was objected to; his sole interests were the disposal of employments, which Pitt did not desire, and retaining the confidence of the King, which Pitt knew he could never win. Newcastle gave trouble only when 'two little lawyers' put ideas into his head which Pitt had to dispel. Mansfield had 'knowledge and parts' but was easily cowed; Hardwicke, 'knew a great deal of the *routine* and of the *Bar,*' talked a lot and had to be listened to, but 'was not of the consequence he imagined.'[1] Of Holdernesse Pitt had never had any opinion. Originally he had wanted to get rid of him; but now he was coldly indifferent. He admitted that he had felt piqued when first Holdernesse had begun to make court to Leicester House, because he 'well knew that it was *à ses depends*,' but had ultimately thought it best to ignore him, and now his only fear was that, being backed by powerful friends, he might do 'great mischief' when peace was in the offing.[2] Of Legge he had been suspicious, not without reason, since the days of the 'interministerium,' and was aware of, and resented, his sly flirtations with Leicester House.

Whether Pitt was right or wrong in this scornful assessment of his colleagues it is evident that he expected no help from them. He was in a real sense friendless, with no follower in the Lords but the insufferable Temple, and few in the Commons beyond the maladroit Beckford and the loyal but mute band of Tories.

[1] Note. Newcastle House, 16th March 1759. Add. MSS. 32,889.
[2] Note. Newcastle House, 28th Nov. 1759. Add. MSS. 32,899.

Yet the almost complete isolation in which he found himself had one compensating advantage—he was his own master in preparing military plans. No one ventured to argue with him on those matters, however strongly they might dislike and oppose his general policy. He was able therefore to turn unhampered to the problem of the next year's campaigns.

His general outlook was summed up in the King's Speech at the opening of Parliament (23rd November 1758). The pendulum was swinging in England's favour. Our enemies, who had been so triumphant in the past, had been made to feel that 'the strength of Great Britain is not to be provoked with impunity'; and France, which had hitherto had the monopoly of threatening invasion, had been taught that 'their own coasts are not inaccessible to his Majesty's fleets and armies.' If the national honour stood high, so did the national wealth. The conquests already made could not fail 'to bring great distress upon the French commerce and colonies; and, in proportion, to procure great advantages to our own'; indeed, our commerce, 'the source of our riches,' had flourished under the protection of the fleet 'in a manner not to be paralleled during such troubles.' Meanwhile Frederick and Ferdinand had 'found full employment for the armies of France,' from which fact we had derived 'the most evident advantage.' On such an inspiriting foundation the new campaigns were to be built.

The main effort must once more be in America, where Pitt envisaged a three-pronged attack, as in the previous year, but on a broader scale. Forbes and Bradstreet had settled the western borders as effectually as Wolfe and Amherst had opened the gateway of the St. Lawrence. There was no need therefore to do more along the western front than display a state of preparedness, rebuild Oswego, and if time and opportunity allowed, push on towards Niagara. In place of the more restricted advance to the Ohio, it was now possible to make a wider sweep, which would menace the French settlements at New Orleans and the mouth of the Mississippi. Pitt had it in mind to capture Martinique and Guadeloupe, the main French possessions in the Lesser Antilles, that group of islands spread like a shield across the entrance to the Caribbean Sea and the Gulf of Mexico, and guarding the approach to the French Colonies of the south. Here was an extension of the operations of war, threatening the last outpost of France in the new world. Pitt's plans were widening.

The expedition against Martinique had been arranged in September. The remainder of the plan could not be finally settled until Pitt knew what, if anything, Abercromby had done between his repulse at Ticonderoga and his recall to England. It was not until the 29th of December 1758, that instructions could be sent to his successor, Amherst. They covered his own advance on Montreal by way of Ticonderoga and Crown Point, and Wolfe's attack on Quebec by way of the St. Lawrence. They also referred to the possibilities at Oswego and Niagara. For the third time Pitt was laying his plans for the invasion of Canada.

(ii)

Though America must come first, Pitt was anxious on all counts to keep the continental war alive and prosperous, the more so as Frederick and the majority of his own Cabinet were hankering after peace. A premature collapse on the Continent might be fatal. Reinforcements for Ferdinand were therefore desirable, and as Pitt neither could, nor would, supply them in any numbers from England, he searched for them in Europe.[1] He was prepared to pay handsomely for them; Newcastle might have said recklessly. But Pitt believed that the time was coming, if it had not already come, when money well spent would be the best economy. In keeping with this view he told Newcastle that he was prepared to renew the Hessian subsidy, and even to add £50,000 as a gift from the King to the Landgrave 'on account of his unhappy situation in having been obliged so often to remove from his capital'—a subtle step, intended not only to encourage the Landgrave, who was becoming restive under the misfortunes of war, but also to sidetrack the awkward question of 'dédommagement.' If there were other powers which could be induced to join the allied cause, so much the better, 'he would forfeit his head rather than not take them'; possibly a friend might be found in Bavaria, at least it was worth exploring.[2] Possibly also Ferdinand could get a couple of thousand men from Brunswick; if so, Pitt would urge Parliament to pay them.[3]

Frederick presented a different problem. For some time now, he and Pitt had felt a growing respect for each other. Frederick

[1] See Sackville to Ferdinand, 23rd Feb. 1759. H.M.C. Stopford Sackville MSS., Vol. I.

[2] Newcastle to Geo. II, 15th Dec. 1758. Add. MSS. 32,886.

[3] Sackville to Ferdinand, 23rd Feb. 1759. Stopford Sackville MSS., Vol. I.

in his forthright manner congratulated England on having at last given birth to a man, and sent complimentary messages through Mitchell and friendly letters in his own hand. Pitt answered in stately and stilted prose. But, for all their mutual admiration, they were treading different paths to their common end and were not prepared to yield up their opinions. Each poured out suggestions which the other politely rejected. At times there was something almost comic about this interchange of incompatible ideas. Take the case of the Princess Electoral of Saxony. She was shut up in Dresden which Frederick was besieging. She was also pregnant. Pitt, who had a strongly sentimental streak, and saw a chance of combining chivalry with political advantage, urged Frederick to allow her to retire to Munich or Warsaw, and so by 'making a favourable impression on the House of Saxony' lead on naturally to a reconciliation.[1] Alas! Frederick had none of Pitt's sentimentality. He was half vexed and half amused, as he answered that he had no wish for a reconciliation; it would mean the loss of an annual revenue of six million crowns which he was levying in Saxony and also the advantage of recruiting troops there. In the circumstances he saw nothing romantic in the Princess's condition, and was quite sure that if she wanted to escape out of Dresden it was in order to hurt him rather than to benefit herself.[2]

Take again the case of Sardinia. Thinking that the King of Sardinia might be persuaded to take an active part in the war if he were offered a sufficient inducement, Frederick proposed that certain Italian Duchies, which on the death of the King of Spain were to go to Austria, should be offered to Sardinia instead. He had no conceivable authority to make the offer, but as he told Mitchell, 'he thought he had as good a right to dispose of other people's territories as they had of his.'[3] Without further ado he dispatched a special envoy to Sardinia and asked Pitt to support him. Pitt thought the object good, but because of possible repercussions in Spain, where he was engaged in delicate negotiations, he took prompt steps to quash the proposal.[4]

In spite of these and many similar rubs, the two men trusted, and so far as they could, supported each other. In Pitt's case the support took the shape of constant though fruitless endeavours

[1] Pitt to Mitchell, 2nd Jan. 1759. Add. MSS. 6,817.
[2] Mitchell to Holdernesse, 21st Jan. 1759. Add. MSS. 6,807.
[3] Mitchell to Holdernesse, 14th March 1759. Add. MSS. 6,807.
[4] Holdernesse to Mitchell, 24th April 1759. Add. MSS. 6,817.

to restrain the northern powers—Russia and Sweden—from invading Prussia, and more successful efforts to keep the Danes and the Dutch out of the war.

(iii)

Though Pitt had prepared his plans with undiminished hope, and Parliament appeared to be united and quiescent, yet this year of victories—1759—opened at home with the gloomiest of prospects. The City was clouded in one of those moods of depression for which there seems to be no accounting; stocks were falling, credit was short; and the financial malaise was inflamed by an unusual delay in the opening of the Budget and a suspicion that the Cabinet was at loggerheads.

The suspicion was justified; never was the coalition nearer disintegration. 'More distressed in administration nobody can be than myself,' Newcastle complained, 'insulted every day by that *chit*, my Lord Holdernesse, not very agreeably or respectfully treated by Mr. Pitt.'[1] Holdernesse was not much happier. He was chafing at the 'dirty court intrigues to lower Mr. Secretary Pitt in the opinion of both the King and the public,' and believed that 'my great crime is that I have not joined in the clamour.'[2] Hardwicke refused to attend any more Council meetings because he thought he was not sufficiently regarded;[3] and Legge who, the previous year, had resigned in a huff and had returned to office only at Newcastle's urgent entreaty, remained sullen and unhelpful. Pitt was in little better case. To begin with, he was full of anxieties over Hester. She was once more to become a mother and during the last few months of her pregnancy Pitt was noticeably often 'dispirited and low.' A lover's devotion was calling him, and on one occasion at least he dismissed affairs of state with a cry from the heart that 'he must go home,' and he went.[4] On the 26th of May (1759) she gave birth to their second son, William. As ever in the Pitt family, the babe was welcomed with unfeigned joy, and soon proved a specific against depression. Within a few weeks Hester was writing, 'I cannot help believing that little William is to become a personage.' It would be pleasant to think that this glimpse into the future was true prophetic

[1] Newcastle to Mansfield, 8th June 1759. Add. MSS. 32,891.
[2] Holdernesse to Mitchell, 28th May 1759. Add. MSS. 6,832.
[3] Memo. for the King, 29th June 1759. Add MSS. 32,892.
[4] West to Newcastle, 27th Jan. 1759. Add. MSS. 32,887.

insight and not merely a mother's foolish fondness; but at least it was enough to bring a sparkle to Pitt's eye and a gaiety to his heart. From that moment he was often to be found in 'good humour.' If private worries had been his only cross, he would have been entirely happy, but private worries were only half the picture. When he left Hayes for London he was not only overwhelmed with business in which he got no help whatever, but was also irritated by the nonsense of Temple's Garter, and stirred to resentment by Legge's now undisguised efforts to supplant him at Leicester House. And over the whole of this restless scene hovered the enigmatical Bute with his unresolved ambitions and his uncertain mind. Nor must Pitt's health be forgotten; as he reminded Grenville, 'without competent strength of body, vain are the efforts of the strongest and wisest minds.'[1]

Before the young William had arrived to spread his beneficent influence, Pitt and the Cabinet had to introduce the Budget. The financial position alarmed Newcastle. To a large extent it was figures not facts that frightened him, but the figures were frightening enough. England had entered the war with a national debt of £72,000,000, and had been out-running the constable ever since. Against a revenue of something under £7,000,000, Pitt's war (as they called it when totting up the expense) had cost £13,000,000 in 1756 and the cost had been increasing ever since. In 1759 it was estimated that £20,000,000 would be needed. The money, said Newcastle, was not there; we should soon come to a standstill for want of pounds, shillings and pence; we must therefore make peace before we were conquered as well as bankrupt. When Newcastle allowed himself to think about the future, his fears became almost unbearable, and he would jot down a series of panic-stricken notes for his next talk with the King: 'to lay before the King the state of the Bank. . . . The impossibility of going on in this way. The country cannot support it. . . . The Bank will shut up. The Exchequer next. . . . The necessity of a peace this summer. My duty to tell his Majesty so.'[2]

But neither King nor Pitt paid any attention. Pitt, who kept a close eye on financial movements both here and in France, had no doubts—trade was prospering and fortunes were being made. Actual specie might be temporarily short because of the large amounts going to the troops in America and the allies on the

[1] Pitt to Grenville, 21st July 1759. Grenville. *Papers*, I, 314.
[2] Memo. for the King, 28th Feb. 1759. Add. MSS. 32,888.

Continent, but it would come back again and there was ample money in the country for all requirements. War expenses which could not be met out of taxation must be covered by borrowing. Newcastle, unable to deny the evidence of prosperity, but not to be done out of his fears, retorted that borrowing required security, and there was no existing tax which was not already mortgaged up to the hilt. How then would the interest on the new loans be met? Newcastle himself could suggest nothing but an increase of the malt tax, and when both Legge and Pitt objected, washed his hands of the whole problem—in precisely the manner which Pitt had described. Legge, forced to act, first suggested a licence duty on shops, which appealed to Pitt, and then substituted a tax on sugar. This was anathema to the City merchants trading to the West Indies, particularly Beckford. They marched, fifty strong, to the Treasury to expostulate, and getting no remedy appealed to Pitt, who influenced perhaps by his friendship for Beckford, persuaded Legge to substitute a tax on dry goods generally, instead of on sugar alone. But Beckford was not to be thus mollified. He continued his outburst in the committee on ways and means, when his fervent but uncouth oratory provoked the House to merriment, and so brought Pitt to his feet. Pitt was always magnificent when handling a derisive House. On this occasion members had raised a 'horse-laugh' at the word sugar, and Pitt, blazing with wrath, thundered out the word again and again till he had reduced the House to a stunned silence, and then glaring round demanded to know who would laugh at it now. He proceeded, in a hushed and crestfallen assembly, to load Beckford with fulsome compliments, showing 'a deference to his judgment that could not but be extremely mortifying to the Chancellor of the Exchequer'[1] and then developed his own ideas on taxation.

No one, he reminded the House, liked paying taxes, and for that reason it was easy enough to create prejudice. Represent a tax on currants as a tax on plum puddings—and out goes the Chancellor. There were many points to bear in mind—not only the revenue obtained but the after-effects. We were a commercial country, and 'the best statesman for England was the man that understood trade and navigation best.' Taxes should be settled on a regular plan and 'permanent foundations'; they should not be chosen haphazard merely 'to serve a pinch.' Personally, he

[1] Symmer to Mitchell, 13th March 1759. Add. MSS. 6,839.

believed in 'an inland duty and a free port,' or, in other words, he preferred excise to customs. But he was speaking out of his province. He had been thrown up by chance and a thousand incomprehensible accidents to fill a gap in Government. It was not for him to settle taxation. He had, indeed, ventured to make a suggestion—a licence duty on shops—but it had not been approved; and so now, though he was sure there were better expedients, he would vote for the Chancellor's proposal, 'not as a mark of approbation, but in consequence of his acquiescing in measures that were in the department of another Minister.'

Though the Budget was passed, this speech was clearly intended as a snub for Legge, and Pitt followed it up three days later by a direct attack on him for procrastination 'to which in a great measure he ascribed the injury the public credit had received.' The loans had not been settled till the middle of February, nor the taxes till the beginning of March, though all should have been prepared during the recess and carried into execution at the beginning of the session. 'One does not need to be a conjuror,' commented Symmer, 'to see that without some extraordinary incident, those two gentlemen cannot go on long together.'[1]

Symmer judged from without. The Sardinian Ambassador found confirmation within. His budget of news was always full of bickerings—how James Grenville gloated over the confusion at the Treasury; how Pitt disparaged, and Bute supported, Legge; how the Grenvilles were 'more violent and outrageous than ever against my Lord Hardwicke'; how Legge's friends were urging Leicester House not to be dependent solely on Pitt 'who was heated in the manner he was half the day'; how Bute disapproved of Temple and so on.[2] By April, the ferment had gone so far that Devonshire and Newcastle took serious council together, and their views depict the opinion of the Whig magnates generally. They saw nothing good in any direction. At home, they were convinced that Pitt meant 'to fling the blame of the miscarriage, that is the low state of credit, the fall of the stocks and the difficulty of going on, upon the negligence, ignorance or ill management of the Treasury.' Abroad, our enemies were more united than ever and there was 'no disposition

[1] Symmer to Mitchell, 13th March 1759. Add. MSS. 6,839.

[2] Notes dated 21st Feb., 3rd March, 16th March and 10th April 1759. Add. MSS. 32,888-9.

in the Courts of Vienna or France towards peace.' On the contrary France was inciting Denmark, Sweden and Holland to take up arms against us and seemed only too likely to succeed. She was also well aware of our financial weakness, and knew that even if we conquered North America we would find it just as expensive to preserve our conquests as to make them. There was only one conclusion to be drawn—'experience shows that it will be impossible to carry on the war another year at this expence.'[1] What made the position hopeless was that although the true state of affairs had never been concealed from Pitt, 'he never owned he saw things in that light.' Because of his blindness or intransigence we must, so Newcastle concluded, go on attempting that 'idlest of all imaginations'—the extirpation of France from North America.[2] But where it would all end did not bear thinking of.

[1] Devonshire's Diary, 18th April 1759. Chatsworth Collection.
[2] Newcastle's Considerations, 19th April 1759. Add. MSS. 32,890.

23

MINDEN

There was living in Paris, at that time, an Irishman, Oliver MacAllester by name. His profession, modestly and somewhat anonymously described as business, was that of a spy, which he carried on with the usual admixture of tarnished glory and shabby enterprise. Provided he was well paid, he was indifferent to whom he sold his services. Hitherto he had been working for France, but in 1759 he noticed that money seemed to be getting short, and that Ministers and officials alike, from Choiseul downwards, were developing a disagreeable habit of putting him off with driblets and promises. He began to think that he had backed the wrong horse, and his suspicion was bulwarked by perhaps the only one of his feelings which was not entirely self-centred. The outlook of spies is not conducive to hero worship, but he had acquired a very genuine admiration for Pitt, who so palpably held all France in awe. He decided to transfer his allegiance, and rightly supposing that he would receive a warmer welcome if he came with useful information in his pocket, set to work to get it. He knew that the French intended to invade England and chance put into his hands a copy of a map of the English coast showing the proposed points of landing. From that moment his one idea was to escape out of France with his trophy. It took him the best part of two years, for the French authorities kept a restraining hand on spies, and his adventures do not concern us. What is of interest is the light which he throws on French hopes and fears. The invasion of England was not, if he is to be believed, a considered military operation, nor was it immediate; it was a policy of despair projected into an uncertain future. The French no longer supposed that they could save Canada, or any other of their overseas possessions which Pitt might choose to attack. Their only hope therefore was to wait until Pitt resigned or was removed, and then by means of an invasion, which was bound to succeed in the confusion of his fall, extort restitution in England itself. Nor—

and this is even more interesting—did they think that they would have long to wait. What grounds they had for this belief in 1759 MacAllester does not explain, but his narrative makes it clear that at least as time went on they were trusting to ministerial dissensions, until in 1761 they could tell him with conviction that 'Lord Bute will break the neck of that damned rascal Pitt.'[1] Meanwhile they went ahead with their preparations against the day of reckoning.

Too much reliance must not, of course, be placed on the tales of spies, but there is no smoke without fire, and one may at least reasonably infer from MacAllester's reiterated statements that the quarrels of the Cabinet were known to the French, and were a source of encouragement to them, prolonging the war, and, MacAllester hints, inducing Spain to renew the Family Compact.

Pitt had his own sources of intelligence which did not include MacAllester, and through them the Cabinet had come to know early in the year of the projected invasion. As usual they were variously affected. Newcastle and Hardwicke promptly took alarm; Pitt remained cool and sceptical. He said that France was in no condition to make the attempt, her preparations not being sufficiently advanced—in which respect his views, though flatly contradicted by Hardwicke and Newcastle, did not differ materially from those of MacAllester. On the other hand he thought that as Newcastle and his friends had alarmed the people, it would be as well to allay their fears.[2] He had already gone some way by giving orders once more for transports and troops to be collected in the Isle of Wight—a proceeding which Newcastle had described as 'a most abominable and a most unheard of measure,' because he had not been told the reason.[3] Pitt now went farther and agreed to strengthen the home fleet at Torbay under Hawke, and dispatched Rodney to bombard the flat-bottomed boats collecting at Le Havre. He also seized the opportunity to encourage the militia, issuing a circular letter on the subject which affords an amusing example of his meticulous attention to words. The first draft, mainly by Newcastle's hand, struck him as too dull; it must be livened up or otherwise the message might be ill-taken and 'produce bad consequences.'

[1] MacAllester, II, 119.
[2] Memo. for the King, 9th May 1759. Add MSS. 32,891.
[3] Newcastle to Hardwicke, 17th April 1759. Add. MSS. 32,890.

He suggested the words 'imminent danger of invasion,' adding dryly that there was all the difference in the world between 'imminent danger *of* invasion' which could be justified by the French plans and orders, and 'imminent danger *from* invasion,' which had no justification whatever.[1]

The circular had a good effect, which, combined with the birth of the young William, put Pitt into a thoroughly good humour. 'Mr. Pitt,' Newcastle noticed with some resentment, 'seems extremely gay; despises the attempts of the French, says we have 40,000 men in Great Britain and Ireland etc., and laughs at everything the French can do.'[2]

Though Pitt was outwardly gay, he was inwardly anxious. Victory still eluded him, and speed was everything. His successes to date were sufficient to encourage the thought of peace but not enough to ensure adequate rewards. Here lay the danger. Many members of the Cabinet wanted peace, Newcastle in particular. It had been Newcastle's one dream at least since the middle of 1758,[3] and he had not ceased to press his views. Pitt had held him at bay, but the failures and half successes of the war, combined with the new threat of invasion, were creating an atmosphere of weariness, if not defeatism, which played into his hands, and there was now a growing body of opinion, both in and out of Parliament, that it was time to come to terms.

So far this opinion had not been very vocal, nor perhaps very widespread, but in June 1759 there came a letter from Prussia which fundamentally altered the position. Frederick it appeared was growing desperate. He knew that the forces against him greatly outnumbered his own; he knew that in spite of his best efforts, he was being slowly ground to pieces. The strain was too great and he was near breaking-point. In fact within a few weeks he was to put his fortunes, in desperation, to the hazard in two ill-judged attempts against the Russians, at Züllichau (23rd July) and Kunersdorf (12th August), in both of which he was bloodily defeated, and after the latter very nearly committed suicide. In a mood of despondency, anticipating defeat, he wrote to George II, suggesting that it would be neither below their dignity nor against their honour to take advantage of the first

[1] West to Newcastle, 22nd May 1759. Add. MSS. 32,891.
[2] Newcastle to Hardwicke, 12th June 1759. Add. MSS. 32,892.
[3] See Newcastle to White, 29th July 1758. Add. MSS. 32,882.

favourable event of the campaign to propose jointly the summoning of a peace congress.[1] Newcastle was overjoyed. He could now face Pitt in Prussian armour. Good European as he was, peace presented no problem; it was just a question of shaking hands and forgetting. The conquests on either side were tiresome details, but could without much difficulty be made to equal one another, and so form a basis for exchange. Nothing really mattered except the cease fire, the end of borrowing, and the beginning of a new era at home.

But to Pitt peace meant something wider. He knew that he would be bargaining for more, much more, than islands in the Mediterranean, or forests in Canada, or even electorates in Germany. He knew that more was at stake even than trade and commerce, important as those were. He would be the trustee for 3,000,000 Englishmen over the seas who had no other representative, and for whom too many people forgot that the war was being waged. They needed protection both now and hereafter, and protection they must have. What form it should take Pitt had not had time to decide. It would be useless to demand too much; it would be criminal to accept too little; and the more or less would be settled by the facts. Pitt had therefore been careful to hide his thoughts; he had refused to back the King's airy notions of universal conquest; he had also rejected with scorn Newcastle's hankerings after another Treaty of Utrecht. England, if he could help it, would never again tarnish her honour by deserting her friends.[2] The debt to Frederick must be paid in full, and, like most debts, hung heavy round his neck. If he was to do all he wished at the peace table, he must have something more substantial in his hand than he possessed at present. He was not ready for peace, whatever Frederick might be.

Yet he was forced to bow to this appeal from Frederick, backed as it was by the growing weight of discontent and fear in the Cabinet. He did so with a sore heart, and a determination to delay progress at least until he had heard from America. In the discussions with Newcastle and the Prussian Ministers, he insisted that any declaration issued to the world should speak of 'the successes we had had.' Newcastle objected, largely on the ground of fact, but also out of impatience because he shrewdly suspected that Pitt wanted to hold up the document 'till we had obtained

1 Frederick to Geo. II, 20th June 1759. Chatham. *Correspondence,* I, 413.
2 Pitt to Mitchell, 12th June 1759. Add. MSS. 6,833.

some signal success.'[1] His suspicions were correct. It was with the same idea at the back of his mind that Pitt refused point-blank to recall a single man from America, insisting that Louisburg and Guadeloupe would be the best plenipotentiaries and speaking of Senegal and Goree as 'good things to make peace with.'[2] As he told Hardwicke, 'perhaps it is not too much to say that sustaining this war, arduous as it has been and still is, may not be more difficult than properly and happily closing it.'[3] That new difficulty was now upon him, and upon him alone, for he had no help from Newcastle; it had come prematurely and he was being hurried. His reaction was natural and obvious.

While he was thus dragging his feet on the path to peace, he was doing his utmost to speed up the war. There was not much that he could do, pending news from the scenes of operation, but what could be done, he did, though at times it earned him black looks. He pressed Newcastle to send ample supplies of specie to America, lest a shortage should retard success, and pressed with such bewildering insistence, that Newcastle was jolted into the sensational remark that we 'have now issued more than we have';[4] he arranged for a parade and march past of the militia in Kensington Gardens, to the great delight of the populace, who so thronged the route that the time-table was upset, the troops were late, and the King had to twiddle his thumbs for half an hour under the portico of the palace;[5] and he urged the Duke of Argyll to enlist 'the well-affected Highlanders' and persuaded Lord Eglinton to raise a troop of light dragoons in the Lowlands.

But there were certain directions in which his efforts could be more effective. Germany was near at hand, and in some respects was becoming the central pivot. In the new campaign, Ferdinand was being pushed back by two French armies, one under the Duc de Broglie in Hesse, and the other, under Contades, on the Rhine, which together greatly outnumbered the forces at his command. Pitt followed his fortunes with intense interest. He supplied him with such artillery as could be spared from England,[6] and encouraged his evident wish to make a stand. Having great faith in his

[1] Newcastle to Hardwicke, 21st July 1759. Add. MSS. 32,893.
[2] Newcastle to Stone, 1st Aug. 1759. Add. MSS. 32,893.
[3] Pitt to Hardwicke, 20th October 1759. Add. MSS. 35,423.
[4] Newcastle to Hardwicke, 3rd June 1759. Add. MSS. 32,891.
[5] Pitt to Hester, 17th July 1759. Chatham. *Correspondence*, II, 4.
[6] Newcastle to Holdernesse, 24th May 1759. Add. MSS. 32,891.

abilities, and noting his 'opinion and desire to risk a battle,' he pressed for stronger orders to be sent to him to fortify his inclination. Newcastle was horrified and urged in opposition opinions expressed, inconsequently, by Ferdinand's Secretary, and, ominously, by Lord George Sackville.[1] Pitt, however, in spite of inevitable forebodings, stuck to his hope. He had already told Grenville 'we expect every moment news of a general action in Hesse; the expectation is big with inquietudes, but hope predominates,'[2] and now he confided to Hester that the parade of the militia in Kensington Gardens 'could engage but in part the attention of such of the spectators as expect, on pretty certain grounds, the accounts of two decisive battles; Prince Ferdinand having moved so as to bring on an action, and Dohna having been almost up with the Russians some days since.'[3] Dohna, Frederick's general, went on to defeat at Züllichau, but Ferdinand fared otherwise. He had been forced back to the Weser and seemed likely to be driven over it when, on the 1st of August (1759), he seized an opportunity given to him by Contades and won the battle of Minden. It was decisive, as Pitt had hoped it might be, but not so decisive as it should have been. By universal consent, the victory was due to the incomparable conduct of the English infantry; but was robbed of its full fruits by the conduct of Lord George Sackville, who disobeying Ferdinand's orders failed to complete the rout of the French, by the use of the cavalry under his command.

Sackville had been Pitt's white-headed boy. He had done his best to push him up the ladder, asking for him as Secretary at War, choosing him for the descents on the coasts of France, and insisting on his appointment to the command of the English troops in Germany when the Duke of Marlborough had died. The charge of disobedience and cowardice must have struck at Pitt's heart. So many English generals had failed, but not one so blatantly as this; the others had fallen short in ability, Sackville in character. To make matters worse, Sackville was a favourite at Leicester House and Bute intervened on his behalf. But with Pitt, failure was final; the fortunes of England were too precious to be left one moment in unworthy hands. The most he could do for Sackville was to give him the chance of resigning before he

[1] Memorandum for the King, 5th July 1759. Add. MSS. 32,892.
[2] Pitt to Grenville, 23rd June 1759. Grenville. *Papers*, I, 307.
[3] Pitt to Hester, 17th July 1759. Chatham. *Correspondence,* II, 4.

was dismissed, and such opportunities of clearing himself as a court martial might provide. His answer to Bute was sad but firm: 'as I have already, so I shall continue to give him, as a most unhappy man, all the *offices of humanity*, which our *first, sacred* object, my dear Lord, the public good, will allow.'[1] To Sackville himself, when he angled for Pitt's aid, he showed himself no less uncompromising and no less grieved: 'Give me leave to say,' he replied, 'that I find myself (from the turn of your lordship's letter) under the painful necessity of declaring my infinite concern at not having been able to find . . . any room (as I wished) for me to offer support, with regard to a conduct, which my incompetence perhaps to judge of military questions leaves me at a loss to account for. I cannot enough lament the subject of a correspondence, so unlike everything I had wished, to a person for whose advantageous situation my poor endeavours had not been wanting.'[2]

But all this sadness was to come; for the moment Pitt could taste the sweets of pleasure unalloyed. He hastened to share them with Hester: 'I cannot let the groom go without a line to my sweetest life, especially as I have the joy to tell her that our happy victory *ne fait que croitre et embellir*. . . . The main of the French army seen to be flying they know not where. . . . To this point has favouring Providence blessed our immortal Ferdinand. . . . May happy peace wind up the glorious work, and heal a bleeding world.'[3]

No event seemingly in this year of decision was to be either simple or isolated. Minden, which saved Hanover and raised hopes of peace even in Pitt's breast, precipitated France, more surely because with less option, into her scheme of invasion. As originally planned by Belleisle, there was to be a concentration at Brest of the French naval forces, under the protection of which 50,000 men from Flanders were to be landed in Essex and march on London; another 20,000 were to sail from Brittany to the Clyde and march on Edinburgh, while by way of diversion Thurot was to make a descent on Ireland. The details had long since been worked out and orders for the preliminary steps had been dispatched while Ferdinand was still retreating. On the 5th of August, four days after Minden, La Clue set out from Toulon with

[1] Pitt to Bute, 15th August 1759. Chatham. *Correspondence,* I, 417.
[2] Pitt to Sackville, 9th Sept. 1759. H.M.C. Stopford Sackville MSS., Vol. I.
[3] Pitt to Hester, 6th Aug. 1759. Chatham. *Correspondence,* II, 7.

twelve ships of the line for Brest, hoping to slip unobserved through the Straits while the Mediterranean fleet under Boscawen was refitting in Gibraltar. But on the 17th of August, as he was creeping along the north African coast, he was sighted by an English frigate, which came flying to Gibraltar to give the alarm. La Clue, knowing that he had been seen and fearing the worst, fled into the night. Five of his ships took refuge in Cadiz. The rest sailed north hotly pursued by Boscawen, who came up with them off Lagos. There was a running fight for forty-eight hours, in the course of which two of the enemy escaped, one hauled down its flag, and the remaining four were driven on to the Portuguese coast. Boscawen, regardless of international law, followed them in, burnt two and captured the others.

When the Portuguese protested at this violation of their territorial waters, Pitt offered profuse apologies in the stately fashion of which he was a master. But nothing more. He had no intention of making restitution or of finding fault with Boscawen. How could he when, by demolishing La Clue's squadron, Boscawen seemed to have ended the threat of invasion? Even Newcastle was satisfied. When the news arrived on the 5th of September, his fears vanished and he confessed significantly, 'I own I was afraid of invasion till now.'[1]

But to the French the outlook was different. What they might have done if Contades had gained the upper hand at Minden is a matter for academic debate; conceivably they might have been content to press forward to Hanover, and postpone the invasion, as MacAllester thought they would, until Pitt had fallen. What is certain is that Minden made the invasion inevitable, as the only remaining alternative. When therefore the news reached Versailles, the French authorities, with Gallic fatalism, decided that Conflans must do alone what he was to have done with La Clue, and must do it at the earliest possible moment. In short, the invasion was now on, more surely than ever before.[2]

Pitt's view of Minden differed from all others. Undoubtedly he looked on it as a 'good thing to make peace with,' but he saw it also in another and very unexpected light. He was not blind to the machinations around him, being well aware of Newcastle's feelings and recognising that Leicester House was no longer favourable. He could have little doubt that the coalition and

[1] Newcastle to Hardwicke, 6th Sept. 1759. Add. MSS. 32,895.
[2] Corbett, II, 44.

probably his own importance[1] would end with the war. Now that peace was on the tapis, his time was growing short, and if he was to cash in on his successes, he must act at once. Surely Minden, added to all he had done, entitled him to some reward. Now, if ever, was the time to press for Temple's Garter. Pitt flared up again like a smouldering volcano come suddenly to life, and the mountain of Minden, after much labour, produced its ridiculous mouse. It is a chastening thought that, in England, the valour and glory of that decisive battle vanished in the disgrace of a second-class general and the decoration of a second-class politician, who between them reduced Minden from a victory to a name.

In his ministerial as opposed to his private capacity, Minden gave Pitt hope that peace was not impossible and not far off. It was not the 'signal success' which he had in mind—that could come only from America—but it was a great victory, and would lend weight to negotiations which Pitt believed could best be made from strength. Hitherto 1759 had not yielded much. The fall of Goree had been reported in January, and the capture of Guadeloupe in June, a useful, but not a big bag. Minden, however, ushered in a new era; it was on the grand scale and it made Pitt talk of 'getting out of this war honourably and gloriously.'[2]

Frederick's letter seemed to have let loose a universal desire for peace; it cropped up everywhere, no longer as a suppressed wish, but openly and vocally. The one place where possibly it lagged was Leicester House. The Prince of Wales chose this moment to ask the King for permission to join the army in view of the threatened invasion. One may hope that the offer was genuine and came from the heart. That at least was Pitt's view; he declared that it would have been inexcusable if the Prince had not made the offer, and to refuse him would be the greatest hardship. He had been brought up in too secluded a manner and was as innocent as a babe. Any opportunity therefore of bringing him out and giving him experience ought to be gladly seized.[3] But Newcastle, with his ingrained distrust of all generous

[1] Cf. his remark to Newcastle: 'the King surely could not think much of his services and might reason "a peace is near and then I shall have no further occasion for him."' Newcastle to Hardwicke, 27th September 1759. Add. MSS. 32,896.

[2] Newcastle to Devonshire, 19th Aug. 1759. Add. MSS. 32,894.

[3] Newcastle to Hardwicke, 27th July, and to Stone, 1st Aug. 1759. Add. MSS. 32,893.

emotions, believed that the offer was merely a scheme to put Cumberland's nose out of joint. The Prince's letter had been very vague; Pitt might ascribe that to innocence, but Newcastle was sure it was designed. What the Prince wanted was not real service but to be appointed 'Captain-General'—a figure-head, occupying the place which Cumberland might reasonably expect to fill if the invasion materialised. Such a request should be dismissed out of hand. The innocuous duties of inspection which Pitt suggested did not commend themselves to the suspicious Newcastle or the prejudiced King. The Prince was 'put off,' and in his vexation complained to Bute, quite unjustifiably, of Pitt's insolence and want of regard.[1] The upshot was more trouble for Pitt when he needed freedom from distraction in order to study the problems of peace.

There were, first, the discussions with Newcastle and Knyphausen on the draft of the Anglo-Prussian declaration, which Pitt insisted on strengthening each time a new victory was announced. But more serious, because it was a new factor the significance of which was not immediately apparent, was the interest which Spain suddenly developed in the war. Her attitude had been a source of anxiety from the first. There were several points of dispute between Spain and ourselves, which though of minor importance, were of long standing, and the possibility could not be overlooked that these small irritations, combined with the pull of 'family' feelings, might bring Spain into the war as an ally of France. So long as Ferdinand VI, that poor mild lunatic, lived and General Wall was Prime Minister, Pitt felt reasonably secure, but all the world knew that Ferdinand was dying, and no one knew for certain the intentions of his successor. Shortly after Minden Pitt was to learn.

Towards the end of August Prince Sanseverino, a representative of Don Carlos, the new King of Spain, asked for an interview. It was not the first, but was the more significant from the fact that Ferdinand VI had died about a fortnight earlier. Just before the meeting Pitt dashed off a note to Hester, the tone of which was a little excited. The King of Spain, he said, was certainly dead and the Prince was at the door. He himself was overwhelmed with variety of business, but was as well as hurry and bile would admit.[2] At the meeting, the Prince hinted at Spanish mediation

[1] Geo. III to Bute, 30th July 1759. Sedgwick, p. 27.
[2] Pitt to Hester, undated but about 25th August 1759. Public Record Office.

between England and France. Pitt side-stepped; surely, he argued, considering our victories, the first overture should come, not from Spain or from England, but from France. Personally, he felt the time was hardly ripe, but he would certainly prefer to treat while still in a condition to fight than wait till he could carry on no longer, which was already the case with France.[1] The meeting was inconclusive, but in true diplomatic style, the door was left open.

Whatever progress Pitt may have made was more than lost in the middle of September when news arrived of Frederick's crushing defeat at Kunersdorf. It came at a moment when the pother about Temple's Garter was at white heat, and the two together thrust Pitt into a slough of despond. In his dejection he confided in Lady Yarmouth the hopes he had cherished and had now lost. He had flattered himself, he told her, that he would have been able to lay before the King 'America, the West Indies, Africa, and such a situation of affairs in Germany as might enable his Majesty to make what peace he pleased,' truly a royal offering; and now Frederick's defeat had thrown everything into confusion, and we were all at sea again.[2] Worse still, it had made Frederick more eager than ever for peace, which, he maintained, was not the less necessary because we could no longer take as high a tone as we could have done a little earlier. Pitt did not wish to be ungrateful, he recognised to the full his debt to Frederick, but the exact time for negotiating peace must be chosen carefully, and the hour of Frederick's despair was certainly not that time.

Affairs were in this state when Sanseverino appeared once more, this time speaking in graver tones; the new King of Spain was uneasy at our conquests in America; we were upsetting the equilibrium long since established between English and French interests, a thing that Spain could not view with indifference. Pitt's treatment of an extremely awkward interview was masterly. He adopted a playfully serious attitude, giving the soft answer which not only turns away wrath but is so uncommonly difficult to parry. Equilibrium!, he said in effect, What a word to use between friends! What would the King of Spain think if we talked about equilibrium in Italy? Not that we had

[1] Newcastle's Note, 27th Aug. 1759, and Hardwicke to Newcastle, 2nd Sept. 1759. Add. MSS. 32,894-5.

[2] Newcastle to Hardwicke, 19th Sept. 1759. Add. MSS. 32,895.

any such intention. We did by our friends as we hoped they would do by us, and would rejoice to see Spain aggrandise herself in Italy at the expense of France. All we asked was reciprocity. We hoped that Spain, in the same spirit, would rejoice at any advantage we might gain in America. Not knowing how to counter this mild thrust, the Prince recommended moderation. That, said Pitt gravely, depended entirely upon the situation. Providence had come down on our side, giving us such great advantages over our enemy that no one, certainly no friend, could expect us to leave it in the power of France to encroach upon us or to insult us hereafter.[1]

1 Devonshire's Diary, 9th October 1759. Chatsworth Collection.

24

AMERICA AGAIN

(i)

The supreme advantage for which Pitt had been panting these many months must come from America. Progress reports reached him from time to time, but the final news was delayed till the middle of October.

The first stage had been the expedition against Martinique. Hopson, who was in command, was an elderly man, nearer death's door than he imagined. He had been in charge of Louisburg when it was handed back to the French in 1748, had served as Governor of Nova Scotia in 1752, and had taken reinforcements out to Loudoun in 1757. He was not therefore without knowledge of American affairs, though his experience was hardly such as to fire his enthusiasm. As a commander he seems to have been kindly and humane, an eighteenth-century prototype of Captain Reece of the *Mantelpiece*, but as a general he was a little finicky and over-anxious; rather slow to take risks, rather prompt to be daunted. He had been the King's, not Pitt's choice, but having been appointed, he received Pitt's full support. When his instructions reached him in the middle of October (1758) he at once began to worry—about the numbers of his men; about the care of the sick; about the precariousness of supplies in America. Pitt indulged him to the full, increasing his strength, providing hospital ships and arranging for provisions to be sent from England. He had merely to express a wish for it to be gratified; so eager was Pitt to make this expedition a success.

Hopson arrived at Barbados on the 3rd of January (1759), where he was joined by his naval colleague, Moore, and ten days later the combined force sailed for Martinique. On the 15th they were off Port Royal, and the next day, after silencing the shore batteries, landed safely on Negro Point. 'I trust in Heaven,' said Pitt on hearing the news, 'that the issue will be prosperous;

though much yet remains after the landing. Facilis descensus—but Fort Royal, which seems to be their first design by landing at Point Negro may have its difficulties, which I trust however will be surmounted. If they mean to march to St. Pierre, I have no doubt of their carrying that place.'[1]

How Pitt in England could see so clearly into the position at Martinique must remain a mystery, but his vision was uncomfortably prophetic. Hopson discovered that Fort Royal was five miles from Point Negro, and the road thither almost impassable for artillery or stores. Completely daunted, he re-embarked and sailed for St. Pierre, forty miles to the north. Here, he and Moore fell into long debates; they agreed that the capture of the town was possible but thought it would be costly; decided that its destruction would lead nowhere and that they had not enough troops to garrison it; so they reached the conclusion that it would be best to leave St. Pierre and Martinique alone and sail off to Guadeloupe, to see whether they might not have better luck there.

To Guadeloupe accordingly they sailed, arriving off Basseterre on the 22nd of January. The next day they bombarded the town, which caught fire and was largely destroyed; the French retired to the hills and Hopson occupied the smoking remains. After making himself as secure as he could, he summoned the French to surrender. They refused and thereafter Hopson, vacant of ideas and resisting suggestions, did nothing till the 27th of February, when he died. It was as well; for the ruins of Basseterre were exceedingly unhealthy, not only for Hopson but for the troops; they were dying at an alarming rate; their morale was cracking and desertions becoming frequent.

Barrington, who now took over the command, was a very different type of man, one much more after Pitt's own heart—stubborn, undismayed, hopeful. He needed all his qualities, for the expedition was in disorder and worse was to follow. His first step was to move the wretched remnant of the troops from the fever-stricken ruins of Basseterre to the other side of the island, where Moore had recently captured Fort Louis. The new site was in many ways admirable, but as a fort was too large and too weak to suit Barrington's much reduced forces. There was anxious debate amongst the higher command, and the opinion of a Council of War was that the place was not tenable—an

[1] Pitt to Newcastle, 3rd March 1759. Add. MSS. 32,888.

opinion which Barrington could not refute but resolutely ignored. His decision to hold his ground was the more courageous because at this moment news came that a French fleet under de Bompart had just arrived at Martinique, and Moore consequently declared that he must leave, to concentrate his ships at Prince Rupert's Bay in Dominica, the island lying between Martinique and Guadeloupe, in order to keep an eye on the French and protect the English islands generally. Not only so, but he asked Barrington for troops, and Barrington, with something of the reckless faith of a Gideon, gave him 300 men. Like Pitt, however, he found that weakness strengthened his determination and troubles stirred his inventiveness. Unable any longer to make regular attacks or besiege towns, he changed, as he said, the entire nature of the war and decided to carry it on 'by detachments.' Thereafter he so harried and harassed the enemy by a series of descents and sudden thrusts that in a couple of months they threw up the sponge and asked for terms. 'I own to you, Sir,' Barrington reported with modest gratification, 'I never expected my talents for treaties would have been tried, and indeed I should have been very happy if that part of the work had been done by some other; but my situation was such that it was absolutely necessary that what was done should not be procrastinated, as I was determined to grant no truce for time enough for the inhabitants to recover from their fears.' The end of his report contained his complete justification. 'I cannot help congratulating myself,' he wrote, 'that I had just signed the capitulation with the inhabitants of the Grand Terre, when a messenger arrived in their camp to acquaint them that Monsieur Beauharnois, the General of these Islands, had landed . . . with a reinforcement from Martinico. . . . This support, had it arrived an hour sooner must have made the conquest of that Island very difficult, if not impossible. As soon as he heard the capitulation was signed, he re-embarked again.'[1] Barrington followed up his success in Guadeloupe by annexing the small adjacent island of Marie Galante.

He returned to England in June, and one bids him farewell with regret. His spirit was higher than his health for during much of the campaign he was afflicted by gout in his feet, head and stomach; but he never faltered, and like most big-hearted men had an eye for the merits of others. If in this little expedition we must

[1] Barrington to Pitt, 9th May 1759. Kimball, II, 100.

regret Hopson, let us remember Colonel Crump, whom Barrington appointed Governor of Guadeloupe because he was 'the man that thinks the noblest, and the most disinterestedly,' and Brigadier Clavering of whom Barrington said 'such men are rare.'

(ii)

The central prong of Pitt's threefold attack was entrusted to Amherst. He was to invade Canada, either up the Hudson route or by way of Lake Ontario and La Galette (Ogdensburg), whichever seemed the most feasible. If he could also spare men to capture Niagara, so much the better, but this must be regarded strictly as a side-show and subordinated to 'the great and main objects of the campaign.' His own lack of enterprise and Wolfe's dramatic success have tended to minimise the importance of his job. Yet it was, in its way, the vital element. Pitt's strategy was always a unified whole, in its several parts as well as in its world-wide aspect. The great object to which he was working was the conquest of Canada. The capture of Quebec, like the capture of Louisburg, was a stage. As Pitt visualised the campaign, whilst Wolfe was making his great diversion from the east, Amherst was to sweep up from the south and put the final touch to the conquest.

Amherst was a soldier by rule. He was not content to be slow and sure; he preferred to be very slow, without, unfortunately, being more sure. His strength was his ability to plod; his weakness, lack of imagination. That there might be no mistake, Pitt gave him very detailed instructions about the arrangements to be made for Wolfe and stressed the need for urgency. For his own allotted task, Pitt did not think it necessary to give precisely detailed orders; he must be allowed his head. Amherst did his work meticulously and not very well. As Commander-in-Chief he rightly took an interest in all parts of his command, but his reports have too much of the arid invoice about them; they refer to every conceivable field and are packed with every conceivable detail. He busied himself with so many things that he tended to miss the obvious. In particular, he failed to observe the import of Pitt's warning about Niagara. It lay to the south-west of Lake Ontario whilst his own direction was to the north-east. It was essentially a side-show, almost one might say a *pis aller*. But

Amherst gave himself no chance to see whether the troops could be spared, or how the expedition would fit in with his main task. Instead, he at once appointed Prideaux for the work, and spent so much time in equipping and dispatching him to Niagara, that he failed to arrive at his own base, Fort Edward, until the 7th of June. There he fell to building forts and block-houses, making roads and clearing woods—so thoroughly that it was not till towards the end of July that he was ready to embark on the waters of Lake George in quest of Ticonderoga. Landing at the north end, and determined not to fall into Abercromby's mistake, he spent two days bringing up his artillery and approaching the fort in form, only to find that the French had retired, leaving a small detachment to fight a delaying action. Three days later, on the 26th of July, the little garrison decamped, after doing their best to blow up the fort. Amherst marched into its remains and began rebuilding it. Six days later scouts reported that the French had also abandoned Crown Point; but Amherst was not to be hurried. The news, he told Pitt, 'makes no alteration in my motions,' and it was not till the 4th of August that he entered Crown Point bloodlessly.

He reported his victories, but they were in a real sense more Pitt's than his. Vaudreuil and Montcalm were feeling the effects of Pitt's stranglehold, and as the noose tightened they were forced to concentrate. They had thought that danger threatened only from two sides—along the Hudson route and by way of Lake Ontario. Suddenly they had found themselves confronted by a third attack, as Wolfe came up the St. Lawrence. If that were successful, Bourlamarque at Ticonderoga, or even at Crown Point, might be hopelessly cut off, and it was to bring him closer to the heart of the defence that he was ordered to retreat to Ile aux Noix near where the River Richelieu debouched into Lake Champlain.

While at Crown Point, Amherst heard news of Niagara. Prideaux had moved swiftly and well. He had ascended the Mohawk with 5,000 men, established posts at both ends of Lake Oneida, passed on to Oswego, where he left nearly half his force to protect his lines of communication, and with the remainder hurried to Niagara. The fort was strong and well garrisoned under an able and energetic commander, Captain Puchot, who, on hearing that the English were approaching, sent an urgent call for help to the numerous bands of French, Canadians and Indians stationed in and around the forts of the Ohio valley—Presquisle, Le Bœuf and Venango.

Prideaux began the siege in form, but was unfortunately killed by an accident. His place was taken by Sir William Johnson, who carried on Prideaux's good work with such energy that the fort was soon reduced to extremity. Puchot's only hope lay in the succours coming from the south, and when Johnson defeated them on the 24th of July, he had no alternative but to surrender. Niagara had been won, and with it the complete mastery of the Ohio valley.

With this news in his pocket, Amherst had the chance, if he still had the time, to fulfil Pitt's dearest wish; he could advance by both the Hudson and the Lake Ontario routes, to meet Wolfe at Quebec and finish off the American war. The idea crossed his mind, and by way of putting it into operation, he sent Brigadier Gage to supersede Johnson, directing him to descend the St. Lawrence, capture La Galette and advance towards Montreal. But Gage, as Parkman says, was not 'by nature prone to dashing and doubtful enterprise,'[1] and by the early days of September had found so many 'difficulties and impossibilities' in the way of doing anything before winter came, that he felt himself obliged to give up the attempt.[2] Pitt when he heard of this decision was coldly disapproving; one may read beneath the restrained rebuke of his letter the heaviness of his disappointment.[3]

Amherst described himself as greatly concerned at Gage's lack of energy, but did little better himself. The French had two or three small vessels on Lake Champlain; it was obvious to Amherst that he could not advance on Ile aux Noix before they were destroyed, and that they could not be destroyed till he had built a navy of overwhelming strength to oppose them. For the next two months he was a busy shipwright, frequently delayed but not dismayed by recurring breakdowns of his saw-mill. By the 11th of October his fleet was ready and three days later came up with the enemy vessels, which refused to fight and scuttled themselves. But by now the winter storms had begun and the tempestuous weather satisfied Amherst that it was waste of

[1] *Montcalm and Wolfe,* II, 249.
[2] Amherst to Pitt, 22nd Oct. 1759. Kimball, II, 196.
[3] Pitt to Amherst, 11th December 1759. Kimball, II, 217.

time trying to reach Ile aux Noix that year. He decided to return to Crown Point and the campaign was over.[1]

(iii)

The third prong was Wolfe's attack on Quebec. The story hardly needs to be retold, but certain features may be stressed for the light they throw on Pitt's genius. First was Pitt's decision to undertake the work at all. The navigation of the St. Lawrence was unknown to the English. The French, whose ships made the passage, regarded it as difficult with pilots and impossible without them; so much so that it never occurred to them that Quebec was vulnerable by that route. No doubt Pitt counted on that fact to lend an element of surprise; but whatever advantages the route offered, his decision to take it was startling—in its way as startling as Hannibal's decision to cross the Alps. Almost more startling was Pitt's complete assurance. Whatever he may have thought, he never betrayed the least doubt or hesitation. Where French ships could go, the English fleet would find a way. Pitt's knowledge of American geography was uncanny in its completeness. He was always ready to receive information from whatever source, but more useful than his receptiveness was his ability to sift the grain from the chaff. Somehow he knew that the St. Lawrence was navigable, and its terrors greatly exaggerated.

Secondly, the expedition was the supreme example of Pitt's attention to detail. Everything conspired to heighten his anxiety to capture the city, and so far as it depended on him, nothing was left to chance. His orders to Amherst covered every conceivable point and were given in extraordinarily meticulous detail. Wolfe was to have 12,000 men. The actual regiments were chosen by Pitt; they were not to be altered except for overwhelming reasons, and under no circumstances were the numbers to be reduced. There were to be 500 Rangers and eighty carpenters, the latter under the command of a provincial—Colonel Gridley. Vessels of various sorts would be needed, and Amherst was to procure forty schooners or sloops and to build seventy whaleboats, all of which were to be ready by the 1st of April and sent forthwith to Louisburg. Arrangements were to be made for provisions, especially fresh meat and spruce beer, as a specific against scurvy,

[1] Amherst to Pitt, 22nd October 1759. Kimball, II, 186.

and battering trains and stores were to be 'put into the most perfect repair and order.' Pitt would provide 20,000 tons of transport from England, but in case of accidents Amherst was to collect a further 6,000 tons in America, imposing, if necessary, an embargo on shipping for the purpose. The whole force was to be assembled at Louisburg on or about the 7th of May.[1]

Amherst was not altogether pleased. He would have liked a little more discretion, and he was put out at having to recall for Wolfe's benefit troops who were 'unluckily in the most advanced and distant parts.'[2] No doubt he did his best, but in the upshot Wolfe did not receive anything like his full quota. Wolfe exonerated Amherst with the generous observation that he had 'forwarded everything to the utmost of his power,' but he allowed himself one caustic remark: 'I writ to General Amherst for money, but he could send me none; this is one of the first sieges perhaps, that ever was undertaken without it.'[3]

Wolfe's equipment was not the only object of Pitt's care. As ever, his strategy was twofold, having a negative as well as a positive side. While Wolfe was to be provided with ample, and if possible overwhelming forces, the French were to be denied all succour. Hawke and Boscawen were sent out to close the ports of France and as a second line, Commodore Durell was given stringent orders to sail from Halifax as early in the year as conditions allowed and cruise off the Ile de Bic, 200 miles up the St. Lawrence, 'in order effectually to prevent and cut off from Quebec all succours of troops and provisions from Europe.'[4] Durell had remained in America through the winter but was only second in command. The man entrusted by Pitt with the naval side of the expedition was Saunders—one of Anson's men—and because of doubts which Wolfe entertained of Durell's capacity,[5] Saunders was told to renew Durell's orders 'in the strongest manner.'[6] But it was all to no purpose. Durell was daunted by the fogs and ice of Canadian waters, and whilst he remained snugly in Halifax, Bougainville with a flotilla of French ships crammed with stores and provisions slipped into

[1] Pitt to Amherst, 29th December 1758. Kimball, I, 432.
[2] Amherst to Pitt, 29th March 1759. Kimball, II, 78.
[3] Wolfe to Pitt, 6th June 1759. Kimball, II, 119.
[4] Pitt to Durell, 29th December 1758. Kimball, I, 444.
[5] 'I will add from my own knowledge that the second naval officer in command there is vastly unequal to the weight of business.'
[6] Pitt to Saunders, 9th Jan. 1759. Kimball, II, 2.

Quebec. The stores and provisions were a source of thanksgiving to the half-starved inhabitants but, far more important, Bougainville brought with him an intercepted letter from Amherst revealing Pitt's whole plan of campaign. On receipt of this unexpected news, Montcalm, who had been taken completely unaware, hurried back from Montreal in order to build the defences of Quebec, and unfortunately he had time. It is an interesting and provoking thought that but for Durell's lapse and Amherst's inopportune letter, Wolfe might have taken Quebec by *coup de main*, and its capture have been another of Pitt's bloodless victories.[1]

Instead, the campaign was arduous, baffling and full of disappointments. Wolfe set out from Louisburg four weeks late, short of stores, with only 9,000 men instead of the promised 12,000, and with the disheartening knowledge that 'succours of all kinds had been thrown into Quebec.' He expected to find most of the Canadian forces concentrated in the city, and indeed Montcalm had collected some 16,000 men. Wolfe admitted to Pitt, and perhaps more ominously, to himself, that 'I could not flatter myself that I should be able to reduce the place.' None the less he was determined to do his best, and spent anxious days and nights seeking a chink in Montcalm's armour. At the end of July he staged an attack at the Falls of Montmorency, but it went awry, and then to make matters worse, he fell seriously ill. His flaming spirit was, like Pitt's, housed in a heart-break body. Health he had none; disease in plenty—scurvy, gravel, rheumatism, tuberculosis of the kidneys; no Caliban was ever more full of cramps and side-stitches. And to illness was added depression and irritability. What was Amherst doing? If Montcalm had 16,000 men in Quebec, how many could there possibly be facing Amherst? Why did he make no move? Why was the whole burden left to a sick and dying man?

On the 2nd of September Wolfe roused himself from a bed of sickness to report to Pitt: 'I wish I could upon this occasion have the honour of transmitting to you a more favourable account of the progress of his Majesty's arms.' What had been done was little enough, what could be done seemed even less. 'We have almost the whole force of Canada to oppose. In this situation, there is such a choice of difficulties that I own myself at a loss how to determine.' He would be happy, if his efforts might contribute,

[1] Corbett, I, 415.

by way of a diversion, to success in any other part of America—at Ile aux Noix, at La Galette, perhaps even in the far south—so low had his expectations fallen.

It was his last dispatch. Eleven days later he had found the answer to his problems on the Heights of Abraham. Quebec had fallen and he himself was among the immortals.

25

'DAPPLINGS FOR PEACE'

(i)

From the moment of Frederick's letter to the King, Pitt realised that peace had become an urgent question. It would require all his skill and all the victories he could collect, if it was to be concluded to his wishes. He had no doubt about the skill, and given time no doubt about the victories, but he was haunted by fear of what Newcastle might do. Newcastle had an abnormal desire to meddle; his fingers itched to be in every pie; his nose was fashioned for poking round corners; and worse still, he fancied himself as a Foreign Secretary. For years he had been carrying on a private correspondence with our Ambassadors abroad, demanding information and giving advice and even instructions—sometimes instructions which ran counter to Pitt's orders. Pitt was aware of the practice and grudgingly acquiesced; after all, Newcastle was First Lord of the Treasury and nominally the First Minister; he had a right to know what was happening, and indeed was encouraged by the King, who liked to discuss foreign affairs with an old crony who never taxed his intelligence too far. But Pitt disliked the practice, and at this critical conjuncture, as he might have said, he disliked it the more, knowing as he did that Newcastle was champing at the bit. What he might do was an ever-present anxiety. He was so ready to seize opportunities that Pitt had to be cautious even in the give and take of friendly conversation. He had once, shortly after Minden, spoken in the exuberance of the moment of ending the war honourably and gloriously, and Newcastle had reacted immediately, pressing him to 'get us out.' His vehemence had sobered Pitt, who had answered with discouraging emphasis, 'But we must have another campaign first.'[1] Pitt was undoubtedly worried and would have been still more so if he had known that

[1] Newcastle to Devonshire, 19th Aug. 1759. Add. MSS. 32,894.

Newcastle was brooding over memories of the Peace of Aix, and of how that peace had been brought about by a letter which Newcastle himself had written.[1] The only real check on his writing another letter now was the thought that if he tried and failed, his position would be hopeless indeed. But if he believed that peace was possible, and some opening presented itself, what might he not attempt? And the attempt, whether successful or not, might place everything in jeopardy.

Pitt had no mind that the risk should be run. He was vigilantly on guard, especially when, in August, the prospects brightened and he began to formulate to himself the terms which he would demand. He kept them secret, and might have smiled had he known how eagerly Newcastle was seeking information about them. But whatever hopes of peace he may have had, they were dashed, first by Frederick's defeat at Kunersdorf, and then by Amherst's failure to advance beyond Crown Point. Pitt was now certain that another campaign was inevitable, possibly two—one to complete the conquest of Canada, and one to restore the position in Europe. But in this view he stood alone, with only the rather embarrassing support of the King whose aspirations had long been alarmingly inflated. Against him there were Frederick, who was the more eager for peace because he had temporarily abandoned hope of victory, and Newcastle and Hardwicke, because they had never entertained any hope at all. It was at this moment, while the question of peace was so precariously poised, that a lady, known to English historians as l'Inconnue, appeared upon the stage to play an unconscious part in as pretty a comedy as a biographer could wish.

The lady in question was the Dowager Princess of Anhalt-Zerbst, whose main achievement was to be the mother of Catherine the Great. In contrast to her daughter, she was herself a butterfly politician, flitting from project to project, and sipping the nectar of innumerable airy intrigues. At this moment she had it in mind to promote peace between Great Britain and France, and wrote under a *nom de plume* to Sir Joseph Yorke, telling him that she was off to Versailles for the purpose. She chose Yorke because he was the British Ambassador at The Hague, which was a sort of European Exchange where all the nations met and business of this type was usually transacted. It was his duty to sift his visitors and his correspondence, sending anything of

[1] Considerations, 19th April 1759. Add. MSS. 32,890.

importance to England and putting the rest aside with diplomatic finesse. He thought very little of the lady's first letter, but when she wrote again he began to wonder if there was anything in it, and in order, as he said, 'to make her talk more,' sent her a playful semi-flirtatious reply. Then, without realising what he was doing, he sent copies of the correspondence to Newcastle 'for his amusement' and as tittle-tattle for the King.[1] The King chuckled over the letters, but Newcastle was obviously in two minds about them. He knew that by rights they should go to Pitt, but he could not rid himself of a niggling hope that 'Joe's correspondent may become a lady of consequence'; if so, there might be developments and he would be the first in the field.[2] The temptation to keep the letters to himself was great and he succumbed.

Developments followed, but in a form vastly different from what he had expected. The lady wrote no more and vanishes from the scene, but a week or so after her letters had reached England, Holdernesse got wind of them. Now Holdernesse disliked Yorke, of whom he was jealous; he also disliked Newcastle's secret correspondence with the Ambassadors in his department. Thinking these letters gave him a rare chance of killing both dislikes with one stone, he whispered in Pitt's ear that peace negotiations were afoot between Newcastle and Yorke. Pitt was alarmed; this was the very thing which he had dreaded; at all costs it must be stopped. He sent Newcastle a short but emphatic note, palpitating with his fears and taut with his determination: 'I understand your Grace has received, some days since, a letter from Mr. Yorke, relating to certain dapplings for peace on the part of some lady. . . . As it is so indispensably the right of a Secretary of State to be informed *instantly* of every transaction of this nature, and as the King's service and the public good must be essentially and incurably prejudiced by such suppressions, in a moment so critical that one false step may prove fatal, I find myself necessitated to mention this matter to your Grace. I know not how far your Grace may have had the King's orders for this clandestine proceeding; if such be His Majesty's pleasure, it is my duty to receive it with all possible respect and submission; but I must find myself thereby deprived of the means of doing His Majesty any service. I beg the favour of your Grace

[1] Yorke to Newcastle, 9th Oct. 1759. Add. MSS. 32,896.
[2] Newcastle to Hardwicke, 15th October 1759. Add. MSS. 32,897.

to lay me at the King's feet and to inform His Majesty that my health requires the air of the country for two or three days.'[1] There was no mistaking his meaning; it was an ultimatum due to expire almost at once; and at the end of it, unless satisfied, Pitt would go.

The thought threw everybody into a dither, and there was a chain reaction highly reminiscent of the old lady driving her pig from market. Newcastle dropped his half-formed schemes like a hot penny, deploring 'poor Joe's' rashness in sending him 'those cursed female letters,' and inveighing against Holdernesse's wickedness. Holdernesse began writing hoity-toity letters to Yorke and Yorke responded in kind, smouldering with wrath at this apparent check to his career. Hardwicke was furious at Newcastle's attempt to make a scapegoat of Joe, and refused to set foot in the House of Lords or go to Court till the slur on his son had been expunged. Newcastle, driven half crazy under the twofold assault of his own uneasy conscience and Pitt's heavy displeasure, came to the conclusion that the only hope of calming the storm was for the King to give Temple the Garter, and began pressing the point with an urgency he had never shown before, to the great and growing annoyance of the King. And in the background hovered Lady Yarmouth apprehending 'the worst consequences.'[2]

Pitt himself was very soon satisfied. Newcastle sent him the correspondence with abject apologies, and Pitt recognised that the letters were innocuous, though he was careful not to admit it till the incident had blown over. For a few days he maintained his show of displeasure, to ensure that Newcastle was properly cowed and would play no tricks in future. 'When I protested to him,' the wretched man wrote to Hardwicke, 'that I would not enter into any separate negotiation for peace on any account in the world, he then said, not very politely, if I did, I should not be able to walk the streets without a guard. I took no other notice of that but to infer still stronger, for that reason, that it was impossible for me to do it.'[3] Newcastle was certainly subdued, but Pitt, only too well aware of his mercurial temperament, was in no hurry to reassure him. On the contrary, he took steps to provide a further safeguard. The incident gave him the chance of

[1] Pitt to Newcastle, 23rd Oct. 1759. Add. MSS. 32,897.
[2] Newcastle to Hardwicke, 23rd Oct. 1759. Add. MSS. 32,897.
[3] Newcastle to Hardwicke, 31st Oct. 1759. Add. MSS. 32,897.

broaching the subject of peace directly to the King, and he was able to extract a promise from him that no peace should be made without Pitt's knowledge, and presumably concurrence.[1] With that in his pocket, Pitt could feel reasonably safe, more safe in fact than before, and by degrees he slipped back into good humour. But it had been a warning.

(ii)

He had other grounds for anxiety. The French project of invasion came slowly to the boil. It was based on the supposition, strategically sound, that it was better to cut the losses in Canada, where the arm of France could no longer reach, and concentrate on the heart of England, where all might yet be retrieved. In Choiseul's hands, such a policy stood a good chance. Choiseul, who had lately come to power, had a great reputation. There were many in France who believed that, if he could only cleanse the Augean stables, he would prove himself in other respects nearly, if not quite, Pitt's equal. Moreover he had an able instrument in Conflans, who, if elderly—he was sixty-nine—was none the less a great sea officer. France, in the midst of her misfortunes, felt an undercurrent of hope.

As confidence grew in France, anxiety deepened in England, or at least in Newcastle, who pestered Pitt to withdraw men and ships from Canada to meet the threat in the Channel. Pitt remained adamant; he was too wise a bird to be caught by the chaff of camps on the French coast. That was a bluff which had been tried so often—admittedly with success—but was now for the first time to fail. None the less Pitt recognised the potential danger and worked hard to meet it in his own way. Too much depended on him, especially in view of his feeble health. He had not only to carry an immense load of responsibility, but was also expected to deal with the smallest minutiæ. 'The poor Norfolk militia,' wrote Lady Townshend, in a note which is not without its comic element, 'by being pent up so long in the barracks at Portsmouth are all dying of the bloody flux. Sir Armand Woodhouse is come to town to see Lord Barrington to endeavour to get them relieved, but Mr. Pitt's being out of town makes it impossible for their having any immediate redress.'[2]

[1] Newcastle to Hardwicke, 25th Oct. 1759. Add. MSS. 32,897.

[2] Lady Townshend to Lady Ferrers, 2nd Oct. 1759. H.M.C. Marquess Townshend's MSS.

Had he been in town Pitt would no doubt have taken the action of which no one else apparently was capable, for he was trusting to the militia, 14,000 strong, to repel the French in the unlikely event of their landing. His main reliance, however, was on the naval defence. It consisted of two parts—the Grand Fleet which was to deal faithfully with the French men-of-war, and a second line of smaller vessels along the coast, which were to cope with any transports that succeeded in getting through. During the second half of 1759 Pitt was busy strengthening the second line by taking into Government service a number of privateers, whose activities he was anxious to curb, and who would so obviously be better employed in defending England than in angering neutrals. The Grand Fleet was under Hawke, whose instructions were to blockade Brest and at the same time to keep an eye open for de Bompart on his return from the West Indies. Hawke went to his station towards the end of June, at about the same moment that Conflans left Paris to hoist his flag at Brest. The two were playing an interesting game. The greater part of the French transports were at Morbihan in Quiberon Bay, and in the original plan it had been La Clue's duty to collect and convoy them to Brest. At the outset, therefore, Hawke had to keep a threefold watch—against La Clue coming from the south, against de Bompart coming from the west, and against Conflans whose movements were uncertain. Boscawen's victory over La Clue (see p. 325) relieved him of one part of his task, and simplified the remainder. The duty of collecting the transports at Morbihan now fell upon Conflans, and Hawke knew that if he came out of Brest his course must be southward. The knowledge was important, for try as Hawke might to keep a strict blockade of Brest, storms would drive him off from time to time, when the way of escape was opened. To be certain what course Conflans would take, if he ever came out, greatly simplified the problem of renewing lost contact.

Towards the end of September there were signs of activity at Brest, and it must have cut Hawke to the heart when, in the middle of October, he was once more driven by storms to England. To make matters worse, he reached Plymouth on a day of universal gloom following the receipt of Wolfe's unhappy dispatch. Even Pitt was shaken. 'Mr. Pitt,' said Newcastle, 'with reason, gives it all over, and declares so publicly.'[1] In the reaction

[1] Newcastle to Hardwicke, 15th October 1759. Add. MSS. 32,897.

which followed three days later, the people at large paid no attention to a significant fact—Thurot had broken out of Dunkirk and disappeared northwards. The invasion had begun.

Hawke, as indifferent to the fact as the rest of England, and now, as ever, sparring irascibly with the Admiralty, returned to his station off Ushant, where he had the grim satisfaction of learning, from an intercepted letter, that Conflans had positive orders to engage him, in order to cover the sailing of the Duc d'Aiguillon with the troops for Scotland. Hawke asked for nothing better. Fate had so far been more than unkind. Time and again he had searched for enemy fleets—under du Guay, La Motte, Galissonière—and searched in vain; they had all eluded him. Ill luck had dogged him with benumbing persistence, and the thought of a French fleet actually seeking him out was too good to be true. So indeed it seemed, for fresh storms drove him back to Torbay and kept him there till de Bompart had reached Brest, adding seven ships, battered but well-manned, to Conflans' force. But now the end was near. Fate was tired of her joke, and on the 20th of November Hawke and Conflans sighted each other to the west of Belleisle. In spite of his orders, Conflans ran for Quiberon Bay, and Hawke, setting his teeth, raced after him through a raging storm. What happened that night in Quiberon Bay is part of England's history. There is no need to retell the tale. Hawke laid the tribute of his daring at England's feet, and England has not forgotten.

(iii)

Whilst Pitt was waiting for news of Hawke, and the more excitable elements of the country were burning him in effigy for letting Conflans escape from Brest, Parliament met (13th November). The King's Speech was notable for its long list of victories, but more interesting for its reference to peace. The King, so the Speech said, had not entered the war from views of ambition and did not wish to continue it from motives of resentment. The desire of his heart was to put an end to the effusion of Christian blood. But there must be conditions. The terms of peace must be just and honourable for the King and his allies; they must procure the advantages to be expected from England's victories; there must be full security for the future; the repose of Europe must be restored on solid and durable foundations and His Majesty's subjects must be ensured the blessings of peace and tranquillity. 'But,' the Speech continued, 'in order to this great and desirable end . . . it is necessary to make ample provision for carrying on the war, in all parts, with the utmost vigour.'

The Speech did all that was necessary in laying down the broad outlines of peace. But Pitt wanted to emphasise the position before the Anglo-Prussian Declaration was published and the wrangling and bargaining at a Congress began. He therefore felt it necessary, though suffering from a painful jaw, to wind up the debate. With peace so obviously on the horizon, there should be no discord in the Cabinet, and Pitt began with a graceful reference to his colleagues. He had once, he said, doubted whether unanimity had produced success, or success unanimity. Now he knew; it was the latter. Success came from Providence; all he could do was to advise, and the merit belonged to all members of the Council alike.[1] Then he launched into his main theme. He spoke cautiously of peace. The best peace was one which followed success of arms. He hoped there would not be another campaign, but he recommended it strongly to the House to enable the King to carry on the war for as many campaigns as might be necessary. We had in a great measure already taken care of ourselves; our next business must be to take care of our allies. The war was now to be carried on with more vigour than ever upon the Continent, and he would propose to send 10,000 British troops to reinforce Prince Ferdinand. As for Frederick, 'he was persuaded there was not a member in the House that would not conceive an indignation at the thoughts of a peace that might promote our own particular interest without a due regard to that of our magnanimous and great ally.'[2]

Walpole cynically observed that Temple's resignation the next day was a sad commentary on the unanimity of the Cabinet. Yet, in a real sense, nothing showed that unanimity more clearly than the measures taken by them all to bring him back. Pitt was sincere in his desire to preserve a united front, for practical reasons. Like Frederick he believed that to show too great a desire for peace was not the way to obtain a good one, and he was sure that he alone could restrain Newcastle's eagerness. They must therefore work together. He strove for that end with

[1] West to Newcastle, 13th Nov. 1759. Add. MSS. 32,898.
[2] Symmer to Mitchell, 13th November 1759. Add. MSS. 6,839.

such success that Newcastle, completely ignorant of his motives, wrote complacently to Hardwicke: 'I may be mistaken, but my real opinion is that Mr. Pitt's present intention is to unite himself most cordially and confidentially with your Lordship and me and our friends.'[1] From Pitt's point of view, the most galling feature was that friendship with Newcastle involved coolness towards Leicester House, where Holdernesse was using his influence to undermine everyone except himself.[2] Patriotism was no paying job. If Pitt was losing ground with the young Court in order to restrain Newcastle, he was equally losing ground with the King by refusing to sacrifice English interests for 'electoral advantages.'[3] Whatever he did added to his isolation amidst a group of self-seeking intriguers. Little wonder that his thoughts turned with longing to the home where all was love and kindness and gentle thoughts: 'after much Court and more House of Commons . . . what refreshment and delight to sit down to address these lines to the dearest object of my every thought. . . . Send me, my sweetest life, a thousand particulars of all those *little-great* things which, to those who are blessed as we, so far surpass in excellence and exceed in attraction all the *great-little* things of the busy, restless world.'[4]

The busy restless world was very prominent in the last weeks of 1759. Agreement had been reached on the Anglo-Prussian Declaration which Prince Louis of Brunswick was about to present to the enemy Ambassadors at The Hague. How they would receive it was a matter for surmise, and in England there were hopes and fears in plenty. Whatever their reaction, the ultimate responsibility would rest with Pitt, who grew weary of the twin tasks of curbing the wild ambitions of the King and of putting iron into Newcastle's soul. Thoughts of retirement flitted through his mind. He confided to Devonshire that he 'had wished to be a Minister and now wished to be out of it.'[5] The wish was a passing mood, but one liable to recur with increasing emphasis. On this occasion it evaporated when the King promised Temple the Garter, but it left a sediment behind. He told Devonshire that he would go on and do the best he could for the public, though he found it difficult 'to hold the

[1] Newcastle to Hardwicke, 21st November 1759. Add. MSS. 32,899.
[2] Note. 10th Nov. 1759. Add. MSS. 32,898.
[3] Newcastle to Hardwicke, 16th Nov. 1759. Add. MSS. 32,898.
[4] Pitt to Hester, 19th Nov. 1759. Chatham. *Correspondence*, I, 457.
[5] Devonshire's Diary, 14th November 1759.

balance between the faiblesse d'un vieillard, the humeur altiere d'une femme and l'ambition démesuré d'un favori.'[1] It was a bitter remark, betraying in particular the wide breach with Leicester House. The bitterness was doubly unfortunate, for Bute was about this time anxious to be reconciled. He was passing through a phase of self-depreciation, when the possibility of the King's early demise and his own summons to high office under a new and inexperienced King loomed exceptionally large and terrifying. It induced him to send Elliot, as a mutual friend, to see what could be done, but in such an atmosphere there was no prospect of success. All that happened was that Pitt had a chance to hold forth on Bute's iniquities. He spoke angrily of his high imperious tone, his habit of monopolising power, the flippant way in which he used the Prince's name for his own ends, his jeers at Pitt's lack of favour at Court. Bute, he said, had once been his friend but had dropped him, and now wanted to forgive and forget only because he was aiming at high office. It was waste of time; they could never act together. Bute would demand the first place and Pitt would not take the second. He refused to be ridden with a check rein; he would not bear a touch of command—particularly, though he did not say so, from an erstwhile protégé. If he was to be responsible, as obviously he must be, no one should dictate to him. Nor, for that matter, did he want to dictate to friends. If he and Bute acted together as such, his hands would be tied; he could never bring himself to contend for mastery in the Closet, or use the weight of popular opinion to drive measures through, as he did with the present Ministers with whom there was no pretence of friendship. It would be better for them to keep apart. If Bute was so anxious for office, Pitt would make way for him, without peevishness, without discontent; all he would ask for would be 'some honourable bystanding office' which carried no responsibility.[2] His attitude was reminiscent of that adopted by him at his darkest hour in 1754. As then, he no doubt meant it at the moment but the feeling was superficial and did not come from the heart. The King had seen more truly into his mind when he had told Newcastle, 'Oh, he won't quit his own schemes and measures.'[3] So long as his work was unfinished, Pitt would be very reluctant to go, but the constant repetition of the thought, springing, as it always

[1] Devonshire's Diary 21st Nov. 1759. [2] *The Border Elliots*, p. 363.
[3] Newcastle to Hardwicke, 25th Oct. 1759. Add. MSS. 32,897.

did, out of frustration, actual or prospective, was familiarising him with the idea, and was one day to lead to action. Elliot's efforts were wasted, but Bute's intervention, whether well-meaning or self-seeking, had one effect which was to bear Dead Sea fruit. The Prince of Wales, with the unreasoning chivalry of youth, was affronted by Pitt's attitude towards his idol and declared that 'he has shown himself the most ungrateful and in my mind most dishonourable of men, I can never bear to see him in any future Ministry.'[1] A disastrous thought had been implanted in a mind as tenacious as it was narrow. Otherwise the incident was merely an excrescence on the problems of peace.

[1] Sedgwick, p. 45.

26

PROBLEMS OF PEACE

(i)

Of all the problems of peace which Pitt had to solve the most serious seemed to be the attitude of Spain. From his earliest days Pitt had been fascinated by her. As a young man, at the time of Jenkins' Ear, he had clamoured for war with her; later, at his own darkest hour, he had paused in the midst of his self-pity to speculate on General Wall's appointment as Prime Minister; at the outset of his own Ministry he had seriously contemplated the cession of Gibraltar, and since then he had time and again been assailed by uneasy forebodings. As King Ferdinand sank into imbecility and death, Pitt maintained an anxious correspondence with our Ambassador—first Sir Benjamin Keene and then Lord Bristol—demanding to be told Wall's standing in the councils of Spain, his latest views on France, and the general feeling towards England. His recent interviews with Sanseverino had done nothing to allay his disquiet, and thereafter Newcastle noted, uncomprehendingly and a little querulously, that Pitt 'is always harping upon Spain.'[1]

His forebodings were justified early in December (1759) when D'Abreu, the Spanish Ambassador, presented a written Memorial, repeating and emphasising all that Sanseverino had said, and adding that the new King offered himself as a mediator between England and France. Pitt had no difficulty in finding a temporary answer; only ten days earlier Prince Louis had published the Anglo-Prussian Declaration, and it was obvious that nothing more could be done until the reaction of France was known. So much was easy, but Pitt felt that more was imperatively necessary. He was, as his colleagues noted, 'much affected' and 'very uneasy.' Spain was an incalculable factor. Her new King was known to dislike England and favour France, and to Pitt it

[1] Newcastle to Hardwicke, 15th Oct. 1759. Add. MSS. 32,897.

seemed ominous that 'before His Catholic Majesty had reached his capital or so much as seen the Ministers of Spain, as well as before an Ambassador had been appointed for the Court of England, Monsieur D'Abreu should receive orders of so delicate and important a nature.'[1] Pitt had no wish to find himself at war with Spain; that might come, but the present was hardly the moment, with America still unsettled and Europe convulsed. He therefore took much time and trouble in drafting a reasoned answer, which might soothe Spain without yielding one iota of our rights or justifiable expectations, and he persuaded his colleagues to approve it. Whether his reply was convincing, or Wall was able to make milder counsels prevail, Carlos drew back for the moment, recalled D'Abreu and sent a new Ambassador, the Conde de Fuentes. But the outlook was clouded.

To add to the general uncertainty, at the end of the year Lord Howe produced a curious story. After Quiberon Bay, he had been sent to negotiate an exchange of prisoners with the Duc d'Aiguillon, who had told him that France would like to conclude a separate peace with England. Indeed, he had declared that the object of the abortive invasion had been to promote peace. He had himself been instructed to begin negotiations immediately he had effected a landing, and had full powers for the purpose. In the new circumstances he supposed his powers were no longer sufficient, but he wanted Pitt to be informed of the facts.[2]

A further and considerable addition to the uncertainties was the absence of any clear-cut division between the belligerents, or community of aims between the allies. Everywhere counsels were divided. In France, Choiseul was supposed to be heart and soul for the Austrian treaty, but other Ministers were eager to drop the continental alliances and make a separate peace with England, while the Court was, as Frederick said, 'entirely governed by caprice and resentment.'[3] Frederick was longing for peace but was more than puzzled how to obtain it. He was certain that if only the menace from France or Russia, or preferably both, could be removed, he could deal with Austria and make sure of Silesia. Peace he needed, but he would not purchase it at the price of any of his possessions. His best hope therefore was to come to terms with France, under the wing of England, who would be able to impose conditions as a conqueror—a fact out of which

[1] Pitt to Bristol, 14th Dec. 1759.
[2] Anson to Newcastle, 27th Dec. 1759. Add. MSS. 32,900.
[3] Mitchell to Holdernesse, 12th Feb. 1760. Add. MSS. 6,807.

Frederick hoped to snatch an advantage. Spain, again, was in two minds, anxious to help France, willing to frighten England, but restrained by Wall's advice and the fear of war. In England, Newcastle and Hardwicke had long been advocates of peace, while Pitt was hesitating between two extremes. Uncertain of the King's life, uncertain of his colleagues, more than uncertain of Bute and the Prince of Wales, he longed at times to take his profit while he could, and be gone, but at other times allowed his victories to inflate his hopes, and gave full scope to his patriotic pride. This vacillation ran counter to what Hester described as 'your wise precept of not wearing the mind to pieces by indecision, but to take one's party, as appears best, and submit the rest to Providence.'[1] Decision and the power to decide was, of course, one of the outstanding differences between Pitt and Newcastle, and it was ironical that in this matter of peace it was Newcastle who never changed, while Pitt was blown hither and thither. But if their usual roles were reversed on the main principle, they were not so on the details. Pitt's terms might expand, but Newcastle's were for ever wavering.

Of one thing Pitt was sure; the best way to make peace was to prepare for war. It was therefore with relief that he turned to the congenial task of preparing the next year's campaigns. Two points stood out clearly. The campaign in America ought to be the last. It should therefore be an omnibus campaign, clearing up outstanding problems and putting as much as possible into the bag. It must 'complete the reduction of all Canada,'[2] secure the frontiers of the Southern Colonies, and include, if possible, the capture of Dominica, St. Lucia and Martinique. All this, together with the demolition of the Louisburg fortifications and a possible expedition against the French settlements on the Mobile and the Mississippi, was to be carried out by the forces already in America. No further troops, nor yet much in the way of stores and ammunition, must be expected from England; they were not, in Pitt's view, necessary and were needed elsewhere. He expected, as he told Mitchell, obviously for Frederick's ear, that 'our American War will probably be entirely over early in the summer.'[3] He said very much the same officially to Amherst, impressing on him the need for haste.[4]

[1] Hester to Pitt, 24th July [1760]. Public Record Office.
[2] Pitt to the Northern Governors, 7th Jan. 1760. Kimball, II, 232.
[3] Wood to Mitchell, 15th Feb. 1760. Add. MSS. 6,823.
[4] Pitt to Amherst, 7th Jan. 1760. Kimball, II, 237.

This contraction of the forces in America and comparative waning of interest went hand in hand with the second point. The time had now come when British troops could and should be sent in some numbers to the Continent. It was there that the war must be ended. Defence was no longer sufficient; there must be a forward movement, a victory, something which would compel France to throw up the sponge. But this movement must be against France, for we were at war with no one else, and it must be under the leadership of Ferdinand. It was no part of Pitt's policy to fight Frederick's battles against the rest of Europe. He must be supported in all practical ways, including money; but the war against Russia and Austria was essentially his; England had no direct part in it, still less interest. Moreover, Pitt thought and said that Frederick should be prepared to make sacrifices in order to get out of an impossible situation; and if Pitt was not willing to fight in order to enlarge the dominions of Hanover, by what sophistry could he justify to himself, let alone to the country, fighting to ensure Silesia for Prussia? So when Frederick at the beginning of the year pointed to his own lack of numbers and asked what troops he could expect from England, Pitt, though sympathetic or, as Newcastle said, 'in pain for the King of Prussia,' replied firmly that whilst we would strengthen Ferdinand's army 'most considerably,'[1] we could not 'detach any part of that army to the King of Prussia's relief';[2] and when a little later Knyphausen returned to the attack, Pitt not only refused absolutely to send a man, but felt 'highly offended.'[3] What troops could be spared were for Ferdinand, not for Frederick.

Pitt's strategy was simple. Realising that Frederick was being slowly squeezed to death by weight of numbers, he wanted to concentrate all available forces under Ferdinand, so that he could make an immediate advance and, as he hoped, gain a decisive victory. For that purpose Pitt sent out reinforcements in a steady stream throughout the first half of the year, until we had 23,000 men in Germany. But the plan did not work out as Pitt expected. As previously with the cavalry, so now with the infantry, Ferdinand no sooner received the British reinforcements than Frederick withdrew the Prussian contingents, so that Ferdinand was no

[1] Memo. for the King, 8th Jan. 1760. Add. MSS. 32,900.
[2] Holdernesse to Mitchell, 25th Jan. 1760. Add. MSS. 6,818.
[3] Business for Lord Hardwicke, 18th Feb. 1760. Stowe MSS. 263.

better off than before, or not much, and instead of the expected advance, achieved nothing. In July (1760), it is true, he raised hopes by winning three minor successes—at Korbach, Emsdorf and Warburg—but he was unable to gain the knock-out blow which Pitt so ardently desired. On the contrary, he seemed to be pitching his hopes lower and lower, until at last he convinced himself that if he could force the French to retire it would be a successful campaign, even without a decisive battle. On hearing this, Pitt rapped out, 'I don't think so. That would not do our business. I declare for one, without a battle, I will not be for the continuance of the measures in Germany another year.'[1]

Frederick's insatiable appetite for troops, and Ferdinand's failure to bring the French to battle, shook Pitt. In his speech on the Address (13th November 1759) he had said that 'he had unlearned his juvenile errors, and thought no longer that England could do all by itself.'[2] But the thought had more content than his detractors usually allow; it cut both ways; if allies were necessary to enable England to conquer France in America, they were also necessary to conquer France in Germany. England by herself could not strengthen Ferdinand sufficiently, and if Frederick would not or could not help, then England must look elsewhere.

There was a further thought in Pitt's mind. From many quarters advocates were pressing for a separate peace with France, but Pitt was doubtful if such a peace would benefit either England or Prussia. Unless there was a general peace, the war in Europe would still be alive, and both England and France were bound, one way or another, to be drawn into it as auxiliaries. The main difference, therefore, would be simply that English troops would be buried deeply in the heart of the Continent, and we should lose the advantage of our naval power.[3] Better, therefore, continue the war in the way best suited to our capacities, until France in sheer desperation coerced her allies into making a general peace. There was, as Hardwicke admitted, 'great weight in Mr. Pitt's reasoning.'[4]

Thoughts such as these, together with the growing menace of Spain, produced for the first time an element of uncertainty in Pitt's attitude. He could not make up his mind whether to continue

[1] Newcastle to Hardwicke, 13th September 1760. Add. MSS. 32,911.
[2] Walpole, *Geo. II*, III, 225-6.
[3] Newcastle to Hardwicke, 2nd Jan. 1760. Add. MSS. 32,901.
[4] Hardwicke to Newcastle, 3rd Jan. 1760. Add. MSS. 32,901.

in Germany or try something else. He had alternative plans in view; being, as Newcastle once said, 'always fertile in schemes and projects.'[1] But they were not welcomed by his colleagues and partly for that reason, partly because he had so great a trust in Ferdinand's abilities, he could not decide whether or when to write off Ferdinand's efforts. At last, he threw the responsibility on to the Cabinet, and when the question of further troops for Germany came up, said simply that 'though he could do no more than he had done, yet if the other Ministers were of opinion that more English troops should be sent, *he* should not oppose it, or be displeased with it.'[2] Such an attitude was so unlike Pitt that Newcastle wondered if it was serious. It was serious, but in a way that Newcastle hardly appreciated. It reflected an anxiety and uncertainty very foreign to Pitt's nature. Probably Pitt would have been wiser to take the plunge, in whatever direction, for the indecision preyed on his mind and he brooded too much. The deluding mirage of another and more decisive Minden was oppressing him. In July 'he was in hopes of having before now some good news to send from Prince Ferdinand; but the glad tidings from that quarter are still most impatiently and anxiously expected,'[3] and three months later he was still sighing his heart out: 'I have waited many a tedious day for the arrival of news from the armies.'[4] He was beginning to believe that it was time for new expedients—and more than time, for the season was far advanced.

(ii)

Germany was not the only quarter from which he expected news. There were other quarters which sent him their quotas—not always welcome—more quickly. First to come was the tale of Thurot and the final spark of the invasion. After escaping from Dunkirk, Thurot had taken refuge in Sweden, and in the belief that he was making for Edinburgh, Commodore Boys had been stationed at Leith to intercept him. But his destination was Ireland, and so while Boys kicked his heels on the east coast of Scotland, Thurot slipped down the west coast and, entering Belfast Lough,

[1] Newcastle to Hardwicke, 18th Oct. 1760. Add. MSS. 32,913.
[2] Newcastle to Hardwicke, 9th April 1760; Barrington to Newcastle, 18th April 1760. Add. MSS. 32,904; and Newcastle to Hardwicke, 1st May 1760. Add. MSS. 32,905.
[3] Pitt to Devonshire, 9th July 1760. Chatsworth Collection.
[4] Pitt to Grenville, 18th Oct. 1760 Grenville. *Papers*, I, 355.

landed his troops at Carrickfergus. For some time Ireland had been misgoverned by the Duke of Bedford. Pitt had exhorted him, not once nor twice, to prepare against possible raids, but Bedford either could not or would not take proper steps. His ineffectiveness was so notorious that Pitt had written him letters which should have resulted in his immediate resignation but, in fact, resulted only in violent antipathy to Pitt and a sullen determination not to carry out orders. It was not therefore surprising that Thurot found little resistance at Carrickfergus. There were a few troops under Colonel Jennings, but they were below strength, had very little ammunition and only crumbling fortifications. When they had exhausted their powder, they tried brick-bats, but, brick-bats proving ineffective, they were forced to yield. As Carrickfergus offered little plunder, Thurot sailed up the Lough to Belfast where he demanded and received victuals. Then, feeling that he had done enough for honour, he sailed away. But not far. Captain Elliot of the *Æolus*, who was in Kinsale revictualling, heard of his exploits and without waiting for orders promptly commandeered two small frigates lying in the harbour and set out in pursuit. Coming up with him off the Isle of Man on the 24th of February, he won a complete victory against a stronger enemy, killing Thurot himself and compelling his three ships to strike. This happy news reached Pitt early in March.

The news from America was more tardy and more agitating. His optimistic guess that the war in that quarter would be over early in the summer proved to be wide of the mark. On the death of Montcalm, de Lévis had succeeded to the command of the French forces, and had spent the winter preparing for the recapture of Quebec. The omens seemed propitious. Through the inhabitants, who, though well treated and now nominally British subjects, were still French at heart, he had a source of constant information. From them he learnt that the severe weather had delayed, where it had not entirely prevented, the repair of the damaged fortifications. Better still, he learnt that the English troops were suffering greatly from the frosts and the lack of proper clothes and provisions. Scurvy was rampant and numbers were diminishing rapidly, while the French were increasing in strength by their concentration at Montreal. There seemed every reason to hope that if de Lévis moved promptly at the first appearance of spring, he could regain Quebec before the slow-moving

Amherst could come to its rescue. He set out towards the end of April, reaching the Heights of Abraham on the 28th.

Meanwhile, in Quebec, Wolfe's death, Monckton's wounds and Townshend's return to England had left Murray in command. He was young as generals went, forceful, enthusiastic, able, but a little over-confident. He had heard rumours throughout the winter of de Lévis's intentions, and knowing that his final relief must await Amherst's arrival, had come to the conclusion that fortifications on the Heights of Abraham would afford a better protection against superior numbers than the shattered walls of the town. Hitherto, however, frost had prevented him from throwing up the necessary works. None the less, when he heard of de Lévis's approach, he marched out to meet him with all available troops—not much more than 2,000—confident in the thought that his little army was in the habit of beating the enemy, and buoyed up by the belief that he could shelter behind the city walls as profitably after a battle as before it. If he were defeated he would retire to the city, hold it to the last extremity, and then retreating to one of the islands in the St. Lawrence, wait for reinforcements. It was a brave resolve, but unavailing against odds of five to one. He was defeated on Wolfe's battlefield and forced back into the city, where, after sending a dispatch to Amherst for help, he set to work cheerfully to reanimate his men and make something of the damaged walls.[1]

His dispatch reached Halifax on the 10th of May (1760), where its bearer had much to say about Murray's plight. The Governor, Charles Lawrence, felt 'unspeakable mortification' at the defeat and was much exercised to know what he should do. Clearly Pitt ought to be informed at the earliest moment. Who else could take effective action? But the dispatch was addressed to Amherst, and if it had to meander half across America and back again before starting on its journey to England, the outlook was bad. At last, after much heart-searching, Governor Lawrence decided to violate the sanctity of letters, and opening the dispatch sent a copy straight off to Pitt, who received it on the 18th of June and with his inflexible honesty at once published it in the *Gazette*. Great was the lamentation. In Newcastle's case without inhibitions: 'You will have an account of the astonishing bad news from Quebec,' he wrote, 'I am afraid Murray has been

[1] Murray to Pitt, 25th May 1760. Kimball, II, 291.

extremely to blame . . . we don't own it, but the most sanguine of us fear that Mr. Murray will be obliged to abandon Quebec to the enemy. . . . This is a sad beginning of our campaign, where we thought all was safe; and will greatly animate and encourage the French in Europe, and make them less inclined to peace.'[1] In 'the most sanguine of us' we may perhaps trace a reference to Pitt and his views, which otherwise are unknown.

But Murray's ordeal and Pitt's misgivings were both short-lived. The lesson of Durell's lethargy had been lost on no one. By Pitt's orders a squadron had been left at Halifax under Commodore Lord Colville, with strict orders to sail for Quebec at the earliest moment, and Governor Lawrence in forwarding Murray's dispatch had been able to report that Colville had already sailed. In addition Pitt himself had early in March dispatched a small squadron, under Commodore Swanton, direct for Quebec with a convoy of store-ships. On the 9th of May, a frigate appeared sailing up the St. Lawrence. Besiegers and besieged alike waited with breathless expectation for the flag to be unfurled. It proved to be the red cross of St. George, and the ship to be the *Lowestoffe*, one of Swanton's squadron which had got separated in the fog, and now brought the glad news that both Swanton and Colville were at hand. With their arrival de Lévis knew that the game was up and retreated to Montreal. Murray's report of his deliverance reached Pitt on the 27th of June. 'Join, my love, with me in most humble and grateful thanks to the Almighty,' Pitt wrote to Hester. 'Happy, happy day! My joy and hurry are inexpressible.'[2]

For all his rejoicing, the news from Quebec, both in its sombre and its gay aspects, was by way of an extra. As Walpole remarked, 'Who the deuce was thinking of Quebec?'[3] Certainly not Pitt. His thoughts were fixed on Montreal, and it must have added to his disappointment to read in Murray's dispatch that Amherst could 'hardly act by the Lakes before the month of July.'[4] The 'early summer' of Pitt's hopes was fading into autumn, and might fade away altogether. Here was another element in his problem, another reason for holding back from Germany.

[1] Newcastle to Kinnoull, 23rd June 1760. Add. MSS. 32,907.
[2] Pitt to Hester, 27th June 1760. Chatham. *Correspondence*, II, 45.
[3] Walpole to Mann, 20 June 1760.
[4] Murray to Pitt, 25th May 1760. Kimball, II, 296.

(iii)

To add to his burdens, the mounting expectation of peace was having its effect on Newcastle. Almost unconsciously he began to push Pitt out—not from the conduct of the war; that, of course, was unthinkable—but from political influence. Somewhere at the back of his mind there was a growing conviction that with the return of peace he would resume his rightful position, and Pitt would be put in his place. What that place might be Newcastle had not as yet considered, but at least many degrees lower than during the war. This new assertiveness showed itself in Newcastle's attitude towards certain Bills which he described as 'popular,' and, apparently for that reason, disliked. There were three in particular, dealing respectively with the qualification of members of Parliament, the Scotch militia, and family allowances for the militia generally. The Qualification Bill came first. Members were supposed to have and maintain a property qualification, but frequently failed to do so. The Tories wished to put the matter right, and sent Sir John Phillips and Alderman Beckford to enlist Pitt's help for a Bill which they were proposing to introduce. He was inclined to give it, partly as a *quid pro quo* for their consistent and devoted support, partly because he approved making 'land a turnpike to get into that House.'[1] Pitt hoped that Government would not oppose, but Newcastle preferred to whittle the provisions down. His reasons are not clear; what is clear is that he treated Pitt in an abrupt and cavalier manner which he had never ventured to show over military matters. He recorded the meeting at which the matter was discussed. Pitt, he said, was 'civil, but plainly extremely hurt' when Newcastle insisted on having his own way, and so 'we differed in our opinions, and he civilly but sullenly submitted to what he could not prevent.'[2] The phrase is significant and becomes more significant in the light of a letter which Newcastle wrote about the Bill to set up a militia in Scotland. This Newcastle regarded as contrary to all the principles on which he, Hardwicke and Devonshire had ever acted, and he was therefore determined to defeat it. 'I went to work,' he wrote, 'in the old way. . . . I summoned avowedly all our friends from every part of the kingdom . . . and we threw out the Bill by 200.'[3] The method

[1] West to Newcastle, 21st April 1760. Add. MSS. 32,905.
[2] Newcastle to Hardwicke, 4th March 1760. Add. MSS. 32,903.
[3] Newcastle to Kinnoull, 1st June 1760. Add. MSS. 32,907.

left nothing to chance. 'On the affair of the Scotch Militia being debated in the House of Commons,' wrote Pyle, who as a Royal Chaplain had much inside information and as a Whig had a strong bias in Newcastle's favour, 'the English ditto has had a thorough roasting, and is scouted out of all credit, as a most ridiculous, expensive, and to the common men (as to morals and industry) ruinous project.'[1] When the murder had been done, West commented, 'All our friends in great glee.'[2] Newcastle, in short, was flaunting his parliamentary majority in Pitt's face, and Pitt thoroughly understood the implications. He made what even Newcastle was forced to admit was 'a very strong, pathetic lamentation that he saw there must be a breach, that he was a single man.' But Newcastle with a smirk of satisfaction decided that 'I will certainly persist in the answer I have given.'[3] Pitt was forced to yield. He did so because, at this stage, union seemed to him essential. It would be disastrous if the coalition fell to pieces at this moment when union had so nearly won the war. So Pitt accepted the Qualification Bill in the form approved by Newcastle, though to him it seemed to have been 'hacked and wounded,'[4] and submitted to a bowdlerised form of the Allowances Bill, and the total loss of the Scotch militia. The only point on which he showed fight was on the Bill to extend the English Militia Act. On this point also Newcastle had defeated him but as Pitt regarded the militia as essential, he declared his intention of reintroducing the Bill on the first day of the next session. 'Our friends,' was Newcastle's retort, 'should be prepared for it, and all summoned to be up the first day.'[5] No doubt he would have acted accordingly had not Hardwicke intervened and arranged a compromise. To Hardwicke and even to the King, Newcastle made no secret of his jubilation, referring jauntily to the doomed Bills, laughing at the King's fears, and poking fun at Devonshire's doubts. He even discussed the fantastic theory that Pitt was supporting these 'popular' Bills in order to destroy Newcastle's influence and credit, and 'to enable *himself with the Tories* to carry everything he pleased. It is,' Newcastle said, 'to be sure a most ridiculous situation. Mr. Pitt by his situation and consequence is at the head of the

[1] Pyle to Kerrick, 26th April 1760. *Memoirs of a Royal Chaplain,* p. 321.
[2] West to Newcastle, 15th April 1760. Add. MSS. 32,904.
[3] Newcastle to Hardwicke, 22nd March 1760. Add. MSS. 32,903.
[4] West to Newcastle, 2nd May 1760. Add. MSS. 32,905.
[5] Newcastle to Hardwicke, 16th Aug. 1760. Add. MSS. 32,910.

House of Commons, of which the Tories scarce make a sixth part; and all *extrajudicial* business is to be agreed and concerted with them, without any notice taken of our friends, who compose the majority of the House of Commons; and then, if they don't come blindly in, there is a confusion of measures, and a disunion and misunderstanding in the Administration upon them. For me, I am unable to act in such circumstances. If I give in to the reasonable objections of our friends, I break *pro tanto* with Mr. Pitt. If I do not, I offend the only real friends we have, and those with whom I must and will abide.'[1] Had the letter been addressed to Pitt instead of to Hardwicke, he would have been warned, but indeed he knew without being warned. He had read the writing on the wall, and the strain grew steadily greater.

From the first days of the year he had been very ill and often confined to his bed. Before long he became nervy, querulous and jumpy. The deterioration in the political scene was heightened by two events—the publication of a pamphlet entitled 'A Letter to two Great Men,' and the renewal of Spanish intervention. The Letter started what Symmer called 'the controversy (and a curious controversy it is) . . . whether we would keep Canada, or Guadeloupe, in consequence of the ensuing Treaty of Peace.'[2] Curious or not, it gave tongue, for the first time, to the desire for peace latent in many hearts, which must have been stirred to re-echo its eloquent exordium: 'we have had bloodshed enough. God forgive those who have occasioned this terrible destruction of the human species, and spread misery and devastation, for so long a time, in almost every corner of the globe.'[3] Walpole with his penchant for Olympian gossip might call it 'very dull,' but even he was forced to admit that it was 'much adopted by the city, and much admired by all who are too humble to judge for themselves.'[4] Its publication could hardly fail to remind Pitt that if his objectives were to be gained, speed had become doubly necessary.

Spanish intervention was renewed with the arrival of Fuentes. He reached England on the 24th of May (1760) when Pitt was too ill to receive him and Holdernesse was out of town. Pitt was therefore obliged to hand him over to Newcastle, at the very moment when Newcastle was feeling particularly elated at the defeat of the 'popular' Bills. He seized his chance, and not only

[1] Newcastle to Hardwicke, 15th March 1760. Add. MSS. 32,903.
[2] Symmer to Mitchell, 13th May 1760. Add. MSS. 6,839.
[3] Douglas. *A letter* etc. p. 4. [4] Walpole to Montagu, 14th Jan. 1760.

welcomed Fuentes on his arrival, but arranged to see him later officially. Pitt was obviously uneasy and suspicious; he neither trusted Newcastle, nor had any faith in his ability to negotiate. From certain phrases that had been used, Pitt was convinced that Newcastle had been indulging in clandestine 'dapplings,' and once more he set about warning him not to interfere. On this occasion, possibly because he was ill and nervy, possibly because of his recent defeats in Parliament, he tried a new method. Instead of haughty demands to be instantly informed of what was taking place, he professed himself unable to express any opinion on the Spanish complaints; the necessary decisions would have to be reached by Newcastle and Hardwicke without his help; they after all had been handling the matter for a long time; they were 'perfectly master of it'; they had given their hints to Wall; they were blessed with the confidence of the King; they had the support of Parliament. All the cards, in short, were in their hands, while his situation was very different; he could not afford either to break with Spain or to give up any English right. Not that he was afraid of Spain, but that he 'wished extremely' to avoid a breach with her in the interests of Europe as a whole. Newcastle was a little nonplussed by this attitude, which he ascribed to jealousy,[1] and might possibly have continued his underground workings but for a hint from Hardwicke. It would be better, that cautious lawyer advised, to make suggestions to Pitt and 'put the execution of it into his hands.'[2] Perhaps it need hardly be added that, for all his peevishness, Pitt had no intention of abandoning the Spanish question. He did, in fact, take an active and commanding part in the discussions, writing a strong protest when Fuentes sent a copy of one of his Memorials to the French Court, and dispatching instructions to our Ambassador so crystal clear, so carefully argued, and at the same time so dignified and firm that they might well be used as a model for all diplomatic correspondence.[3]

Concurrently with these pricks at home, events abroad worried him. He began to brood. 'I was repining,' wrote Hester, 'before the arrival of your sweet note that I was not with you to sit by your dear side and to try to divert your thoughts from too constant an attention to unpleasing circumstances.'[4] So wrote his guardian angel, but the facts were patent also to the outside

[1] Memo. 4th July 1760. Add. MSS. 32,908.
[2] Hardwicke to Newcastle, 20th Aug. 1760. Add. MSS. 32,910.
[3] Pitt to Bristol, 26th Sept. 1760.
[4] Hester to Pitt, 26th August 1760. Public Record Office.

world, as, for instance, Hardwicke's nephew, Hugh Valence Jones, who reported that 'Mr. Pitt is uneasy and out of humour on account of the inactivity of the campaign. He says it neither enables this country to make peace, or to carry on the war,'[1] and Pitt confirmed both views in a letter to Granby: 'may one happy day on the Dymal dissipate every cloud that for some time has hung somewhat heavily on the scene.'[2] There were ups and downs in the fighting, but nothing decisive. Fouquet, one of Frederick's generals, was annihilated with 10,000 men at Landshut on the 23rd of June, and though Frederick by a superhuman effort recovered some of the lost ground at Liegnitz on the 15th of August, yet even Frederick, as Carlyle says, 'does not deceive himself as to the difficulties, almost the impossibilities that still lie ahead.'[3] The whole weight of the European war was pressing on Pitt's shoulders. To him alone everyone looked—Frederick for help, Ferdinand for instructions, Newcastle for peace, the King for glory. And Pitt, uncertain and depressed, chose this moment to add to his distractions—perhaps by way of a counter-irritant—by making what Hardwicke called 'a very interesting operation in your family,' and what he himself described as an 'anxious undertaking.' He arranged for his two little girls to undergo the new, uncertain and much doubted process of inoculation against small-pox, and suffered all 'a parent's sensibility' till the trial was safely surmounted.[4]

The period of vacillation, however, was nearly over. It was cut short by news that the French were sending a fresh army, under St. Germain, to the Lower Rhine. Pitt, reacting immediately, 'flung out' to Newcastle and Lady Yarmouth his intention to create a diversion by a descent on the coast of France. He had, throughout the year, been turning over, or as Newcastle said, harping on, the idea of attacking Belleisle. Now he made up his mind, and Newcastle promptly, one might almost say automatically, objected. Pitt without further ado went straight to the King, obtained his hearty consent—he was 'violently for it'—and then ordered the Admiralty to prepare the transports. This was the old, incisive Pitt, sure of himself, sure of his aim. The harping, of which Newcastle complained, had done its job; the plan had

[1] Jones to Hardwicke, 29th August 1760.
[2] Pitt to Granby, 26th August 1760. H.M.C. Rutland MSS., Vol. II.
[3] Carlyle. *Frederick the Great,* IX, 54.
[4] Pitt to Hardwicke, 2nd Oct. 1760. Add. MSS. 32,912.

grown insensibly in his mind and was now cut and dried; he knew what he wanted to do and how to do it.

His renewed vigour brought its own problems. Newcastle, piqued at this breaking loose from the bonds he was so neatly tying, came limping behind, intent on mischief. What he had done to Pitt in Parliament, he would now do in the Cabinet; he would convince the King; he would collect his friends together and show Pitt who was master. He had an ideal chance; the war fever was abating; the season was late, and his opposition was not concerned with actual operations, but with a new venture in a new quarter, which was not likely to rouse popular enthusiasm and could be dropped without obvious harm. He began operations at once, pestering the King and plying Anson and Barrington with dinners, all in preparation for the meeting of the Cabinet. It met on the 2nd of October, but to Newcastle's chagrin approved Pitt's proposals, in spite of the fact that Newcastle had continued 'positive in my opinion against such a monstrous project as going in November with almost all our army to conquer and take the Island of Bellisle.'[1] Not to be beaten, he next enlisted Hardwicke's willing aid, and continued his culinary assaults on Anson and Ligonier, whom for this purpose he described as 'my admiral and general.' His hopes ran high when on the 5th of October (1760) news at last came that Amherst had captured Montreal and the whole of French Canada had capitulated. Surely, he argued, that should be sufficient.

Pitt—for a few fleeting moments—allowed his mind to stray to other projects in the hope that they might be less distasteful. He glanced towards the East. Throughout the year victories had been coming thick and fast from India, where Pitt had sent a few troops and some ships to help Clive and Coote, and just at this moment 'Pocock is arrived in the Downs with seventeen rich India ships, value above two millions.'[2] It occurred to Pitt as a possibility that the expedition might be used against Mauritius, which was a port of call on the way to India, but he soon reverted to his first idea. India was a problem of which he fought a little shy; the time might come when it would have to be tackled seriously, but for the moment he was content to leave it in the hands of Clive and Coote, and to concentrate himself on France which remained at once the core of the problem and its answer.

[1] Newcastle to Hardwicke, 3rd Oct. 1760. Add. MSS. 32,912.
[2] Pitt to Hester [? September 1760]. Public Record Office.

Newcastle urged that the success in America should turn their minds from 'such a speculative, chimerical expedition' to thoughts of economy, or better still, of peace, but to Pitt the fall of Canada seemed an added reason for pressing ahead. Neither would give way, and as 'these vague conversations at Court produced little but altercations,' it was finally agreed to refer the matter to a further Cabinet meeting, at which Keppel, as the proposed commander, should be ordered to attend. Newcastle repeated his dinners, though without the success he had hoped. The Cabinet thought peace was still distant, and were not as yet prepared to shake Pitt off, so that, as Newcastle sadly admitted, there was 'a disposition in almost everybody to forward this scheme, or (what is juster) such a fear in everybody to do, or say, anything which may obstruct or prevent it.' But one point Newcastle gained. Keppel doubted if there was sufficient depth of water for the ships, and thought that the only landing place had recently been strongly fortified. It was therefore agreed to refer these two points to Hawke and await his report.[1]

Hawke's reply came on the 24th of October. After his victory, Hawke had returned to England to receive the thanks of Parliament, and had remained ashore till August, when he had once more hoisted his flag. Returning to Quiberon Bay, he had resolved to finish off the work he had begun nine months earlier, by seizing and destroying the ships which had escaped into Morbihan and the Villaine. When he received the Cabinet's letter about Belleisle, he was completing the plans for his own scheme. Hawke was by nature testy, tactless and impatient; it irked him to be put out of his stride. His answer therefore threw plentiful cold water on Pitt's project, emphasised the difficulties, criticised the strategy and extolled his own plan as far superior, though agreeing, if ordered, to put it on one side. Perhaps worst of all, he completely ignored the two questions put to him. Newcastle was delighted and sent Anson to the King with the report before Pitt could see it. His manœuvre succeeded to admiration. When Pitt entered the Closet, the King at once told him that as Hawke was opposed to the scheme, he would not send his troops 'à la boucherie.' Pitt, as ever, bowed to the King's wishes, but coming out of the Closet gave vent to his feelings. His fury was tremendous and reduced his hearers to quaking silence. 'He attacked Sir Edward Hawke most bitterly, and dissected his letter from

[1] Newcastle to Hardwicke, 11th October 1760. Add. MSS. 32,913.

one end to the other.' Why had he not answered the questions put to him? Why had he indulged in reasonings which nobody wanted? He might be a very good sea officer, but he was no Minister, and if he did not know what use to make of Belleisle, Pitt did. The whole thing was a put-up job to hamstring an expedition which Pitt knew was both practicable and of the highest consequence. Someone would pay for it; the whole intrigue would be dragged to light in the House. Pitt's wrath was very real and very bitter, and his disappointment no less; it drove him, as so often, into intractability. He was not content to inveigh against Hawke but refused to accept responsibility for the lesser scheme. It was, he stormed, fantastic to use the whole great expedition on a plan which Hawke had proposed to carry out with his own marines, but if the Cabinet wanted to do it, they could. Pitt would not stop them. He washed his hands of the whole affair. After he had gone, Newcastle supposed that if Pitt was against Hawke's plan 'nobody would be so mad as to undertake it.' Otherwise he was delighted. But Lady Yarmouth, who had listened to the whole outburst, remained thoughtful.[1]

The next morning all schemes were in the melting pot, for shortly after seven o'clock George II dropped down, suddenly, dead.

[1] Newcastle to Hardwicke, 25th Oct. 1760. Add. MSS. 32,913.

27

THE NEW KING

The death of a King can hardly fail to be a matter of moment, for in spite of egalitarian theories, the fact remains that morale descends from the top downwards, and a change in the hand that holds the tiller is felt, for good or ill, throughout the ship. George II was dead. As Kings went in those days, he had been a good King, comparing not unfavourably with most of his contemporaries. Kings then, whether good or bad, were more than figureheads; they might have little influence over Parliament, but in administration they were the ultimate authority. George II had not been very wise or very moral, and by nature had been irascible and prejudiced, but he had a strong sense of duty and, as Devonshire observed, 'a good notion of the constitution of this country';[1] given time he could generally overcome his personal feelings and, however ungraciously, act as he was required. The hall-mark of his character, Pitt said many years later, was 'justice, truth and sincerity in an eminent degree,'[2] qualities which were in harmony with Pitt's temperament and gave him a secure background; whatever the storms, whatever the snags, he knew where he stood. And now another King had come to the throne, a King whose character had yet to unfold; a King who had been shut away from the busy haunts of men, cooped up with his mother, a German Princess of small intelligence and much dissimulation, and moulded by an obscure Scottish peer of amateur status and no experience. His education in the arts of government had consisted of copy-book maxims—a farrago of pious hopes and woolly aspirations. In years, he was twenty-two; in age, still adolescent, full of childish loyalties, full of violent, unreasoning hatreds. The one hope for him in these early days was that the sudden glare of public life might frighten him into seeking the counsels of wiser men. To some extent it did; he was inwardly diffident, shrinking from responsibility; but

[1] Diary. Chatsworth Collection. [2] Speech, 14th March 1770.

the person to whom he looked for guidance was, not unnaturally, his boyhood's hero—Bute. For good or ill, England's fortunes lay in Bute's hands.

George III had long been expecting the event with some impatience, for he had no love for his grandfather, but when the news reached him at Kew in a message from the old King's valet de chambre, it threw him into a panic. The only idea in his mind was that he must see Bute; Bute would tell him what to do. He dashed off a hurried note to say that he was keeping the news secret and would wait for advice; but, a little later, on receipt of fuller details from his aunt, Princess Amelia, he sent a further scribble, saying simply: 'I am coming the back way to your house,' and set off for London.[1] On his way he met Pitt, coming to break the news officially, who told him there were some formalities immediately necessary. But he was far too agitated to talk to Pitt, and replying that he would give orders in due course, made straight for Carlton House, where he remained closeted with his mother and Bute. They were all in a flurry together, so much so that they left the Duke of Cumberland waiting for a couple of hours at Savile House, before realising that they had summoned him to the wrong address.[2]

As the first flurry died down, they called to mind the schemes they had previously discussed among themselves. Now was the time to put them into operation. It was no doubt arrogance as well as ignorance which induced them to draft the new King's address to the Privy Council without consulting any of the old Ministers. The address was not undignified, but it ended with what appeared to be a back-handed slap at Pitt. 'As I mount the throne,' George said, 'in the midst of a bloody and expensive war, I shall endeavour to prosecute it in the manner the most likely to bring on an honourable and lasting peace.' To Pitt, the epithets applied to the war and the absence of reference to our allies seemed deplorable, and he insisted on having the words altered, in the printed version, to read 'an expensive, but just and necessary war' and a 'peace in concert with my allies.' Whether, as is usually supposed, the original version was meant as a deliberate challenge to Pitt is not easy to determine, because the many accounts which have come down to us vary in precisely those details which might give a clue. Certainly the King

[1] Geo. III to Bute, 25th October 1760. Sedgwick, p. 48.
[2] *Life and Letters of Lady Sarah Lennox*, p. 4.

disliked Pitt and would have been glad to get rid of him,[1] but one must not too readily endow the inexperienced trio who drafted the speech with either deep-laid schemes or clear foresight. Very probably the words were a natural expression of George III's feeling, used without much thought of possible repercussions. What is clear is, that the incident raised doubts and suspicions in many minds—Pitt, for instance, saw Newcastle's hand in it[2]—and did not make for peaceful developments.

Developments there had to be, for a new reign cannot simply proceed as though nothing had happened, and they must in fact arise from clashes between the old and the new. The existing Ministers were well aware of the fact; so, within limits, were the new protagonists. Much depended on the motives by which they were severally swayed.

The King was well-meaning and conscientious, but owing to his youth and inexperience, entirely dependent upon Bute. If he could have had his way he would at once have appointed Bute Prime Minister and Lord High Everything Else. So far as he could, he did; but Bute was unable to fill this multiple role. Other Ministers there must be, and unfortunately the King had been taught to distrust them all in general, and had taught himself to hate Pitt in particular. At the outset, the exhilaration of novelty, and some natural aptitude, joined with his conscience to keep him at his task. He performed the ceremonial functions of a King with a youthful dignity and grace which proved very appealing; but in matters of government he could do little but repeat Bute's lessons and shuffle out of personal decisions. In the circumstances the pains of kingship tended to exceed its pleasures, and George soon allowed his thoughts to wander. His ambition was to get married, and his elevation to the throne gave him the opportunity. Surely a King might indulge himself to that extent. The idea was entrancing, and came to monopolise his attention more and more—as was very understandable in a young man whose flirtatious tendencies had been rigorously suppressed by 'the voice of truth,' as expounded by Bute—but it meant a still greater delegation of the humdrum functions of government. George III's good intention to be present in person at all Council meetings[3] died stillborn.

[1] Sedgwick, p. 49.
[2] Newcastle to Hardwicke, 26th Oct. 1760. Add. MSS. 35,420.
[3] Devonshire's Diary, 27th Oct. 1760.

Bute's motives are difficult to fathom. Everyone assumed that he aimed at becoming all-powerful, and were frightened at what he might do in his want of experience. Devonshire summed up this aspect in a discussion with Newcastle. They must, he argued, have time to decide 'what was to be done with Lord Bute, who, by all that appears, seems not only ignorant of business but visionary, for it was plain by every step that he meant to be the Minister over them all and yet had no plan of administration or even thought of the practicability of effecting it.'[1] Yet perhaps Bute was neither so ambitious nor so helpless as Devonshire supposed. He yearned for political power as something that he had never yet enjoyed and for which he believed himself to be fitted, but he shrank from responsibility, and would much rather be joint than sole Minister. His choice of colleague had been Pitt, to whom he had from time to time before the old King's death made blundering approaches. They had been rebuffed—to his own chagrin and the future George III's fury; but the rebuff had borne fruit. Bute was not prepared to take office in isolation or in opposition; he must wait until he had formed his own bodyguard. If the old Ministers had properly appreciated this fact, they could with ease have kept him out. But Bute was clever enough to hide his hesitations and skilful enough to set his rivals by the ears. Some four years earlier Edmund Pyle, speaking of the internal arrangements at Leicester House, had remarked that 'there is a sly Scotchman, at the head of this settlement, whom the Duke of Newcastle could not help taking in (for he has got the length of the Princess-Mother's foot) that will soon *out* all he don't like. His name is Lord Bute.'[2] Pyle had put his finger on the spot. Undoubtedly Bute had parts, but they shone brightest in intrigue; he was only too able to oust others, but not necessarily so able to fill the vacancy they left. It was one thing to get the length of a widow's foot or excite a passionate admiration in a backward boy; it was quite another thing to put on Pitt's armour or even Newcastle's faded livery. Bute had mistaken his capacity; being able to make himself useful in a domestic milieu, he thought that with patience and a little practice, he could learn to run an empire. He was to find out his error, but at the moment he was intent on winning the coveted position—on his own terms.

[1] Devonshire's Diary, 27th Oct. 1760.
[2] *Memoirs of a Royal Chaplain*, p. 271.

Of Newcastle it is not necessary to say much. He had no views beyond a very normal reluctance to retire and a very natural pleasure in being pressed to remain. Having no convictions, he canvassed his friends. With the exception of Hardwicke and Stone—incidentally, his two most able advisers—all, to his great delight, urged him to stay; but they did so, not for his own advantage, not for the benefit of the King, not for the good of the country, but solely for party purposes. They told him that 'he owed it to his friends, and the Whig Party who would be broke to pieces and turned adrift' if they lost him.[1] Their reasons mattered not at all to Newcastle; the great point was that they urged him to stay. Fortified—or weakened—by this general consensus, he became as putty in Bute's hands. Bute needed him temporarily for his own purposes, and, ably seconded by the King, had no difficulty in playing on his vanity and persuading him that he was indispensable.

There remained Pitt. Of all the actors concerned in the coming tragedy he was by far the most capable, and the only one who tried to guide himself by patriotic, as opposed to personal, views. Perhaps for that very reason all looked on him as essential and none looked on him with favour. To a large extent he had only himself to blame. He was neither gracious nor ingratiating, nor was his character simple. He recognised the fact regretfully, and on one occasion told Devonshire that 'he was an odd mixture of a creature, the most obstinate on one hand and the most diffident on the other.'[2] The inferiority complex of his schooldays still haunted him, making him sometimes obsequious and cringing, sometimes haughty and arrogant, and never thoroughly at ease, except in his own home. But however prickly he might be, his views were not prejudices; they were rooted in principle; and he found it particularly hard to adjust himself to the facts of the new reign. He was well aware of Bute's ambitions, which he had himself described as unbounded; and he was equally aware that Bute wanted him as a prop. The thought revolted him for many reasons, both personal and constitutional. To work with Bute seemed wrong; to continue without Bute seemed impossible. Pitt was much exercised in mind, but came to the conclusion that the war must take precedence over everything, and until

[1] Devonshire's Diary, 27th Oct. 1760.
[2] *Ibid.*, 9th April 1761.

it was brought to a successful issue, he must do the best he could with the materials to hand.

To sum up, the King was governed by his prejudices; Bute by ambition; Newcastle by the habits of a lifetime; Pitt by patriotic pride. The mixture of these various motives was to be the soil out of which the weeds of disaster were to grow.

28

THE SEARCH FOR PEACE

(i)

The first year of George III's reign coincides closely with the last year of Pitt's Ministry. Its story has four main motifs running through it—the progress of the war, the negotiations for peace, the manœuvres of Spain, and the isolation of Pitt. The first three are intimately connected; the last stands by itself, dominating everything. It is preferable to speak of the isolation of Pitt rather than the rise of Bute because, in spite of appearances, Bute never rose. He began as a favourite in favour, which was little enough, and ended as a favourite out of favour, which was less. His tragedy, and indeed England's, was that a positive contribution was demanded of him, and he was unable to give it. When he had ousted Pitt, the war continued simply through the momentum imparted by Pitt; and when peace was made, it was made simply by the mutilation of Pitt's terms. Bute solved difficulties by giving them up.

His presence created confusion from the first. In a sense the tug-of-war was not between Bute and Pitt, or Bute and the old Ministry; it was between Bute and the King. To the King, Bute represented all wisdom and all ability: Government must be placed in his hands; he must contrive everything. Flattering as that might be, Bute found it oppressive and the other Ministers bewildering. Hardwicke, Newcastle, Pitt and Holdernesse all came up against the same extraordinary phenomenon. The King was lavish of compliments but silent as a clam on state affairs. 'His Majesty,' Newcastle reported, 'said these remarkable words, "My Lord Bute is your good friend; he will tell you my thoughts at large."'[1] The words, of course, were not remarkable; they were a confession of ignorance, but to Newcastle, who had not read Dickens and knew nothing of the Bagnets, they were

[1] Newcastle to Hardwicke, 26th Oct. 1760. Add. MSS. 35,420.

fraught with all manner of sinister meaning. Hardwicke was baffled by the same enigma. 'In short,' he told Newcastle, 'he [the King] said everything that a most gracious Prince could say of that kind but not one word of any business.'[1] Pitt's treatment was more cavalier but no more enlightening. At one time he 'complained that he was nobody, that he knew nothing, that he was consulted on no occasion, that it was impossible it should go on long';[2] and at another 'that he and my Lord Holdernesse dangled at Court with a bag in their hands, but they were not ministers.'[3] It was, of course, shocking treatment for a man of Pitt's eminence, but unpremeditated rather than deliberate, and springing out of the King's ardent wish to have Bute as his sole Minister. Bute, meanwhile, was unable to make up his mind. What he had originally hoped to do was to take Newcastle's place, but Pitt had been emphatic that Newcastle must remain. Bute struggled to get his way, partly at the dictates of ambition and partly at least in obedience to the King's wishes, but after sounding everyone, came to the reluctant conclusion that the wisest course would be 'to hold the situation of a private man at the side of the young King and give his best support to public measures.'[4] That was what he had told Pitt on the evening of the old King's death, and though he had apparently gone back on it two days later by allowing the new King to make him a member of the Council, it was for practical purposes the position in which he found himself during the early months of the reign. He was not yet strong enough to insist on a ministerial post. It followed that the old Ministers must be retained. What was important from Bute's point of view was to sow distrust among them, so that by dividing he could rule, and when the time came, discard. His methods were masterly enough. He saw the Ministers separately and played on their weaknesses—on Pitt's inferiority complex, on Newcastle's vanity, on Hardwicke's family ambitions.

Walpole remarked that Pitt was 'too quick-sighted not to perceive what would be the complexion of the new reign,'[5] but, indeed, Pitt was no quicker-sighted than the others. They all recognised the impact of the 'succession'; they all knew the influence of the Favourite; they were all—except Pitt—regretting

[1] Hardwicke to Newcastle, 28th Oct. 1760. Add. MSS. 32,913.
[2] Devonshire's Diary, 12th Nov. 1760.
[3] Hardwicke to Newcastle, 29th Oct. 1760. Add. MSS. 32,913.
[4] *The Border Elliots*, p. 364. [5] Walpole. *Geo. III*, I 8.

that they had not made warmer court to the Dowager Princess. Realising the dangers, they all felt that they ought to unite against the interloper; and they spent much of their time asserting the fact. But there was a snag, the snag which had been at the bottom of all the uneasiness of the coalition since its inception—Pitt was suspect as not being a true Whig. If only he would come back to the fold! Devonshire pleaded with Temple to use his influence. The country, he declared, would certainly be ruined unless there was union, and 'Mr. Pitt might, if he pleased, with taking very little pains, gain the Duke of Newcastle and make his party friends to him . . . if he would show a little more regard to them and less to his Tories.'[1] The coalition had never been more than a suspension of arms, and the atmosphere always one of suspicion; the two elements had different aims, different outlook, different methods; they were connected at only two points—Newcastle trusted Pitt for the war; Pitt trusted Newcastle in the Closet—and even on these points they trusted only because they must. On all others they were divided. Close union now, when Bute was busy sowing suspicions, was more impossible than ever. For every step forward, Newcastle sooner or later took two backwards, and whenever Bute or the King smiled on him, was only too ready to make his court at Pitt's expense.[2] Pitt, on his side, was ready to act as a genuine colleague so far as his solitary nature allowed, but was much hampered by the conflict in his mind between his belief in his own right to lead and the frustration of his inferiority complex. His motives were partly personal and partly patriotic. He was clear that if Newcastle went, Bute would step into his shoes, and Bute as First Lord was more than Pitt could stomach. But more important was the probable effect on the war. Newcastle's influence in the City, where the money had to be raised, was much greater than Bute's; and Newcastle, again, was not tarred with Sackville's brush. Leicester House had championed Sackville, and were now welcoming him to Court, much to Pitt's dismay. It looked like a direct snub for Ferdinand and might induce him to resign which, said Pitt, 'would at once break the whole system.' He was so worried at the prospect that when Devonshire called on him to discuss the political situation, 'there was no getting him to talk upon

[1] Devonshire's Diary, 28th Oct. 1760.

[2] Cf. 'The Duke of Newcastle in high spirits. The King most gracious to him and his conversation with Lord Bute friendly and well. It looked much as if they now preferred him to Pitt and Lord Temple.' Devonshire's Diary, 31st Oct. 1760.

any other subject.'[1] Pitt's views were coloured not only by his confidence in Ferdinand as a general, but also by his conviction that peace depended upon Ferdinand's ability to hold the French in Germany. His attitude, with its insistence on the country's good, was in marked contrast with the petty intrigues of the others for party and personal power. It seems to have been beyond their comprehension that anyone should have lofty or selfless views, and when Pitt happened to remark, surely innocently enough, that the King ought to have a Parliament representative of all classes, their only reaction was 'that Pitt's meaning was evidently to get a Tory Parliament or as many of those people as (he) could, which would be a strength to him.[2] Such were the troubled waters at the outset of the new reign. Suspicions were rife, confidence at a discount.

(ii)

George II's death had one advantage; it enabled Pitt to revive the question of the Belleisle expedition, and gave him an excuse to praise the militia in the King's Speech. Needless to say the Whig magnates opposed him on both points; they could see no virtue in the expedition, and no merit in the militia. He found a supporter, however, in Bute, possibly to his surprise. Yet the reason was simple. Bute, though neither original nor creative, was at least shrewd, and he saw that if Pitt was to be kept in office in order to run the war, he should be allowed to run it in his own way. The time for criticism was past. He had succeeded hitherto and there was no reason, other than Newcastle's trepidations, for supposing he would fail now.

The Cabinet meeting on the Belleisle expedition was hardly edifying. Bute made what Devonshire described as 'a strange, bombast speech.' Devonshire was speaking at second-hand, but with the quick suspicion of the Whigs, had no hesitation in calling it 'plain proof of giving in to Mr. Pitt's measures.' Pitt, intent only on assessing probabilities, asked Anson and Ligonier for their professional advice. When both approved, Mansfield, poised uncomfortably between Newcastle and Pitt, tried to avoid trouble by disclaiming knowledge of military matters and acquiescing in the experts' opinion. But he was not to escape so lightly. Newcastle, indignant at this flagrant apostacy, accused him of selling his vote to save his position as Chief Justice, while

[1] Devonshire's Diary, 1st Nov. 1760. [2] *Ibid.*, 5th Dec. 1760.

Temple openly exulted at this schism in the ranks of the enemy.[1] It was to the accompaniment of this hubbub that the expedition was blessed. But though Pitt appeared to have gained his way, actually he had failed. Consent had come too late, and the expedition had perforce to be postponed till the following spring. By then it had lost much of its original meaning. It had not been an isolated idea, but part of a wider scheme. What Pitt desperately wanted was a victory from Ferdinand which, he believed, might end the war. Throughout the first half of the year, he had tried to promote it by sending troops to Germany, but had been checkmated by the dispatch of an equal number of troops from France. He was forced to admit that on those lines we, as the smaller country, could not compete. A new method was necessary, and he proposed to find it by threatening the coasts of France with an expeditionary force which could, if taken seriously, immobilise many times its own numbers. The type of descent which had been tried in the early stages of the war had lost its efficacy, but the capture and retention of an island, such as Belleisle, at the entrance to Quiberon Bay, was another matter altogether. It was, Pitt knew, feasible; it would have an immediate and a lasting effect, proving useful as a pawn if peace negotiations began and serving as a strategic barrier between the French and Spanish fleets if Spain were rash enough to join in the war. From every point of view, the expedition against Belleisle was desirable. The mere threat imposed a check on French activities, but the threat alone was not enough. Ferdinand remained outnumbered and not only failed to win his victory, but was forced to abandon Hesse. The situation on the Continent was in part retrieved by Frederick's victory over the Austrians at Torgau (3rd November), but from Pitt's point of view the campaign ended sadly.

His demand that the militia should be commended in the King's Speech was, after much fuss, grudgingly allowed. A modest paragraph was drafted for the purpose and adopted without further comment in the excitement caused by the King's decision to insert a sentence of his own, boasting of his British birth and education. This created a furore in the political world —with Pitt because the information came so late that he had barely time 'to get the razures made in the Speech and to adapt

[1] Devonshire's Diary, 12th Nov. 1760.

the Address to the alteration';[1] and with the Whig magnates because they saw a sinister meaning in the word 'Briton,' which clearly betrayed the hand of Bute, dragging the King over the Tweed! To the world at large the King's bearing was much more important than his words, and the Duchess of Northumberland was content to record that 'the crown, like to fall, sat down upon his nose and misbecame him greatly. He faltered a little at first but afterwards spoke like an angel.'[2]

With the King's Speech safely over (18th November 1760), the last session of the old King's last Parliament had begun. Strictly speaking it should hardly have met; it was moribund and there must be a general election in six months; but at that late hour it was thought best to let the arrangements stand. More interesting was the question who was to 'manage' the elections for the new Parliament. Newcastle, having stayed in office to please the King, thought it was his prescriptive right; Bute, on the other hand, meant to have a finger in the pie. Parliament had been engaging his attention for some time. Only the year before he had had a passage of arms with Legge for refusing to stand down in favour of Bute's candidate in a by-election at Southampton,[3] and now he was determined that the King—that is to say Bute—should exercise the right of nomination to the various Government boroughs. Newcastle was thrown into a fluster, which was in no way soothed when Bute, consulting no one but Pitt, appointed several Tories to the Bedchamber. Indeed, the Tories were reviving: 'the gentlemen of the Cocoa Tree are come to Court';[4] and as Pitt openly supported this trend, arguing that no one 'could take umbrage at a few of the principal Tories being taken in the King's Service,' the Whigs looked still more askance at him and were the more anxious to control the elections.[5]

Ireland provided further grounds for distrust. Under Poyning's Law of 1495 no Parliament could be summoned in Ireland until the King had been informed of, and had given his consent to, the Bills which it was proposed to pass. To comply with this law, the Irish Privy Council was in the habit of sending over two or three Bills for approval, one of which was by custom a Bill of Supply. For some time, however, there had been a growing feeling in Ireland that money Bills should take their rise in the

[1] Pitt to Newcastle, 17th Nov. 1760. Add. MSS. 32,914.
[2] *Diaries of a Duchess*, p. 14.
[3] *History of the Late Minority*, p. 17.
[4] G. L. Scott to Mitchell, 24th Nov. 1760. Add. MSS. 6,858.
[5] Devonshire's Diary, 5th Dec. 1760.

Irish House of Commons and not in the unrepresentative Privy Council, a view to which the Privy Council itself subscribed. This feeling found expression on George III's accession. A couple of Bills were sent over, as an acknowledgment of the English Parliament's rights, but instead of a Supply Bill, the Privy Council sent a reasoned explanation why it had been omitted. The Whigs were shocked at what they could only see as a case of rank insubordination. Pitt alone took a more liberal view; he doubted if a Money Bill was legally necessary and was sure that on this occasion it was inexpedient, as it could only create 'a great flame' at a very critical moment. No one supported him; not even Temple; not even Bute; he was overborne and became 'much out of humour,' refusing to attend the next meeting of the Cabinet when the reply to Ireland was finally settled.[1] The Irish Privy Council yielded, and by way of punishment the Irish Chancellor of the Exchequer was dismissed—to Pitt's disgust.[2] Though the incident seemed at the time to be a storm in a teacup, it is of more than passing interest. Ireland was then regarded as a colony, subject to the will of Parliament, and this small clash was a forerunner of the greater and more disastrous quarrel with the American Colonies. The action of the Whigs and Pitt's instinctive reaction were both symptomatic. Had Pitt been able to win his point, had he even received any support, the history of both Ireland and America might well have been modified, if not fundamentally altered. It was not wise counsels, but the capacity to appreciate them, that the Whig magnates lacked.

(iii)

Whatever his treatment, whatever his health, Pitt knew that his shoulders must carry the war and his brains devise the peace. Both problems were pressing. So far as America was concerned, he had no doubts. The war there was flickering to its death, though a few islands still remained to be conquered. Of these, the most important was Martinique; Hopson's failure could not be regarded as the last word; if Martinique had escaped in 1759, it must certainly fall in 1761. For climatic reasons the attack could not be made till the end of September, and to Pitt's impatient mind the delay was infuriating. Searching round for

[1] Devonshire's Diary, 2nd and 3rd Dec. 1760.
[2] See Pitt to Bedford, 10 March 1761. Bedford. *Correspondence,* III, 6.

something to be done in the interim, he noted that there were a couple of islands—Dominica and Sta. Lucia—lying between Guadeloupe and Martinique. Could Amherst snap them up before the hurricane months arrived? 'If,' he wrote imploringly, 'some interesting attempt could be made, with success, during the earlier part of the year, the impression whereof could not but have a very beneficial influence in Europe, both at home and abroad,' why, then Dominica and Sta. Lucia would be treasures indeed. But—and here Pitt's strategy overcame his longings—the reduction of Martinique was the 'main expedition,' and if Sta. Lucia and Dominica could not be reduced before the hurricane months, they must be treated as sour grapes.[1]

Apart from America, there were two main theatres of war, India and Europe. In India, though the news could not arrive for many months, the power of France was tottering to its fall and was, in fact, to disappear on the 15th of January (1761) when Pondicherry capitulated. But in Europe, the military position was much less clear. France might be battered and bankrupt, but under the skilful guidance of Choiseul she was making a last and not unsuccessful effort. The full effects of his policy had yet to be revealed, but he had already succeeded in checking Ferdinand, and was busy collecting forces which he hoped would give him Hanover in the coming year. He was also casting sanguine eyes in the direction of Spain. While France thus appeared to be reviving, Frederick was undoubtedly declining. Each year saw him pushed farther back, and this very October (1760) he had, for a while, lost possession of Berlin itself. Pitt's countermove was to have been the Belleisle expedition, and its postponement left him at a loss. For a short while he once more played with the idea of diverting the expedition against Mauritius, and even summoned a Cabinet meeting to consider the matter, or, as he put it, to 'find if possible a proper and timely operation, without which the coming year will move very heavily under the load of twelve millions and not the most promising aspect of affairs in Germany.'[2] But he soon reverted to his original plan, feeling that the European position was not only the more important but the more uncertain.

The question of peace raised different problems. The desire which had first found voice in the Letter to the Two Great Men

[1] Pitt to Amherst, 7th Jan. 1761. Kimball, II, 384.
[2] Pitt to Newcastle, 29th December 1760. Add. MSS. 32,916.

became more vocal as 1760 drew to its close. There were many reasons: the year had not been prolific of victories as 1759 had been, and had given rise to a feeling of anti-climax; the fact that the King and Bute were known to regard the war with disfavour inflated the hopes of peace; people felt that the main objectives had been achieved; only the profitless struggle in Germany was left. This yearning for peace found its most effective expression in a pamphlet which appeared about this time, entitled *Considerations on the present German war,* written by one Israel Mauduit. Though it achieved a great vogue at the time and has since received high praise, it was no more than a clever piece of propagandist journalism. As Symmer sagaciously remarked, 'there is nothing new in the arguments the author employs, but they are handled in a manner not unlikely to raise a flame among the vulgar and abet the prejudices of many.'[1] The sting of the pamphlet lay in its ingenious distortion of Pitt's old arguments against a continental war, used without admitting or perhaps realising the altered circumstances. In the old days, Pitt had observed that Hanover invariably swallowed America, and that the real fighting invariably took place on the Continent where we could never hope to win advantages for the Colonies. He had therefore argued that we must leave Hanover to its fate and concentrate on America, where we could not only gain all we needed, but an overplus which would serve to redeem Hanover at the end of the war. Since coming to power he had put this theory into practice with brilliant success. But that was not all. Fortune had given him another card. Before he had come to power, France by involving herself in the plot to dismember Prussia had been given a new enemy and a fresh objective, and he had consequently found her preoccupied with something more than Hanover. Here was an opportunity not to be missed: France, thus entangled, might be kept out of Hanover, and so deprived of any claim upon our conquests at the end of the war. In this lay the possibility of a final solution of the ancient American problem. So Pitt thought, and so his ambitions grew. But Mauduit appreciated neither the negative nature of the German war nor the positive values in America. Indeed, he ignored the whole American continent, except for a passing statement that he was 'as thankful as any man for the taking of Montreal.' What Mauduit urged again and again was that Hanover should be defended 'in a practicable way; by attacking the

[1] Symmer to Mitchell, 28th November 1760. Add. MSS. 6,839.

French in their islands, by which only they can ever be formidable to Britain, and thereby securing an ample indemnification for that part of Germany for which alone we ought to have any concern.'[1] It was apparently nothing to Mauduit that Pitt had already conquered Canada, Nova Scotia, Newfoundland, the Ohio valley, Guadeloupe, Marie Galante, Senegal, Goree and large tracts of India. It was nothing to him, indeed he did not know, that Pitt was preparing to conquer Dominica, Sta. Lucia and Martinique, not to mention Belleisle, and was casting his eyes on Mauritius. If the conquest of islands could produce peace, Pitt had done all and more than all that could be expected. But Mauduit was looking at the problem with the myopic cleverness of the armchair critic, which plays with dichotomies and logic, and has no constructive solution for the difficulties of life. Peace cannot be obtained by a well-turned epigram. What Pitt was seeking was the argument of the mailed fist, which would coerce France into ending the war.

Whatever means he was adopting, Pitt was consciously pursuing the search for peace. His attitude came as a great relief to Newcastle, who had been infected with Mauduit's arguments and was oppressed at the thought that 'all these successes of the King of Prussia, and the keeping our ground on the frontiers of Hesse, is no more than that we are where we began this campaign, after having spent near seventeen millions; and so we may be another year; and indeed there is no end of it.'[2] It was truly a disturbing thought, especially for one brought up on the 'old system' which ignored the world outside Europe. It was a disturbing thought even for Pitt, who appreciated more fully than the others the difficulty of ending a war, and the immediate problems involved in the pursuit of peace. Among them was the need to find some method of approaching France. The Congress, set up at Augsburg the previous year, had lost itself in shallows, and the several tentative feelers thrown out by d'Affry, the Duc d'Aiguillon, l'Inconnue and others had come to nothing. Pitt, as the conqueror, had no intention of weakening his position by being the first to sue for peace. The bridge between the belligerents had still to be built.

Frederick's attitude too was important. Our treaty required us to make peace only in conjunction with him. It was on this point that the efforts of the previous year had been shipwrecked.

[1] Pp. 51-2. [2] Newcastle to J. Yorke, 2nd Dec. 1760. Add. MSS. 32,915.

France had wanted to deal with England alone, and Frederick had refused to be left out. Had he as yet any real inclination for peace? Did he still insist on being included in any negotiation we might have with France? A knowledge of his views was an essential preliminary and both Pitt and Newcastle 'talked strongly to the Prussian Ministers' about it.[1] As it happened, Frederick was only too anxious, and at the very moment when Newcastle was sounding the Prussian Ambassador, was confessing as much in a personal letter to Pitt. It arrived on the 1st of December (1760)—full of compliments which made Pitt blush, but full also of information which made him think. Frederick admitted sadly that the victories were not all on one side; he had suffered reverses too, and when he thought of his enemies' superiority in numbers, he despaired of ever gaining a decisive advantage, or humbling their pride. He therefore relied on 'Mr. Pitt's superior talents to find out *un tempérament* to put an honourable end to this war, equally ruinous to all parties.'[2] It was very flattering, and Pitt, a little shyly in view of the compliments, gave it to Bute to show to the King. Neither Bute nor the King seemed impressed. One may perhaps hazard the guess that Bute was both jealous and disappointed—jealous at this testimonial to a rival, and disappointed because he may have hoped to win for himself the merit of making peace. But with or without encouragement, Pitt could obviously not ignore this *cri de cœur,* nor, on the other hand, could he afford to be rushed. Frederick must be more explicit; he must say what terms he expected for himself, what sacrifices he would make to appease Russia and Maria Theresa, and in particular whether he had in mind a congress for a general pacification or simply negotiations with France alone; and in the latter event whether he expected to be included, or would consent to a separate peace between England and France.[3]

On the wider aspects Frederick answered readily enough; he had no hopes of a general pacification; his only idea was to divide his enemies, and in particular to detach France from her allies; as he himself had no credit at Versailles, he not only consented to a separate peace but was eager for it. If and when that peace was made, he would expect such assistance in his own

[1] Newcastle to Yorke, 28th Nov. 1760. Add. MSS. 32,915.
[2] Frederick to Pitt, 7th Nov. 1760. Chatham. *Correspondence,* II, 77.
[3] Newcastle to Hardwicke, 3rd Dec. 1760. Add. MSS. 32,915.

war as the King might think reasonable. The reply delighted Newcastle, who wanted to 'begin without waiting for anything else,' a view in which he was supported by Hardwicke. But Pitt held back; he wanted to know exactly what assistance Frederick would need, and Frederick was extremely unwilling to answer. Neither Hardwicke nor Newcastle could understand Pitt's reluctance, which they attributed to pique of one sort or another. Later historians have assumed that he was not in earnest pending the results of his expedition. No doubt this latter reason had its weight, but surely Pitt had others as well. If, after making peace with France, England had still to support Frederick, she would no longer be fighting for any interest of her own; in effect, she would be declaring a fresh war on fresh enemies without any clear objective. It was very necessary to know how far England would be implicated. The secret of Pitt's military success had been meticulous preparation in advance, and the same thoroughness could and should be applied to diplomacy. Moreover, there was still the question of prestige, depending upon who should make the first advance. Whatever his reasons, Pitt's reluctance was justified in the event. France cracked first. She made a tentative approach in February (1761) when a certain La Borde wrote to Sir Joshua Vanneck, a City financier, offering on Choiseul's behalf to send over an agent to discuss peace. Vanneck passed the letter to Newcastle, who decided 'to communicate it tomorrow morning, first to Lord Bute, afterwards to the King, then to Lord Holdernesse, and then *at noon* to Mr. Pitt.'[1] So low in the list had Pitt fallen. What happened to that letter history does not relate, but the movement, once begun, progressed. At the end of March Prince Galitzin, the Russian Ambassador, presented a formal declaration from all the enemy powers proposing a new Congress at Augsburg, and at the same time a letter from Choiseul to Pitt suggesting immediate negotiations for a separate peace between France and England.

[1] Newcastle to Hardwicke, 22nd Feb. 1761. Add. MSS. 32,919.

29

THE WILES OF BUTE

Prince Galitzin handed the peace proposals and Choiseul's letter to Pitt. It seemed the most obvious course in the world. Who was there in England to be compared with the great Minister? No sooner had he done so than the stocks began to rise and the country at large to have high hopes. But one man was annoyed. Bute, who six days earlier had become Secretary of State for the Northern Department, sent a message to Pitt to say that while he exonerated Pitt from blame, 'he resented in the highest manner Prince Galetzin's behaviour, who a foreign Minister in his [Bute's] department carried his despatches to the other Secretary [Pitt], and that he [Bute] would not suffer the least slight or diminution of his employment whilst he held it, no, not for two minutes.'[1] Pitt, who had supped on slights all his parliamentary life without allowing them to warp his sense of justice, agreed that Bute was in the right, and Prince Galitzin offered a thousand apologies.

The incident was a straw, but it throws into startling relief the profound change in Pitt's position from what it had been only six months earlier. Then, though harassed by Newcastle and the Whigs, he had been admittedly master of all England. Now, not even his best friend could deny the existence of a serious and widespread opposition. How deep the change had gone, not only in high places but in low, can be seen by contrasting two extracts from a royal chaplain's letters to a country parson. In 1757, Edmund Pyle had written to his old friend, Kerrich: 'The new Minister, Mr. Pitt, out-did his usual outdoings in the House of Commons last week . . . and spake so for the subsidy of £200,000 for the King of Prussia, that it was carried Nem. Con.' Now, four years later—years full of victory, of growing trade, of rising prosperity—the same unthankful chaplain wrote to the same country parson: 'You seem to mean Mr. Pitt by the "unus

[1] *Life and Letters of Lady Sarah Lennox*, p. 42.

homo qui nobis restituit rem." And to rejoice in the boasted extinction of parties. This has always been the Tory method of getting into influence. . . . Mr. Pitt knows—nay confesses—that were the Duke of Newcastle to withdraw, he could not carry on the public affairs a fortnight;—for he is no more able to secure a majority in the House of Commons, than you are able to do it. What therefore is all this rout made about Mr. Pitt for? Why, in good truth, for talking more against German attachments, than ever man did, till he got into the Ministry; and then going greater lengths in expense of British money, for the preservation of German Dominions, than ever any Minister did, or dare, I wont say advise (tho' that is the right word) but consent to. This is Mr. Pitt.'[1] Pyle's outburst was not due simply to hatred of war but to bitterness against Pitt. 'I can see,' Scott, a Commissioner of Excise, confided to Mitchell, 'a sympathy between those who dislike Mr. Pitt and those who talk against the Prussian system.'[2] He was probably right, for officials see most of the game. Pitt's stock was falling; 'his popularity,' as Bute told Newcastle, 'was sunk.'[3] What had caused the change? It is a sorry story of intrigue, of disloyalty, of innuendoes and plain downright lies, starting from the first moment of the new reign.

A few days before his accession, George III had hoped that the nation would see that 'her popular man is a true snake in the grass,' and a few days after, that they would have nothing to do with 'the man who from his own ambition, pride and impracticability, means to disturb my quiet and (what I feel much stronger) the repose of my subjects.'[4] This peculiar view of Pitt had been instilled into this peculiar young man by Bute. He had done it deliberately and without visualising the probable consequences. Now, those consequences were upon him, and he had at once to stoke up, and to damp down, the fires he had lighted. Pitt was necessary for the time being, and Bute, like Newcastle, like Hardwicke, like Lady Yarmouth, decided that 'they must keep him to make the peace, and then they hoped to be in a situation to get rid of him.'[5] Until the day of deliverance, Bute intended to play Pitt and Newcastle off against each other, extracting in the meantime as much as possible out of them. Bute had many ambitions—an English peerage, for instance—which they could

[1] *Memoirs of a Royal Chaplain*, pp. 287 and 334.
[2] Scott to Mitchell, 24th Nov. 1760. Add. MSS. 6,858.
[3] Devonshire's Diary, 10th March 1761.
[4] Sedgwick, pp. 47 and 50.
[5] Devonshire's Diary, 8th December 1760.

serve. He showed a surprising skill in this species of trickery in which the interests of the country played no part. It would, however, be wrong to suppose that Bute was working solely for his own hand; far from it; he had many aims which he regarded as patriotic, and the temptation to feather his own nest vanished in January (1761) when his wife inherited a vast fortune on the death of her father.

Whatever his motives—and of course they were mixed—his intrigues started at once, but at the outset may have been as much the result of ignorance as intention. He allowed the King to neglect his Ministers through lack of knowledge, and by giving audiences almost at haphazard to create the atmosphere in which intrigue most readily flourishes. If it was deliberate it was clever, but more probably it was just thoughtlessness. Bute was, in modern parlance, a doctrinaire, who had been suddenly called on to give effect to his ideologies. He meant well, he was devotedly loyal to the King, he was full of high-falutin ideas, but he was uncertain of himself and mistook intrigue for statesmanship. His main object was to turn George III into a benevolent despot, or, in the jargon of his own days, to increase the royal prerogative; and forgetting that George was no longer a child, tended to regard himself, and indeed was so regarded by George, as the King's trustee; it was his duty to run the country in the best interests of the King, and, broadly speaking, the best interests of the King were that the old Ministers should give place to Bute, who alone understood the King's inchoate ideals.

It would be unprofitable to trace in detail the course of Bute's manœuvres. His method was a nicely adjusted distribution of smiles and frowns which kept everyone guessing and was a wonderful begetter of jealousies. And to press the matter home, he encouraged Count Viry to circulate stories, coloured to the right tint, to Newcastle, Pitt, Devonshire and the like—with the sole object of widening breaches or closing them up, as circumstances demanded. What he wished principally to do was to depress Pitt's reputation without actually driving him from office. He forwarded this object in a variety of ways—by tittle-tattle in the coffee houses,[1] by pamphlets such as Mauduit's, who was promptly rewarded with a place;[2] by innuendoes, and especially by isolating Pitt from his friends. He offered Temple the post of

[1] Dodington, p. 427. [2] Walpole. *Geo. III*, I, 25.

Lord Lieutenant of Ireland and pressed him—unsuccessfully—to accept it,[1] knowing that Temple was Pitt's main support and that his absence from the Council would leave Pitt practically alone. He bribed James Grenville with the post of Cofferer; he fostered George Grenville's budding antipathy to Pitt; and in exchange for a seat at the Treasury, persuaded Elliot to renounce Pitt's friendship. In short, he tried to get rid of, or win over, Pitt's closest friends, and there can be no doubt that his efforts were both widely and quickly successful.

The wiser part of the world shrewdly suspected his aims, and without difficulty saw the Ministers' obvious riposte. 'It would seem,' said Symmer, 'as if His Majesty did not intend to put the administration into the hands of any one Minister, but by holding the balance between two be more master of his measures than some of his predecessors have been. How far so difficult an undertaking may become successful may be a matter of doubt; especially as the person he is supposed to consult with in intimate confidence cannot but become the object of jealousy with those who are put at the head of the administration, and who therefore may be induced to make up what misunderstandings may be among themselves to get the better of him.'[2] Unfortunately the misunderstandings were too deeply seated. For Pitt, the coalition meant rising above sectional interests; it meant that none were for a party and all were for the state; it suited him well enough, since he was by conviction a Tory in foreign, and a Whig in home, affairs. But, for Newcastle, the coalition meant simply enduring Pitt for the sake of the war, and solely for its duration. There was no making up this misunderstanding. It followed that while at the outset the old Ministers were disposed to close their ranks, their differing motives made it easy for Bute to keep them apart. Newcastle and the Whigs objected to Bute mainly on personal or party grounds, and whenever he showed a disposition to be friendly, were quite willing to be wooed. Pitt's objection was more fundamental. In his eyes Bute's position was unconstitutional; he was a Favourite, and whilst in the past there had been Favourites in plenty, 'the nation would never suffer them to be both favourites and ministers.'[3] Bute had chosen to be a courtier, which for ever barred him from administration, and being not

[1] Devonshire's Diary, 6th Feb. 1761.
[2] Symmer to Mitchell, 28th November 1760. Add. MSS. 6,839.
[3] Devonshire's Diary, 21st Jan. 1761.

only a Favourite but outside Parliament, it was wholly improper that he should govern the country through his influence over a young and inexperienced King, and without bearing the least shred of responsibility. When such was Pitt's belief, his opposition must be implacable; he might, in practice, have to endure Bute's interference, but in principle he could never approve. Nor at any point did he show signs of weakening. At a very early stage he had 'warm words' with Bute, attacking him 'very roughly' for his habit of transacting affairs without informing the Minister, and as he was to all appearances extremely angry, Bute quailed before him.[1] But no improvement followed, and so two months later, Pitt was again found declaring 'in very high and strong terms that there was no business done, no system, and though he had great patience, yet he was tired and it could not last in this way.'[2] Had he but known, Bute did not intend it to last in that way; he had his own schemes, the success of which depended upon the submission not of Pitt, but of his colleagues, and those colleagues were succumbing.

At first sight, any one of the Whigs might have proved the weak link in the chain. They were not an impressive crew. Hardwicke was perhaps the best; he was an eminent judge, had considerable influence—especially with Newcastle—and was not easy to hoodwink, but he was growing old and was disinclined any longer to take an active interest in politics. Granville had what are called parts, but drank too much and was now regarded with curiosity rather than admiration. Mansfield was sapient, but being timid cut less ice than he should. Newcastle was obstinate and strongly fortified against argument, but, as Devonshire told Bute, 'was easily to be managed and at any time set right by a kind word added to good usage.'[3] Holdernesse was a turncoat whom everyone distrusted; Legge was out of favour and George Grenville ignored as a precisian. Amidst this welter of mediocrity, Bute chose Devonshire as his instrument, probably for much the same reason that George II had chosen him to be Pitt's First Lord. Devonshire was just forty; he was a man of high rank and great wealth, honest, upright, conscientious, modest and retiring. He inspired confidence as a worthy man, but did not shine as a statesman. In politics his main asset was what might be described as short-sighted commonsense, which

[1] Devonshire's Diary, 17th Nov. 1760. [2] *Ibid.*, 29th Jan. 1761.
[3] *Ibid.*, 5th Nov. 1760.

enabled him to see very clearly indeed to the end of his nose. Had he been able to see farther, he might have behaved differently, for he meant well. On George II's death he summed Bute up with his usual good sense; recognising his ambitions, his unfitness for office, and the tremendous pull which the King's favour gave him. The idea of Bute's supremacy frightened him, and he was as strong as anyone that the continuance of the Newcastle-Pitt coalition was 'absolutely necessary for the preservation of this country, that if the present system was broke, this country would again fall into confusion and in the present crisis would be in danger of being ruined.' On the other hand, if Pitt and Newcastle 'were strongly united, they might easily get the better of a Favourite.'[1] Feeling so acutely on the point, he made it his business to preach union to them on every possible occasion, and took what steps he could to bring them together and explain away misunderstandings.

Bute noticed his activities and very soon made a determined and skilful effort to win him over. He began indirectly, through Viry, who mentioned, as a mutual friend, how grieved Bute was to think that though he had paid Devonshire great civilities and done him real service with the King, Devonshire 'was the only one of the great people that had not made him professions or said something personally obliging to him.'[2] It was clever flattery, both in its suggestion of hurt feelings and its hint of royal favour. Devonshire was so far mollified that, two days later, when telling Pitt how necessary it was for him and Newcastle to act in concert, he added 'and if they could, to take Lord Bute along with them.'[3] After this first beginning progress was rapid. In November he advised Bute 'to hold the balance even' between Pitt and Newcastle; in December he urged him to unite with Newcastle but 'in such a manner as should not give umbrage to Mr. Pitt,' and in January (1761) he was listening complacently to the first open suggestion of Pitt's possible dismissal.[4] So far as Devonshire was concerned, the Newcastle-Pitt coalition had given place to a Newcastle-Bute coalition, which would be equally effective in preventing this country from falling into confusion, and on the whole much more comfortable for all concerned—except perhaps Pitt. But Devonshire had never really cared for Pitt, and indeed had once 'resolved never to have a private conversation with

[1] Diary, 28th October 1760. [2] *Ibid.*, 3rd Nov. 1760.
[3] *Ibid.*, 5th Nov. 1760. [4] *Ibid.*, 5th Nov., 9th Dec. 1760 and 23rd Jan. 1761.

him.'[1] If the country were not ruined, did Pitt matter so much?

By this time Devonshire was malleable enough for Bute to take his next step. Again Viry was the channel. He told Devonshire 'in great confidence that the King was displeased with Lord Holdernesse and had pressed Bute to be Secretary of State in his room'; Bute had so far declined. Viry himself imagined that Bute and Pitt might act very well together and jointly make peace, but he would be interested to learn Devonshire's opinion. Brought face to face with this inevitable outcome of all the political gerrymanderings, Devonshire was, or professed to be, antagonistic. No one, he said, ought to advise such a step; it was very dangerous, especially when Pitt's views were not known.[2] His irrepressible commonsense told him that Viry's story was at best only half the truth; Bute obviously meant to absorb them all. None the less, that very evening he was weak enough to urge Newcastle and Hardwicke to adopt an attitude of benevolent neutrality. As the Whig magnates all hoped they were stealing a march on Pitt, his advice was taken.

But clearly Pitt's views had to be canvassed. Someone must bell the cat and nobody fancied the job. There followed a comic interlude—a sort of hesitation grand-chain. Viry suggested Devonshire; Devonshire suggested Bute; Bute suggested Newcastle; there was no end to the suggestions—George Grenville, Viry, the Duke of Bedford. All held back, and the universal reluctance was heightened when Newcastle mentioned that Pitt had harangued him for nearly an hour in 'a very long, friendly and most extraordinary conversation' on 'the impossibility of a Favourite, or a certain particular person to be Minister.'[3] No one knew whether the harangue was accidental or designed, but it was uncommonly apposite and damped their ardour. When all declined the task, Bute became impatient. He could, of course, achieve greatness with a high hand, but prudence told him that it would be best to have greatness thrust upon him. So Viry returned to Devonshire, and casually let fall that Bute was thinking of withdrawing from business, and hinted that perhaps 'the King might entirely give up Germany and the Continent and then make a Ministry of his own, independent of the present Ministers.' Once more Devonshire's uncomfortable commonsense forced him to blurt out that if the King had any such intention, it was

[1] Diary, 14th Nov. 1759. [2] *Ibid.* 12th Jan. 1761.
[3] Newcastle to Hardwicke, 20 Jan. 1761. Add. MSS. 32,917.

'a very idle one';[1] but the threat was not lost on him. Viry meanwhile took advantage of one of Pitt's outbursts to suggest to him that things might go better if Bute could be induced to take a ministerial office. This seemed to crystallise the vague rumours which had been flying round, and Pitt's reaction was immediate and unmistakable: 'Pitt was startled and seemed displeased but made no reply, grew cool and then said, for his part he should be glad to retire from business himself. If the King would place him in some honourable post in the Cabinet, he should like it, or, if not, he could retire and live in the country.'[2]

Pitt's views were now known, and it is significant that the knowledge made no difference. However frightened the Whig magnates might be, they had in fact, even if unconsciously, made up their minds; their only thought was how to shun responsibility and avoid Pitt's wrath. As for Bute, he had all along believed, as George II had believed, that Pitt would never consent to leave his work half finished; for the sake of the work he would endure Bute. If his feelings became too much for him he might retire—perhaps in dudgeon, but he would go without a fuss. His reaction to Viry's hint confirmed Bute in his belief; Pitt could be written off. But there still remained public opinion. Pitt had a large following in the country, and there had been signs of restiveness—placards stuck up at the Royal Exchange and in Westminster Hall with the words 'No Petticoat Government; No Scotch Favourite,' and insulting remarks hurled in public at Bute, at the Dowager Princess, and even at the King.[3] Bute must not show himself too eager; he must not thrust himself forward. On the contrary he must hang back and pretend reluctance. What he had in mind was, as Viry explained to Devonshire, to be 'made Secretary of State at the instigation of you great people.'[4] How were the great people to be moved? It meant a good deal of shameless lying, but the method was simple. Bute began making veiled threats that unless Newcastle recommended Bute's promotion to the King, his patronage would be curtailed and he would not be allowed to have any say in the 'management' of the coming elections. Bute also visited Temple and George Grenville in an ostentatiously private fashion, to enable Viry to hint that, unless the Whigs moved

[1] Diary, 27th Jan. 1761.
[2] *Ibid*, 29th Jan. 1761.
[3] Walpole. *Geo. III*, I, 13.
[4] Diary, 31st Jan. 1761.

swiftly, Pitt and Temple would get in first and secure Bute for themselves. Devonshire was so much impressed by these and similar innuendoes that he capitulated, horse, foot and artillery. He told Viry, shamefacedly and at great length, that as Bute had been extremely civil to him, he would be 'very ready to do him personally any service'; he had 'never suffered private friendships or connections to stand in the way of the good of the whole,' and as—so one must infer—he thought it obviously to the good of the whole to put an inexperienced Favourite over Pitt's head, he would forward Bute's machinations to the utmost of his power.[1] It was a sorry exhibition, but sincere so far as it went. Having capitulated, Devonshire did his best to prod Newcastle into action.

Newcastle had so far declined to be made a catspaw.[2] Torn as he was with doubts and suspicions, at bottom he had never wavered in his conviction that Pitt was necessary for the war; nor did he doubt that Bute intended to be 'sole Minister.' But by now he had become a pathetic figure—old, uncertain, lost, fit only to be snubbed by Bute or cajoled by Devonshire. At last on the 6th of March (1761) he gave way, and as shamefacedly as Devonshire, recommended the King to promote Bute. He did it unwillingly and even unhappily, trying to justify it to himself by emphasising the handicap of Pitt's ill-health. At the end, something which may have been fear, remorse or a belated feeling of loyalty, compelled him to add that Pitt's 'credit and influence were of great service to his majesty and therefore nothing ought to be done that would give him offence'—an interesting peep into his mind, but surely a *non sequitur* to his request.[3]

What was to prove a tragedy for the Whig magnates was a comedy for Bute and the King. They played their parts to perfection. The King thanked Newcastle for his suggestion and promised to use his influence with Bute. Bute declared solemnly that he was taking the office to which he had the most repugnance, and then condescendingly sketched his programme; he would 'leave Mr. Pitt master of foreign affairs except where his Grace [Newcastle], the Duke of Devonshire and Lord Hardwicke shall think he goes too far, and in regard to peace he will act with these

[1] Diary, 31st Jan. 1761.

[2] Cf. 'Viry admits that the proposal cannot come from me.' Newcastle to Hardwicke, 7th Feb. 1761. Add. MSS. 32,918.

[3] Diary, 6th March 1761.

three.'[1] In short, Bute would keep Pitt in his place. He must have been persuasive for Devonshire noted in his Diary 'The Duke of Newcastle convinced that Lord Bute means to act confidentially with him.'[2]

To the end, everyone fought shy of telling Pitt personally—so frightened, perhaps so ashamed, were they all. In craven fashion, they arranged that the King should announce the appointment to the assembled Ministers; but that plan failed owing to Pitt's absence through gout. Finally, Bute had to go down to Hayes and break the news himself. The King, he said, had forced him to accept office. To which Pitt answered dryly, 'The thing is done, and I have all duty and submission to the King.' He was not surprised though he could hardly be enthusiastic. What was important was to define his own position. He would not act through Bute; he must have free access to the King and the right to make recommendations to him. Bute gave the most ample assent, adding with what must have been veiled irony, that 'if Pitt chose that method and thought it the most likely to succeed, to be sure he was in the right.' So the matter was settled, and Pitt with some impatience turned from this lost battle to his proper business of war and peace.[3] But the deceit and chicanery employed did not make for happy relations, nor did Bute's touchy insistence on his rights in the matter of Prince Galitzin.

[1] Devonshire's Diary, 13th March 1761. [2] *Ibid.*, 10th March 1761.
[3] Newcastle to Hardwicke, 13th March 1761. Add. MSS. 32,920.

30

IS IT PEACE?

(i)

It was perhaps inevitable, and certainly unfortunate, that Pitt and Newcastle should have approached the interwoven problems of peace and war from diametrically opposite directions. To Pitt it seemed obvious that there must be no slackening of effort; on the contrary, it was precisely when an opponent began to stagger that blows should be redoubled. Pitt's views sprang naturally out of his achievements and were backed by his self-confidence; but they roused no echo in his colleagues. So long as peace had been at a distance, Newcastle had been content to sigh for it, but now that it was rising over the horizon, his eagerness knew no bounds. It must be grasped at once and on almost any terms. Delay meant the possibility, which steadily mounted in his mind through probability to certainty, that France would crush Ferdinand and overrun Hanover, and we should then be obliged to sacrifice all our conquests to redeem it. He described this possibility as an 'argument so strong that I defy anybody to answer it.'[1] In this conviction he was bound to oppose fresh adventures; our proper course was to lie quiet, so that France should not be discouraged in her first shy advances. 'What I most fear,' he confessed, 'are proposals for some other expeditions. I think that would be extremely wrong in every respect.'[2] It was, no doubt, an arguable position, it may even have been right in itself. What made it impossible was the fact that Pitt was in charge and no one else was as yet prepared to take over. For Newcastle to insist on his view was merely to hobble Pitt, without even gaining his end; but he had the support of all his Whig colleagues, while Pitt could rely on no one but Temple. Much, consequently, depended on Bute, whose attitude, though

[1] Newcastle to Devonshire, 28th June 1761. Add. MSS. 32,924.
[2] Newcastle to Hardwicke, 14th June 1761. Add. MSS. 32,924.

it seemed to incline towards Pitt, was unknown. In any event Pitt could not count on him and did not welcome his support—amongst other reasons because he had no opinion of Bute's abilities.

The nervous strain upon him was thus greater than ever, as he pushed forward with his plans for the new campaign. So far as America was concerned he was given a fairly free hand. No one pretended to know what was happening in that distant part of the world, and France was thought to be as indifferent about it as the Whigs. Newcastle expressed a mild hope that some of the troops might be brought back, but his hope was small and easily forgotten. Pitt was left to write to Amherst as he wished, and sent his new orders in January, with an urgent reminder in March.[1]

Over the Belleisle expedition there was more difficulty. It was nearer at hand and so more obvious; the troops, marching down to the coast, passed by Claremont, Newcastle's stately home, and kept him twitteringly mindful of their destination. Nor were fears the only obstacle. The Whig magnates were shocked at the idea of violating French soil; Bedford even babbled of doing as we would be done by, and remembering that Belleisle was to France what the Isle of Wight was to England.[2] But on this occasion Bute came down on Pitt's side—perhaps as a gesture in return for Pitt's acquiescence in his promotion. The expedition was approved; Hodgson and Keppel were appointed the military and naval commanders, and on the 25th of March, the day on which Bute received the Seals, Pitt sent them their instructions. They sailed four days later, reached Belleisle on the 7th of April and on the 8th made an unsuccessful attempt to land. Thereafter the course of events was singularly like that at Quebec. Hodgson and Keppel reconnoitred the island from end to end, only to come to the conclusion that 'it is quite impracticable to make good a landing.'[3] But before their report could reach home, they had, like Wolfe, discovered a point which was poorly guarded because it was supposed to be inaccessible, and there, on the 22nd of April, made good their footing. Pitt poured in reinforcements, and on the 8th of June the French finally capitulated. As soon as victory became reasonably certain, Pitt ordered Keppel to reconnoitre the western ports of France, having it in mind to

[1] Kimball, II, 407. [2] Bedford. *Correspondence,* III, 18.
[3] *Life of Keppel,* I, 310.

employ the troops on 'further operations on the coast of France.'[1] But no opportunity arose.

In Germany, Pitt was content to hold his own, and fortune was on his side. Choiseul launched what should have been overwhelming forces against Ferdinand, with the object of occupying Hanover before the peace negotiations began. He gained some temporary successes. But the two French generals—Soubise and Broglie—failed to work in harmony. While Soubise and his men were sitting back twiddling their thumbs, Broglie was soundly beaten at Vellinghausen on the 16th of July. The campaign ended, as the others had done, without decision.

So much for the war. In waging it, Pitt was left to his own devices because none of the others knew how to fight. In negotiating peace he was isolated, except for Temple's dubious help, because all the others knew how to surrender. It is incredible how fierce they were against Pitt, how faltering towards France. But this is anticipating.

In the matter of peace, Choiseul and Pitt confronted one another, nominally on level terms; but as it happened all the advantage of position was to lie with Choiseul. The two had much in common; they were both men of strong character, both able statesmen, both true patriots; but on the moral plane they were widely separated. Choiseul was moved by the Gallic sense of honour; he could flame into wrath at any affront to himself or his country; but when honour was not involved, he approached his problems unhampered by principles. At will, he could be serious; he could be gay and light-hearted; he could dissemble and play a part; and he was consequently dangerous and hard to interpret. Pitt, too, had a highly developed sense of honour, but it was controlled by a Christian outlook. The utmost extent of his dissembling was to hold his tongue. In a world much given to chicane, his constant and consistent truthfulness was utterly bewildering, so that often in the diligent search for a hidden meaning that was not there, the true and obvious meaning became mysterious. His strength had none of Choiseul's suppleness. Bowed down, as he was, by incessant pain, it would have been difficult for him in any case to switch at will from grave to gay. It was impossible for him to play more than one part, and so far as peace was concerned it was the part imposed on him by nature and surroundings alike, the part of a lonely Athanasius,

[1] Pitt to Hodgson, 18th June 1761. Add. MSS. 36,995.

upheld by a consciousness of moral right. He could not believe that the cornucopia crammed with victories was to be tossed aside; Providence had been too clearly with us, and it was our duty as well as our right to take and be thankful for the blessings so bountifully bestowed. Buoyed up by this belief, he showed himself from the first more strong, more forceful, perhaps more grasping than his colleagues, certainly more unbending and more determined. His attitude frightened smaller men, who dropped away from him, partly out of fear, and partly, to do them justice, out of a leaning towards moderation.

The coming cleavage cast its shadow in front, even before the arrival of Choiseul's letter. In the middle of March, Hardwicke visited Pitt to discuss the draft for the King's Speech at the end of the session. Pitt was 'in his easy chair in his fore room, full of complaints of his health and his very bad sleepless night; but on the whole in better spirits and better humour' than Hardwicke had expected. Neither ill-health nor pain clouded Pitt's intellect; he at once put his finger on the point where the split was likely to come. Hardwicke had written of the 'public-spirited concern for the honour of the nation and the maintenance of its undoubted rights and possessions.' That, said Pitt, was not enough; true, it had been the original cause of the war, but it could no longer be regarded as 'the total of our present object, after so great a success.' Some reference must be made to our conquests, some hint of acquisitions to be secured at the peace. Hardwicke gave way reluctantly, not because he was convinced but because he believed that without some such words Pitt would 'disclaim the Speech.'[1]

Parliament was dissolved on the 19th of March, and at the end of the month Choiseul's letter arrived. In it, Choiseul suggested that the two countries should be regarded as rightful owners of any conquests made on each other of which they might be in possession on the 1st of May in Europe, the 1st of July in the West Indies and Africa and the 1st of September in the East Indies; and on that basis of '*uti possidetis*' should negotiate such exchanges or compensation as they might think fit; if the dates or 'epochs' were not considered suitable, others could be discussed. The 'epochs' did not suit Pitt who had three expeditions on hand—against Pondicherry, against Dominica and against Belleisle. Any or all of them might fall to his arms

[1] Hardwicke to Newcastle, 17th March 1761. Add. MSS. 32,920.

in the near future, and he saw no reason why they should be wasted. There were other questions that arose in his acute mind. What in particular did Choiseul mean by the conquests made on each other? Did he include the conquests made by France in Germany on the King as Elector and on the King's allies? Or did he mean only the conquests made on England? The letter was loosely worded and obscure—a great sin in Pitt's eyes—but none the less to be accepted for what it was worth, and if possible developed into something more. He replied on the 8th of April, suggesting that Choiseul should send a representative to London. Hardwicke was surprised and pleased; Pitt's letter, he said, 'goes further and shows more disposition to close; and the offer to receive a person authorised from France to negotiate *here*, is rather more full than I expected.'[1] The fact is that Hardwicke had not penetrated Pitt's mind. Pitt was not a hard-faced conqueror riding roughshod over his victims. There were limits to his wishes, and he had in fact been hankering after peace for some time, but had felt that the appropriate moment had not yet come. Probably, if Frederick had not made his appeal and Choiseul had not written, Pitt would have preferred to wait till the end of the campaign—there were still loose ends to be tied—but undoubtedly his mind was inclining towards peace and undoubtedly that inclination had been influenced by the appeals. It was also influenced by another factor which was to play an increasingly powerful part. Pitt had meant intensely all that he had said about Bute; he disapproved his presence in the Council, he disapproved still more his promotion as Secretary; he disapproved most of all the intrigue which had led to that promotion. 'He talked,' Newcastle noted in one of his numerous memoranda, 'upon the new arrangement of my Lord Bute as done in concert with me, the Duke of Devonshire, Lord Hardwicke, and the Duke of Bedford, and without his knowledge. That if he had been previously consulted, he should have given my Lord Bute the same advice he had done before—to remain where he was.' There can be little doubt that Bute's elevation gave an added content to Pitt's reiterated wish to withdraw, and it is no mere coincidence that Newcastle's memorandum continues: 'At last he concluded that if he differed in opinion with the rest of the King's servants, either on these terms of

[1] Hardwicke to Newcastle, 6th April 1761. Add. MSS. 32,921.

peace or otherwise, he desired to retire.'[1] He foresaw retirement at no long distance, and was consequently the more ready to negotiate peace; for he knew that a peace negotiated by him was likely to be more favourable for England than one negotiated by Newcastle,[2] and he may well have doubted if a war conducted by Newcastle could be anything but a disaster.

Choiseul accepted Pitt's suggestion, and asked in his turn that an English representative should be sent to Paris. The necessary preliminaries proceeded smoothly and at the end of May, Bussy arrived in London and Stanley in Paris as the duly accredited representatives of France and England respectively.

As the negotiations failed, the various proposals and counter-proposals may be ignored; they are of little interest. In great matters, such as peace and war, details rarely, if ever, cause a breakdown; they are the excuse, not the reason. Far more interesting are the objectives at which the two sides aimed, and the causes which led to the failure.

Pitt had four main objectives. First and foremost, the colonists in America must be given security; that had been the original purpose of the war. The ties of kinship were involved, which corresponded, on the public stage, to love and loyalty in the bosom of the family. No one ever took greater delight in the family circle than Pitt, and it was no effort, it was natural, to extend that feeling to the wider circle of the Empire. Secondly, Hanover, Hesse, Brunswick and Prussia must be lifted out of the morass into which they had fallen; they were our allies, and to help them was a debt of honour. Thirdly, there must be a settlement in India satisfactory to the East India Company; this was a matter of trade, and trade was still our 'last entrenchment.' Finally, England, as the victor, should receive her prize—the American fisheries and the African trade; their acquisition would pay England for the war, and their loss to France as a nursery for the French marine would guarantee the peace.[3] How these objectives were to be reached was a point of cardinal importance which Pitt was anxious to discuss at the earliest moment. He sounded Newcastle, only to find him timorous, yielding and

[1] Memo. 10th April 1761. Add. MSS. 32,921.

[2] 'It would be seen, he believed, that he should be against signing a treaty with respect to our conquests which I should be ready to sign.' Newcastle to Hardwicke, 14th May 1761. Add. MSS. 32,923.

[3] Cf. Bute's remark to Devonshire: 'we ought, after our successes, to reap some advantage . . . if we had not the fishery, we really got nothing.' Devonshire's Diary, 14th Aug. 1761.

obsessed by fears of what 'the other powers of Europe, and particularly Spain,' might think.[1] His attitude irritated Pitt, and the irritation was increased by the fact that under the first impact of Choiseul's attack, the position in Germany was deteriorating. Ferdinand ascribed his setback to the failure of the commissariat, which Pitt in his exasperation supposed must be due to 'the want of care, economy and attention in the Treasury,'[2] and should be enquired into. Newcastle, mightily flustered and quailing before Pitt personally, restored his self-esteem by scuttling to the King and telling him that he 'defied all that Mr. Pitt could do,' and then informing Hardwicke that though he expected the worst from Pitt and 'his bloodhounds' still 'Mr. Pitt shall neither frighten me, nor change me.'[3] Newcastle's antics are better than a play in retrospect, but at the time helped to create that atmosphere of suspicion and distrust to which ultimately the failure of the negotiations was due. Nor, of course, can Pitt escape all blame; he was moody and extravagant, violent and overbearing; but at least it can be said in mitigation that he was in almost constant pain, and that he was greatly tried.

The suspicion and distrust grew as the time approached for the negotiations to begin. Never was so unhappy a company. Pitt was clear on the procedure that should be adopted; he should be empowered to tell Bussy the definite terms which we were prepared to offer and from which we would not depart, and for that purpose we should make up our minds at once, before Bussy arrived; at the same time we should inform Stanley so that he could avoid mistakes in Paris.[4] Except for Temple, not one of the magnates agreed. Their plan, if it can be called a plan, was that the negotiations should take place in London, and in order to ensure that desirable end, nothing should be discussed, let alone settled, until Bussy had come and had explained the views of France. For the same end Stanley's instructions should be of the briefest 'in order that as little material as possible might be put into his hands.'[5] In the upshot Stanley's instructions amounted to no more than permission to accept Choiseul's general proposition of negotiating on the basis of '*uti possidetis*,' with the 'epochs' still to be fixed, and to intimate

[1] Memo. 10th April 1761. Add. MSS. 32,921.
[2] Memo. 18th April 1761. Add. MSS. 32,922.
[3] Newcastle to Hardwicke, 17th April 1761. Add. MSS. 32,922.
[4] See Devonshire's Diary, 22nd April 1761.
[5] Hardwicke to Newcastle, 16th May 1761. Add. MSS. 32,923.

that we expected the negotiations to lead to peace between England and France irrespective of the general Congress at Augsburg. For the rest, he was to listen to Choiseul's proposals and transmit them to England.

To Pitt it seemed fantastic to leave the initiative to France and to allow the defeated country to propose the terms of peace. It was foolish to send Stanley to France in blinkers; what could he do but fumble when he had no knowledge of his Government's views or intentions? It was fatuous to expect Pitt himself to negotiate with Bussy without any idea of his goal. There was in short no rhyme or reason in the Council's attitude; it would not have been sensible if France had been the conqueror; in existing circumstances it was madness. Let us at least discuss the matter among ourselves and come to some conclusion, however tentative. Pitt laboured his point with, as Newcastle said, 'all the malice, the skill and art that he was able.' But in vain. Whatever he did was wrong. If he pressed his own views, they were too haughty and peremptory and would result in negotiations being broken off at once. When, changing his tactics, he offered to express no opinion but to accept the views of others, provided only some decision was reached, he was obviously laying a trap for his colleagues, and would misrepresent them to the King, to the Allies, to the Common Council, to the 'City of all ranks,' to Alderman Beckford: 'there can be nothing truer,' said Newcastle with the foolishness of fear, 'than that his view was, and is, to have this in his power; and for that reason, as well as others, we ought the more carefully to avoid it.'[1] Under no circumstances apparently must Pitt know the views of his colleagues.

The outcome was inevitable, and should have been obvious. The magnates' proposal that Pitt should discuss the peace with Bussy was in itself both wise and sound. Bussy was no match for Pitt; he had been frightened by Pitt's reputation before he set out from France, and was overawed when they came face to face. Apart from personalities, England was in a position to dictate terms, and Bussy's job should have been to soften and reduce them where he could. But by their methods, the Whig magnates made their own proposal unworkable. They threw the ball to Choiseul, and by so doing made certain that the negotiations

[1] Newcastle to Hardwicke, 14th May 1761. Add. MSS. 32,923. See also Devonshire's Diary, 23rd April 1761.

would take place in Paris, not London, and that the blinkered Stanley would be the king-pin of the proceedings. They deliberately left it to Choiseul to dictate the terms—with, it must be added, an eager desire to accept them—and so laid upon Pitt the unenviable task, not of softening them down, but of screwing them up. Success in such an undertaking would have been difficult in any circumstances, and became incredibly difficult when Pitt had to proceed by means of letters to the unbriefed Stanley. It was in accordance neither with the rights of the case, nor with Pitt's nature, for England to go cap-in-hand to France. His letters, therefore, naturally and indeed justifiably, assumed the high tone of a conqueror, and the Whig magnates were correspondingly shocked at what they called his 'very haughty and dictatorial style.'[1] Newcastle complained that 'this negotiation has been conducted, from the beginning, as unskilfully as possible'[2] and Bute protested that 'the negotiation was transferred to Paris.'[3] They were right, but in both cases the blame lay, not with Pitt, but with themselves; they had created an impossible situation.

The suspicions entertained of Pitt were a reflex of the magnates' hopes. They longed for peace, and believed that Pitt was intent only on war. If that had been all, they must surely have come to a better understanding, for most of them realised sooner or later that their attitude was unreasonable and based solely on fear of responsibility.[4] But mixed with their longing for peace was a hope that was neither innocent nor innocuous. They were yearning for the time when they should be freed from the incubus of Pitt's overshadowing greatness, from the terrors of his blistering sarcasms, and the affront of his vast popularity; they were panting for the time when they might be able once more to strut in the rays of their own stars and garters, peddling their bishoprics and tidewaiterships, and busying themselves with their unending game of parliamentary Snakes and Ladders. The shifting sands of intrigue were taking on a new and compelling importance. With the prospect of peace, Pitt was no longer in the ascendant; the days of his inevitability were numbered. The

[1] Hardwicke to Newcastle, 2nd August 1761. Add. MSS. 32,926.
[2] Newcastle to Hardwicke, 31st May 1761. Add. MSS. 32,923.
[3] Hardwicke to Newcastle, 23rd June 1761. Add. MSS. 32,924.
[4] Cf. e.g. 'An opinion must be given sooner or later, and Mr. Pitt must give his opinion too; or everybody else will have an equal, nay a better, pretence to excuse himself.' Hardwicke to Newcastle, 16th May 1761. Add. MSS. 32,923.

time had come to hitch the Whig wagon to Bute's rising star, and float off into new empyreans of power and prosperity.

The prime mover was Devonshire. He set to work in good earnest and even deluded himself into thinking that he was doing well by the country. The Newcastle-Pitt coalition, which a few months earlier had been 'absolutely essential,' had now drifted into incompatibility of temperament; there must be a divorce and a new marriage. Devonshire began to woo Bute with an appearance of brisk manliness which he had never dared to display towards Pitt. All the world, he told him, knew that he enjoyed the King's favour, and he personally had no objection to his having the weight and power to which the King's favour entitled him; but he must not try to go too fast. Newcastle and Devonshire were both taking great pains to bring their friends over to his side, but it was a question of time, and Bute's best hope was to keep on good terms with Newcastle, so as to step into his shoes when in the course of nature Newcastle fell out of the race. If Bute was so foolish as to throw himself on the Tories 'he would by that means lose two-thirds of the nation and besides he might be assured that if he and Mr. Pitt differed that he would lose great part of the Tories.'[1] A month later Devonshire went farther and assured Bute that it was impossible for him to stand alone, and as he must have some support, he could judge for himself 'which would be the least burdensome, the Duke of Newcastle or Mr. Pitt.' Devonshire was certain that 'a ministry composed of his Lordship and Mr. Pitt would not go down in this country' and moreover, if such a union took place, Devonshire could not undertake to persuade his 'nearest and best friends to support it.'[2] Pitt, in short, had become a liability, and his handling of affairs a disaster.

This view was widespread among the magnates and was expressed in its extremest form by Bedford. As a politician, Bedford was a pacifist, a pessimist and a defeatist, and like most of that ilk, fiery and pugnacious in his dealings with individuals. The magnates relied on him to confront Pitt in the Council. None of them could outargue Pitt face to face, and the majority were far too frightened to do more than mutter behind his back; but Bedford had at least the courage of his pusillanimous convictions, and was ready to support them openly.[3] He chose this time, in the

[1] Devonshire's Diary, 11th July 1761. [2] *Ibid.*, 14th Aug. 1761.
[3] Rigby to Bedford, 22nd April 1761. Bedford. *Correspondence*, III, 6.

full flow of victory, when Pondicherry had just fallen, when Dominica had just been captured and Belleisle taken, when Ferdinand had won Vellinghausen, and the glories of 1759 seemed to be repeating themselves, to proclaim that he differed from others 'in not thinking the war we are now engaged in, a prosperous one, but on the contrary thinking it a most ruinous one.' 'As,' he continued, 'I cannot close in opinion with those who think we have gone as far as we should in order to obtain peace . . . and as I consider our affairs in Germany, the British and the other troops at the mercy of the enemy, and in the same state do I consider the country of Hanover, Hesse and Brunswick, and as in addition to all this I look on carrying on the war on the continent (should it be possible to continue it) as reducing this kingdom immediately to a state of bankruptcy, or should that be impossible the King's troops and countries must fall into the enemies' hands, as I see no prospect of a retreat from thence in the face of a superior enemy, and as . . . another victory in either of the Indies would undo us,' he must beg to be excused from taking any further part in the country's counsels. He must, forsooth, throw up the sponge because 'whilst Mr. Pitt has any weight, and even whilst he carries the pen, I am convinced there will be no peace made. The continuance of the war, especially should Spain take a part against us, I look upon as bringing absolute ruin on this country.'[1] It is difficult to feel any patience with such a man, but one must admit that, holding such views, it was his patriotic duty to work night and day for the downfall of Pitt. In this respect he went farther than the others. There can be no reasonable doubt that the magnates were conspiring to cement an alliance between Bute and the Whigs, with the intention of getting rid of Pitt at the first convenient opportunity; but, except for Bedford, they did not imagine the hour had yet struck, nor did they really believe that the war, if it had to go on, would result in 'absolute ruin.'

Ironically, such progress as Pitt was able to make was owing to Bute. As the man who possessed the King's ear, and to whom the Whigs were turning with sycophantic deference, his opinion carried great weight. He could hardly overlook the fact, and

[1] Bedford to Newcastle, 14th Sept. 1761. Add. MSS. 32,928.

By way of contrast, Lady Hervey wrote at about this time: 'let the envious and Mr. Pitt's enemies say what they please, good fortune and glory have attended our affairs ever since he had the management of them. Victory comes one day from Pondicherry, and the next from Germany; wherever we attack we succeed; we have "Cæsar and his fortunes" with us.' *Lady Hervey's Letters*, pp. 216-7.

no doubt felt the burden of responsibility. Either for that reason, or because it suited his book to create uncertainty, he kept a wavering middle course, swaying now to one side, now to the other, though on the whole inclining more towards Pitt. In the circumstances, it was perhaps unfortunate that Pitt's uncompromising nature would not allow him to be grateful, still less to pay court, to Bute, though possibly it mattered the less as it was unlikely that any alliance between them could have lasted for long or been productive of much good. As it was, their connection was never easy, and the break came at the end of June.

The immediate cause was the American fisheries. Choiseul had taken full advantage of the initiative offered to him, and amongst other things had claimed the right for France to fish in American and Canadian waters and to have appropriate places assigned to her where the fish could be dried. Pitt was for rejecting the claim out of hand; it should be a *sine qua non* that the fisheries were to be ours and ours alone.[1] The magnates were for conceding the claim. Bute was for what he called 'making the trial'; we ought to ask for the exclusive right to the fisheries but not as a *sine qua non*; it would be 'a vast thing for us, if we could procure it,' but he entertained no great hopes. Pitt said impatiently that such a procedure was puerile and illusory. Pained to the quick, Bute argued his point 'with great firmness and resentment' until at last, borne down by numbers, Pitt, though wholly unconvinced, agreed to tell Choiseul that we would concede his claim in return for 'some very important compensation.' But although Pitt had thus given way, his epithets were not forgiven. 'Puerile and illusory' turned Bute from an uncertain ally to an inveterate enemy.[2] Nor did his yielding mollify the rest of the Cabinet. Characteristically, they had no sooner worn him down, than they began to be frightened at their own success. It involved them in responsibility, which Pitt must be made to share. Pitt, said Hardwicke, would not have deferred to their views, had he not felt an undercurrent of conviction that at least they would do the country no hurt. It was enough for each of them to answer for his own opinion; to answer for the opinion of others would be too heavy a burden, and one which Hardwicke was 'not willing to take any share of.' Pitt's reply has not been recorded, but Hardwicke made a special note of this 'one particular which

[1] Cf. the French view that 'the fisheries were the principal object which made those colonies (Canada) valuable.' Grenville. *Papers*, I, 342.

[2] Newcastle to Devonshire, 28th June 1761. Add. MSS. 32,924.

was said by Lord Hardwicke,'[1] presumably for his exculpation in the eyes of posterity.

(ii)

Choiseul, meanwhile, was playing his own game. He had asked for peace, but he was a difficult man to fathom, and his real aim was, and is, uncertain. He had three strings to his bow, or, perhaps more aptly, three plates in the air, two of which might be allowed to crash, provided the third came safely to hand. Peace had obvious charms for a country almost on its last legs, but Choiseul knew that it could be bought only at a tremendous price. There was likely to be a popular outcry, and it would ease his path if he could claim that he had beaten down Pitt's original terms and won concessions. Unfortunately, the methods of the magnates, though it gave him unexpected openings in other directions, deprived him of that particular advantage, so necessary as propaganda. It did even worse; it was so unusual that it cast doubts on England's sincerity. Choiseul's Macchiavellian mind was just the type to lay undue emphasis on the old tag '*Timeo Danaos*.' From his standpoint the negotiations were tainted from the first.

Then there was the continental war, and in particular the Westphalian operations. If France was on her last legs, so was Frederick; at any moment he might succumb, when either universal peace would ensue, or France might expect more active help from her ally. It was a race against time and the odds were on France. Apart from that wider aspect, Choiseul hoped that the effort he was making in Westphalia would crush Ferdinand and lead to the French occupation of Hanover. Such a victory would give a new complexion to the Anglo-French negotiations, tipping the scales in Choiseul's favour. He planned accordingly, and seemed at first to be heading for success; but he was checked at Vellinghausen.

Lastly there was Spain, which was bound to France by family ties and had material inducements not to break them. Neither country was altogether pleased with the course of events. Neither wanted Frederick to be completely crushed. His disappearance would leave Austria too powerful. She might so easily renew her old alliances, and having disposed of Prussia, join England to dispose of France. Or again, after recovering Silesia, she might,

[1] Note dated 24th August 1761. Add. MSS. 35,870.

with whetted appetite, set out to recover her lost provinces in Italy. Perhaps it might be better for France and Spain to take less interest in the heart of the Continent and unite to smash, or at least scotch, England before it was too late. As Spain and her new King had their grievances against England, now was the time to renew the Family Compact, and perhaps bring Spain into the war.

Spain was by no means averse. If she had serious thoughts of breaking with England—and she had—obviously it would pay her to join in the war whilst France still had something to offer. What gave her pause was her own unprepared condition; she had yet to arm herself and collect her revenues from America. With her, therefore, it was mainly a question of time, which was the one thing Choiseul could not afford. His position was such that he must act at once. The Spanish alliance meant burning his boats and was a gamble. If Spain had been ready and could bring an immediate accession of wealth, a fresh army and an unscathed navy, she might well have produced the same result as a blood transfusion in the nick of time. As it was, these benefits were deferred to an unknown future which might so easily be too late. In the circumstances, one may suppose that at the outset Choiseul was genuinely seeking peace, his future conduct depending partly on the speed of Spanish rearmament, and partly on the terms proposed by England and his views of her sincerity. Pitt was psychologically right in his belief that 'if we were at first firm in our proceedings and did not yield to France, we should soon have a very good peace.'[1] But Pitt was overruled, and Choiseul having no idea of England's terms and every reason to doubt her sincerity, began to turn more seriously towards Spain; and the more he turned, and the longer the time, the more he felt disposed to withdraw and boggle over his own previous proposals to England. France, said Hardwicke, 'don't appear to be in haste, probably waiting in expectation of some events that may mend their circumstances; and there is so much unreadiness, unpreparedness, timidity, or watching for another, here that I begin to despair almost of seeing anything brought to a conclusion.'[2] The defects which Hardwicke deplored could by no conceivable juggling be ascribed to Pitt.

When momentous decisions have to be taken, it is with

[1] Devonshire's Diary, 27th April 1761.
[2] Hardwicke to Newcastle, 7th June 1761. Add. MSS. 32,923.

statesmen as with humbler mortals; there is a period of hesitation, followed by a sudden plunge. Exactly when Choiseul made up his mind to throw peace overboard is not certain; but he went through a period of hesitation in June and July, when possibly, if Pitt's method had been adopted from the first, peace might have prevailed. But the whole course of the negotiations had bred doubts in his mind. As he wrote in his last memorial (9th Sept. 1761), 'France is sensible how opposite it is to principles of conciliation, that the party which cedes should propose to the party who has conquered,'[1] and the puzzlement of this method was not lessened when he noted that Stanley 'did not appear to be authorised by his Court to come to any agreement . . . nor even to elucidate those obscurities which occurred in the English answers.'[2] There was clearly a strong undercurrent of suspicion towards England and a drag towards continuance of the war from Spain. In retrospect, the issue could hardly be in doubt. A break was inevitable and the moment of decision came in the middle of July.

On the 13th of that month Choiseul handed Stanley a memorial to be forwarded in the normal course, but on this occasion he also sent through Bussy two further memorials, which, whatever their intention, at least marked the end of his own hesitations. The one informed Pitt that Maria Theresa had agreed to France making a separate peace, provided the conquests made on Frederick were retained, and neither France nor England helped their allies in Germany. The other required England to settle her differences with Spain before concluding with France, and to agree to invite the Spanish King to guarantee the treaty of peace.

Pitt received the first memorial on the evening of Monday, the 20th of July, and was presented with the other two on the following Thursday. Choiseul could hardly have chosen a less propitious moment, for Tuesday morning had brought news of the capture of Pondicherry, Tuesday evening of the conquest of Dominica and Wednesday morning of Ferdinand's victory at Vellinghausen. This striking contrast served to inflame Pitt's natural indignation. He was now convinced that the shilly-shally must end, and the firm line, which he had always advocated, be taken. It might be too late to secure peace, but at least it would spoil Choiseul's game. There was, he told Stanley, 'no room to doubt that the main object of the Court of France has been to

[1] Choiseul's Historical Memorial, etc. Jenkinson, III, 155. [2] *Ibid.*, p. 153.

gain time, hoping by the amusement of an ineffectual and delusive negotiation to be able to push her one great operation in Germany, and in the meantime to slacken and suspend those of Great Britain in all other parts of the world.'[1] Pitt would endure it no longer. Henceforth the negotiations must take their tone from him. What help did he, or could he, get from his colleagues? At the moment, Newcastle was petulant and pouting because he had not been allowed to nominate the new Bishop of London. Devonshire was brooding over his political manœuvres to hitch Bute on to the Whigs; Bute was busying himself with preparations for the King's wedding; Granville was still tippling, and Hardwicke and Bedford were still preferring the comforts of home to the labours of the Council Chamber. Pitt must now be his own master.

His indignation carried all before it. The Cabinet agreed to his demand that the Austrian and Spanish memorials should be returned as totally inadmissible. They also agreed to a strong reply to Choiseul, setting out at long last the conditions on which England would make peace. The drafting was left to Pitt. He went to work with a will, and in transmitting what he called his 'ultimatum' told Stanley, for Choiseul's information, that 'France in no time has a right to meddle in discussions between Great Britain and Spain,' that the English terms were 'fixed and unalterable,' and that, as the first effect of Choiseul's memorials, Pitt had sent 'decisive orders to General Amherst.'[2] When the magnates saw his reply, they were horrified. 'I never was less edified,' said Hardwicke, 'with any performances that have come from *that hand*. The compositions are inelegant and awkward, and full of rough and offensive expressions.'[3] Newcastle, though too much absorbed in his personal woes to be greatly interested, complained to Bute, who, ruffled by the friction over the Bishop of London's appointment, snapped back that the magnates had only themselves to thank if they would 'all run out of town, and not stay to read the letter and Paper of Points before they went.'[4] So far, Pitt had gained his way; but the opposition was mounting and had been stemmed for the moment only because Bute and Newcastle were at loggerheads over a trifle of patronage.

[1] Pitt to Stanley, 25th July 1761. Add. MSS. 32,925. [2] *Ibid.*
[3] Hardwicke to Newcastle, 2nd Aug. 1761. Add. MSS. 32,926.
[4] Newcastle to Devonshire, 5th Aug. 1761. Add. MSS. 32,926.

When Bute recalled those epithets of puerile and illusory, there might be another story to tell.

(iii)

To take a strong line with France was easy. More obscure was to know how to deal with Spain. Pitt had long realised that war with her was likely. At first he had dreaded the prospect, but as his plans matured and his victories piled up, he became increasingly confident, though not for that reason the more pugnacious. Originally, he had relied for peace on Wall's friendly disposition, but that hope was waning. The atmosphere had changed directly Charles III came to the throne. Pitt noted the difference at once, and thereafter kept an even sharper outlook on Spanish affairs. Two things in particular roused his suspicions—the intercepted correspondence between the Spanish Ambassadors in London and Paris, which showed conclusively that they, at any rate, were working for France against England; and the feverish activities in the Spanish ports of which the British Consuls sent early, and not always accurate, information.[1] The omens became so threatening that they influenced his strategy. He was thus ready when Choiseul's memorial arrived. More than that, he recognised that if an extension of the war was inevitable—as he believed it to be—there was no point in delaying its outbreak merely to allow Spain time in which to complete her preparations. It would be a tremendous advantage to get in the first blow, which might well knock Spain out before she had properly begun. The French memorial gave him an excuse for urgent action. His first step was to cross-examine Fuentes, who 'talked backwards and forwards,' but declared—and stuck to it—that the memorial had been authorised by Spain.[2] His next step was to instruct Lord Bristol to ask Wall if he avowed 'this strange piece,' and if he did, to 'remonstrate with energy and firmness,' and at the same time to demand 'a proper explanation with regard to the naval armaments that have been so long preparing in the various ports of Spain.'[3]

His promptness had very different effects abroad and at home. Abroad, Choiseul was much put to it to keep up his pretence.

[1] Compare e.g. Consul Goldworthy's letters of 20th and 28th Feb. 1761. Add. MSS. 32,919.
[2] Newcastle to Hardwicke, 1st Aug. 1761. Add. MSS. 32,926.
[3] Pitt to Bristol, 28th July 1761. Add. MSS. 32,926.

He had now gone too far to recede even if he had wished; the Family Compact was on the point of being signed, and with it a further Convention under which Spain was to declare war on the 1st of May (1762). At all costs England must be kept 'amused' for the next few months, so that Spain could get her treasure ships safely across the Atlantic. Choiseul had two methods; he toyed with Stanley, chopping and changing his proposals almost daily, and he instructed Bussy to toy, or attempt to toy, with Pitt by contradicting whatever Choiseul might have said. Stanley, though puzzled, continued to believe that France was sincere. Pitt had no such illusions: 'How reconcile with that view,' he asked, 'her whole conduct? I can find no solution for this political enigma, except that perhaps the French Ministry claim by prescription to perplex by chicane, deceive by perfidy, and impose by insolence, whenever they treat of peace with England.'[1] In Spain, Wall was perhaps less equivocal, but not more ruthful than Choiseul; he admitted that France and Spain were cordially united; brushed the naval preparations airily aside; spoke with respect of England's strength, and declared that Spain was invariably anxious 'to cement and cultivate the friendship so happily subsisting between the two courts.'[2] Bristol was half disposed to believe him, but Pitt was more than dubious.

At home, the magnates became increasingly restive. To Bedford, war with Spain meant 'absolute ruin'; Hardwicke did not see 'how we should be able to deal with such an alliance notwithstanding all our high spirits,'[3] and Newcastle in melancholy mood recorded his conviction that we should be invaded, and have to evacuate not only Germany but 'our acquisitions in the East and West Indies,' after which, 'what peace might we not then be forced to accept.'[4] Of them all, only Bute was unaffected,[5] which Newcastle ascribed to a disposition 'to give in to and support Mr. Pitt in his warlike notions,' as a corollary to his hurtful indifference to Newcastle's patronage claims.

It was a distracted company that sat down on the 13th of August to consider Choiseul's reply, which had come under cover of a letter from Bussy—said to have been drafted by Choiseul himself—protesting at Pitt's imperious tone and

[1] Pitt to Temple, 10 Aug. 1761. Grenville. *Papers*, I, 385.
[2] Bristol to Pitt, 31st Aug. 1761. Add. MSS. 32,927.
[3] Hardwicke to Newcastle, 2nd Aug. 1761. Add. MSS. 32,926.
[4] Some thoughts, etc., 7th Aug. 1761. Add. MSS. 32,926.
[5] 'Lord Bute seems not at all alarmed with the junction of Spain.' Newcastle to Hardwicke, 6th Aug. 1761. Add. MSS. 32,926.

asking for an interview. The Whig magnates were mostly preoccupied with other issues, Newcastle, in particular, whose mind was fully taken up with the terms and conditions which he 'must insist upon with my Lord Bute' to enable him 'to go on with some sort of inward comfort.'[1] Pitt himself was in no happy mood; he believed 'the pleasing prospect of approaching peace . . . at an end,' and to make matters worse was 'a good deal out of order with a bilious complaint.'[2] The decision of these sick and sorry men, reached after a stormy meeting of six hours' duration, was that Pitt should answer Bussy's letter and agree to see him. The next day the same sick and sorry men met to discuss Pitt's draft. In it Pitt expressed regret that 'the happy moment to put an end to so many miseries is not yet come,' defended the form and substance of his ultimatum, and made a most telling comparison of the conduct of the negotiations on either side.[3] It was undoubtedly an effective letter. But it did not please the magnates. Hardwicke objected that it was 'much too long and too irritating';[4] and Granville remarked crushingly that 'some called the letter a fine piece of oratory, a classical and elegant performance,' but as all his experience had taught him that in negotiation plain language and style did best, he was of opinion it ought to be altered and made less offensive. Pitt might have been annoyed even in the best of health, and now, being bilious, he 'flew into a great passion,' declaring that the letter should not be 'cobbled' by anyone; that it was written in the plainest language and he would not allow one iota to be altered; that, rather than alter it, he would take it to the King, and if the King disapproved then, 'he must employ some other Lord to frame another.' In short, he 'would not bear the treatment he met with.'[5]

Pitt's outbreak was but too clear evidence that he was reaching the end of his tether. The letter to Bussy was not in itself of vital importance, but the lack of importance made this negative carping the more intolerable. The Whig magnates were displaying their ill-will, and they followed it up with a threat of a sit-down strike. If, said Bedford, letters were not to be altered, there was no use in his attending Council. On which he left the room. Others showed signs of following.

[1] Newcastle to Hardwicke, 7th Aug. 1761. Add. MSS. 32,926.
[2] Pitt to Temple, 10th Aug. 1761. Grenville. *Papers*, I, 385.
[3] Jenkinson, III, 144.
[4] Hardwicke to Royston, 15th Aug. 1761. Yorke, III, 320.
[5] Devonshire's Diary, 15th Aug. 1761.

Their attitude, childish as it was, began to affect Bute, who had hitherto in general supported Pitt. Now he began to veer round, and showed which way his mind was working by telling the King, in Pitt's presence, that 'when he saw so many Lords of great consequence and character taking a view opposed to his own . . . he should as far as he could in conscience for the sake of unanimity give up his opinion.'[1] It was a concession to authority rather than conviction, but it was also a symptom which Pitt could not ignore. With no one but Temple to support him, Pitt could do little but submit under protest. There were consequently no further flurries over the memorials to France. Stanley was told that in order to test once more 'the too justly suspected sincerity of France,' England would make a few further concessions. Choiseul must understand that this was the final offer, and if it was not accepted, Stanley was to return home without further ado.[2] When this final offer reached Choiseul, on the 1st of September, the Family Compact had already been signed (15th August 1761). Choiseul could not therefore accept the terms even if he had wished to. All he could do was to hold Stanley in parley for a few precious weeks.

(iv)

Meanwhile, in England, Government was rapidly falling to pieces. The strike mania was spreading. 'The Duke of Bedford,' Newcastle wrote to Hardwicke, 'has already taken his resolution to come [to Council] no more; the Duke of Devonshire the same, after the present consideration of the peace is over, which will now be very soon at an end. Your Lordship (my great and first adviser and assistant there) will not, I believe, come oftener than shall be absolutely necessary. My Lord Mansfield, I conclude, the same.'[3] In the circumstances, and especially bearing in mind Bute's snub, Newcastle was, or thought he was, determined to resign. The magnates, in general, excused themselves on the ground of Pitt's offensive behaviour, but one may believe that they were moved by something less petty, and were at bottom protesting against the continuance of a war which they did not know how to end. Whatever their motives, this dead set at Pitt could hardly encourage him. He was worn out, and the urge to retire grew so strong that he began to speak of it, not only when

[1] Devonshire's Diary, 18th Aug. 1761.
[2] Pitt to Stanley, 27th Aug. 1761. Add. MSS. 32,927.
[3] Newcastle to Hardwicke, 17th Aug. 1761. Add. MSS. 32,927.

frustrated or out of humour, but deliberately and in cold blood, to the King, to Bute, to Newcastle, to Devonshire.[1]

The one man who was satisfied was Bute. He had originally feared three things—his own inexperience, his lack of parliamentary strength and Pitt's popularity. But time was changing all that. He had now been in office some months, the strangeness had worn off, and he was beginning to fancy himself as a Minister. More than that, he had been practising, with no small skill, the art of creating a party, and had found, as Pitt had long ago realised and as North was soon to prove, that it was an easy task when the King was assisting. Hardwicke was under no delusion: 'the Court,' he noted, 'has strengthened itself and created many new dependencies. The gratifications to the Tories; the new Queen's Family [i.e. household officers], must have attached many persons, and, on that account, even the state of the House of Lords may be found to be a good deal changed.'[2] Bute was no longer worried by fears of Parliament. Nor was he any longer so nervous of Pitt's popularity. He had always grudged it because in his eyes popularity belonged to the King; Pitt had no business to come between a sovereign and his people. Once, when speaking to Newcastle about Pitt, he had abruptly ended the conversation with the seemingly irrelevant words, 'My Lord, all the nation looks up to the King.'[3] The remark had a touch of pathos about it and more than a touch of loyalty, but above all it was revealing. Bute had grudged Pitt his popularity, but now he believed that it was on the wane and would disappear with the return of peace. Pitt was not so necessary after all.

Such was, broadly, the position in the Cabinet when Choiseul's answer to Pitt's final letter was received. Choiseul had, of course, no option. Instead of either accepting or rejecting Pitt's terms, he forwarded another temporising memorial which he knew could not be accepted. Bedford and Newcastle still clung to their pitiful hope that peace might be possible, but for the rest the conviction was growing that the end had come. Pitt was certain of it. They had tried appeasement—in vain; they had tried severity—too late. The only course still left was to drive both France and Spain into the open, turn the cold war into a hot war, and batter the enemy till they cried for mercy. On the 15th of

[1] Newcastle to Bedford, 13th Sept. 1761. Bedford. *Correspondence,* III, 43.
[2] Hardwicke to Newcastle, 8th Aug. 1761. Add. MSS. 32,926.
[3] Note dated 21st April 1761. Add. MSS. 32,922.

September the Cabinet reluctantly but unanimously decided that Stanley must be recalled and the negotiations broken off. Pitt sent instructions accordingly.

Meanwhile, there was Spain. Bristol's report arrived with confirmation of Wall's 'total and entire avowal of the offensive step taken by France, and of an entire union of councils between France and Spain.'[1] There were other letters and reports, all tending to the same end—letters from Stanley, speaking of Franco-Spanish agreements, of Spain's intention to declare war, of great sums lent by Spain to France, of Spanish ships of war preparing, and, not less significant, of Choiseul's changed demeanour;[2] there were intercepted letters from Grimaldi to Fuentes, speaking of signed documents and the need to hold back till the safe arrival of the treasure ships; there was the implication of Bussy's memorial and not least there were Choiseul's own admissions. Spain's intentions were clear beyond reasonable doubt, and Pitt summoned the Cabinet, on the 18th of September, to discuss them. He set out the evidence and urged, with all the eloquence and fervour of which he was capable, the need to break with Spain and to strike at once. His preparations were complete; he had ships off Finisterre in sufficient strength to capture the treasure fleet on its way home and smash any naval force sent to protect it, and by land he was ready to attack Panama and the Philippines. The plans were cut and dried and could scarcely fail. As things stood, it was actually easier to fight France and Spain combined than France alone, for the two were more vulnerable than the one; France had been sucked dry, but Spain would broaden the target and offer fresh prizes. If we were prompt and decisive and declared war at once, peace might be won with the minimum of effort and the maximum of gain.

But the Cabinet were afraid. They knew in their hearts that war was not to be avoided, but they told themselves that it was neither just nor prudent to begin it at once. Instead, they would send reinforcements to the West Indies and the Mediterranean, 'as if a war with Spain were certain,' and at the same time make a 'further trial' of Wall. Bristol should ask him categorically what were Spain's intentions, and unless he received a satisfactory answer should come away 'without taking leave.'

[1] Hardwicke. Memo., 18th Sept. 1761. Add. MSS. 35,870.
[2] Stanley to Pitt, 2nd, 6th and 8th Sept. 1761. Add. MSS. 32,927-8.

So it was proposed and so it was decided, in spite of all Pitt's arguments. No one supported him but Temple; even Bute no longer tried to find a middle course, but swung over to the majority—to the 'Lords of great consequence and character.' But Pitt could not agree—too much was at stake—and being desperately in earnest, he fell back on the only expedient left. He declared that he would appeal direct to the King, setting out his views and recommendations in a written memorial.

His decision shook the magnates, but it is significant that what worried them was not the doubt, which they certainly felt, about the rightness of their decision, but fear of the effect of Pitt's memorial on the public. They were frightened that his 'absurd and offensive' paper might be quoted in Parliament if and when they were proved to be wrong, and give him the chance of representing that they had 'lost the opportunity of putting it out of the power of Spain to hurt us.' They must, if possible, prevent him from signing, or at least from presenting the paper; they must hinder him 'from going out and thereby leaving the impracticability of his own war *upon us*.'[1] Curious, that the war he was not allowed to wage should be *his* 'impracticability'! But indeed the proper course for the magnates to take was the subject of much debate. The two points which emerged were the determination to postpone the war as long as possible, and the fact that, to Newcastle's delight, Bute 'acted with as much cordiality and concert with us as possible; and for the first time exactly as one of us.'[2] Pitt was now cut off, not only from his colleagues—they had long been against him—but, owing to the final defection of Bute, from all influence with the King. Like another Gulliver at Lilliput he was bound hand and foot by a multiplicity of cords. None the less, he did not give up hope. On the 21st of September he presented his memorial to the King, who, no doubt on Bute's advice, refused to consider it until Stanley had returned and could be consulted. His attitude put off the evil day a bit longer.

That afternoon the discussion was renewed in the Council. The magnates, one by one, repeated their former opinions, without adding anything to the argument. All, that is to say, except Mansfield, who confessed his own blindness by saying that he did not see what operations could be undertaken against Spain which could suffer by the delay. His remarks pained Newcastle because 'it gave Mr. Pitt a great advantage, to expatiate upon his

[1] Newcastle to Hardwicke, 20th Sept. 1761. Add. MSS. 32,928. [2] *Ibid.*

great schemes, and the almost certainty of success against the united forces of the House of Bourbon; but then there was not an hour to be lost.' As Pitt spoke, they were listening, not merely to a great orator, but to a master of strategy. The rest deliberately shut their ears, but Mansfield remained troubled, for he was intelligent enough to appreciate Pitt's arguments. Unfortunately, he was timid and ineffectual; he did not like swimming against the stream; so after a hesitating glance in Pitt's direction and a half whisper that 'if that were the case, it would then appear in a very different light,' he succumbed to the will of the majority, without doing either Pitt or himself any good. Pitt was overruled on the spot, and Mansfield was afterwards disparaged in private by Bute.

When the meeting had broken up, Bute summoned Newcastle and Devonshire to a private conference. He had made up his mind that Pitt must go; the time had come to get rid of him; and the only question was how. His two hearers were ready to declare bravely that 'no consideration or threat from Mr. Pitt would make us depart from our opinion,' but they shied away from the thought of losing him. Bute, however, persevered and ultimately prevailed; and Newcastle, as he grew accustomed to the idea, began to find a nostalgic pleasure in discussing the names of persons to fill the vacancy—George Grenville, perhaps, or Lord Egremont. What delight, after these barren years, to be once more Cabinet-making! In the end, the three of them, like conspirators, swore 'to stand by one another,' and tried to still their involuntary quakings by deciding that their great point was 'to do right by the public,' by which they meant doing nothing which might 'give Mr. Pitt great handle against us.'[1]

The method they chose was not ineffective. They would not answer Pitt in writing since they could not hope to hold their own against him in a paper warfare. He should present his memorial to the King, and then the rest of the Council should go in one by one, and give their opinion verbally. The King, who was allowing his old venom against Pitt full play, would be primed and the end of the farce would be a foregone conclusion. What might happen thereafter remained to be seen. Possibly Pitt would resign; possibly the King would have to get rid of him; but one way or another Pitt must go. As arranged, the magnates trooped in to the King on the 26th of September, and all 'spoke their

[1] Newcastle to Hardwicke, 21st Sept. 1761. Add. MSS. 32,928.

opinion boldly and clear to His Majesty'—and none, sad to say, more boldly and clear than Mansfield.[1]

Still a decision was delayed pending Stanley's arrival. His latest letters had suggested that peace was yet possible. Pitt had brushed the letters aside as 'amusements'; but they might represent fact. If so, Bristol's instructions would be different from anything as yet suggested by either side; and more, Pitt's dismissal would be the easier. He had burnt his boats when he presented his memorial, and if France really meant peace, he could be laughed out of office. The magnates saw many good reasons for delay.

At last Stanley arrived, only to dash their hopes. 'I have,' Newcastle lamented, 'had a very long day and fruitless conversation with my friend Stanley, the whole tending to war and not peace. Former facts alleged by him softened, and not quite verified and supported. Present dispositions stated in a favourable light for the views and measures of those who differ with us.'[2] It seemed, after all, that Pitt had been right. Even Hardwicke had to admit that the evidence showed Spain to be 'more determined than ever before.' But the King and Bute and the magnates were not interested in evidence. They had decided that Pitt must go, and they had agreed that his demand for war with Spain gave them an opportunity not to be missed. War with Spain was probable, but with any luck would hold off long enough for them to work their will on Pitt.

The Cabinet met on the 2nd of October, ostensibly to decide the orders to be sent to Bristol, but in fact to seal Pitt's fate. One and all they gave their opinion against war with Spain. They did more; they had planned to crush Pitt with expert advice, and now brought Anson and Ligonier, well primed, to blow his schemes sky-high. Anson declared that our ships were foul and the time needed for their overhaul and repair would afford a breathing space for further discussions. Ligonier, now eighty-three years of age and dreaming of the past, spoke of the ancient glories of Spain, and deplored the prospect of throwing 70,000 of her valorous troops into the scale of France. So it continued, until at last Pitt rose to reply. He did not attempt to argue the merits of the case; the time for that had gone; the magnates had no intention of listening. Instead, he made a valedictory speech.

[1] Newcastle to Hardwicke, 26th Sept. 1761. Add. MSS. 32,928.
[2] Newcastle to Hardwicke, 1st Oct. 1761. Add. MSS. 32,929.

He had never, he said, asked for one single employment in his life, but he had been called by his Sovereign, and, he might say, in some degree by the voice of the people, to assist the state when others had abdicated. He had answered that call and had gone through more difficulties than ever man did; and, perhaps by good fortune, he had succeeded in the measures he had taken for the honour and interest of the nation. In the execution of those measures he had met with great obstruction from some who had no wish that they should succeed. There was hardly one expedition which he had proposed, however hopeful in its prospects and however successful in the upshot, that had not been scouted at first as chimerical and ridiculous. The war had been imputed solely to him; it had been called his war. Well, it had succeeded. Now, the case had altered; he had little credit in the Council; he had little influence in Parliament. But he had in his bag papers which, unless proper measures were taken, would fix an eternal stain on the Crown of England. It would be criminal in him, as Secretary of State, to put those papers to sleep in a pigeon-hole. The greatest indignity had been offered to the Crown of Great Britain by Spain, who was now carrying on the worst species of war on behalf of France—covering her trade, lending her money, abetting her in negotiations. We were actually at war with the whole House of Bourbon, and he could not acquiesce in sending no answer to Spain, or indeed any answer other than the one he had proposed. In his situation, he was responsible; and he would not continue to hold that situation unless he could direct affairs. That being the case, no one could be surprised that he could go on no longer. He would repeat that he would be responsible for nothing which he did not direct. Fortunately, he could hand over to a union of the greatest and most considerable men in the kingdom, who, he hoped, would carry on the King's business with success.

It was a dignified and a touching speech of farewell, and might have been accepted graciously. But the magnates were not magnanimous. Granville, in what was supposed to be a complimentary speech, went out of his way to argue that Pitt claimed too much unless he also claimed to be infallible. The King could decide on foreign policy with his Secretary of State alone, but if, as in this case, he referred a matter to his Council, the opinion of the majority must prevail, and the Secretary's duty was merely executive.

Pitt, with much greater dignity, acknowledged his many obligations to Granville and the assistance and support he had in particular instances received from his old colleagues. And so the meeting ended. Three days later, Pitt resigned the Seals. The news was not published for five more days, but the rumour ran round the astonished world that the little men had gained their little ends and the great man had fallen.

Bibliography

Almon, John — *Anecdotes of the Life of William Pitt*. 3 Vols. 3rd edition. 1793.
History of the Late Minority. 1766.

Bancroft, George — *History of the American Revolution*. 3 Vols. 1852.

Bedford — *Correspondence of John, Fourth Duke of Bedford*. 3 Vols. 1842-6.

Burrows, M. — *Life of Edward, Lord Hawke*. 3rd edition. 1904.

Butterfield, H. — *The Reconstruction of an Historical Episode*. 1951.

Cambridge Modern History. Vol. VI. 1934.

Carlyle, T. — *Frederick the Great*. 5 Vols. 1903.

Chalmers, G. — *An Estimate of the Comparative Strength of Great Britain*. 1794.

Charteris, Hon. Evan — *William Augustus, Duke of Cumberland, and the Seven Years War*. 1925.

Chatham — *Correspondence of William Pitt*. Edited by W. S. Taylor and J. H. Pringle. 4 Vols. 1840.
Speeches. *The Modern Orator*. 1848.

Chatham Papers — MSS. in the Record Office.

Chatsworth Collection — MSS. at Chatsworth.

Chatterton, Lady H. G. M. — *Memorials of Admiral Gambier*. 2 Vols. 1861.

Chesterfield — *Lord Chesterfield's Letters*. Edited by J. Bradshaw. 3 Vols. 1926.

Churchill, Sir W. S. — *Marlborough*. 4 Vols. 1939.

Clark, G. N. — *The Wealth of England*. 1947.

Corbett, Sir J. — *England in the Seven Years War*. 2 Vols. 1907.

Coxe, William — *Memoirs of Lord Walpole*. 2 Vols. 1808.
Memoirs of Sir Robert Walpole. 4 Vols. 1816.

Devonshire — MSS. Diary of the Duke of Devonshire. Chatsworth Collection.

Dickins and Stanton — *An Eighteenth-century Correspondence*. 1910.

Dodington, B. — *The Diary of the late George Bubb Dodington*. 1784.

Douglas, J. — *A Letter addressed to Two Great Men*. 1760.

Dowell, S. — *History of Taxation*. 4 Vols. 1886.

Doyle, J. A. — *The Colonies under the House of Hanover*. 1907.
The Middle Colonies. 1907.

Elliot, G. F. S. — *The Border Elliots*. 1897.

Examination of the Principles . . . of the Two Brothers. 1749.

Franklin, Benjamin — *Autobiography and Letters*. Edited by John Bigelow.

Glover, Richard — *Memoirs of a Celebrated Literary and Political Character*. 1813.

Grenville — *The Grenville Papers*. Edited by W. J. Smith. 4 Vols. 1852.

Hannay, D. — *A Short History of the Royal Navy*. 2 Vols. 1909.

Hardwicke — Hardwicke Papers in the British Museum.

Hartshorne, Albert — *Memoirs of a Royal Chaplain, 1729-63*. 1905.

Hervey, Lady — *Letters of Mary Lepel, Lady Hervey*. 1821.

H.M.C. — Records of the City of Exeter.
Stopford Sackville MSS.
Townshend MSS.

Horn, D. B. — *Sir Charles Hanbury Williams and European Diplomacy* (1747-58). 1930.

Hotblack, K. — *Chatham's Colonial Policy*. 1917.

Ilchester, Earl of — *Henry Fox, First Lord Holland*. 2 Vols. 1920.
Life of Sir Charles Hanbury-Williams. 1928.
Lord Hervey and his friends. 1950.

Jenkinson, Charles — *A Collection of Treaties*. 3 Vols. 1785.

Journal of the Campaign on the Coast of France, 1758.

Journal of the Commissioners for Trade and Plantations (1754-58).

Keppel, T. — *Life of Augustus, Viscount Keppel*. 2 Vols. 1842.

Kimball, G. S. — *Correspondence of William Pitt*. 2 Vols. 1906.

Lecky, W. E. H. — *History of England in the 18th century*. 8 Vols. 1883.

Lennox, Lady Sarah — *Life and Letters*. 2 Vols. 1901.

MacAllester, O. — *A series of Letters discovering the Scheme projected by France, etc*. 2 Vols. 1767.

Maitland, F. W. — *Constitutional History of England*. 1909.

Mauduit, I. — *Considerations on the Present German War*. 1761.

Mitchell, Sir A. — Mitchell Papers in the British Museum.

Newcastle, Duke of — Newcastle Papers in the British Museum.

Northumberland, Elizabeth, Duchess of — *The Diaries of a Duchess*. Edited by James Greig. 1926.

Parkman, F. — *Half-century of Conflict*. 2 Vols. 1892.
Montcalm and Wolfe. 2 Vols. 1919.
Old Régime in Canada. 1909.

Parliamentary History

Phillimore, R. — *Memoirs and Correspondence of George, Lord Lyttelton*. 2 Vols. 1845.

Potter, T. — *The Expedition against Rochefort,* etc. 1758.

Rashed, Z. E. — *The Peace of Paris, 1761*. 1951.

Riker, T. W. — *Henry Fox, First Lord Holland*. 2 Vols. 1911.

Robertson, Sir C. Grant — *Chatham and the British Empire*. 1946.

Rosebery, Lord — *Chatham, His Early Life and Connections*. 1910.

Sedgwick, R. — *Letters from George III to Lord Bute, 1756-66*. Edited by R. Sedgwick. 1939.

Seeley, Sir. J. R. — *Expansion of England*. 1895.

Sherrard, O. A. — *Lord Chatham, A War Minister in the Making*. 1952.

Sparks, Jared — *Life of George Washington*. 2 Vols. 1839.
Stowe — Stowe MSS. in the British Museum.
Taswell-Langmead, T. P. — *English Constitutional History*. 6th edition. 1905.
Trevelyan, G. M. — *The Peace and the Protestant Succession*. 1934.
Trevelyan, Sir G. O. — *The American Revolution*. Part I, 1766-76. 1899.
Torrens, W. M. — *History of Cabinets*. 2 Vols. 1894.
Tunstall, B. — *Admiral Byng*. 1928.
William Pitt, Earl of Chatham. 1938.
Waldegrave, James, Earl — *Memoirs from 1754 to 1758*. 1821.
Walpole, H. — *Letters*.
Memoirs of the Reign of George II. 3 Vols. 2nd edition. 1847.
Memoirs of the Reign of George III. 4 Vols. 1894.
Waugh, W. T. — *James Wolfe, Man and Soldier*. 1928.
Whitten, F. E. — *Wolfe and North America*. 1929.
Williams, B. — *The Life of William Pitt, Earl of Chatham*. 2 Vols. 1913.
Woodward, W. H. — *A Short History of the Expansion of the British Empire*. 2nd edition. 1907.
Yorke, P. C. — *Life of Lord Chancellor Hardwicke*. 3 Vols. 1913.

Index

Abercromby, General James (1706-81), *succeeds Loudoun,* 257, 281; *fails at Ticonderoga,* 284-7, 288, 289, 291, 292, 294, 311, 334
Abraham, *Heights of,* 339, 358
Abreu, Comte d', 351, 352
Acadia (Nova Scotia), 14, 24, 25, 28, 29, 30, 32; *Le Loutre and,* 34-6, 50, 60, 73, 81; *Monckton and,* 85-7, 91, 223, 330, 383
Æolus, H.M.S., 357
Affry, D' (1713-90), 182, 383
Aiguillon, Duc d' (1720-98), 279, 346, 352, 383
Aix, Ile d', 224, 225
Aix-la-Chapelle, *Treaty of,* 19, 32, 44, 49, 92, 341
Albany, 285, 287
Albemarle, William Anne Keppel, 2nd Earl (1702-54), 35, 49, 50, 54, 55
Alcide, 60
Aldborough (Yorks), 153
Alexandria, 80, 82
Alleghany Mountains, 53
Alleghany River, 37, 39
Aller River, 267
Allowances Bill, 361
Amelia, Princess (1711-86), 369
America, *Problems of,* 18
American Independence, *War of,* 14
Amherst, Jeffrey (1717-97), 257, 280; *captures Louisburg,* 281-4, 285, 289, 294, 301, 310, 311; *captures Ticonderoga and Crown Point,* 333-6; *and Wolfe,* 336-8, 341, 353, 358, 359; *captures Montreal,* 365, 381, 397, 411
Ancram, Lord, 278
Anhalt-Zerbst, Princess of, 341, 383
Annapolis, 18, 25, 27, 29
Anne, Queen, 24, 25, 27, 145
Anson, Lord (1697-1762), 52, 60, 112, 113, 140, 144, 176, 198, 208, 210, 224, 269, 272, 337, 365, 366, 377, 420
Anstruther, General, 102
Antwerp, 72
Apraxin, Field-Marshal, 222
Argyll, Archibald, 3rd Duke of (1682-1761), 174, 322
Army, *Control of,* 73, 238, 239, 242, 243, 244
Army of Observation, 159, 177, 183, 184, 190, 191, 228, 230, 231, 232, 235, 241, 242, 247, 248, 249, 263, 267, 268, 297, 298
Ashburnham, John, Earl of (1724-1812), 198
Augsburg, 383, 385, 403
Austrian Succession, *War of,* 14, 29, 85, 110

Baltic, 127, 128, 179; *Pitt's view on fleet in,* 216-20, 222, 223, 268
Bancroft, George, 14, 86
Barbados, 330
Barrington, General Hon. J. M., 296; *captures Guadeloupe,* 331-3
Barrington, 2nd Viscount (1717-93), 94, 150, 152, 155, 172, 175, 178, 189, 196, 208, 211, 254, 301, 344, 365
Basseterre, 331
Bath, 100, 101
Baye Verte, 74, 86
Beaubassin, 35, 36
Beauséjour, 34, 35, 49, 74, 80, 85, 86
Beckford, William (1709-70), 102, 161 183, 238, 309, 315, 360, 403
Bedford, John, 4th Duke (1710-70), 143; *and Ireland,* 174, 296 and 357, 245, 392, 397, 400; *pacifist views of,* 405-6, 411; *and peace negotiations,* 413-16
Belfast, 356, 357
Belleisle, 346; *Pitt plans to attack,* 364-7; *revives proposal,* 377-8, 381, 383; *captured,* 397, 399, 406
Belleisle, Maréchal (1684-1761), 105, 112, 324
Bergen-op-Zoom, 53
Berlin, 64, 247, 381
Bernstorff, J. H. E. (1712-72), 267, 268
Bestuzheff, Alexis, 64, 65
Bienville, *see* Céloron
Bic, Ile de, 337
Bigot, François, 86
Black Hole of Calcutta, 120, 129, 156, 216, 238
Blackfriars Bridge, 15
Blakeney, General (1672-1761), 116, 117
Bligh, General (1685-1775), 278, 279, 293
Bompart, de, 332, 345, 346

Boscawen, Sir Edward (1711-61), *captures Alcide and Lys,* 60-1; *at Louisburg,* 281-4, 301; *defeats La Clue,* 325, 337, 345
Boston, 24, 25, 26, 27, 28, 86, 121
Bougainville, de (1729-1811), 337, 338
Boulogne, 271
Bouquet, Colonel, 291
Bourlamarque, de, 334
Boys, Commodore, 356
Braddock, General Edward (1695-1775), *his character,* 52-3, 59, 71, 73, 75; *expedition and defeat of,* 80-5, 86, 87, 88, 89, 90, 91, 94, 113, 114, 122, 123, 223, 290, 295
Bradstreet, Colonel John (1711-71), *captures Fort Frontenac,* 287-9, 291, 310
Brest, 218, 274, 324, 325, 345, 346
Bristol, George, 3rd Earl (1721-75), *at Madrid,* 294, 351; *and Wall,* 412-13, 417, 420
Broglie, Duc de (1718-1804), 322, 398
Brown, Lieutenant, 283
Browne, Field-Marshal, 178
Brunswick, Duke of, 72, 73, 127, 311, 401, 406
Bunge (Swedish Minister), 105, 106, 112
Bussy, F. de (1699-1780), 401, 402, 403, 410, 413, 414, 417
Bute, John Stuart, 3rd Earl (1713-92), 99; *and Princess of Wales,* 124-5, 132, 135, 138, 191, 204; *takes part in forming coalition,* 210-11, 230, 300, 301; *character and early history,* 304-8, 314, 316, 319; *and Sackville,* 323-4, 327; *estranged from Pitt,* 348-50, 353; *at George III's accession,* 368-73; *and George III,* 374-7, 380, 382, 384, 385; *his aims,* 386-90; *courts Devonshire,* 391; *becomes Sec. of State,* 392-5, 396, 397, 400; *and Whigs,* 404-5; *supports Pitt,* 406; *and fisheries question,* 407, 411, 412; *and Spanish problem,* 413, 414, 415, 416; *decides to get rid of Pitt,* 418-20
Byng, Admiral John (1704-57), *at Minorca,* 112-20, 154, 155, 162; *his trial and death,* 163-9, 170, 184, 200, 223, 238, 239, 240

Cadiz, 325
Calais, 271
Canada, French, 19
Cancale Bay, 273, 280
Cape Breton, 28, 35, 60, 87, 281; *Wolfe lands on,* 283; *Newcastle and,* 293-4
Carlos, Don (Charles III of Spain, 1715-88), 327, 351-2, 412
Carolina, 289
Caribbean Sea, 310
Carrickfergus, 357
Cartier, Jacques, 23
Cassel, 229
Catherine II (the Great) (1729-96), 54, 341
Céleron de Bienville, 33-4
Champlain, Lake, 24, 30, 50, 87, 90, 334, 335
Chandernagore, 23
Charente, River, 221, 224
Charles II, 17, 18
Châtelaillon, 225
Chaudière, River, 121
Cherbourg, 278
Chesapeake Bay, 80
Chesterfield, Philip, 4th Earl of (1694-1773), 204, 230
Chitty, Sir T., 15
Choiseul, Etienne, Duc de (1719-85), 318; *his reputation,* 344; *his political outlook,* 352; *his policy,* 381; *asks for peace,* 385-6; *compared with Pitt,* 398-9; *and peace negotiations,* 400-13, 415-17
Claremont, 186, 254, 255, 273, 397
Clavering, Brigadier, 333
Clermont, Louis, Comte de (1709-70), 268
Clive, Lord (1726-74), 238, 365
Closterseven, *Convention of, signed,* 235, 237, 239; *Pitt and,* 240-2, 247, 263, 268
Cocoa Tree Club, 201, 379
Colbert, Jean Baptiste, 19, 23
Cologne, Elector of, 127
Colonies, *System of Administration,* 46, 47
Colonisation, *Forms of,* 16
Colville, Lord (1720-70), 359
Conflans, H. de B., Comte de (1690-1777), 325; *at Quiberon Bay,* 344-6
Considerations on the present German war, 382
Contades, Maréchal (1704-95), 322, 323, 325
Contrecœur, 39
Conway, Hon. H. S. (1721-95), 223
Coote, Sir Eyre (1726-83), 365
Cornwallis, Hon. Edward, *in Acadia,* 34-6; *at Rochefort,* 223
Coureurs de Bois, 21
Coventry, George, 6th Earl of (1722-1809), 198
Crevelt, *Battle of,* 274
Cromwell, Oliver, 17
Crown Point, 50, 80, 81, 87; *Johnson's campaign against,* 88-9, 121; *Abercromby and,* 285-6, 311; *captured by Amherst,* 334, 336, 341
Crump, Colonel, 333
Cumberland, William, Duke of (1721-65), 50, 51; *and Braddock,* 52-5; *on Council of Regency,* 70; *in control of army,* 73; *and Shirley,* 121-2, 125, 134, 135, 136, 158; *hampers Pitt,* 174-6, 185,

186; *demands Pitt's dismissal,* 189-96, 198, 199, 204, 207, 208, 210, 212, 214; *on Continent,* 218-19, 221; *views on Continental War,* 228-9; *defeated at Hastenbeck,* 229-30, 231, 233; *signs Convention of Closterseven,* 234-5; *and Pitt,* 237-8; *recalled,* 240; *and King,* 242-4, 247, 269, 305, 327, 369
Cumberland, Fort, 82, 85
Cumming, Thomas (d. 1774), 184, 269-70

Dashwood, Sir Francis (1708-81), 165-6
De Lancey, James (Governor of New York), 81, 88
Denmark, 179, 217-18, 232, 234, 268, 313, 317
Devonshire, William, 4th Duke of (1720-64), 142; *becomes First Lord,* 143, 150, 152, 157, 160, 174, 175, 191, 195; *and Newcastle,* 199; *opposed to maritime war,* 220, 301; *and Temple's Garter,* 304-5, 316, 348, 360, 361, 368; *and Bute,* 371, 372; *and Pitt,* 376-7, 388; *helps Bute to become Sec. of State,* 390-5, 400; *urges Bute to break with Pitt,* 405, 411, 415, 416; *conspires with Bute,* 419
Dieskau, Baron, 90, 122
Digby, Lord, 133
Dinwiddie, Robert (Governor of Virginia) (1690-1770), 32, 33; *and Ohio Valley,* 37-8; *and Washington,* 39-40, 42, 50
Dodington, Bubb (1691-1762), 51; *and Fox,* 115-16, 192, 201; *and Bute,* 306
Dohna, General, 323
Dominica, 332, 353, 381, 383, 399; *conquest of,* 406, 410
Dresden, 64, 312
Dublin, H.M.S., 382
Dumas, Captain, 120
Dunbar, Colonel, 83, 84, 85
Dunkirk, 346, 356
Dupplin, Lord (1710-87), 198, 199
Duquesne, Fort, *built,* 39, 50; *Braddock and,* 80-3, 120, 121, 257; *Forbes and,* 290-2, 300
Duquesne, Marquis, 32, 37, 39, 42
Durell, Admiral Philip, 337, 359
Durham, Bishop of, 254-5
Dury, General, 278
Dymal, River, 364

East Friesland, 267
East India Company, 17, 184, 401
East Prussia, 222
Edward, Fort, 89, 90, 285, 334
Egg Island, 28
Eglinton, Lord, 322
Egmont, John, 2nd Earl of (1711-72), 142, 198
Egremont, Charles, 2nd Earl of (1710-63), 419
Elbe, River, 229, 234, 248, 267, 277
Elizabeth, Tzarina (1709-61), 44, 62, 64, 65, 67, 68, 126
Elliot, Sir Gilbert (1722-77), 154, 162; *and Pitt,* 349-50, 389
Elliot, Captain John, 357
Emden, 229; *Holmes and,* 267-9, 274
Ems, River, 267, 268
Emsdorf, *Battle of,* 355
Erie, Lake, 37, 50, 87
Erskine, Sir Henry, 104
Estrées, Maréchal Comte d' (1695-1771), 229, 234
Exeter, 201

Family Compact, 319, 409, 413, 415
Ferdinand of Brunswick, Prince (1721-92), 158; *commands Army of Observation,* 242, 247, 249, 253; *Pitt and,* 264-5; *minor operations of,* 267-8, 271, 272; *wins Crevelt,* 274-7, 279, 280, 295, 298, 305, 310, 311; *wins Minden,* 322-4, 347; *minor successes of,* 354-6, 364, 376, 377, 378, 381, 396; *wins Vellinghausen,* 398, 402, 406, 408, 410
Ferdinand VI of Spain (1713-59), 55, 327, 351
Finisterre, 417
Finkenstein, Prussian Minister, 249
Five Nations, The, 30, 89
Flushing, 72
Foquet, General, 364
Forbes, Admiral John (1714-96), 165
Forbes, General John (1710-59), 257, 281, 285; *and Fort Duquesne,* 289-92, 310
Fort Necessity, 41, 84, 89
Fort St. Philip, 116
Fowke, General Thomas, 113, 114, 119, 120, 233
Fox, Henry (Lord Holland) (1705-74), 45, 48, 51, 54, 55, 56, 59, 61, 64; *breaks with Pitt,* 70-1, 77, 79, 92; *and the Militia,* 95-6, 102, 103, 104, 109; *contemplates leaving Govt.,* 115-16; *and Shirley,* 121-2; *resigns,* 130-6, 140, 142, 143, 150, 152, 153, 155, 160; *and Byng,* 165-8, 178, 182, 183; *intrigues with Cumberland,* 185-94, 195, 196, 197, 198, 199; *and Enquiries,* 201-3; *and Waldegrave,* 207-9; *becomes Paymaster,* 211, 218, 220, 233, 259, 269, 279, 305
Franklin, B. (1706-90), 47, 82, 83
Fraser, Simon, 174
Frederick Augustus II of Saxony, 178
Frederick II (the Great) (1712-86), 44, 45, 62, 63, 65; *enters into Convention of Westminster,* 66-9, 73, 75, 98, 105; *and*

Frederick II (the Great)—*continued* *Silesian loan,* 110, 114; *begins war,* 126-9, 158, 159, 162, 177; *doubts about England,* 178-82, 203; *at Prague,* 204, 212; *at Kolin,* 214-16; *and Pitt,* 217-20, 221, 222; *and Cumberland,* 228-9, 231, 232, 235, 240, 241; *at Rossbach,* 247-50; *and Pitt,* 252-4, 262, 264, 265; *and subsidy treaty,* 268-9, 270, 271; *at Olmutz,* 274-5, 276, 277; *at Zorndorf and Hochkirch,* 279, 280, 295, 301, 310; *and Pitt,* 311-12; *at Zullichau and Kunersdorf,* 320; *writes to George II,* 320-1, 323, 328, 340, 341, 347, 352, 353, 354, 355, 364, 381; *attitude towards peace,* 383-5, 386, 400, 401, 408, 410
Frederick, Prince of Wales (1707-51), 76, 147, 304
French Creek, 37
French East India Co., 23, 270
Frontenac, Fort, 88, 121, 123, 288, 300
Fuentes, Conde de, 352, 362, 363, 412, 417
Fundy, Bay of, 86, 287
Fur Trade, 30, 32, 33

Gabarus Bay, 283
Gage, General Thomas (1720-87), 335
Galissonière, Marquis La (1693-1756), 15; *Governor of Canada,* 33-4, 36, 37; *at Minorca,* 113-14, 119, 346
Galitzin, Prince (1735-1803), 385, 386, 395
Galway, Lord, 85
Ganges, River, 238
Garraway's Coffee House, 116
Gaspereau, Fort, 86
George II, 15; *founds Halifax,* 34, 45; *on Braddock,* 52; *goes to Hanover,* 62; *and Frederick the Great,* 63; *signs Convention of Westminster,* 66-8, 70, 71; *on continent system,* 72, 75, 76, 104, 108; *offers his grandson an allowance, etc.,* 124-5, 127, 129; *and Bute as Groom of Stole,* 132-3; *at Fox's resignation,* 135-7, 139; *and Pitt,* 140-2; *sends for Fox,* 143; *and Pitt,* 150-1, 156; *and foreign policy,* 157-8, 162; *and Byng,* 166-9, 178; *and Frederick the Great,* 180-3; *dislikes Pitt and Temple,* 185-6, 188; *dismisses Pitt,* 190-4; *attempts to obtain new Ministry,* 195-200, 203; *his conditions for accepting coalition,* 205-13, 214, 215; *opposes Rochefort expedition,* 220-1; *appoints Mordaunt,* 223; *and Cumberland,* 228-31, 234; *after Closterseven,* 240-3, 247, 252, 254, 259, 269, 271, 275, 293, 296, 298; *and Temple's Garter,* 302-3, 314; *receives letter from Frederick,* 320; *and Prince George,* 326-7; *and "dapplings for peace,"* 440-4, 348, 349, 361; *and Belleisle expedition,* 364-7; *death,* 367; *character,* 368, 393
George III *and George II,* 124-5, 143, 190; *and Bute,* 304-7; *asks to join army,* 326-7, 350; *ascends throne,* 368-70, 372, 373; *and Ministers,* 374-6; *his speech to Parliament,* 378-9; *regards war with disfavour,* 382, 384, 385; *and Pitt,* 387-8, 393, 395, 402, 411, 414, 415, 416; *and peace negotiations,* 418-20
George, Lake, 87, 89, 90, 237, 285, 286, 287, 334
"German War," 14
Gibraltar, 112, 113, 114, 115, 117, 119, 130, 232, 233, 295, 325, 351
Glover, Richard (1712-85), 200, 201, 204
Goldworthy, Consul, 412
Goree, 23, 269, 270, 296, 322, 326, 383
Granby, John, Marquis of (1721-70), 198, 243, 364
Grant, Major, 291
Granville, John, Earl (1690-1763), 48, 50, 51, 60, 135, 136, 142, 186, 189, 190, 230, 390, 411, 414, 421, 422
Great Meadows, 40, 41, 43, 47, 50, 82, 83
Grenville, George (1712-70), 101, 137, 145; *retires with Pitt,* 195, 198; *Pitt wants him as Chancellor of Exchequer,* 206; *and Newcastle,* 209-10; *and payment of Army of Observation,* 231-2, 248, 274, 295, 314, 323; *growing antagonistic to Pitt,* 389, 390, 392; *visited by Bute,* 393, 419
Grenville, Mrs. George, 101
Grenville, Henry (1717-84), 107
Grenville, Lady Hester, *see* Pitt, Lady Hester
Grenville, James (1715-83), 195, 316, 389
Gridley, Colonel, 336
Grimaldi, Marquis de (1720-85), 417
Gross-Jägendorf, *Battle of,* 242
Grosvenor, Sir Richard (1731-1802), 300
Guadeloupe, 310, 322, 326, 331, 332, 362, 381, 383
Guay, Comte du, 346

Habeas Corpus Bill, 258-62, 263, 264, 272
Hague, The, 114, 171, 182, 341, 348
Halifax, George, 2nd Earl of (1716-71), *at Board of Trade,* 46-8, 49, 50, 74, 142, 192, 198, 269
Halifax, Nova Scotia, 34, 105, 173, 235, 236, 237, 256, 281, 283, 284, 337, 358, 359
Hamilton, James (Governor of Pennsylvania), 33, 34

Hanbury-Williams Sir Charles (1709-59), *appointed Ambassador to Russia,* 63-5, 126, 179

Hanover, *influence of on George II,* 45 and 71-2; *King visits,* 62-3, 65, 67, 74, 92, 94, 98; *Pitt's views on,* 100; *and France,* 105, 107, 109, 114; *Frederick and,* 127-9, 140, 141, 148; *altered position of,* 158-9; *Hanoverian troops returned,* 177-8; *George II desires neutrality for,* 180-1, 184; *Cumberland and,* 190, 215, 222; *Cumberland at Hastenbeck,* 228-31; *and Closterseven,* 234-5, 237, 239, 242, 248, 249, 293, 298, 300, 302; *and Bute,* 305; *and Minden,* 324-5, 354; *and Choiseul,* 381; *and Mauduit,* 382, 396; *Pitt's peace aim for,* 401; *and Bedford,* 406, 408

Hanoverian Dynasty, *characteristics,* 124

Hanoverian soldier, *Case of,* 133, 138, 141, 188

Hardwicke, Philip, 1st Earl of (1690-1764), 48, 50, 52-3, 55, 59, 60, 70, 72, 74, 78; *opposes Militia Bill,* 97, 103; *and Shirley,* 121, 130, 131, 132, 134, 135; *invites Pitt to meeting,* 136-9; *and Pitt's plan,* 140; *further interview with Pitt,* 141, 142, 143; *on Tory "petitions,"* 149, 151; *conversation with Pitt,* 153-4, 155; *and Byng,* 167, 174; *sounds Pitt,* 187-8, 192, 193; *and Legge,* 198-200, 202; *arranges coalition,* 208-13; *opposes Rochefort expedition,* 221; *despair after Hastenbeck,* 230; *supports Ligonier's appointment,* 243, 245; *visits Pitt,* 251-2; *opposes Pitt's Habeas Corpus Bill,* 259-62, 264, 275, 276; *proposes to give up Louisburg,* 293, 294, 299, 307; *Pitt's opinion of,* 309; *refuses to attend Council meetings,* 313, 316, 319, 322, 341; *and l'Inconnue,* 343, 348; *advocates peace,* 353, 355; *attitude towards "popular" Bills,* 360-2, 363, 365, 372; *and Bute,* 374-5, 385, 387, 390, 392, 394; *visits Pitt on draft of King's Speech,* 399; *on peace negotiations,* 400, 402; *on fisheries,* 407-8, 409, 411; *on Bussy's letter,* 413-14, 415, 416; *on Spanish question,* 420

Hardy, Admiral Sir Charles (1705-80), 284

Hastenbeck, *Battle of,* 229

Havre, Le, 319

Hawke, Sir Edward (1705-87), 61; *supersedes Byng,* 113, 115; *at Rochefort,* 223-5, 272, 284, 319, 337; *at Quiberon,* 345-6; *on Belleisle proposal,* 366-7

Hay, Dr. George (1715-78), 153

Hayes, 106, 114, 162, 171, 172, 184, 237, 273, 314, 395

Henley, Sir R. (1708-72), 153, 212

Hervey, Lord, 14

Hesse, 63, 74, 75, 98, 231, 297, 298, 311, 322, 323, 378, 383, 401, 406

Highland Regiments, 50, 295

Hill, Brigadier John, 27

Hochkirch, *Battle of,* 279

Hodgson, Field-Marshal (1708-98), 397

Holburne, Admiral Francis (1704-71), 184, 235-7, 239, 256

Holdernesse, R. d'a., 4th Earl of (1718-78), *with the King at Hanover,* 71-5, 132; *and Hanoverian soldier,* 133; *Pitt wishes to dismiss,* 150, 151, 155, 159, 162; *visits Pitt,* 172; *and Mitchell,* 179, 181, 182, 184, 188, 190, 196, 198; *threatens to resign,* 208, 217, 230, 233, 241, 250; *Pitt revises his drafts,* 252, 265, 268, 269, 273, 275, 276; *on Temple's Garter,* 302; *deserting Pitt,* 306-7; *Pitt's opinion of,* 309, 313; *and l'Inconnue,* 342-3, 348, 362; *and George III,* 374-5, 385, 390, 392

Holland, 106, 110, 179, 181, 218, 232, 248, 295, 313, 317

Holmes, Admiral Charles (1711-61), 268-9

Honduras, Bay of, 233, 295

Höpken (Swedish Foreign Minister), 106

Hopkins, Lieutenant, 283

Hopson, General, 276, 330, 331, 333, 380

Howe, George Augustus, 3rd Viscount (1725-58), 285, 286, 294

Howe, Admiral Richard, 4th Viscount (1726-99), 224, 272, 279, 352

Huntingdonshire Instructions, 149

Hudson, River, 30, 87, 237, 257, 281, 285, 333, 334, 335

Hudson's Bay, 22, 29

Ilchester, Earl of, 133

India, 114, 156, 184, 218, 238, 365, 381, 383, 401

Invasion of England, *projected,* 106

"Invective," 99, 119

Iroquois, 30

Jamaica, 102, 184, 270

Jenkins's Ear, *War of,* 351

Jenkinson, Charles, 183

Jennings, Colonel, 357

Johnson, Sir William (1715-74), 80, 87; *defeats Dieskau,* 88-91; *captures Niagara,* 335

Jones, Hugh Valence, 364

Jonquière, Marquis de la, 34, 35, 36, 37

Jumonville, Coulon de, 40

Kaunitz, Prince (1711-94), 44, 45, 62, 68
Keene, Sir Benjamin (1697-1757), 172, 233, 234, 237, 263, 294, 351
Kensington Gardens, 322, 323
Keppel, Augustus, 1st Viscount (1725-86), 75, 76; *and Byng,* 166; *at Goree,* 270 and 296; *and Belleisle,* 366 and 397
Kerrich, S. (1696-1768), 386
Kinsale, 357
Knowles, Admiral Sir Charles, 102
Knyphausen, Baron von (1729-89), 253, 327, 354
Kolin, *Battle of,* 214, 215, 216, 219, 229, 247
Korbach, *Battle of,* 355
Kunersdorf, *Battle of,* 320, 328, 341

La Borde, 385
La Clue, 324, 325, 345
La Galette, 333, 335, 339
Lagos, 325
La Motte, Comte de (1720-91), 236, 346
Landshut, *Battle of,* 364
La Rochelle, 225
La Salle, 23, 33
Lawrence, Brigadier Charles, *at Beaubassin,* 35-6, 81; *at Louisburg,* 283; *Governor of Nova Scotia,* 358-9
Le Bœuf, Fort, 37, 39, 335
Lecky, W. E. H., 14, 185
Legardeur de St. Pierre, 39
Legge, Hon. H. B. (1708-64), 56, 125, 145, 149; *Chancellor of the Exchequer,* 150, 152, 178; *resigns,* 195, 197; *promotes coalition,* 198-200; *and Pitt,* 201, 204, 206; *and George II,* 208; *Chancellor again,* 210-11, 260; *wants peerage,* 263, 300; *foments friction between Pitt and Bute,* 306-7, 309; *at enmity with Pitt,* 313-16, 379, 390
Leicester House, 99, 125, 132, 135, 142, 186, 190, 191, 192, 204, 208, 210, 212, 230, 246, 254, 304, 305, 307, 309, 314, 316, 323, 325, 326, 348, 349, 371, 376
Leipzic, *Siege of,* 247-8
Leith, 356
Le Loutre, Abbé, 34, 35, 36, 86, 87
Lesser Antilles, 310
Letter to two Great Men, 362, 381
Leuthen, *Battle of,* 248
Levant, 114
Lévis, Duc de (1720-87), 357, 358, 359
Liegnitz, *Battle of,* 364
Ligonier, Lord (1678-1770), 18, 60, 191, 241, 243, 244, 365, 377, 420
Lippe, River, 181
Lobositz, *Battle of,* 140, 179
L'Orient, 271
Loudoun, John, 4th Earl of (1705-82), 122, 123, 174, 191, 235-8, 255-7, 284, 288, 330
Louis, Prince, 158
Louis XIV, 19, 23, 28, 29
Louis XV, 15, 29, 66, 68
Louisburg, 28, 29, 32, 34, 60, 173, 175, 235-6, 256-7, 274, 281, 283-4, 287, 292-3, 295, 297, 300, 322, 330, 333, 336-8, 353
Louisiana, 23, 33, 289
Lowestoffe, H.M.S., 359
Lys, 60
Lyttelton, George, 1st Lord (1709-73), 59; *Chancellor of the Exchequer,* 102-4, 107, 109, 136; *becomes a peer,* 144; *offers seat to Pitt,* 153; *comments on Pitt's speech,* 160-1, 259

MacAllester, Oliver, 318, 319, 325
Madagascar, 23
Magdeburg, 235, 247
Magnanime, H.M.S., 224
Mahon, Lord, 14
Maine, 30
Man, Isle of, 357
"Management" in Parliament, 146-7, 153, 379
Mansfield, (William Murray) Earl of (1705-93), 45, 48, 50, 56, 59, 71, 115, 129, 130, 131; *becomes a peer,* 144, 145; *and Byng,* 165 and 167, 192, 193, 212, 221; *co-opted into Cabinet,* 240; *and Ligonier,* 244; *opposes Habeas Corpus Bill,* 259-61; *Pitt's opinion of,* 309; *and Belleisle expedition,* 377, 390, 415; *and Spain,* 418-20
Maria Theresa (1716-80), 44, 45, 62, 63, 68, 128, 216, 230, 384, 410
Marie Galante, 332, 383
Marlborough, John, 1st Duke of (1650-1722), 23, 25, 27
Marlborough, Charles, 3rd Duke of (1706-58), 271, 273, 275, 277, 278, 323
Marsh, Captain, 270
Martinique, 296, 310, 311, 330-2, 353, 380, 381, 383
Maryland, 32, 120, 289
Masham, Abigail, 27
Mason, Major, 270
Massachusetts, 23
Mauduit, Israel, 382-3, 388
Mauritius, 365, 381, 383
Memel, 216
Mexico, Gulf of, 37, 310
Michel, A. L. (1712-82), 265, 268
Middleton, Lord, 300
Militia, The, 94; *Pitt's scheme,* 95-7, 109, 138, 149; *national militia foreshadowed,* 159, 161, 174, 177, 184, 203;

riots over, 226-7; *Newcastle opposed to,* 276; *Pitt's encouragement of,* 319-20; *the Norfolk militia,* 344-5; *Scotch militia* 360-1; *mentioned in the King's Speech* 377-8
Minden, *Battle of,* 323-7, 340, 356
Minorca, 105, 108, 109; *French capture,* 112-20, 122, 129, 130, 156, 164, 202, 223; *Spain and,* 232-3, 293, 296
Miré Bay, 283
Mirepoix, Duc de, 61, 121
Missaguash, River, 86
Mississippi, 23, 33, 93, 310, 353
Mitchell, Sir Andrew (1708-78), *and Russian treaty,* 126-7, 129, 152; *in Berlin,* 158; *and Hanoverian troops,* 177; *and home politics,* 179, 181, 214-16, 219-20; *and Cumberland,* 229; *after Rossbach,* 248-9; *and Pitt,* 250-4, 262, 271, 297, 312, 353, 387
Mobile, 353
Mohawk, River, 286-8, 334
Monckton, General Hon. R. (1726-82), 80, 81, 85, 86, 87
Monongahela, River, 40, 83, 114
Montagu, Mrs. (1720-1800), 106
Montcalm, Marquis de (1712-59), *captures Oswego,* 122-3; *captures Fort William Henry,* 237; *defeats Abercromby at Ticonderoga,* 286-7, 334; *defeated at Quebec,* 338-9, 357
Montmorency, Falls of, 338
Montreal, 24, 87, 123, 257, 285, 311, 335, 338, 357, 359, 365, 382
Moore, Admiral Sir John (1718-79), 296, 330-2
Morbihan, 345, 366
Mordaunt, General Sir John (1697-1780), 223, 238, 239, 240
Morlaix, 278
Munchausen, Baron von, 190, 242, 266, 299
Murray, General Hon. James (1719-94), 258, 259
Murray, William, *see* Mansfield

Napoleonic Wars, 176
National Debt, 314
Negro Point, 330
Nelson, Lord, 176
Newcastle, Thomas Pelham Holles, Duke of (1693-1768), 14, 18; *and Beaubassin,* 35-6; *First Lord,* 43, 45, 46; *and French encroachments,* 47, 48; *and Washington's defeat,* 49, 50; *consults Pitt on American affairs,* 51; *and Braddock,* 52-3, 54, 55, 56; *attacked by Pitt,* 57-8; *and prospect of war,* 59-61; *his foreign policy,* 62; *and finance,* 71; *and strategy* 72-4; *approaches Pitt,* 74; *and Braddock,* 75; *and Pitt,* 76-9, 80; *on Braddock's defeat,* 85, 91; *and Fox,* 103; *and secret service,* 105-6, 109; *and Minorca,* 112-18; *and royal squabbles,* 124-5; *and Russian treaty,* 125-6; *and Frederick,* 127-8; *falls,* 129-44, 145; *and Parliamentary management,* 147, 148; *and Pitt,* 149-51, 155, 163, 174, 176; *and Hanoverian troops,* 177, 185; *views on resigning,* 186-93; *and coalition,* 195-213, 216, 220, 221; *and Rochefort expedition,* 223; *after Hastenbeck,* 230-2; *and Gibraltar,* 233, 238; *and Closterseven,* 239, 240; *and Ligonier,* 243-4; *in coalition,* 245-7; *and Mitchell,* 250-4; *and America,* 254-5; *opposes Habeas Corpus Bill,* 259-62; *and expenses of Army of Observation,* 264-6, 268; *and continent,* 273-7, 296; *and finance,* 297-300; *and Temple's Garter,* 302, 304; *and Bute,* 304-8; *Pitt's opinion of,* 309; "*distressed in administration,*" 313; *and taxes,* 314-17; *alarmed at prospect of invasion,* 319; *desire for peace,* 320-3, 325; *and Leicester House,* 326-7; *and l'Inconnue,* 340-4, 345, 347, 348, 349; *and peace terms,* 353, 354, 356, 358; *and* "*popular Bills,*" 360-1; *and Fuentes,* 362-3; *and Belleisle,* 364-7, 370; *on George III's accession,* 371-3; *and Bute,* 374-7, 379; *and peace,* 383-5, 386, 387; *and Bute's intrigues,* 388-95, 396, 397, 400, 401, 402; *and peace negotiations,* 403-4, 405, 411, 413, 414, 415, 416; *and Spain,* 418-20
Newfoundland, 23, 29, 383
New Orleans, 37, 310
New York, 30, 47, 87, 89, 197, 236, 237
Niagara, 50, 80, 81, 87, 88, 121, 310, 311, 333, 334, 335
Nieuport, 216, 221, 275
Noix, Ile aux, 334, 335, 336, 339
North, Lord (1732-92), 416
Northumberland, Elizabeth, Duchess of (1716-76), 379

Ohio, 32, 33, 37, 38, 39, 47, 50, 58, 78, 79, 81, 87, 91, 257, 288, 290, 291, 310, 335, 383
Ohio Company, 32, 33, 38, 47
Okehampton, 153, 161
"Old System," 14, 44, 45, 48, 62, 63, 74, 125, 159, 219, 222, 383
Oléron, 224
Olmutz, 274, 275, 276
Oneida, Lake, 334
Onondaga, River, 288
Ontario, Lake, 50, 87, 88, 121, 123, 288, 289, 333, 334, 335
Opposition, H.M., 145, 148, 149

Osborne, Admiral Henry (1698-1771), 284, 301
Ostend, 72, 216, 221
Oswald, James (1715-69), 145, 198
Oswego, 88, 120, 123, 129, 288, 310, 311, 334

Panama, 417
Passaro, *Battle of Cape,* 113
Parkman on French Canada, 19
Pelham, Henry (1696-1754), 35, 36, 43, 45, 47, 48, 148, 185, 305
Pelham, Lady Katherine, 103
Pennsylvania, 30, 33, 41, 47, 82, 120-2, 289-91
Pepperell, Sir William (1696-1759), 50
Peter the Great, Tsar, 64
Peter, Grand Duke ,65, 179
Philadelphia, 85, 289, 292
Philippines, 417
Phillips, Sir John, 360
Pichon, Thomas, 86
Pirna, 179
Pitt, Harriot (1758-86), 272
Pitt, Lady Hester (1721-1803), 48, 51, 77, 100-1, 106-7, 137, 237, 272, 274-5, 277, 294, 313, 323-4, 327, 348, 353, 359, 363
Pitt, John, of Encombe, 255
Pitt, William, Earl of Chatham (1708-78), *and Blackfriars Bridge,* 15; *and Beaubassin,* 36; *passed over for promotion,* 43; *represents colonial interests,* 44; *on Pelham's death,* 48; *marries,* 48; *advice on American War,* 51, 56; *attacks Newcastle,* 58; *attacks Robinson and Murray,* 59; *breaks with Fox,* 70; *approached by Newcastle,* 74; *rejects subsidy treaties,* 75; *his policy compared with Newcastle's,* 76; *his views on office,* 77-9; *dismissed,* 79; *on navy estimates,* 92; *on sale of prizes,* 93; *on Walpole,* 83-4; *on army estimates,* 94; *on militia,* 95-7; *on subsidy treaties,* 98; *his invective,* 99; *his "insular plan,"* 100; *at Bath,* 100; *buying houses,* 100-1; *on Admiral Knowles,* 102; *and Lyttelton,* 102-3; *on Government grant for American troops,* 103; *on Prevôt,* 104; *buys Hayes Place,* 106-7; *on mercenaries,* 106-8; *on wartime administration,* 108-9; *on vote of credit,* 109; *on Convention of Westminster,* 110; *and Minorca,* 118-20; *his relations with C.O.s,* 119; *and Fowke,* 119-20; *and Fox,* 130; *and Newcastle,* 131-2; *and the Hanoverian soldier,* 133; *on birth of eldest son,* 137; *and Hardwicke,* 137-9; *sees Lady Yarmouth,* 139; *his "plan,"* 140; *rejected by King,* 141; *and Fox,* 143; *Sec. of State,* 143; *early political career,* 147; *views on foreign policy,* 147-8; *woos the Tories,* 148-9; *his "visionary notions,"* 149; *administrative arrangements,* 151; *proposed course of action,* 152; *reliance on Tories,* 153-4; *attitude towards Whigs,* 154; *self-reliance,* 154-5; *drafts King's Speech,* 155-60; *speech on the Address,* 160-1; *M.P. for Okehampton,* 161; *his health,* 161-2; *and Byng,* 165-9; *his statesmanship,* 170; *his position in Parliament,* 171; *conducts affairs from Hayes,* 171-2; *his first administration,* 172-3; *and Highland regiments,* 174; *meets obstructions,* 174-5; *his naval policy,* 175-6; *his war objectives,* 176; *and mercenaries in England,* 177; *and Frederick the Great,* 179-80; *his continental strategy,* 180-2; *supports Hessian subsidy,* 182; *and Army of Observation,* 183; *results of first administration,* 184; *and George II,* 185; *and Hardwicke,* 187-8; *Fox's enmity,* 189; *friction with Cumberland,* 191; *gains ground,* 192; *dismissed,* 194-5; *relations with colleagues,* 197; *"it rains gold boxes,"* 200-1; *and Enquiries,* 202; *influence in Parliament wanes,* 203; *urged to enter coalition,* 204; *his terms,* 204-5; *reluctant to compromise,* 206; *his plan rejected,* 207; *King's requirements,* 209; *and Hardwicke,* 209-10; *enters coalition,* 210-11; *his doubts,* 212; *and Frederick,* 214, 217-19; *and Rochefort expedition,* 218-19; *and Whig magnates,* 220-1; *meets obstructions,* 223-4; *his mortification,* 225-6; *resistance to his Militia Bill,* 226-7; *sends fleet to Emden,* 229; *refuses troops for Germany,* 229-30; *and Hastenbeck,* 230-1; *estranged from Grenville,* 232; *offers Gibraltar to Spain,* 232-4; *affected by disasters abroad,* 237-8; *and control of army,* 238, 243-4; *and Mordaunt,* 239-40; *and Closterseven,* 240-2; *effect of coalition on,* 245-6; *and Rossbach,* 248-9; *and Mitchell,* 250-3; *American plan,* 254-5; *new naval strategy,* 256-7; *and Habeas Corpus,* 258-62; *and finance,* 262-3; *obtains control over Army of Observation,* 264-5; *despatches Holmes to Emden,* 267-8; *and Michel,* 268-9; *and Senegal and Goree,* 269-71; *renews descents on French coast,* 271-4 and 277-9; *meets obstruction,* 274-7; *selects Amherst,* 281-2; *and Abercromby,* 284-5 and 294-5; *and Forbes,* 292; *and Martinique,* 296; *war objectives,* 297; *and dédommagement,* 298; *and German estimates,* 299-300; *Speech on the Address,* 300-1; *and Temple's Garter,* 302; *and Bute,* 305-8; *opinion of colleagues,* 309; *and King's Speech,* 310; *extends plans,* 310; *relations with continent,* 311-12; *his son William,*

313-14; *and taxation,* 314-16; *and projected French invasion,* 318-20; *fear of premature peace,* 320; *views on peace,* 321-3; *and Sackville,* 323-4; *and Boscawen,* 325; *and Prince of Wales,* 326-7; *and Sanseverino,* 327-8; *hopes of peace dashed,* 328; *and Hopson,* 330; *and Canada,* 334-6; *and peace moves,* 340-4; *and King's Speech,* 346-7; *on unity in Cabinet,* 347-8; *views on Leicester House and Bute,* 348-50; *and Spain,* 351-2; *final campaign in America,* 353; *European strategy,* 354-6; *and "popular" Bills* 360-1; *and Newcastle,* 361-3; *and Belleisle expedition,* 364; *on George II,* 368; *at George III's accession,* 369-72; *his treatment by George III and Bute,* 374-5; *and the Whig magnates,* 376-7; *revives Belleisle expedition,* 377-8; *and Poyning's Law,* 379-80; *and Martinique,* 380-1; *and Mauduit,* 382; *and peace,* 383-5; *his waning influence,* 386; *and George III,* 387; *and Bute,* 389-93; *accepts Bute as Sec. of State,* 395; *and Choiseul,* 398; *on war aims,* 399; *foresees retirement,* 400; *peace objectives,* 401; *and peace negotiations,* 402-7; *and Bussy's memorials,* 410-11; *ultimatum to France,* 411; *and Spain,* 412; *and Bussy's letter,* 414; *deserted by magnates,* 415; *breaks off negotiations with France,* 416-17; *urges war with Spain,* 417; *his written memorial,* 418; *isolated,* 418; *his valedictory speech,* 420-1; *resigns,* 422
Pitt, William (1759-1806), 313-14, 320
Pittsburg, 39 292
Plate Tax, 107
Plymouth, 345
Pocock, Admiral Sir George (1706-92), 365
Podewils, Herr von (Prussian Minister), 249
Pomerania, 222, 248
Pompadour, Jeanne, Marquise de (1721-64), 44, 59, 60, 68
Ponchartrain, M. de, 22
Pondicherry, 23, 381, 399, 406, 410
Port à l'Anglois, 28
Port Mahon, 113, 115, 116, 239
Port Royal (Acadia), 25, 27
Port Royal (Martinique), 330
Portsmouth, 117-18, 163, 282, 344
Potomac, River, 39, 80
Potter, Thomas (1718-59), 149, 197-8, 222, 238-9
Poyning's Law, 379
Prague, *Battle of,* 203-4, 212, 214
Pratt, Sir Charles (1714-94), 212, 258, 260
Presquile, Fort, 37, 335
Prevôt, Augustine (1725-86), 104
Prideaux, Colonel John (1718-59), 334-5
Prince Rupert Bay, 332
Puchot, Captain, 334-5
Puysieulx, Marquis de (1702-63), 35, 36
Pyle, Edmund (1702-76), 361, 371, 386-7

Qualification Bill, 360
Quebec, 24, 27, 60, 73, 87, 121, 173, 175, 235-7
Quiberon Bay, 345, 346, 352, 366, 378

Redstone Creek, 40
Reversal of Alliances, 67
Rhé, Island, 224, 240-1
Rhine, 158-9, 179, 267-8, 272, 274-5, 279-80, 322, 364
Rhone, 103
Richelieu, Marquis de (1696-1788), 113, 114, 116, 233-5, 240, 242, 248, 267-8
Richelieu, River, 87, 334
Rider, Sir Dudley, 115
Rigby, Richard (1722-88), 99
Robertson, Sir C. Grant, 15
Robinson, Sir Thomas (1695-1770), 43, 44, 45, 48, 49, 56, 59, 71, 166, 197, 198
Rochefort, 218-19, 221-2, 224-6, 229-30, 237-40, 248, 263, 272, 274
Rodney, Admiral George (1718-92), 226, 282, 319
Romans, King of, 62
Rossbach, *Battle of,* 248, 264
Rouillé, Antoine (1689-1761), 49
Royal American Regiment, 85
Royston, Lord (1720-90), 136, 139, 140
Russian Treaty, 65, 68, 71, 75, 98, 105, 126, 156, 179
Ryswick, *Peace of,* 24

Saale, River, 248
Sackville, Lord George (1716-85), 191, 211, 223, 243, 271-2, 275; *at Minden,* 323-4, 376
St. Briac, 279
St. Cas, 279
St. Clair, Sir John, 287, 291
St. Domingo, 129
St. Germain, Comte de, 364
St. James's Square, 237
St. John, Henry (Viscount Bolingbroke), 27
St. John, Fort, 85, 87
St. John, River, 74, 86
St. Lawrence, 23-4, 28, 60, 81, 87, 256, 281, 287, 310-11, 334-7, 358-9

St. Lucia, 353, 381, 383
St. Malo, 273-4, 278-9, 282
St. Petersburg, 63-4, 126
St. Pierre (Martinique), 331
St. Servan, 273
St. Vincent, Lord, 176, 233
Sanseverino, Prince, 327-8, 351
Saône, River, 103
Sardinia, 312
Saunders, Admiral Sir Charles (1713-75), 115, 337
Saxe, Maréchal de (1696-1750), 90
Saxony, 129, 132, 178, 235, 312
Scandinavia, 127, 217
Schuyler, Peter, 25
Scott, G. L., 387
Seeley, Sir J. R., 14
Senegal, 23, 269-70, 322, 383
Shippen, "Honest," 146
Shirley, William (1693-1771), 50, 80-1, 87-9, 91, 121-2
Silesia, 44, 62, 248, 352, 354, 408
Silesian loan, 110
Soubise, Prince de (1715-87), 235, 240, 248, 398
Southampton, 379
Spain, 110, 232-4, 237, 294, 312, 319, 327-9, 351, 353, 355, 362-3, 374, 378, 381, 402, 406, 408-13, 416-18, 420-1
Spithead, 224-5
Spörcken, General, 240
Stade, 229, 234-5, 239, 268, 277
Stanley, Hans (1720-80), 401-4, 410-11, 413, 415, 417-18, 420
Stanwix, Brigadier John (1690-1766), 285-6
Stockbridge, 153
Stockholm, 106
Stone, Andrew (1703-73), 133-4, 145, 193, 372
Surat, 23
Swanton, Commodore, 359
Sweden, 179, 217, 313, 317, 356
Symmer, Robert, 152, 155, 184, 209, 249, 316, 362, 382, 389

Talon, Sieur, 20
Temple, Richard, Earl (1711-79), 51, 137, 160; *at Admiralty*, 164; *and Byng*, 165, 176; *distasteful to King*, 185; *dismissed*, 193-4, 197-8, 206-8, 231, 295; *and the Garter*, 302-4, 308, 309, 314, 316, 326, 328, 343, 347-8, 376, 378, 380; *offered Lord Lieutenancy of Ireland*, 388-9, 393-4, 396, 398, 402, 415, 418
Thurot, François (1727-60), 324, 346, 356-7
Ticonderoga, 90, 121-3, 286-7, 294-5, 311, 334
Torbay, 319, 346
Torgau, 247, 378
Tories, The, *Views on Militia*, 95; *position in Parliament*, 145-6; *adopted by Pitt*, 151; *become Pitt's party*, 153, 178, 186, 188, 195, 201, 204, 218, 246, 306, 309; *and "popular" Bills*, 360-2, 376-7, 379, 387, 405, 416
Toronto, 121
Toulon, 114, 118, 218, 233, 324
Townshend, Charles (1725-67), 46, 211
Townshend, George (1724-1807), 96, 103, 145, 171, 174, 201, 211, 358
Townshend, Lady, 344
Trade, *Board of*, 46
Tyrawley, James, 2nd Earl of, 130, 233

Ultimatum, *French*, 105
Upper Brook Street, 100-1, 137, 139
Ushant, 282, 346
Utrecht, *Treaty of*, 25, 28, 91, 321

Vanneck, Sir Joshua, 385
Vaudreuil, Marquis de (1724-1802), 334
Vellinghausen, *Battle of*, 398, 406, 408, 410
Venango, 37, 335
Verden, 267
Vergor, Duchambon de, 86
Versailles, *Treaty of*, 68, 181
Vetch, Captain Samuel, 24, 255
Vienna, 64, 317
Vilaine, River, 366
Villeray, 86
Vine, Mr. M. P., 183
Virginia, 32, 33, 38, 81-2, 120, 289, 291-2
Virginia Company, 17
Viry, Comte de, 306, 316, 388, 391-4

Waldegrave, James, 1st Earl (1685-1763), 99, 160, 185-6, 191-3, 196, 207-8
Wales, Dowager Princess of, 60, 124-5, 133, 304, 368-9, 371, 376, 393
Walker, Sir Hovenden, 27
Wall, General Richard (1694-1778), 233-4, 327, 351-3, 363, 412-13, 417
Walpole, Horace (1717-1797), 18, 52, 56, 58, 61, 85, 87, 96-9, 107, 135, 139, 140, 142, 144, 166, 182, 185-6, 197, 200, 202, 223, 240, 282, 285, 347, 359, 362, 375
Walpole, Sir Robert (1678-1745), 18, 29, 73, 76, 93-4, 145, 148, 157, 188
Warburg, *Battle of*, 355
Warburton, Dr. William (1698-1779), 198
Warsaw, 64
Washington, George (1732-99), 32, 38-43, 48, 81-3, 121, 290

Watson, Admiral Charles (1714-57), 238
Wesel, 128
Weser, River, 228-9, 267, 277, 323
West, James (1704-72), 246, 361
West, Admiral Temple (1713-57), 165
Westminster, *Convention of*, 66, 73, 105, 109-10, 126, 159, 180-1
Westphalia, 183, 222, 408
West Wickham, 107
White, John, M.P., 276
Whitmore, General Edward (1691-1761), 283
Wight, Isle of, 271, 319, 397
Willes, Sir John, 129
William III, 23, 148
William VIII, Landgrave of Hesse Cassel, 63
William Henry, Fort, 89, 123, 237, 285
Williamsburg, 82
Wills Creek, 39, 82
Winchilsea, Daniel, 8th Earl of, 194, 208, 210
Wolfe, General James (1727-59), 80, 223, 225-6, 283-4, 287, 294, 310-11, 333-8, 345, 358, 397
Wood Creek, 24
Woodhouse, Sir Armand, 344
Wotton, 48, 51, 274

Yarmouth, Amalie Walmoden, Countess of (1709-65), 75, 134-6, 139, 140-1, 190, 231, 235, 244, 259, 261, 302-3, 328, 343, 364, 367, 387
Yorke, Charles (1722-70), 74, 187, 198
Yorke, Sir Joseph (1724-92), 52, 114, 171, 248, 252-4, 274, 277, 341-3

Zorndorf, *Battle of*, 279
Züllichau, *Battle of*, 320, 323